As the parent of a mentally ill son, I found this book to contain a wealth of information. I wish it had been available twenty years ago.

—Marilyn Meisel, Director and
Cofounder of the Training and
Education Center Network,
Mental Health Association of
Southeastern Pennsylvania

. . . An ideal guide and workbook for those with the illness and their relatives . . .

—Richard S. E. Keefe, Ph.D., and
Philip D. Harvey, Ph.D.; Mount Sinai
School of Medicine; authors of
*Understanding Schizophrenia*

Mueser and Gingerich bring their impressive knowledge and experience to life in this book, providing just the right balance of information, advice, and practical tools . . . It is must reading not only for families of persons with schizophrenia, but for those who seek to help them.

—Anthony F. Lehman, M.D., M.S.P.H.;
Professor of Psychiatry, University of
Maryland; coauthor of *Working with
Families of the Mentally Ill*

Written in a clear-cut but empathetic manner, this book is . . . essential . . . for concerned family members and professional caregivers alike.

—Hans-Dieter Brenner, M.D., Ph.D.;
Professor of Psychiatry, Director,
Social Psychiatric Clinic of the
University of Berne

—Anette Schaub, Ph.D.; Psychiatric
Clinic of the University of Berne

. . . An invaluable family's guide to the demanding mental illness. Families have traditionally received very limited support and information: this book says it all.

—*The Bookwatch*, December 1994

*Coping With Schizophrenia* is an outstanding achievement. I will recommend it enthusiastically.

—Herbert Y. Meltzer, M.D.;
Bond Professor of Psychiatry,
Case Western University

This manual should be on the desk of all those who work with the seriously mentally ill!

—Robert Paul Liberman, M.D.;
Professor of Psychiatry, University of
California at Los Angeles;
Director, Clinical Research Center
for Schizophrenia and Psychiatric
Rehabitation

—Alejandro Kopelowicz, M.D.;
Medical Director, San Fernando
Mental Health Service

... A sophisticated set of tools to help family members cope with the disorder. I highly recommend this book ...

—Alan S. Bellack, Ph.D., A.B.P.P.;
Director of Clinical Psychology,
Eastern Pennsylvania Psychiatric
Institute, Medical College of
Pennsylvania

... [This] book was the most complete of any [on the subject] that I have read.

—Gerard E. Hogarty, M.S.W.; Professor
of Psychiatry, University of Pittsburgh

The text delivers what the title promises ... and it is now up to professionals to make this book available to the public at large and their clients and families ...

—Cyril M. Franks, Ph.D.; editor of
*Child & Family Behavior Therapy*

Simply put, this is the best source of information on schizophrenia for families that is currently available ... I wish that I could send a copy to every family that has been affected by schizophrenia.

—Robert E. Drake, M.D., Ph.D.;
Professor of Psychiatry,
Dartmouth Medical School

*COPING WITH SCHIZOPHRENIA* HAS BEEN SELECTED AS A
RECOMMENDED TITLE BY THE LITERATURE COMMITTEE OF THE
**NATIONAL ALLIANCE FOR THE MENTALLY ILL.**

# Coping with Schizophrenia

## A GUIDE FOR FAMILIES

KIM T. MUESER, Ph.D
SUSAN GINGERICH, M.S.W.
Foreword by Harriet P. Lefley, Ph.D.

NEW HARBINGER PUBLICATIONS, INC.

*Publisher's Note*

This publication is designed to provide accurate and authoritative information in regard to the subject matter covered. It is sold with the understanding that the publisher is not engaged in rendering psychological, financial, legal, or other professional services. If expert assistance or counseling is needed, the services of a competent professional should be sought.

Cover art by Roman Tybinko, "Keening Clouds," oil on canvas, 1985
Cover design by SHELBY DESIGNS & ILLUSTRATES
Editing by Leslie Tilley
Text design by Tracy Marie Powell

Distributed in the U.S.A. primarily by Publishers Group West; in Canada by Raincoast Books; in Great Britain by Airlift Book Company, Ltd.; in South Africa by Real Books, Ltd.; in Australia by Boobook; and in New Zealand by Tandem Press.

Library of Congress Catalog Number: 94-067043
ISBN 1-879237-78-4 Paperback

1st printing, August, 1994, 8,000 copies
2nd printing June, 1995, 2,000 copies
3rd printing May, 1996, 1,500 copies
4th printing August, 1996, 3,000 copies

To our parents, Roland, Sonja, Dave, and Dorothy; our spouses, Rachel and Ted; and our extended families and friends, Genie, Naomi, Billy, Shep, Sonia, Adrienne, and Nancy.

# Contents

Problem Solving Techniques to Plan for the Future
• Special Issues to Consider When Planning for the
Future • Optimizing Your Ill Relative's Independence

# List of Worksheets

# Foreword

Consider what happens if you have a relative with cancer or heart problems who needs hospitalization and ensuing care. Chances are the attending physician or nurses will provide information about the disease and its treatment, together with a description of the progress the hospital staff is making with your relative. Before discharge, family education will be provided about medications and post-hospital illness management, so that the patient's relatives can function as informed caregivers. With the cost of medical care today, and the even more important costs of human suffering and pain, it only makes sense that both patients and their support systems receive education that can help them deal with the illness and hopefully deter its recurrence.

For many years the situation has been completely opposite in the case of mental illness. Practitioners and treatment systems have not only failed to offer family education, but in too many cases they have intentionally avoided any communication with families except for collecting background information about the circumstances of the disorder. Family members' questions, their very natural attempts to obtain information about what is wrong with their relative and what they can do to help, have been carefully deflected or ignored by the treating professionals.

Traditionally, this failure to communicate with family members was the deliberate policy of many mental health facilities. Although its effects were cruel and often damaging to the patient and family, the policy was considered necessary for effective treatment. It was based on a model of mental illness in which recovery was viewed as evolving from a therapeutic alliance between the patient and therapist. In this model, it was felt that any communication with family members would be experienced as a breach of trust by the patient and would gravely interfere with progress in treatment. Most models, in fact, viewed the family as the source of "toxins" rather then help, so even when families were involved in the treatment process, honest information from professionals was the exception rather than the rule.

Today the field is much more knowledgeable about major psychiatric disorders such as schizophrenia. The therapeutic alliance, which now takes place in many settings, including psychosocial-rehabilitation and case-management programs, no longer automatically excludes families. Practitioners now know that families do not cause schizophrenia, and acknowledge its biological base. They also understand that they alone cannot ensure their patients' adherence to the treatment regimen they have prescribed, and recognize the value of support systems. Research has clearly demonstrated the value of psychoeducational interventions in enabling families both to cope with mental illness and to help their relatives deter relapse. Unfortunately, this knowledge has not transferred into any widespread practice. Except for a few enlightened cases, in most psychiatric hospitals and in most mental health systems, family education is still the rare exception rather than the rule.

This book, then, fills a yawning gap in our treatment system. During the past few years there have been some heroic attempts to address the many questions raised by families, largely through the initiatives of the National Alliance for the Mentally Ill. Family-resource books and manuals have been produced by professional educators and clinicians who have an additional source of special expertise: they are family members of persons with mental illness. Notable among these professionals are Dr. Agnes Hatfield of Maryland and Dr. Joyce Burland of Vermont. Based on years of work with families, their books have dealt with specific diagnoses, but have focused on generic issues that are common to a range of severe and persistent mental illnesses.

The current book by Kim Mueser and Susan Gingerich, also based on years of work with families but in a more clinical setting, adds to this literature an extremely comprehensive and comprehensible manual for family education in schizophrenia, arguably the most difficult of the major psychiatric disorders. The authors give us a state-of-the-art background on the precursors, symptoms, and treatment of schizophrenia and debunk the myths surrounding the illness. With graphic media that include checklists and tables, they provide a compendium of information on accurate diagnosis, on psychotropic medications together with their effects and side effects, and on warning signs of relapse. Tools are provided for assessing and logging the progress of the illness. Families are taught how to make systematic observations and how to evaluate the behaviors they observe. They learn how to recognize and deal with stressors, techniques for family communication, and illness-management strategies. They are informed about the functions of the treatment team, and how they can interface and work with the mental health professionals who treat their loved ones.

This is an extremely unique book in terms of the tools provided for family members. Family members reading this book are actually treated like valued collaborators; they are given objective instruments to record and measure, the same type of instruments used by agency staff or researchers. But even more, they are given tools that allow them to observe themselves as well as the behaviors of their loved ones. Harmonious family life is often contingent on effective negotiation of needs, expectations, and performance. This book provides mechanisms for families to record their own behaviors: their expectations of performance and their assessment of their mentally ill relative's actual ability to fulfill their expectations in ordinary household living. They are given step-by-step instructions for rule setting, for establishing limits, for coping with positive and negative symptoms, for helping their relatives increase motivation and activity. Problem-solving strategies are outlined, including dealing with substance abuse and suicidal thoughts. Ideas for improving their relative's quality of life and planning for the future are provided, all with worksheets and charts, so that a plan can actually be worked out at each level for specific needs.

We know that families, like their mentally ill relatives, are very different, that they have varying needs, problems, and strengths. Some readers may find these tests and worksheets burdensome (although they are options rather than demands). But many more readers will welcome them and use them to good advantage. This book provides a wealth of information for families, and more, it provides tools for addressing specific areas of concern. Authors Mueser and Gingerich have provided an extremely valuable addition to the literature on family education in schizophrenia. Families will thank them for making their lives easier, for giving them the knowledge and problem-solving techniques they have long desired, and for helping them and their relatives attain a better quality of life.

—Harriet P. Lefley, Ph.D.
Department of Psychiatry and Behavioral Sciences
University of Miami School of Medicine

# Preface

Countless times, in the more than ten years we have been working with the families of persons with schizophrenia, we have heard someone exclaim, "If only someone had told me that before!" Many other times these clients have presented us with specific problems and asked for suggestions on how to cope with them: "My son doesn't want to do anything. He just lies around the house all day." "My daughter is terrified to go anywhere. She always thinks people are talking about her."

Schizophrenia can have a devastating effect on the lives of both patients and their families. You yourself have undoubtedly experienced the turmoil of trying to deal with this strange and unpredictable illness. Understanding your relative and being able to cope with his or her behavior is critical to both your own well-being and that of your relative. And, as someone who cares deeply about your relative, you have an important role to play in improving his or her long-term health and quality of life.

Our goal is to help enable each family member and his or her ill relative to live as full a life as possible, to fulfill his or her potential as an individual. We have found that, in general, people enjoy being as independent as they can, taking pride in doing things for themselves whenever possible. People with the illness of schizophrenia are no exception to this, in spite of the many challenges they face. We believe that families and their ill relatives can further the goal of increasing independence, while still enjoying good family relationships, by learning as much as they can about coping and managing this illness.

## How to Use This Book

Coping with Schizophrenia is intended to be a comprehensive guide to living with the illness. We have attempted to collect here the information that families have requested over the years, including specific suggestions for managing the illness and coping with problems. In coping optimally with the illness, both basic information about the disorder and practical strategies for coping with common problems can help.

Individuals and their families are affected in extraordinarily different ways by the illness of schizophrenia—no two situations are identical. To give you access to the information most useful to your particular circumstances, we have covered a wide variety of subjects and provided examples from the hundreds of families we have worked with. As a result, it is inevitable that you won't relate to every family or problem described here, since different people have different difficulties and choose different solutions, particularly with regard to their level of involvement with their ill relative. Thus, we encourage you to pick and choose among the information and examples offered, find those most relevant to your circumstances, and ignore the rest.

Similarly, we have included many worksheets and checklists, which families have found useful when applying our suggestions to their own particular situation. It is unlikely that anyone would find all these worksheets helpful, nor do we expect anyone to complete them all. They are provided as a tool and an aid to understanding and applying the techniques you choose to work with to benefit your relative and your family.

Each of the five main sections of the book focuses on a different aspect of the task of living with schizophrenia.

Part I provides a factual introduction to the illness, including the history of the disorder and its treatment; theories about its causes; and its onset and course, diagnosis, and symptoms.

Part II presents information on how to prevent relapses of the illness, including encouraging medication compliance, monitoring your relative's early warning signs of relapse, and making use of community resources. An overview of antipsychotic medications is also provided.

Part III focuses on helping you create a more supportive environment for both you and your relative, which involves communicating effectively, solving problems, managing stress, and establishing and enforcing household rules. Such a supportive environment reduces stress on all family members and promotes gradual improvement in your relative.

Part IV addresses coping strategies for common difficulties related to schizophrenia, including persistent delusions and hallucinations, social withdrawal, depression, anxiety, substance abuse, and crises.

Finally, Part V offers suggestions for steps you can take to improve your relative's future—improving personal relationships and leisure activities and planning for ongoing care. Also addressed are the special concerns siblings often have and important role they can play in their relative's life.

Although this book was written mainly with families in mind—since until recently they have had limited access to the information and guidance they deserve in responding to this complex, confusing, and often distressing illness—we hope that others will also find it beneficial, including persons with schizophrenia and mental health professionals involved in its treatment. The more everyone involved can understand and talk to one another, the better.

If you have a family member with the illness, or if you suffer from schizophrenia yourself, you have likely endured much hardship and pain. In this respect you are a survivor; but we believe you deserve more than just survival. With time and effort, we are optimistic that you can learn to cope with the illness, enjoy your life, and make the most of all your relationships. We hope that this book will help you in these efforts.

## Acknowledgments

This book would not have been possible without the assistance, input, and inspiration of many people. Among our colleagues and members of the family consumer movement, we are especially grateful to the following people: Tim Ackerson, M.S.W.; Julie Agresta, M.S.S.; Susan Balder, M.S.W.; Debbie R. Becker, M.Ed.; Alan S. Bellack, Ph.D.; Amy Brodkey, M.D.; Robert Drake, M.D., Ph.D.; Ian R. H. Falloon, M.D.; Shirley M. Glynn, Ph.D.; Sylvia Gratz, M.D.; Michele Hamilton, M.S.N.; Richard Jossiasen, Ph.D.; Samuel M. Keith, M.D.; Harriet Lefley, Ph.D.; Douglas L. Levinson, M.D.; Robert P. M. Liberman, M.D.; Edie Manion, M.F.T.; William R. McFarlane, M.D.; Christine McGill, M.S.W., Ph.D.; Marilyn Meisel; Maggie Meshok, M.S.W.; Eric Pfeiffer, M.A.; Carole K. Rosenthal, M.Ed.; Nina R. Schooler, Ph.D.; and George M. Simpson, M.D.

We are also indebted to the many patients with schizophrenia and their families with whom we have worked. We admire the great strength and courage shown by these families who are struggling to cope with schizophrenia, and have learned much from their resourcefulness and determination.

Finally, special thanks goes to Ruthanne Vendy for her tireless energy in typing, modifying, designing forms and tables, and preparing this book for publication.

# PART I

## Introduction

# 1

# An Overview of Schizophrenia

Schizophrenia is a major psychiatric illness that can have a devastating impact on the lives of both patients and their family members. For many years, the families of persons with schizophrenia were treated unfairly by mental health professionals, who erroneously believed that the family was responsible for either causing the illness or worsening its course. Fortunately, over the past 20 years the mental health profession has undergone a dramatic shift in its perception of the importance and value of families of patients with schizophrenia. Once viewed as a nuisance or as contributors to the problem, families are now recognized by professionals as important members of the patient's treatment team who can work alongside them to improve the outcome of this serious illness.

As a family member you are in a unique position to help your relative with schizophrenia. You care deeply for your relative and know him or her better than any professional can. You probably have more contact with your relative and are in better touch with his or her moods, feelings, and needs than anyone else. Your special relationship with your relative places you in the "frontline" of his or her treatment, since you are aware of changes, for better or worse, before others are.

But this special relationship has a high cost. Living with a person with schizophrenia can be nerve-wracking, because his or her behavior can be unpredictable, even frightening at times. It may be difficult for you to find friends who understand the stress you experience coping with your relative. Feelings of isolation, anxiety, depression, and frustration are common among family members with an ill relative, even when they are doing an excellent job.

However, there is hope. By learning more about schizophrenia and how to cope with common problems, you can reduce the strain involved in dealing with the illness and improve the quality of your life and that of your relative. As you become able to communicate more effectively, to recognize the early warning signs of relapse, to support adherence to treatment recommendations, and to encourage small steps toward greater independence, the course of your relative's illness will improve. Improvements are common in areas such as symptom relapse, rehospitalization, social relationships, and capacity to work. And when your relative's life improves, so does yours!

This book is designed to give you the information about schizophrenia your family needs to manage this difficult illness. We also provide practical suggestions for coping with common problems, such as establishing household rules, that other families have found helpful. We believe in the power of your family to overcome obstacles and to move forward into a more positive future.

In this first chapter we review basic information about schizophrenia that will enable you to better understand your relative's illness and help develop realistic expectations for the future. Our discussion here is intended to be a primer to schizophrenia—focusing on the most important facts—rather than a comprehensive review of everything that is known about the illness. For those interested in learning more, including the latest in research findings, we suggest some additional readings in the Resources section at the end of the book.

## What Is Schizophrenia?

Schizophrenia is a complex and confusing illness for mental health professionals, patients, and family members alike. One reason for much of the misunderstanding is that the term *schizophrenia* and *schizophrenic* have so many different uses in everyday language, the popular media, and the medical community.

In everyday language, *schizophrenic* is often used to describe a state of contradictory or incompatible elements. For example, a person who says one thing and then does another might be described in everyday speech as schizophrenic. Likewise, *schizophrenic* is sometimes used to describe the contradictory actions or policies of an entire group of people, such as an organization or a nation. For example, a nation with a friendly foreign policy toward one country and an unfriendly foreign policy toward another, similar country might be described as having a schizophrenic foreign policy.

In the popular media (television, radio, newspaper), the word *schizophrenic* is often used to describe any person with psychotic symptoms, such as hallucinations or delusions, or who is "out of touch" with reality. People in the media also sometimes assume that anyone who has a chronic psychiatric illness has schizophrenia. Professionals who realize schizophrenia is a medical illness view these common descriptions of schizophrenia in the media as inaccurate. Not all people with psychotic symptoms have schizophrenia, and people with schizophrenia are not always psychotic. Similarly, not all people with schizophrenia are chronically ill, nor do all chronic psychiatric patients have schizophrenia.

Among medical professionals who treat persons with mental illness, *schizophrenia* refers to a specific psychiatric illness characterized by severe problems in social functioning and self-care skills and difficulty distinguishing reality. There is a strong consensus among researchers that schizophrenia has biological origins, likely due to an imbalance in chemicals in the brain that regulate thinking and feeling.

Medication plays an important role in treating the illness by correcting this imbalance. However, there is also evidence that environmental stress contributes to the severity of the illness, with high levels of stress resulting in more frequent relapses of symptoms and rehospitalizations. Thus, while biological factors are the major cause of the symptoms of schizophrenia, the amounts of overall stress and support your relative experiences also have a significant bearing on his or her level of functioning.

In summary, schizophrenia is a major psychiatric illness that is probably caused by imbalances in chemicals in the brain, but which is also influenced by the environment. This interplay between biology and the environment provides you with unique opportunities to help improve your relative's illness by reducing stress and actively supporting positive steps toward better coping and increased independence.

## What Is Schizophrenia?

- Schizophrenia is a medical (biological) illness that is probably due to an imbalance in chemicals in the brain.

- Common problems in schizophrenia include impaired social functioning and self-care skills and difficulty distinguishing reality.

- Medication can improve the symptoms but is not a cure for schizophrenia.

- Stress can worsen the symptoms.

- Family members can help improve the course of the patient's illness.

# Common Myths

Almost everyone in our society has heard of schizophrenia, but there are many misconceptions about the illness. These misunderstandings are often created by inaccurate or distorted depictions of the illness in the popular media, and by misuse of the term *schizophrenia* in everyday speech. Now that we have given a brief, accurate description of schizophrenia, it is important to dispel some of the most common myths people have about the illness.

*Myth 1: People with schizophrenia have a "split personality."* A split personality, in which two or more distinct personalities simultaneously exist within the same person, is a rare psychiatric illness called a *multiple personality disorder.* Examples of popular depictions of persons with a multiple personality disorder include *The Three Faces of Eve* (based on the life of Evelyn Lancaster) and *Sybil* (by Flora Rheta Schreiber). People with schizophrenia do *not* have a split personality. It's true that the behavior of someone with schizophrenia may vary at different times during the illness, usually depending on the severity of particular symptoms such as suspiciousness. This does not mean, however, that the person has more than one personality.

*Myth 2: People with schizophrenia are prone to violence.* It is common for newspapers, radio, and television to overemphasize violent crimes committed by psychiatric patients as opposed to those committed by persons who are not mentally ill. Crimes committed by nonpatients often appear less sensational to the public, and consequently receive less media attention. This bias in reporting leads to the impression that schizophrenia is a violent illness. In truth, the opposite is more often the case. Rather than becoming more violent when their symptoms worsen, most people with schizophrenia withdraw from others and prefer to spend more time alone.

Although most people with schizophrenia are not violent, there are *some* patients who become violent. For example, patients are sometimes violent when they have delusions that others intend to injure them, or when they hear voices that threaten them or tell them to hurt others. The most important predictor of future violence is violent behavior in the past. Therefore, if your relative has been violent in the past, it is vital for you to take steps that will minimize your risk of exposure to his or her violent behavior in the future. Further information on minimizing this risk of violence is provided in Chapter 4 ("Early Warning Signs of Relapse"), Chapter 9 ("Establishing Household Rules"), and Chapter 13 ("Responding to Crises").

*Myth 3: Families cause schizophrenia.* The media alone cannot be blamed for the common notion that schizophrenia is caused by problems in early family life, since until recently this myth was endorsed by many mental health professionals. Although there are still a few professionals who hold onto the outdated belief that problematic family interactions play a role in causing schizophrenia, the vast weight of evidence is against them and indicates instead that the behavior of the family has no role in causing the illness. Even if you look back at your own family and identify problems and tensions that you think contributed to the development of your relative's illness, these problems did not *cause* schizophrenia, and no one is to blame for the illness. Modern theories of schizophrenia emphasize that the disorder is biological in nature and that families can, in fact, play a key role in helping the patient cope more effectively with the illness.

*Myth 4: Drug and alcohol abuse can cause schizophrenia.* Street drugs such as marijuana, LSD, heroin, cocaine ("crack"), PCP ("angel dust"), and amphetamines ("speed"), can cause symptoms that closely resemble schizophrenia in individuals who do not have a mental illness. For example, hallucinogens such as LSD and PCP can cause distortions in visual and auditory perception that are quite similar to those found in persons with schizophrenia. Marijuana use can sometimes cause temporary feelings of panic or paranoia. Stimulant drugs, such as cocaine and amphetamines, can cause frightening delusions, especially if these drugs are used frequently over long periods of time. Finally, alcohol abuse and withdrawal from alcohol can also result in many of the symptoms described above.

Despite the similarity between the symptoms of schizophrenia and the negative effects of drugs and alcohol, substance abuse does not *cause* this illness. Most people who experience schizophrenia-like symptoms while using drugs or alcohol stop having these symptoms soon after their substance abuse ceases. The vast majority of people who abuse drugs and alcohol never develop schizophrenia. And research suggests that those people who do develop schizophrenia after substance abuse would probably have developed the illness anyway.

Although substance abuse does not cause schizophrenia, it can worsen the symptoms of the illness. Strategies for coping with drug and alcohol abuse in schizophrenia are discussed in Chapter 12.

# Basic Facts About Schizophrenia

## History of the Concept

There is some debate about how long schizophrenia has existed. There are writings dating back thousands of years that describe the behavior of individuals who appear to have had schizophrenia. However,

## Common Myths About Schizophrenia

| Myth | Reality |
|------|---------|
| People with schizophrenia have a "split personality." | Each patient has only one personality. |
| People with schizophrenia are prone to violence. | Persons with schizophrenia are rarely violent. |
| Families cause schizophrenia. | Schizophrenia is a biological illness that is not caused by families. |
| Drug or alcohol abuse can cause schizophrenia. | Drug or alcohol abuse can worsen the symptoms of schizophrenia, but cannot cause the illness itself. |

it is difficult to determine from these old accounts whether these people actually had schizophrenia as we understand it today or whether they had forms of dementia that could be caused by a variety of factors other than schizophrenia, such as head injury, stroke, or a brain tumor.

The modern concept of schizophrenia as a psychiatric illness with a specific group of symptoms has developed mainly over the past hundred years. Although there are many different individuals who have contributed to our current understanding of schizophrenia, the work of two pioneers stands out above all others: Emil Kraepelin (1855–1926) and Manfred Bleuler (1857–1939).

Kraepelin is most often credited with first describing the symptoms of schizophrenia and suggesting that these symptoms are due to a single illness. Kraepelin described schizophrenia using the term *dementia praecox*. This Latin term refers to two major characteristics of the illness, according to Kraepelin's theory: early onset of the illness (*praecox*) and deterioration in intellectual functioning (*dementia*). He distinguished schizophrenia from manic depression and identified characteristic symptoms of the former, such as hallucinations, delusions, impaired attention span, and social withdrawal.

Bleuler focused more on the nature of symptoms of schizophrenia and less on its course than Kraepelin did. Bleuler believed that the illness did not necessarily have an early age of onset or always result in a gradual deterioration in mental functioning. He rejected the term *dementia praecox* and proposed the word *schizophrenia* to describe what he saw as the essential feature of the illness: a split (*schizo*) in the mind (*phren*) between perception and reality—rather than a split between different personalities. However, he agreed with Kraepelin's description of many of the basic symptoms of the illness. Most of the same symptoms are used to diagnose schizophrenia today.

## Diagnosis

There is no laboratory test, such as a blood test or x-ray, that can be used to diagnose schizophrenia in your relative. The illness must be diagnosed based on a careful clinical interview with the patient conducted by a trained professional, usually a psychiatrist or psychologist. The interview is conducted in conjunction with a physical exam, which is performed to determine whether the patient has any known physical problem that could cause symptoms resembling schizophrenia. For example, if the patient has a brain tumor, an untreated endocrinological disorder (such as hyperthyroidism), or is currently abusing drugs or alcohol, a diagnosis of schizophrenia cannot be made until the physical condition has first been treated.

During the clinical interview, the professional evaluates whether the patient has experienced any of a particular set of symptoms used to define the illness of schizophrenia. These symptoms need not be present all the time, but they must be present for at least some time in order for a diagnosis of schizophrenia to be made. Specific guidelines have been established for making psychiatric diagnoses, so that different hospitals and clinics use the same criteria in making diagnoses, as discussed further in Chapter 2.

Common symptoms of schizophrenia include hallucinations, delusions, reduced emotional expressiveness ("blunted affect"), and problems in social functioning. The patient need not have every symptom of schizophrenia in order to be diagnosed. In fact, each person with the illness has a unique set of symptoms. However, all people with schizophrenia experience at least some problems in one or more of three major areas of social functioning: work, close interpersonal relationships, and self-care skills.

There are several other psychiatric diagnoses that are closely related to schizophrenia: schizoaffective disorder, schizophreniform disorder, and schizotypal personality disorder. The symptoms and course of each of these diagnoses overlap considerably with schizophrenia. Even more importantly, the same treatments that have been found to be effective for schizophrenia are also effective for these related disorders. For this reason, all of these illnesses are commonly referred to as *schizophrenia-spectrum* disorders. If your relative has any of these disorders, the information and suggestions provided in this guide will be helpful to you. In Chapter 2, "Diagnosis and Symptoms" we provide further information on the diagnosis of schizophrenia-spectrum disorders and the nature of the specific symptoms of these disorders. For the sake of simplicity, however, the term *schizophrenia* is used throughout this book.

## What Is the Experience of Schizophrenia Like?

In an educational-support group meeting that included both patients and relatives, one patient emphatically told the relatives: "You *think* you know what it's like to have schizophrenia, but you really don't. No one knows what it feels like to have these problems unless they've actually had them." This statement summarizes the extreme difficulty of truly understanding the experience of schizophrenia when you don't have the illness yourself. However, it is helpful to try to understand how your relative feels.

One useful way of describing the experience of schizophrenia is that it is similar to dreaming when one is wide awake. Usually when you dream you believe that the experience is real and not part of your imagination. This is similar to your relative's experience with schizophrenia. At times he or she has difficulty distinguishing between reality and illusion even when awake. In addition to this difficulty, patients frequently report problems of being overwhelmed by stimuli, difficulty focusing their attention, and lack of motivation and enjoyment. One patient described the experience of overstimulation as similar to playing tennis when there are many balls coming over the net at the same time.

Practically every person with schizophrenia has problems with attention. One patient told us, "It's hard for me to concentrate on anything because I'm so easily distracted—like right now I'm listening to the cars on the highway outside the hospital." This difficulty can interfere with the ability of your relative to work or to sustain any focused activity.

Problems with motivation and enjoyment are also commonplace. Another patient we were working with told us, "We used to be a beach family and I loved going to the beach. Now, the beach is just a few blocks away and I can't get the motivation to go there. Or if I do go, it's not fun." This problem can result in your relative having few leisure activities or not enjoying social relationships as much as he or she used to.

In short, the experience of schizophrenia is difficult to fully comprehend. If your relative is willing to talk about the experience, you may be able to understand more by engaging him or her in a discussion about what it is like. Written first-person accounts of the experience of schizophrenia are also available. A few of these are listed in the Resources section at the end of the book.

## Schizophrenia Facts: History and Diagnosis

- Current conceptualizations of schizophrenia date back about 100 years.

- Schizophrenia is diagnosed with a clinical interview, not a laboratory test, such as blood test or x-ray.

- Specific symptoms include hallucinations, delusions, lack of motivation, poor social functioning, and problems with concentration.

- Schizophrenia, schizoaffective disorder, schizophreniform disorder, and schizotypal personality disorder are all very similar and are called *schizophrenia-spectrum* disorders.

- The experience of schizophrenia is like dreaming when you are wide awake.

## *Prevalence*

Approximately one out of every hundred people (1 percent) develop schizophrenia at some time during their lives. In the United States, there are between two and three million persons with this illness. Schizophrenia occurs in both men and women, and in all races, social classes, religions, and cultures. Some research has indicated that schizophrenia is more common in some cultures than others, but most researchers have found a fairly similar rate of the illness across different cultures. These figures indicate that schizophrenia is one of most common serious psychiatric illnesses. For comparison, about one out of every *two* hundred people (.5 percent) develop manic depression, another serious psychiatric illness that is usually not quite as severe as schizophrenia.

One indication of the magnitude of the problem of schizophrenia is the resources devoted to the treatment of this illness. More hospital beds are occupied by persons with schizophrenia than any other psychiatric illness. A majority of patients in state psychiatric hospitals have this diagnosis. Approximately one-fifth of all chronic disability (including both physical and mental illnesses) is due to schizophrenia. The majority of patients are unable to live independently and live either with relatives or in supervised community residences. About 10 percent of all homeless individuals have schizophrenia. When one includes the costs of treating schizophrenia, the expenditures by families, and the lost income, the total costs of schizophrenia are staggering.

## Development of Schizophrenia

Schizophrenia usually develops sometime during late adolescence or early adulthood, most often between the ages of 16 and 25. Schizophrenia rarely develops after the age of 35, although a very small proportion of cases have an onset of the illness later in life (after the age of 50). Childhood schizophrenia, in which the onset is before puberty (usually before the age of 10), is quite rare and is considered a different disorder than adult schizophrenia. Childhood schizophrenia should not be confused with autism (also referred to as "pervasive developmental disability"), which is more common and also has an onset during childhood. This guide is intended for families in which a relative has developed schizophrenia in adolescence or adulthood.

Although the prevalence of schizophrenia is approximately the same in men and women, the onset of the illness tends to occur at a slightly later age in women than in men. The reasons for the later age of onset for women than men are not understood at this time, although it does not appear that the difference can be explained simply by a tendency for families to report problematic symptoms for men sooner than for women.

The onset of schizophrenia usually follows one of two different patterns: Either the symptoms emerge gradually over a period of several months, or the symptoms emerge very slowly over a period of several years. In the second case, the onset of schizophrenia can be quite imperceptible, and it is not possible to identify a specific age when the illness developed.

The earliest signs of the onset of the illness are most often a disruption in the person's social relationships, such as withdrawal from friends and family members, which is accompanied somewhat later by a gradual deterioration in other areas of functioning, such as the ability to perform in school, to work, or to care for him- or herself. From the patient's perspective, these early problems are often reflected by mild perceptual aberrations, such as colors appearing brighter or noises sounding louder, and difficulty in concentrating.

At first, family members may not recognize these changes, or they may attribute the changes to a "stage" that the person is going through or to normal adolescent behavior. Sometimes when families *do* recognize that something is wrong and seek a professional opinion, they are told that their relative's behavior is normal and they need not worry. Many professionals who do not work with the seriously mentally ill (such as general practitioners) are not trained to recognize the symptoms of schizophrenia. However, even professionals who are trained to diagnose schizophrenia often find it difficult to diagnose it during its earliest stages.

The question of whether people who develop schizophrenia differ from others in childhood or adolescence before they become ill has intrigued researchers for decades. The answer is both yes and no. Many people who develop schizophrenia were well adjusted, both socially and personally, before they became ill. We know many patients who had a normal and happy childhood and adolescence before they became ill. We have met a variety of individuals who accomplished many things before they developed schizophrenia: a high school class valedictorian, a virtuoso cellist who soloed with a major city orchestra, a writer and illustrator who published his work in high school.

However, some individuals who develop schizophrenia *are* less well-adjusted before they become ill, and these people's difficulties often date back to childhood. Two patterns of abnormal or maladjusted behavior have been described. First, some persons tend to be withdrawn and have fewer childhood and adolescent friendships because they were very shy, had poor interpersonal skills, or were less interested in making friends. These individuals usually lag behind others in romantic interest and involvement, such as dating experience, having a steady boy or girlfriend, and sexual activity. These difficulties in social relationships often go unnoticed by others because the person is not a "problem." The impairments in social functioning experienced by these persons early in life usually persist at a more severe level after the onset of schizophrenia.

The second pattern of maladjustment is that some persons display disruptive behavior problems that predate the development of schizophrenia. The most common behaviors include hyperactivity, attention problems, conduct disorder, and impulsivity that first appear in childhood. These behavior problems usually interfere with academic and social functioning, and may result in recommendations for treatment, such as counseling, parent training, family therapy, and medication.

Although some people who develop schizophrenia display one (or both) of these patterns of maladjustment before they become ill, most children and adolescents who experience these problems never develop schizophrenia. Therefore, it is not possible at this time to predict who will and who will not develop schizophrenia.

## Course of the Illness

Schizophrenia is an episodic illness with symptoms that vary in intensity at different times. When episodes of the illness occur, chronic symptoms worsen and symptoms that have been in remission may reappear, at times requiring treatment in the hospital. Inpatient treatment is usually provided for relatively brief periods of time, ranging from a few days to several months. A small proportion of patients become extremely ill and require long-term treatment, such as in a state hospital. In most cases, these patients pose a grave risk to themselves in the community and thus require institutional care. However, new approaches to caring for even the most severely debilitated patients in the community (based on the Community Treatment Team Model developed by Drs. Mary Ann Test and Leonard Stein in Madison, Wisconsin) have shown much promise, and the era of institutional care for the seriously mentally ill may soon be coming to an end.

The course of schizophrenia is different for each individual. In general, the course of the illness can be described as following one of three different patterns:

- About one-third of people with schizophrenia have a few episodes of the illness, but with treatment are able to regain their former level of functioning after a period of recovery. These individuals' schizophrenia may have a fairly mild course, and a good level of social adjustment can be achieved, although they still need to learn how to manage their illness.

- Another third of patients experience more frequent episodes of the illness throughout their lives, and only partly regain their former level of functioning between episodes. People in this category may have many hospitalizations, but they are still able to spend most of their time living in the community. Schizophrenia handicaps these patients in many ways. But despite these handicaps, with help, these patients are able to pursue personal goals and achieve a degree of independence.

- The last third of patients have a more severe course of the illness. These patients experience symptoms nearly all the time and require much closer supervision, whether they are in the hospital or in the community. Treatment may be less effective for these individuals. Schizophrenia disrupts many aspects of their daily functioning and interferes with their ability to manage their everyday lives.

Despite the serious effects of schizophrenia over a patient's lifetime, there are good reasons to be optimistic about the long-term outcome. Research studies indicate very gradual improvements over time in symptoms and social functioning. It is common for patients during the early years of their illness to have severe symptoms, to deny any problems, and to be uncooperative with treatment (such as medication). Over time these same patients often become more aware of their need for help and participate more actively in their own treatment, leading to improved symptoms. A significant number of persons with schizophrenia become relatively free of symptoms later in their lives, after the age of 50.

Can the course and outcome of schizophrenia be predicted? For the most part, we are not able to predict which patients will do better in the long run. There is a tendency for people who had problems in social functioning *before* they became ill to have a worse course of their illness. Early recognition and treatment of schizophrenia tend to result in a less severe course of illness. There is also a tendency for women to have a slightly less severe course of illness than men. However, it is interesting that people who develop schizophrenia at an earlier age do *not* tend to have a worse course of their illness.

For example, one patient we worked with first developed schizophrenia at the age of 16. His illness had a rocky course over the next 15 years, with inconsistent medication compliance and frequent hospitalizations. Then, with the help of family education, he became more compliant with treatment and his symptoms slowly improved. He is now 39 years old and he has not been hospitalized for the past eight years. Even more remarkably, five years ago he married, and he now has two children and is employed. Despite his progress, he still has mild symptoms of schizophrenia and sees his psychiatrist and nurse every month to have his symptoms monitored.

Our inability to predict which patients will have a good course and outcome of schizophrenia may reflect the fact that stress in the environment, in addition to biological factors, can influence the course of your relative's illness. We will take up this point again later in the chapter, when we discuss the stress-vulnerability model of schizophrenia and the role you can play in improving the outcome of your relative's illness.

## Schizophrenia Facts: Prevalence, Development, and Course

- About 1 in 100 people (1 percent) develop schizophrenia.
- The illness occurs worldwide regardless of gender, culture, race, and religion.
- Schizophrenia is the most severe of the major adult psychiatric illnesses.
- Schizophrenia usually develops between the ages of 16 and 25.
- The first signs of the illness are usually social withdrawal and decline in functioning.
- Some people who develop schizophrenia have social problems growing up; others do not.
- Schizophrenia is a lifelong illness with an episodic course and symptoms whose severity fluctuates over time.
- The symptoms gradually improve over the patient's lifetime.

# The Cause of Schizophrenia

Over the past 100 years many theories have been proposed by scientists to explain the development of schizophrenia. The majority of scientists who have theorized about the causes of schizophrenia have believed that the illness is biological in nature, and involves some type of disturbance in the brain. For example, Kraepelin, as far back as a hundred years ago, firmly believed that the illness was a type of brain disease with origins that would eventually be discovered through biological research.

For a period of several decades, mostly from the 1940s to the 1960s, some mental health professionals argued that schizophrenia was caused by problematic family relationships while the person was growing up, rather than disordered brain functioning. For example, one theory suggested that the illness developed after the individual was repeatedly exposed to "double bind" messages from a parent, that is, communications that were contradictory, such as a mother saying "I love you" while grimacing and pushing her child away. Another theory was that a pattern of coldness and rejection by the mother eventually caused her offspring to develop schizophrenia. Several theories proposed that schizophrenia was due to marital problems, either because the parents were "immature" or because there was conflict between the partners in the marriage.

These theories enjoyed some popularity for a number of years, but advances in biological research on schizophrenia led them to be abandoned by all but a few in the field. For example, the profound effects of antipsychotic medications on the symptoms of schizophrenia suggest that the illness is related to disordered brain functioning and is *not* a psychological response to disturbed family relationships.

There is now a strong consensus that schizophrenia is a biological illness. However, little agreement exists as to which specific factors are responsible for the symptoms of schizophrenia. The task of researchers is further complicated by the fact that no consistent biological differences have been found between patients and nonpatients. One possible explanation for this lack of consistent differences is that schizophrenia is not one disease but is instead several different or overlapping diseases. Extensive research continues to be conducted on the biological underpinnings of schizophrenia to evaluate whether the illness is a unitary one or is composed of multiple diseases.

## The Biology of Schizophrenia

Many of the current theories of schizophrenia are quite complex and involve the interaction between different brain structures or areas (referred to as *neural networks*). For example, many recent theories stress the importance of the *prefrontal cortex,* a region of the brain required for planning and abstract thinking, and the *hippocampus,* a brain structure that is critical for memory. Although it is beyond the scope of this book to explain the nuances of different biological theories of schizophrenia, we believe that it can be helpful to briefly describe one major theory of the illness.

The most prominent theory of schizophrenia is that persons with the illness have an imbalance in the chemicals in the brain. These chemicals play a vital role in all aspects of adaptive functioning, including the ability to think, feel, perceive, and act in a planned, goal directed fashion. In order to understand why a chemical imbalance may be involved in schizophrenia, it is first necessary to review some basic facts about how the brain works.

The brain is composed of billions and billions of nerve cells, called *neurons*. These neurons are densely packed and are distributed throughout the entire brain. All neurons contain chemicals called *neurotransmitters*, which act as messengers communicating information from one part of the brain to another.

The neurotransmitters are stored inside small sacs (called *vesicles*) in the neuron and are released to send a message to another neuron. When the neurotransmitter is released from the vesicle, it leaves the neuron itself (the *presynaptic neuron*) and enters a small space (called the *synaptic cleft*) to another neuron (the *postsynaptic neuron*). Some of the neurotransmitter is absorbed by the postsynaptic neuron, some of it is broken down by other chemicals and excreted through bodily fluids, and some of the neurotransmitter is reabsorbed back into the vesicle of the presynaptic neuron. The entire process of a neurotransmitter release and absorption is referred to as *neurotransmission*. See in Figure 1.1.

## Neurotransmitters and Schizophrenia

Scientists have identified over 50 different kinds of neurotransmitters. An imbalance in a neurotransmitter called *dopamine* is believed to exist in schizophrenia. Dopamine is an important neurotransmitter that is used in many different parts of the brain. It is involved in the regulation of thoughts and feelings, both of which are disturbed in schizophrenia.

Animal studies of the effects of antipsychotic medications (the most effective medications for schizophrenia) on neurotransmitters have consistently found that these types of medication block dopamine neurotransmission in the brain. This finding has led scientists to hypothesize that people with schizophrenia have an excess of dopamine in certain regions of the brain. Research has not yet directly shown that patients have an imbalance in brain dopamine, since this is a difficult question to answer with the technology currently available to scientists. Nevertheless, the dopamine hypothesis of schizophrenia is the most widely accepted biological theory of the illness, and it continues to stimulate much research into the causes of schizophrenia.

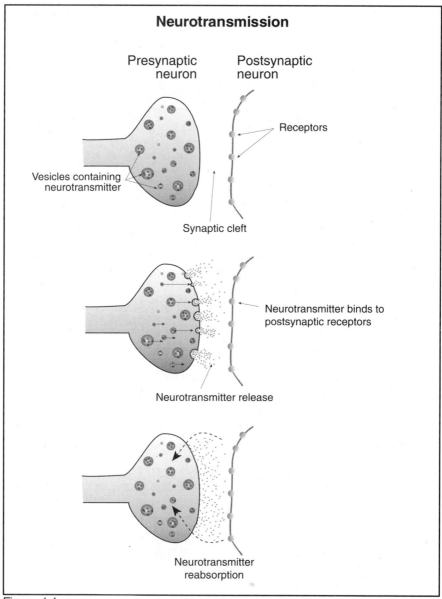

**Neurotransmission**

Presynaptic
neuron

Postsynaptic
neuron

Receptors

Vesicles containing
neurotransmitter

Synaptic cleft

Neurotransmitter binds to
postsynaptic receptors

Neurotransmitter release

Neurotransmitter
reabsorption

Figure 1.1

## Genetic and Environmental Factors

Scientists do not yet understand why some persons may have a chemical imbalance leading to the development of schizophrenia. Research indicates that the vulnerability to develop schizophrenia may be partially caused by genetic factors, because the chances of a person developing schizophrenia are higher if a close relative also has the illness. This is similar to many other diseases in which genetic factors play a role, such as hypertension, diabetes, depression, and coronary artery disease.

As we previously discussed, about 1 percent of people in the general population develop schizophrenia. If the person has a first degree relative with schizophrenia, the chances are higher, about 1 in 10 (10 percent). If someone has more than one ill family member, the chances may be even higher, although in all cases the chances are still less than 50%, as follows:

| Relative | Chance |
|---|---|
| No ill relative | 1 in 100 (1%) |
| Ill uncle or aunt | 3 in 100 (3%) |
| Ill parent or sibling | 5–10 in 100 (5–10%) |
| Both parents ill | 15–20 in 100 (15–20%) |
| Nonidentical (dizygotic) twin ill | 5–10 in 100 (5–10%) |
| Identical (monozygotic) twin ill | 25–45 in 100 (25–45%) |

The fact that a person with an identical twin (a twin with the same genes) with schizophrenia has a greater chance of developing schizophrenia than a person with a nonidentical twin who is ill suggests that schizophrenia is influenced partly by genetic factors. However, not every identical twin of a person with schizophrenia becomes ill, which suggests that genetic factors alone cannot explain who becomes ill. Although family studies on schizophrenia indicate that genes may play a role in determining vulnerability to the illness, a specific pattern of inheritance has not been identified, nor has any "bad" gene been found.

If genes are involved in schizophrenia, most scientists believe that multiple genes may act together to determine vulnerability, rather than a single gene. The possibility that genetic factors lead to the development of schizophrenia is an important *theory*, but it has not yet been proven. There is no test currently available to predict who will develop schizophrenia, because scientists do not know which genes are involved.

Despite the finding that people with schizophrenia are more likely to have relatives with this illness, many families have only one person with this illness. You may wonder how your relative developed schizophrenia if there are few or no other relatives with mental illness in your family. One possibility is that some individuals may carry the genes that predispose for schizophrenia without themselves developing the illness. In such a case, the critical genes are said not to be "expressed" (or are only partially expressed) by the healthy relative, but they may neverthe-less be transmitted to another relative who develops the illness.

Another possibility is that some cases of schizophrenia may occur for reasons other than genetic vulnerability, or because of interactions be-tween very subtle genetic factors and the environment. There is now a growing body of evidence indicating that certain environmental factors to which a baby may be exposed in the mother's womb or at birth are related to small increases in vulnerability to developing schizophrenia later. For example, some researchers have hypothesized that the offspring of mothers who were exposed to influenza epidemics during pregnancy have a higher chance of developing schizophrenia. Children who are born in the winter are slightly more likely to develop schizophrenia than chil-dren born in other seasons, possibly because of the greater chances that the pregnant mother was exposed to influenza-like viruses in the winter. Other environmental risk factors have also been identified. One study found that children who were born during a famine were more likely to develop schizophrenia, and several studies have reported that obstetric complications (such as forceps delivery, fetal distress) are related to a higher rate of developing schizophrenia.

---

## Causes of Schizophrenia

- The cause of schizophrenia is not known.
- Major theories of the illness suggest that:

  Patients may have an imbalance in the brain chemical dopamine

  Genetic factors may play a role in determining vulnerability to schizophrenia

  Exposure to early environmental "risk factors" before or during birth (such as maternal influenza, obstetric complications) may play a role in some cases of schizophrenia

  Schizophrenia may have multiple causes or may even be multiple illnesses

---

Scientists do not understand how these environmental factors act, either in concert with genetic factors or alone, to influence vulnerability to schizophrenia. Some have suggested that exposure to these types of environmental "insult" may cause small amounts of brain damage. This damage may only become apparent later in the person's development, when certain critical parts of the brain fail to mature in a normal fashion, such as during adolescence and early adulthood, eventually resulting in schizophrenia.

In summary, there is compelling evidence that schizophrenia is a biological illness, but beyond this, scientists do not agree as to the specific causes of the illness. Schizophrenia may be one illness with one cause, one illness with multiple possible causes, or multiple illnesses with multiple causes. There are many theories that suggest which specific disturbances in the brain are responsible for the symptoms of schizophrenia and why some individuals are vulnerable and others are not. We continue to learn more every day about schizophrenia as research progresses. Although we are optimistic that research on normal brain functioning and schizophrenia will shed more light on the biological causes of the illness, we also believe that this knowledge will accumulate gradually, over a long period of time, and will not be the result of a dramatic breakthrough in research that explains all cases of this complex illness. In the meantime, millions of people already have the illness and need practical help.

## The Stress-Vulnerability Model of Schizophrenia

Over the past two decades the stress-vulnerability model has emerged as a valuable framework for understanding the factors that determine the severity of schizophrenia. No single scientist alone claims credit for this important model. Rather, it has evolved over the years through the contributions of many different scientists.

According to this model, the severity and course of schizophrenic symptoms are determined by three different factors: biological vulnerability, stress, and patient coping skills:

- *Biological vulnerability* refers to the biological predisposition to experience the symptoms of schizophrenia. As previously discussed, this vulnerability may reflect an imbalance in brain chemistry caused by genetic factors, exposure to early biological risks, or both. If the person does not have this vulnerability, he or she will not develop the symptoms of schizophrenia. Among individuals who have schizophrenia, there appears to be a correlation between the degree of biological vulnerability and the severity of symptoms and course of illness. (There is currently no direct measure of biological vulnerability.)

- *Stress* refers to negative aspects of the environment in which patients currently live. Research has shown that several types of stress can have a negative effect on persons with schizophrenia. Significant life events, such as the death of someone close, loss of a job, or change in residence can be stressful and lead to relapses in some patients. Living in an environment in which there is a great deal of conflict, criticism, or negativity between the patient and others (either family members or professional staff) can be stressful to patients and increase their risk of relapse. Also, an environment that either places heavy demands on the patient or that lacks structure can be stressful and worsen symptoms of schizophrenia.

- *Coping skills* refers to patients' ability to handle stress effectively and thereby to reduce the negative effects of stress. Examples of good coping skills are social skills and the ability to relax. Effective social skills enable patients to resolve interpersonal conflicts, thus lowering stress in relationships. The ability to relax can help patients cope with noninterpersonal stresses, such as increased demands at work.

The interaction between biological vulnerability, stress, and coping skills influences the severity of symptoms and the patient's risk of relapse and rehospitalization, as illustrated in Figure 1.2. This same model also applies to a variety of other medical disorders whose outcome can be influenced by stress and coping, such as hypertension, diabetes, and survival from cancer. In addition to providing a framework for understanding the factors that influence the severity and course of schizophrenia, the stress-vulnerability model is also helpful in guiding the treatment of the illness, as described next.

## Treatment

The treatment of schizophrenia is guided by three general principles that follow directly from the stress-vulnerability model.

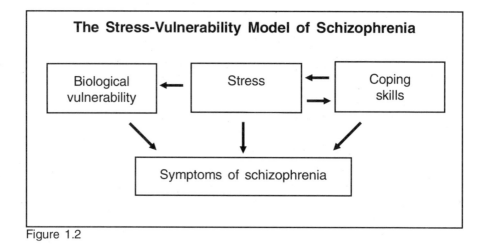

Figure 1.2

*Reduce biological vulnerability.* There is no cure for the biological vulnerability that causes the symptoms of schizophrenia in your relative. However, antipsychotic medications can reduce both symptoms and the risk of relapses. These medications are currently the most powerful tools in treating persons with schizophrenia, although they are by no means perfect. In addition to taking medication, it is important that your relative have his or her symptoms monitored on a regular basis, so that medication can be adjusted if changes in symptoms are detected.

If your relative has a substance abuse problem, treating this (in addition to providing antipsychotic medications) will reduce his or her biological vulnerability and improve the course of the illness. Abusing street drugs, such as cocaine, can worsen the patient's biological vulnerability, leading to more severe symptoms and relapses. Alcohol abuse can render antipsychotic medication ineffective.

*Reduce environmental stress.* Depending upon the source of the stress, there are a number of ways of reducing the stress on your ill relative. Stress resulting from tense family relationships can be lowered by strategies such as developing specific and realistic expectations for your relative's behavior and improving your skills at communicating and resolving problems with him or her.

If your relative has little meaningful structure in his or her life, attempts can be made to develop more structure, while avoiding the pitfall of creating excessive demands and expectations for rapid change. Striking a balance between understimulation and overstimulation in your relative's environment is vital to minimizing stress at home, a day treatment program, vocational program, or at work.

*Improve coping skills.* The third treatment strategy involves teaching persons with schizophrenia more effective coping skills, so that they are better able to handle everyday types of stress. One common strategy for improving patients' coping has been social skills training, in which they are systematically taught how to improve their skills for interacting with others. Good social skills can reduce stress in relationships as well as help patients achieve goals, such as making friends or dating.

Many patients benefit from learning stress reduction techniques to cope with problems of anxiety and depression. In addition to learning how to cope with these types of stress, patients often benefit from developing specific strategies to cope more effectively with persistent symptoms, such as hallucinations and delusions.

## Treatment of Schizophrenia

Reduce biological vulnerability:

- Antipsychotic medication to correct chemical imbalance
- Regularly monitor symptoms to adjust medication when necessary
- Reduce substance abuse

Reduce stress:

- Lower tension in the family environment through establishing realistic expectations, and developing good communication and problem-solving skills
- Create a supportive family milieu by reinforcing small improvements made by the patient
- Strive for a balance between overstimulation and understimulation in the patient's environment

Improve coping skills:

- Teach social skills
- Teach stress reduction techniques
- Help patients develop strategies to cope better with persistent symptoms

# 2

# Diagnosis and Symptoms

*Diagnosis* is a medical term that refers to the classification of an illness. A pattern of symptoms or signs of an illness is necessary in order to establish a psychiatric diagnosis. A diagnosis cannot be made on the basis of a single symptom. In fact, many of the symptoms of schizophrenia are also sometimes present in patients with other psychiatric disorders. It is the unique combination of symptoms that distinguishes schizophrenia from other major psychiatric disorders.

In many ways you are already familiar with the symptoms of schizophrenia; through your close relationship with your family member, you have been able to directly or indirectly observe many of the characteristic symptoms. However, you may wonder which of your relative's problems or behavior patterns are due to schizophrenia and which may be due to other factors, such as personality. Furthermore, your relative may have received a variety of different psychiatric diagnoses over the years, and you may wonder how much confidence you can have in your relative's current diagnosis.

In order to cope effectively with your relative who has schizophrenia and to help him or her manage the illness most successfully, you need to be familiar with how a diagnosis is established and the specific nature of different symptoms. This chapter provides information about the diagnosis of schizophrenia-spectrum disorders, a group of closely-related disorders that have a similar course and respond to the same treatments. The symptoms most commonly present in these disorders are also discussed in detail. This information will help you understand your relative's behavior and monitor his or her symptoms in the future.

## Diagnostic Systems

For many years, particularly in the United States, the diagnosis of schizophrenia was not applied consistently; instead, it was given to anybody with serious psychiatric problems who could not clearly be classified as having another psychiatric disorder, such as depression. As a result of this lack of agreement on how to diagnose schizophrenia, doctors often disagreed about a patient's diagnosis, the diagnosis frequently changed over time, and family members were often confused as to the nature of their relative's disorder.

Over the past several decades significant advances have been made in how psychiatric diagnoses are established. A *diagnostic system* is a set of specific criteria (rules) used to systematically establish a medical diagnosis. By carefully evaluating each objectively-defined criterion specified in a diagnostic system, different diagnosticians can usually agree upon the same specific diagnosis for a particular patient. In recent years several different diagnostic systems for psychiatric disorders have been explored, with two systems being used most commonly throughout the world. In the United States the psychiatric diagnostic system that is used is the *Diagnostic and Statistical Manual*, now in its fourth edition *(DSM-IV)*, developed by the American Psychiatric Association. Throughout the rest of the world, the psychiatric diagnostic system most often used is the tenth edition of the *International Classification of Diseases (ICD-10)*. The specific criteria used in *DSM-IV* and *ICD-10* to classify schizophrenia and related disorders are very similar.

## Establishing a Psychiatric Diagnosis

As mentioned in Chapter 1, the diagnosis of schizophrenia in your relative cannot be made with any type of laboratory test or x-ray. Rather, the diagnosis must be based on interviews with the patient, and sometimes with relatives as well. These interviews focus on evaluating specific symptoms your relative may have, the duration of those symptoms, problems in functioning, and the possible role of drug or alcohol abuse in these symptoms or problems. Medical tests are occasionally conducted to rule out possible organic (physical) factors that could cause symptoms similar to those found in schizophrenia, such as a thyroid problem or brain tumor. If such an organic factor is identified, the person is not diagnosed with schizophrenia. The information obtained from the interviews (and, when necessary, medical tests) is then used to arrive at a diagnosis, based on the *DSM-IV* criteria.

A number of different mental health professionals may be qualified to make the diagnosis of schizophrenia in your relative. All psychiatrists are qualified to make the diagnosis, because it is an essential part of their training. Many psychologists are also qualified to diagnose schizophrenia, provided they have received the necessary training. Psychiatric social workers and nurses usually are not specifically trained in making psychiatric diagnoses, but some have received training and are also qualified to establish diagnoses.

Although the specific criteria for diagnosing schizophrenia are contained in *DSM-IV*, differences between diagnosticians are still possible. For example, one person may make the diagnosis of schizophrenia after a half-hour interview with the patient, while another prefers a longer interview and a meeting with another family member. Interviewers may also differ in the specific wording they use to find out about a symptom. In order to make the process of establishing a psychiatric diagnosis more consistent across different diagnosticians, structured clinical interviews have been developed to evaluate symptoms using a standardized approach. For example, the Structured Clinical Interview for DSM-IV (SCID) provides specific questions for assessing all the symptoms of the different psychiatric disorders. A disadvantage of structured interviews, such as the SCID, is that they may take a long time to administer, sometimes as long as two or three hours (though the time may be divided over several days). For this reason, structured interviews usually are not used in everyday clinical practice. However, research has shown that psychiatric diagnoses made with structured clinical interviews are very reliable (consistent across different interviewers).

## The Reliability of Psychiatric Diagnosis

Your relative may have received many different psychiatric diagnoses since he or she first became ill. If so, you probably found this to be frustrating and confusing, and you may have wondered "Why can't they just make up their minds?!" There are several reasons different psychiatric diagnoses may be given to the same patient over time. As mentioned above, one reason diagnoses vary is because of differences in how the diagnosis is established. Diagnoses made on the basis of structured clinical interviews are more reliable than diagnoses made using less standardized interviews. However, structured clinical interviews are less commonly used in clinical practice. During the course of your relative's illness he or she may have seen a number of doctors who have used their own unstructured interviews.

Another reason diagnoses may change is that the symptoms themselves change, and this can result in different diagnoses at different times, depending upon which symptoms are currently most prominent. For example, most patients with schizophrenia experience some problems with depression during their illness. If the patient is evaluated by a mental health professional during a period of severe depression, he or she may be given a diagnosis of major depression instead of schizophrenia. Similarly, if the patient is evaluated during a period of extreme excitement, a diagnosis of bipolar disorder may be made instead of schizophrenia. Misdiagnosis of schizophrenia appears to be most common during the early stages of the illness, when the diagnostician has less psychiatric history upon which to base the diagnosis.

Sometimes schizophrenia is misdiagnosed (usually underdiagnosed) during the early years of the illness because mental health professionals do not recognize the disorder or they do not want to alarm family members by giving such a serious diagnosis to a young person. When the symptoms of schizophrenia first appear during adolescence, professionals sometimes try to reassure concerned family members by saying that it is "just a stage" the person is going through, and delaying action. These professionals may not recognize the symptoms of schizophrenia at the early stages, or they may want to "protect" family members from the diagnosis. During the first few episodes of schizophrenia, a patient will sometimes be diagnosed with a less debilitating disorder (such as major depression, bipolar disorder, or adjustment disorder), which is switched to schizophrenia if the symptoms persist and the patient continues to have significant problems. Too often the result is that patients and their family members must wait years before receiving an accurate diagnosis.

One last reason different diagnoses may be given to a patient is that there are some patients whose symptoms do not clearly fall into one distinct category. While the majority of psychiatric patients can be classified as having one particular diagnosis, a few cannot, and there is no easy solution to this problem. Despite the many reasons psychiatric diagnoses sometimes change, a reliable diagnosis can be made in most cases.

## Common Reasons for Changes in Psychiatric Diagnosis

- Differences in diagnosticians' interviewing style
- Use of structured diagnostic interview versus nonstructured interviews
- Changes in symptoms over time
- Difficulty recognizing schizophrenia during the early stages
- Mental health professionals' attempts to "protect" relatives from the diagnosis
- Symptom combinations that do not clearly fit into one diagnosis

# Schizophrenia-Spectrum Disorders

The "schizophrenia spectrum" is a group of psychiatric disorders that are similar in terms of the onset and course, characteristic symptoms, levels of impairment, response to treatment, and long-term outcome. This book is written for family members who have a relative with any of these disorders.

The schizophrenia-spectrum disorders include schizophrenia, schizophreniform disorder, schizoaffective disorder, and schizotypal personality disorder. The diagnostic criteria for each of these disorders according to *DSM-IV* is contained in Figure 2.1, at the end of the chapter. The specific symptoms referred to in the figure are described in more detail a bit later in the chapter. We briefly summarize below the common and unique aspects of each disorder.

## Schizophrenia

Schizophrenia is the most common schizophrenia-spectrum disorder. In addition to certain symptoms lasting at least one month, the patient must have significant impairment in some aspect of social functioning, work, or self-care. Overall, the problems must have persisted for at least six months. For the diagnosis of schizophrenia, the patient must also not have prominent symptoms of a mood disturbance (such as severe depressive or manic symptoms), or if such symptoms are present, they must be relatively brief in relation to how long the patient has been ill.

## Schizophreniform Disorder

The diagnostic criteria for this schizophreniform disorder are identical to those for schizophrenia, except that the duration of impairment is less than six months. If the patient has the symptoms for at least one month, but they completely subside before six months, then the patient has a schizophreniform disorder. If the symptoms return for periods of time less than six months, the diagnosis would remain schizophreniform. Most patients who develop schizophreniform disorder eventually develop schizophrenia.

## Schizoaffective Disorder

The primary feature of schizoaffective disorder that distinguishes it from schizophrenia is the presence of a mood episode that has been present for a substantial portion of the time that the patient has been ill, but not all the time. A *mood episode* is a period of time in which the patient has experienced significant symptoms of depression or mania. Common symptoms of *depression* include feeling sad or "blue"; feelings of helplessness, hopelessness, or worthlessness; loss of appetite or increased appetite; difficulty sleeping or excessive sleeping; inappropriate feelings of guilt (for example, feeling responsible for a crime that the person did not commit); loss of energy; thoughts of hurting oneself; and loss of pleasure. Common symptoms of *mania* include decreased need for sleep, increased irritability or hostility, grandiosity (for example, the person thinks he or she has skills, talents, or resources that don't exist), and increased goal-directed behavior (for example, the relentless pursuit of a business deal or romantic conquest). Patients with a schizoaffective disorder have experienced these mood symptoms for a significant period of time, but have also had symptoms of schizophrenia at times when they did not have mood symptoms.

There are two reasons it is sometimes difficult to distinguish schizoaffective disorder from schizophrenia. First, the symptoms of a mood syndrome overlap with those of schizophrenia. For example, grandiose delusions (such as believing that one is the king of England) can be present in either mania or schizophrenia. Second, if significant mood symptoms are identified, it is difficult to determine how long they have been present and whether this time period could be considered substantial.

However, the difficulties in distinguishing between schizophrenia and schizoaffective disorder, are largely moot, even if your relative has been given both diagnoses at different times. The distinction between these two diagnoses has no treatment implications at this time. Both disorders respond to the same treatments and have a similar long-term course.

## Schizotypal Personality Disorder

Schizotypal personality disorder is a little different from the disorders described above in that the symptoms tend to be milder than those present in schizophrenia or schizoaffective disorder. Patients with a schizotypal personality disorder tend to be hospitalized less often, and many patients are never hospitalized. Despite the milder symptoms, most patients with this disorder function only marginally better than patients with schizophrenia; they tend to have few friends, work is difficult or they may work at menial jobs, and they get little satisfaction out of life. A significant number of people who have a schizotypal personality disorder at a younger age gradually develop schizophrenia, schizoaffective disorder, or schizophreniform disorder.

## Subtypes of Schizophrenia

Since schizophrenia was first described over a hundred years ago, different subtypes of the illness have been proposed. The subtypes of schizophrenia that are included in the *DSM-IV* include paranoid type, catatonic type, disorganized type, undifferentiated type, and residual type. These subtypes summarize the patient's most prominent symptoms. Other subtypes of schizophrenia have also been proposed. However, there is no consistent research evidence indicating that any subtypes of schizophrenia respond differently to treatments or have a different course of the illness. It is also unclear how stable subtypes are over time. Therefore, you need not be concerned about your relative's subtype of schizophrenia.

For the sake of convenience, the remainder of the book will refer to all of the schizophrenia-spectrum disorders as "schizophrenia."

## Symptoms of Schizophrenia

The symptoms of schizophrenia can be divided into five broad categories: positive symptoms, negative symptoms, mood problems, disturbances in thinking, and behavioral disturbances. Within each category several specific symptoms are possible. You may be familiar with many of these symptoms from your relative. In fact, with the exception of behavioral disturbances, almost all patients with schizophrenia have some symptoms in each of these categories. However, your relative will not have *all* of these symptoms. No two patients with schizophrenia have exactly the same symptoms; each patient is unique. To help you better understand the nature of different symptoms of schizophrenia, we will describe specific symptoms for each of the broad categories. The examples provided are from actual patients with schizophrenia.

### Positive Symptoms

The terms *positive symptoms* and *negative symptoms* can be confusing. They do not refer to "good" and "bad" symptoms but rather to different types of symptoms. We have chosen to use the terms here because they are commonly used by clinicians and researchers of schizophrenia, and because once you understand the terms they will make sense to you. *Positive symptoms* refer to perceptions or beliefs patients have that are not shared by people who do not have a mental illness. For example, hearing voices when other people are not around (auditory hallucinations), is a positive symptom. *Negative symptoms,* on the other hand, refer to the *absence* of behaviors or feelings that are ordinarily present in persons with no mental illness. For example, not expressing one's feelings through facial expressions, voice tone, and gestures when interacting with another person (*blunted affect*) is a negative symptom. Thus, positive symptoms are characterized by their unique *presence,* whereas negative symptoms are characterized by their unique *absence.*

Two types of positive symptoms are most common in schizophrenia: hallucinations and delusions. For many patients these symptoms fluctuate over time. They may be intense at certain times of the illness, requiring the patient to be hospitalized. At other times they may be quite mild or not present at all. Some patients have persistent positive symptoms; others do not.

### Hallucinations

*Hallucinations* are "false perceptions"—sensations that the patient experiences but other people do not. These perceptions include hearing, seeing, feeling, tasting, and smelling things that are not present in the environment, called *auditory, visual, tactile, gustatory*, or *olfactory hallucinations*. About 70 percent of patients with schizophrenia experience auditory hallucinations, 25 percent have visual hallucinations, and 10 percent have other types of hallucinations.

Auditory hallucinations are usually experienced in the form of voices heard through the ears. Less often, the patient hears the voices inside his or her head. The voices can seem quite real, as though they are coming from the next room or the street. Sometimes patients think the hallucinations are real; other times they know they are not. Examples of auditory hallucinations include:

- Two voices talking about you and commenting on your actions

- A voice telling you that you are a bad person and calling you names

- The murmuring and talking of many people, but it isn't clear what they are saying

Auditory hallucinations are very distressing and distracting to most patients. Some patients readily admit to having hallucinations, while others do not. One indication that your relative may be experiencing hallucinations is if he or she talks or laughs when no one is around. When this happens often the patient is responding to the hallucinations.

### Delusions

A *delusion* is a "false belief," or a belief that the patient holds, that is not shared by others in his or her culture or religion. Delusions appear quite real to the patient but seem impossible or untrue to others. Many different types of delusions exist. Some of the most common types of delusions in patients with schizophrenia are described below.

*Persecutory (or paranoid) delusions.* The patient believes that he or she is being unfairly persecuted or that people want to harm him or her for no good reason. This type of delusion is quite common. Examples of persecutory delusions include:

- Family members are secretly trying to poison your food

- The Mafia, the CIA, and the FBI are conspiring to kill you

- A network of family members and friends are working together in order to drive you crazy

**Delusions of reference.** This type of delusion involves the belief that something or someone is making a reference to the patient when this is not the case. The patient may believe that the TV, radio, or newspaper has a special message for him or her or is referring specifically to him or her. Things in the patient's immediate environment (such as the arrangement of objects, numbers, or letters) may be interpreted as conveying a symbolic message intended especially for him or her. Delusions of reference are quite common in schizophrenia. Some examples of this type of delusion include:

- The TV newscast referred to you last night on the news (when it did not)

- The police are investigating you for a murder you did not commit (when they are not)

- You see the number 666 on the license plate on the car in front of you and you believe it is a message from the devil that you are condemned to go to hell

- Other people on the subway are talking about you

Sometimes patients will have a thought similar to one of the examples provided above, but will then question that thought, rather than immediately believing it. For example, a patient may think, "Those people who are laughing at the front of the bus might be laughing about me. But then again, maybe they aren't." When a patient is capable of questioning these types of thoughts, the symptom is called an *idea of reference*, because it is less firm than a belief. Patients with a schizotypal personality disorder often have ideas of reference. Patients with schizophrenia sometimes have ideas of reference when their symptoms are less severe.

**Delusions of control.** This type of delusion involves the belief that another person or force can control one's thoughts or actions. Examples of delusions of control include:

- An electrical transmitter has been implanted in your stomach that controls your thoughts

- Other people can put thoughts into your head (called *thought insertion*) and take thoughts away (called *thought withdrawal*)

**Grandiose delusions.** The patient believes that he or she is a special person, has unique talents, or is rich, when this is not the case. Examples of this type of delusion include:

- You are the King of Kings, the Lord of Lords, the Master and Creator of the Universe

- You invented the Boeing 747

- You are an unrecognized genius in art

*Other delusions.* Delusions of persecution, reference, control, and grandiosity are the most common types of delusions in schizophrenia. Other types of delusions are also possible. Some examples include:

- Other people can hear your thoughts (*thought broadcasting*)

- Your brain is rotting away (a *somatic delusion*)

- You have committed a terrible crime (a *delusion of guilt*)

- You are an animal

- You are a monster

## Negative Symptoms

You may find it easy to recognize positive symptoms in your relative as the symptoms of a psychiatric disorder, because they obviously appear to be the result of something wrong. It seems clear to most people that hearing voices that others do not hear or believing things that are clearly false reflects some kind of a problem in the brain. You may have more difficulty recognizing negative symptoms as a part of your relative's illness, because they are defined by the absence of normal thought processes, behaviors, or feelings.

However, once you become familiar with your relative's specific negative symptoms you will probably notice that these symptoms are quite prominent. You may also observe that your relative's negative symptoms tend to be fairly stable over time, in contrast to positive symptoms, which may fluctuate more. The negative symptoms described below are very common in schizophrenia.

### Blunted Affect

This symptom (which is also called *affective flattening*) refers to the decreased expressiveness of feelings in facial expressions and voice tone. When your relative discusses something humorous or sad, his or her facial expression and voice tone may not be consistent with the topic but may be flat or bland instead. Despite this lack of expressiveness, blunted affect in your relative may not be an accurate reflection of how he or she is actually feeling at the time. He or she may feel the emotion but be unable to show it.

### Alogia

If your relative tends to say very little (called *poverty of speech,*) or if when he or she talks it does not add up to very much (called *poverty of speech content*), he or she has the symptom of *alogia*. Poverty of speech is much more common in schizophrenia than poverty of speech content. You may have observed alogia in your relative when you tried to engage him or her in conversation and found that it was difficult to keep the conversation going for very long. It is not that your relative doesn't want to talk with you (although this is possible), but rather that he or she doesn't have that much to say.

### Apathy

Your relative may not feel motivated to work toward personal goals or improve his or her ability to function more independently. This lack of motivation, called *apathy*, can interfere with completing even the most basic tasks, such as simple hygiene, and may be reflected by excessive sleep or avoiding others. For some patients, apathy reflects discouragement and a sense of hopelessness about the future, while for others it is simply a genuine state of not caring.

### Anhedonia

*Anhedonia* refers to a decrease in the ability to feel pleasure or enjoyment. Your relative may have difficulty experiencing pleasure from activities he or she used to enjoy, such as watching a sunset, seeing a movie, playing a game, or talking with other people. Some patients have a painful awareness of the change from when they were able to enjoy things to the present. Others may have always had a lower capacity to experience pleasure, which has only gotten worse since developing schizophrenia. If your relative has anhedonia, you may find it difficult to engage him or her in activities because of the expectation that the activity will not be enjoyable.

## Mood Problems

You have probably noticed that your relative has had some problems with his or her mood. These problems can be either chronic and long-standing or more transient. Your relative's mood problems may be related to other symptoms he or she is experiencing, such as hallucinations, but this is not necessarily the case. Some of the problems with mood that your relative may have experienced are described below.

### Depression and Suicidality

Depression is one of the most common problems for patients with schizophrenia. You may have seen some of the following signs of depression in your relative: feeling sad, "blue," or unhappy; thoughts of hopelessness, helplessness, and worthlessness; a sad facial expression. Some patients with schizophrenia have an awareness of their disorder, the limits it imposes, and the social stigma associated with it, and this awareness contributes to their depression. Others may experience depression without being aware of their illness and its social consequences.

Your relative may have talked about hurting himself or herself, or may have made a suicide attempt. Many patients think about suicide (called *suicidal ideation*), and a significant number make suicide attempts. About 10 percent of patients with schizophrenia die from suicide. Suicidal ideation and suicide attempts occur most often in patients who are depressed. Sometimes these patients also have chronic positive symptoms, which can be very troubling. For example, some patients may experience persistent auditory hallucinations of voices that insult them, tell them they are no good, and instruct them to kill themselves. Steps that you can take to reduce the chances that your relative will attempt suicide are addressed in several chapters in this book, including Chapter 4 ("Early Warning Signs of Relapse"), Chapter 10 ("Persistent Positive and Negative Symptoms"), Chapter 11 ("Depression and Anxiety"), and Chapter 13 ("Responding to Crises").

### Anxiety

Many people with schizophrenia experience problems with anxiety. Often this anxiety is related to positive symptoms. It is understandable that delusions, such as the belief that others want to hurt you, and hallucinations, such as hearing voices that put you down, can lead to anxious feelings. If your relative has had these feelings, they probably resulted in his or her avoiding certain situations. For example, a patient may be afraid and avoid riding public transportation because she believes others talk about her on the bus and subway. On very rare occasions patients with intense fears (such as paranoid delusions) become aggressive when they feel they are threatened and have no escape. In many such instances, patients believe they are defending themselves.

### Anger, Hostility, and Suspiciousness

When patients are angry and hostile, they have a strong effect on everyone around them, including relatives, mental health professionals, and peers. Your relative may have expressed anger to you or been hostile, so you know how uncomfortable that can make you feel. Sometimes patients with schizophrenia have a "short fuse"—they become easily angered, but then they get over it quickly. Others may be more consistently hostile or suspicious, making it difficult to get along with them. In many patients, angry, hostile, or suspicious feelings reflect positive symptoms, even when the patient denies the presence of such symptoms. For example, delusions, such as thinking that others are plotting against you or reading your mind, can lead to feelings of resentment and suspiciousness. Auditory hallucinations, such as hearing voices that yell at you, can be annoying, resulting in angry feelings. In addition, angry and hostile feelings can be due to the many frustrations experienced by patients, who often face limited prospects for work, social life, and standard of living because of their illness.

### Labile Mood

Your relative's mood may fluctuate rapidly from happy to sad or angry, for no apparent reason. When this happens (called *labile* mood), it can be confusing for people to understand what the patient is feeling. When mood is very labile, usually many other symptoms are also quite severe, such as hallucinations or delusions.

### Inappropriate or Incongruent Affect

Another less common mood disturbance is when the patient expresses emotions inconsistent or inappropriate with the situation. For example, the patient may smile or laugh when talking about a serious topic, such as the death of a friend. As when a patient has blunted affect, inappropriate affect can make it difficult to understand what the patient is feeling.

## Disturbances in Thinking

Problems in cognition (thought processes) are one of the fundamental disturbances of schizophrenia. Undoubtedly, you have noticed some of these problems in your relative. In some ways, thinking disturbances in schizophrenia are demonstrated in positive symptoms, such as delusions. Delusions reflect a profound inability to check out the reality of one's beliefs and to modify them accordingly. In addition to thinking disturbances being displayed in positive symptoms, you may observe these problems in your relative's ability to process information accurately (cognitive impairments) or in his or her use of language.

### Cognitive Impairments

A variety of different problems in processing information are common in schizophrenia. Your relative has almost certainly experienced some difficulties with attention and concentration. Patients easily become distracted by their own thoughts or stimuli in their environment. For example, a patient may be distracted during a conversation by another person crossing his or her legs or by the sound of a bus passing in the street. Memory problems are also quite common. Memory for recent events tends to be more impaired than distant memories. For example, you may ask your relative to pick up something for you at the store, but he or she forgets. Another area of cognition that is sometimes a problem is abstract reasoning. Abstract reasoning refers to the ability to put information together to reach logical conclusions. Thus, your relative may not reach conclusions about things that would seem obvious to other people.

These cognitive impairments can also be reflected in problems with social perception. *Social perception* involves accurately recognizing important signals during social interactions. Recognizing another person's feelings through facial expressions and voice tone, or understanding what someone is upset about, are examples of social perception. You may have seen problems in social perception in your relative when he or she has had trouble "getting the point" during a conversation with you.

Problems in cognition are occasionally evident in the peculiar logic or reasoning of some patients. For example, one patient of the famous psychiatrist Eugene Bleuler thought that she was the country of Switzerland. Her logic went as follows: Switzerland loves freedom. I love freedom. Therefore, I am Switzerland.

### Language Problems

Difficulties with thinking are immediately evident when a patient uses language oddly, in a way that is hard to understand. Your relative may jump from one topic to another remotely related topic (*loose associations*) or an unrelated topic (*derailment*), making the conversation difficult to follow. He or she may stop talking in the middle of a sentence, having forgotten what he or she was going to say (*thought blocking*). Patients sometimes make up new words (*neologisms*) that others do not understand, or give an existing word a meaning that is confusing to others. For example, one patient coined the word *ingrowability* to describe the ability to grow inward, as toenails can, or to have inner development, inner strength. Sometimes, a patient's speech may be incoherent, either because the patient does not speak clearly or because the syntax is mixed up (*word salad*). Language problems such as those described here are relatively uncommon in schizophrenia. When they appear, it is usually during a period of symptom worsening or in patients who experience severe, persistent symptoms.

## Behavioral Disturbances

Compared to some of the other types of symptoms described above, behavioral disturbances are quite rare in schizophrenia. *Catatonia* is a state in which the patient maintains the same body posture for many hours or days, even though it may appear quite awkward or uncomfortable. The person may be in a stupor, dazed, and not able to engage in any purposeful behavior. Sometimes patients with schizophrenia will engage in excited motor activity that is apparently purposeless and is not influenced by external stimuli (*catatonic excitement*). *Mutism* is when the patient refuses to talk to others, because he or she is either unable or unwilling to talk. These types of behavioral disturbances occurred more frequently in patients with schizophrenia before antipsychotic medications were discovered.

# Understanding Your Relative's Symptoms

You have probably recognized many of the preceding symptoms described above in your relative. Other symptoms may be more difficult to recognize if you have not talked with your relative about them. Some patients are reluctant to talk about their symptoms, while others are quite willing. If you decide to talk with your relative, it can be helpful to remember that he or she is the *expert*, because he or she knows the experience of the symptoms. We have found that many patients we have worked with were willing to talk about their symptoms with family members, once we had explained to them that they were the real experts.

The purpose of talking with your relative about symptoms is to understand what the experience is like and how the symptoms affect his or her life. If your relative prefers not to talk about it, respect this desire for privacy. If your relative does talk, avoid challenging him or her. For example, your relative may deny having symptoms that you have observed, or he or she may insist that certain delusions are true. Instead of questioning your relative on these issues, show that you are interested and want to listen, and try to understand his or her perspective. It is not helpful to press your relative to talk about subjects that make him or her uncomfortable.

To summarize the specific symptoms that your relative has experienced, complete the Symptom Checklist. This checklist will provide you with a brief overview of your relative's past and current symptoms. If your relative's checklist is like that of most other patients with schizophrenia, it probably includes many symptoms that he or she is currently experiencing or has experienced in the past. By appreciating the different symptoms your relative has, you can also understand how the illness has affected his or her life. Positive symptoms such as delusions and hallucinations make the world an unpredictable, frightening place to live. Negative symptoms, like the loss of pleasure and apathy, lead patients to be withdrawn and to give up. Thinking disturbances in concentration, memory, and social perception make it difficult for patients to engage in rewarding interpersonal relationships, as well as to pursue goals.

# Understanding Symptoms' Effect on You

It is clear that your relative's symptoms have had a profound impact on his or her life. Similarly, these symptoms have probably also had a major effect on your life and those of other close relatives. It hurts to see a family member who is not able to realize his or her full potential, and it is frustrating for an adult to be so dependent upon you for basic living needs. In addition to these feelings, you may have also felt irritated or angry at times, such as when your relative ignores something you say, forgets to do things, or won't "listen to reason." These reactions to your

## Symptom Checklist

*Instructions:* Place a checkmark next to each symptom that your relative has experienced in the past (more than one month ago) or has experienced more recently. If you are unsure, leave the spaces for that symptom blank.

| *Symptom* | *Past* | *Present* |
|---|---|---|
| *Positive Symptoms* | | |
| Hallucinations | _____ | _____ |
| Delusions | _____ | _____ |
| *Negative Symptoms* | | |
| Blunted Affect | _____ | _____ |
| Alogia | _____ | _____ |
| Apathy | _____ | _____ |
| Anhedonia | _____ | _____ |
| *Mood Problems* | | |
| Depression | _____ | _____ |
| Suicidality | _____ | _____ |
| Anxiety | _____ | _____ |
| Anger, hostility or suspiciousness | _____ | _____ |
| Labile mood | _____ | _____ |
| Inappropriate or incongruent affect | _____ | _____ |
| *Disturbances in Thinking* | | |
| Attention or concentration problems | _____ | _____ |
| Memory problems | _____ | _____ |
| Abstract reasoning impairment | _____ | _____ |
| Social perception problems | _____ | _____ |
| Peculiar logic | _____ | _____ |
| Language problems | _____ | _____ |
| *Behavioral Disturbances* | | |
| Catatonia | _____ | _____ |
| Mutism | _____ | _____ |
| Disorganized or agitated behavior | _____ | _____ |

relative are quite natural, but they can have negative effects if you begin to blame your relative for having symptoms or if your feelings lead to arguments. The symptoms of schizophrenia are not your relative's fault, even though it may seem that he or she could try harder. You can help your relative function better and manage symptoms more effectively by working together as a team and by avoiding blame and minimizing conflict. Part III of this book offers help in these areas.

## Distinguishing Schizophrenia from Mood Disorders

After becoming familiar with your relative's symptoms, you may still have some questions about whether his or her diagnosis is correct. In particular, you may wonder whether your relative has a mood disorder, rather than schizophrenia. There are specific differences between these two types of disorders that help to determine which diagnosis is correct for your relative.

The symptoms of schizophrenia overlap most prominently with the symptoms of mood disorder, in particular, bipolar disorder (manic depression) and major depression. As we have previously discussed, the chances are very high that at some point in your relative's illness he or she has had some mood symptoms, such as depression, mania, or both. What distinguishes schizophrenia from mood disorders is the *timing* of the schizophrenia symptoms. Patients with schizophrenia have at least some periods of time when they have positive symptoms but do not have significant mood symptoms (such as depression). On the other hand, if your relative has positive symptoms only when he or she also has mood symptoms, the correct diagnosis may be a mood disorder, not schizophrenia.

In addition to the different timing of symptoms between schizophrenia and mood disorders, these disorders differ in other ways. Patients with schizophrenia tend to become ill at an earlier age and usually have symptoms that persist throughout their lifetime. In contrast, patients with bipolar disorder or major depression tend to become ill at a later age and experience symptoms less persistently and more episodically. Many patients with mood disorders have no symptoms between episodes of their illness, and are able to function quite well. Consequently, the functioning of patients with schizophrenia is usually somewhat lower than that of patients with a mood disorder.

In the final analysis, a diagnosis is a judgment call that is not always easy to make. However, if your relative has many of the symptoms described in this chapter and does not function optimally, the recommendations provided in this book will be helpful, regardless of the diagnosis.

### *DSM-IV* Criteria for Schizophrenia-Spectrum Disorders

**Criteria for Schizophrenia**

A. *Characteristic symptoms.* Symptoms include positive symptoms, such as hallucinations, delusions, inability to communicate coherently, catatonic or random behavior; and negative symptoms, such as apathy, blunted affect, or alogia (poverty of speech and thought). Two or more of these symptoms persisting over the space of a month indicate a diagnosis of schizophrenia (unless they are treated successfully prior to that time). One of these symptoms is sufficient to indicate a diagnosis of schizophrenia if it is "bizarre," for example, one or more voices discussing the person's behavior, control by outside forces.

B. *Difficulty functioning socially or occupationally.* In conjunction with criterion A symptoms, the person's ability to work, maintain interpersonal relationships, and care for self is markedly impaired.

C. *Duration.* For a diagnosis of schizophrenia to be indicated, the altered behavior must persist for at least six months, with at least one month of symptoms in criterion A *(active symptoms)*. Either before or after these active symptoms, negative symptoms or other mild symptoms (such as unusual perceptual experiences) may be present.

D. *Mood and schizoaffective disorders excluded.* The symptoms of schizophrenia overlap with those of schizoaffective disorder and mood disorders. For a diagnosis of schizophrenia to be indicated, these diagnoses must have been ruled out either through absence of a concurrent manic or depressive episode or because the concurrent mood disturbance was brief in comparison to the duration of active and residual symptoms.

E. *General medical condition and substance abuse excluded.* Similarly, some diseases and drugs can cause symptoms similar to those of schizophrenia, so these diagnoses must also have been ruled out.

*continued on next page*

Figure 2.1

# *DSM-IV* Criteria for Schizophrenia-Spectrum Disorders

## Criteria for Schizophreniform Disorder

A. A diagnosis of schizophreniform disorder is indicated if criteria A, D, and E for schizophrenia are met, along with criterion B below.

B. Duration of the episode is less than six months but is of at least one month. If episode is still occurring at the time diagnosis is made, diagnosis should be classified as provisional.

## Criteria for Schizoaffective Disorder

A. During an active period, a major depressive or manic episode occurs.

B. During the same active period there must also have been a span of at least two weeks during which hallucinations or delusions occurred but no prominent symptoms of mood disturbance were exhibited.

C. The mood disturbance must be present during a substantial portion of the active and residual periods.

D. A general medical condition and substance abuse must be ruled out.

*continued on next page*

Figure 2.1

### *DSM-IV* Criteria for Schizophrenia-Spectrum Disorders

**Criteria for Schizotypal Personality Disorder**

A. The general indicators of this illness are a lack of close relationships, mild hallucinations, and eccentric behavior, and they must be in evidence by early adulthood and in a variety of situations. Five or more of the following must be present to indicate this diagnosis:

- Thoughts (not beliefs) that one is being talked about
- Actions based on eccentric ideas that are not accounted for by cultural factors
- Mild hallucinations
- Eccentric thought and odd verbal expression, such as vagueness or overelaboration
- Paranoia or excessive suspicion
- Facial or physical expression that is blank or inconsistent with circumstances
- Eccentric actions or appearance
- Lack of attachments other than to close relatives
- Excessive, persisting anxiety in social situations that is associated with paranoia rather than low self-esteem

B. Schizophrenia and other psychotic disorders, mood disorders, and pervasive developmental disorders (for example, autism) have been ruled out

Figure 2.1

# PART II

# Preventing Relapses

# 3

# Medication

Before the 1950s, few effective treatments were known for schizophrenia, and patients were condemned to spend their lives in institutions with little hope for change or improvement. The subsequent discovery of antipsychotic medications (also referred to as *neuroleptics* or *major tranquilizers*) and their impact on the symptoms of schizophrenia represented the most important breakthrough to date in the treatment of this disorder. Medication is now widely accepted as a mainstay in the treatment of schizophrenia. Medication is not a *cure* for the disorder, and it cannot suffice as the only treatment, but the vast majority of patients benefit from medication when it is prescribed and monitored carefully and systematically. For you to be most effective in helping your relative manage his or her illness, you need a thorough understanding of the role of medication in treatment. This chapter is devoted to providing you with practical information about the specific medications used to treat schizophrenia: their clinical effects and side effects, how to handle common problems (such as noncompliance with medication), and how to evaluate the quality of your relative's pharmacological treatment.

## A Brief History of Antipsychotic Medications

The discovery of the effects of antipsychotic medications on schizophrenia was accidental. In the early 1950s, a number of different scientists were in the process of trying to develop more effective medications for the treatment of hypertension (high blood pressure). One of these newly invented medications was the drug Thorazine (chemical name chlorpromazine). When this drug was administered to animals in laboratory tests, its effects on blood pressure were disappointing. However, the scientists observed that Thorazine appeared to have a mildly tranquilizing effect, and began to explore the possibility that it might have other beneficial effects. After further laboratory testing had confirmed that the drug could be safely given to humans, a number of trials were initiated.

As it had in tests with laboratory animals, Thorazine was found to have a tranquilizing effect on people. (The term *major tranquilizer* was first used to describe antipsychotic medications, including what later came to be known as Thorazine.) However, the most astonishing finding was that when this drug was given to patients with schizophrenia, it resulted in dramatic reductions in psychotic symptoms such as hallucinations and delusions. In some cases, these symptoms were completely eliminated. Although Thorazine's effect appeared to be tranquilizing, since it calmed down some agitated patients, for many withdrawn patients it had the opposite effect of perking them up and drawing them out of their psychosis.

Thorazine was first given to patients with schizophrenia not in carefully controlled drug studies, but rather in *open* drug trials, which are exploratory in nature. In an open drug trial patients (who consent to participate in the trial) are informed that they will be given a new drug, and they are then given that drug. Both the patient and physician know when the patient is given the experimental drug. Since both patients and physicians often have positive expectations for a new drug that may bias their ratings of the effects of the drug, open trials of drugs often produce unreliable results. In a *controlled* drug study, on the other hand, patients are informed that they will either receive the experimental drug *or* a placebo (a pill with no clinical effects) that is indistinguishable from the drug. In the best type of controlled drug study, neither the patient nor the physician is aware of whether the patient is receiving a placebo or the experimental drug. (The pills are coded so that their true classification is known only when the data is analyzed.) This type of drug study is called a *double-blind* study, because both the patient and physician are "blind" as to whether the drug or a placebo was given. Double-blind studies minimize the possible role of patient or physician expectations for the effects of a particular drug.

After open drug trials of Thorazine suggested it had positive effects for schizophrenia, rigorously controlled double-blind studies were conducted. In study after study, controlled research supported the initial observations that Thorazine had a beneficial impact on the symptoms of schizophrenia. As these remarkable effects became accepted, Thorazine became widely used for patients with schizophrenia, and played a role in shifting the treatment of many patients from state hospitals to the community. With the success of Thorazine, scientists began to develop other antipsychotic medications with similar clinical effects. In the two decades following the discovery of Thorazine, over ten other types of antipsychotic medications were developed and found to produce similar, positive effects. Even more advances have been made recently in the development of new antipsychotic medications for schizophrenia, as we describe later in this chapter.

# The Effects of Antipsychotic Medications on Schizophrenia

Antipsychotic medications have been found to be helpful both in treating the symptoms of schizophrenia and in improving the long-term outcome of the disorder. In general, these medications have two different roles in the treatment of schizophrenia: symptom reduction and relapse prevention.

## Symptom Reduction

Antipsychotic medications are effective at reducing the *acute symptoms* (the most severe symptoms) of schizophrenia. For many patients, the most prominent effects are on the positive symptoms of the illness, such as hallucinations, delusions, bizarre behavior, and odd speech. Antipsychotics can also reduce some of the negative symptoms of schizophrenia, such as poverty of speech (saying little) and apathy, but to a lesser extent.

When a patient's symptoms worsen significantly and he or she has a relapse, antipsychotic medications are helpful in decreasing these symptoms. If the person was taking medication before the relapse occurred, the dosage level is often temporarily increased. Sometimes antipsychotics have rapid effects on symptoms, within a few hours. More often, medication takes at least several days to begin to take effect, and several weeks or months are usually needed before the patient achieves maximum benefit.

Antipsychotic medication can substantially reduce the symptoms of schizophrenia, but usually some symptoms continue, even when optimal levels of medication are provided. The enduring symptoms of schizophrenia (also called *residual symptoms*) are often troublesome and interfere with day-to-day functioning. Most patients with schizophrenia experience some negative symptoms when they are taking medication, and 20 to 40 percent have positive symptoms, although these symptoms are often mild. This is one of the reasons why antipsychotics alone are not a sufficient treatment for schizophrenia.

## Relapse Prevention

In addition to reducing the severity of symptoms, antipsychotic medications have a profound effect on lowering patients' vulnerability to symptom relapses and rehospitalizations. In the year after leaving the hospital, about 7 out of 10 patients (70 percent) *not* taking medication will have a relapse, compared to only 3 out of 10 patients (30 percent) who take medication regularly. Thus, even after symptoms have been effectively reduced, taking antipsychotics on a regular basis can stabilize the episodic course of the illness.

Despite the effects of antipsychotic medication on reducing risk of relapses, some relapses occasionally happen. However, if the patient is taking medication, relapses tend to occur less frequently. In addition, when relapses do occur, they tend to be less severe and can be treated more rapidly. For these reasons, it is important that your relative take medication on a regular basis in order to keep his or her symptoms to a minimum.

## How Are Antipsychotics Taken?

Antipsychotic medications can be taken a number of different ways. The most common method is to take the medication orally, either in the form of pills or liquid. When oral medication is prescribed, it is taken on a daily basis, usually ranging from once to three times per day. Some antipsychotic medications can be taken in the form of long-acting injections which are given once every two to four weeks. Between the injections, the patient need not take any more antipsychotic medication, although occasionally additional medication may be temporarily prescribed. These injections distribute the medication throughout the body on a constant basis over the following weeks, similar to over-the-counter "time-release" medications available for colds and allergies. This results in approximately the same level of medication being present in the body throughout the two- to four-week period. It should be noted that the antipsychotic medication remains in the body even after the two to four weeks have passed. If additional injections are not given, the level of medication in the body gradually declines over the next several months until none is left.

Sometimes very high doses of antipsychotic medication are given by injection to patients who are extremely agitated. This treatment approach, called *rapid tranquilization*, is used only for brief periods of time in emergency situations, to calm patients down. Although rapid tranquilization has been used extensively over the past several decades, its benefits have not been clearly established.

## Specific Types of Antipsychotic Medication

Since the discovery of Thorazine, many other antipsychotics have been developed and found to be beneficial to persons with schizophrenia. From your experience with your relative you may be familiar with several different medications. To understand the differences between various types of antipsychotic medication, it may be helpful to first look at the two categories these medications fall into: traditional antipsychotics and atypical antipsychotics. The different types, clinical effects, and side effects of medications in each of these broad groups are discussed next.

## Traditional Antipsychotics

Traditional antipsychotic medications, such as Thorazine, are the most commonly prescribed throughout the world, and until recently were the most widely available of this type of medication. Figure 3.1 lists the most commonly used antipsychotics (brand and chemical names), the average daily dosage for each drug, and its potency relative to Thorazine. The effects of these different antipsychotics on symptoms and relapse rates are essentially the same, and their side effects are also quite similar. However, the *potency* of these medications differs. This means that higher doses of a less potent medication must be given to achieve the same clinical benefits as a more potent medication. For example, you can see by inspecting Figure 3.1 that the dosage range for Thorazine, a low-potency

### Traditional Antipsychotics

| Brand Name | Chemical Name | Estimated Dosage Ratio[a] | Average Daily Dosage (mg/day) |
|---|---|---|---|
| Haldol[b] | haloperidol | 1:50 | 1–40 |
| Loxitane | loxapine | 1:10 | 4–250 |
| Mellaril | thioridazine | 1:1 | 50–800 |
| Moban | molindone | 1:10 | 15–250 |
| Navane | thiothixene | 1:20 | 6–60 |
| Prolixin[b] | fluphenazine | 1:50 | 1–40 |
| Serentil | mesoridazine | 1:2 | 25–400 |
| Stelazine | trifluoperazine | 1:20 | 4–60 |
| **Thorazine** | **chlorpromazine** | **1:1** | **50–1250** |
| Trilafon | perphenazine | 1:10 | 8–64 |

[a] Estimated dosage ratio in relation to Thorazine. For example, a dose of 10 mg of Haldol is equivalent to 500 mg of Thorazine, since Haldol is 50 times as potent.

[b] Also available in long-acting (*depot*) injections.

Figure 3.1

antipsychotic, is much higher than the dosage range for Haldol, a high-potency antipsychotic. When a low-potency medication is given in higher doses, it has the same clinical effects as a high-potency medication.

### Side Effects

Many effective medications for treating illnesses have undesirable side effects. For example, medications for hypertension can cause sexual side effects in men, and antibiotics can cause yeast infections in women. Traditional antipsychotics also produce side effects. Some common side effects include:

- Drowsiness
- Muscle stiffness
- Dizziness
- Mild tremors
- Increased appetite
- Blurred vision
- *Akathisia*—an inner feeling of restlessness often associated with pacing, fidgeting, or an inability to sit still
- *Akinesia*—a decrease in spontaneous behaviors, such as gestures and facial expressiveness
- Sensitivity to the sun—sunburn
- Sexual dysfunction—such as difficulty maintaining an erection
- Tardive dyskinesia—abnormal involuntary movements, usually in the hands, feet, tongue, or lips (this is discussed in more detail below)

All of these side effects, including stiffness, tremors, akathisia, and akinesia, are referred to as *extrapyramidal*, because they involve the extrapyramidal motor system in the brain. It is rare for patients to experience all of these side effects, and many patients have few or no side effects from their medication. Except for tardive dyskinesia, all of these side effects are temporary and cease when the patient stops taking the medication.

### Recognizing and Managing Medication Side Effects

It is important to be able to recognize possible medication side effects in your relative, for two reasons. First, some of the side effects are unpleasant, but your relative might not be aware that medications are causing these unpleasant experiences and may consequently suffer needlessly. By becoming aware of your relative's side effects you can take steps to minimize them and the discomfort they cause. Second, some patients *are* aware of medication side effects, and respond to them by skipping doses or otherwise becoming noncompliant with medication. For example, akathisia can be very disturbing, often leading to noncompliance. Monitoring side effects and taking action when necessary can prevent problems with noncompliance that may lead to relapses and rehospitalizations.

In order to evaluate whether your relative may be experiencing side effects of antipsychotic medications, complete the Side Effects Checklist. This checklist will help you identify *possible* side effects of antipsychotic medications, but be aware that some of the signs of medication side effects overlap with symptoms of the illness. For example, drowsiness and diminished emotional expressiveness can be due to either the symptoms of schizophrenia or to medication side effects. It may be helpful for you to get further information about your relative's possible side effects by discussing your impressions with him or her, or by talking it over with your relative's psychiatrist. Identifying possible side effects of medication is your first step toward either reducing them or helping your relative cope with them more effectively.

In general, there are two broad strategies for dealing with the side effects of traditional antipsychotic medications (not including tardive dyskinesia): pharmacological management and coping strategies.

### Pharmacological Management of Side Effects

Medication side effects can often be dealt with by modifying the patient's pharmacological treatment. Three primary pharmacological strategies are available to the psychiatrist: reducing medication dosage, prescribing additional medication for the side effects, and switching to another class of traditional (or atypical) antipsychotic medication.

Reducing the dosage level of antipsychotic medication is often the simplest method for dealing with unpleasant side effects. With some patients, reducing dosage level increases the risk that their symptoms will worsen or they will become more vulnerable to relapses. Other patients, however, tolerate dosage reduction well, and benefit from experiencing fewer side effects. Unless a careful reduction of your relative's dosage has been tried in the past, it is difficult to predict whether your relative will benefit from taking less medication. If your relative and his or her psychiatrist agree to try dosage reduction, your relative's symptoms need to be carefully monitored in case symptoms begin to worsen, so that additional medication can be given in time to prevent a relapse.

The most common method for reducing medication side effects is to prescribe additional medications. A range of different side effect medications can be used, with anticholinergic medications most frequently prescribed. For example, you may be familiar with Cogentin, a routinely prescribed anticholinergic medication for antipsychotic side effects. Anticholinergics operate by reducing the activity of choline, a brain

## Side Effects Checklist

*Instructions:* On the following list, check which antipsychotic medication side effects your relative currently has and those he or she has had in the past.

| Side Effect | Possible Signs | Currently | In the Past |
|---|---|---|---|
| Drowsiness | Increased need for sleep or naps; appears more lethargic than usual. | _____ | _____ |
| Dizziness | Light-headedness when rising quickly. | _____ | _____ |
| Muscle stiffness | Awkward gait or posture, muscle spasms. | _____ | _____ |
| Tremors | Trembling hands, shakiness in legs. | _____ | _____ |
| Akathisia | Restlessness, difficulty sitting still, pacing, fidgeting; complaints of "feeling restless inside"; shakiness in legs. | _____ | _____ |
| Akinesia | Lack of facial expressions, gestures; diminished arm swing; slowed movements. | _____ | _____ |
| Increased appetite | Weight gain. | _____ | _____ |
| Photosensitivity | Increased susceptibility to sunburn. | _____ | _____ |
| Tardive dyskinesia | Involuntary, nonrhythmic movements of the hands, feet, lips, or tongue. | _____ | _____ |

chemical. Other types of medication are also used to treat side effects, such as benzodiazepines, beta-blockers, and dopamine agonists. Figure 3.2 contains a list of the most commonly prescribed drugs for antipsychotic side effects, including the brand name, chemical name, and the dosage range.

In almost all cases, side effect medications are taken orally, in the form of pills. However, anticholinergic medications are sometimes given by injection to treat an *acute dystonic reaction*, a dramatic stiffening of muscles or a muscle spasm affecting such areas as the jaw, tongue, eyes, spine, and neck caused by a high dose of antipsychotic medication. These reactions can be uncomfortable and frightening, but they can be quickly treated with injectable anticholinergic medication. Oral medication can also be effective in less severe forms of acute dystonic reaction.

Side effect medications can produce their own side effects. For example, anticholinergic medications can cause dry mouth or blurred vision. A list of the most common side effects of side effect medications is provided in Figure 3.3.

If other efforts are unsuccessful, the final pharmacological strategy for managing side effects is to switch the patient to another type of antipsychotic medication. There is no consistent evidence that shows that one kind of patient with schizophrenia responds better to one type of antipsychotic medication than another type. Nevertheless, there are subtle differences in the side effects caused by different types of antipsychotic medi-

### Medications for Side Effects of Antipsychotics

| Type of Drug | Brand Name | Chemical Name | Average Oral Dosage (mg/day) |
|---|---|---|---|
| Anticholinergics | Artane | trihexyphenidyl | 5–15 |
| | Benadryl | diphenhydramine | 50–300 |
| | Cogentin | benztropine | 0.5–8 |
| | Kemadrin | procyclidine | 5–20 |
| Benzodiazepines[a] | Ativan | lorazepam | 0.5–10 |
| | Restoril | temazepam | 7.5–60 |
| | Valium | diazepam | 2–60 |
| Beta blockers[a] | Corgard | nadolol | 40–120 |
| | Inderal | propranolol | 60–120 |
| Dopamine agonists | Symmetrel | amantadine | 100–400 |

[a] Used mainly for the treatment of akathisia.

Figure 3.2

## Possible Side Effects of Side Effect Medications

| Drug Class | Side Effects |
| --- | --- |
| Anticholinergics | Dry mouth, constipation, blurry vision, drowsiness, urinary retention, memory loss |
| Beta blockers | Fatigue, depression |
| Benzodiazepines | Drowsiness, psychological or physiological dependence, psychomotor impairment, memory loss |
| Dopamine agonists | Increase in psychotic symptoms |

Figure 3.3

cation (for example, Thorazine tends to be more sedating than Prolixin), so that a change in type of medication will sometimes benefit the patient.

### Coping Strategies for Medication Side Effects

Even with optimal pharmacological treatment, your relative may experience some side effects from his or her antipsychotic medication. Helping your relative develop effective coping strategies may reduce the discomfort that these side effects cause. However, before you can help your relative cope better with possible side effects, it is important to first discuss your observations and to find out whether he or she feels discomfort and is motivated to cope better with the side effect. We describe below some strategies for coping with side effects.

*Drowsiness.* Patients often report feeling sedated from taking medication, which can interfere with their ability to remain attentive and interact with others. Scheduling a brief nap may help cope with this drowsiness. Sometimes patients feel more tired when they take their medication in the morning, and can benefit instead from taking all their medication in the evening before going to bed. This possibility should be discussed with the psychiatrist.

*Increased appetite.* Antipsychotic medications often stimulate appetite, leading to weight gain. This problem can be managed by cutting down on fattening foods, such as sweets, sodas, fried foods, butter, and fast food. Instead, eating fresh fruits and vegetables and using sugar substitutes can keep weight down. In addition, regular exercise, such as brisk walking, jogging, aerobics, bicycling, or sports, can minimize weight gain.

There is some evidence to suggest that Loxitane and Moban do not cause weight gain.

*Akathisia.* Some patients find that exercise or vigorous work activity reduces the discomfort and restlessness caused by akathisia.

*Muscle stiffness.* Antipsychotics are most likely to cause muscles to stiffen in the shoulders and neck area. Physical exercise or muscle stretching and isometrics (tensing muscles tightly, counting to 5 and slowly relaxing) can help alleviate muscle stiffness.

*Dizziness.* Dizziness is one of the most common side effects of antipsychotic medication, because all of these drugs lower blood pressure. In most cases, dizziness occurs when the person rises quickly from a prone or sitting position, or from a tub. It is caused by an abrupt lowering of blood pressure (called *orthostatic hypotension*). You may personally have had similar experiences of dizziness when you've stood up too quickly. Dizziness can be avoided by the patient's first moving from a prone to a sitting position and then rising slowly.

*Blurred vision.* This side effect can result from either antipsychotic medications or from anticholinergic medications. Often vision improves spontaneously as the patient becomes accustomed to the medication. Reading glasses, including those available from a drug store, may help improve vision.

*Photosensitivity.* Your relative can remedy the increased sensitivity to sunburn caused by antipsychotic medications by using a sunscreen lotion. Sunscreens with a SPF (sun protection factor) of at least 10 are recommended.

*Tremor.* Mild tremors of the hands or other extremities are most common soon after a patient has begun to take antipsychotics or after the dosage has been increased, and they often improve spontaneously. If your relative has hand tremors, avoid filling cups and glasses to the brim to prevent spilling.

*Tardive Dyskinesia.* Tardive dyskinesia is one side effect of traditional antipsychotic medications that is of special concern. It is a neurological syndrome of involuntary movements in muscles of the tongue, mouth, lips, or the extremities, such as hands, fingers, and toes. Usually these movements are mild, although sometimes they can be more prominent. The term comes from the Latin words *tardive*, meaning "appearing late," and *dyskinesia*, meaning "involuntary, nonrhythmic movement." The term is used because the syndrome develops only after a patient has been receiving antipsychotic medications for an extended period of time, usually after several years, although it can also develop sooner.

Estimates of how common tardive dyskinesia is vary usually between 1 and 3 out of every 10 patients (10 to 30 percent). If your relative is more seriously ill than most other patients with schizophrenia, chances are higher that he or she has at least mild tardive dyskinesia. Patients who have received higher doses of antipsychotic medications for longer periods of time are more vulnerable to develop tardive dyskinesia. Women are also more likely to develop tardive dyskinesia than men.

Tardive dyskinesia can be bothersome to some patients because they may be aware that this side effect makes them appear different from others. However, patients are often unaware that they have the movements. At the present time, there are no known effective treatments for tardive dyskinesia. Sometimes the syndrome goes away on its own and sometimes it does not. Even though antipsychotic medications cause tardive dyskinesia, the movements can worsen if medications are stopped altogether, and low doses of these medications can keep the movements to a minimum. One important strategy used to lower the risk of developing tardive dyskinesia is to give low doses of antipsychotic medication to patients whose symptoms have been stabilized.

If your relative has severe tardive dyskinesia, he or she may benefit from taking the atypical antipsychotic medication Clozaril. As discussed in more detail in the following section, Clozaril does not appear to cause tardive dyskinesia, and can be effective at reducing the abnormal movements of this syndrome.

## Atypical Antipsychotics

The term *atypical* is used to describe antipsychotic medications that have different side effects and are believed to operate by different mechanisms of action than the traditional antipsychotics. At this time, there are only two atypical antipsychotics available on the market in the United States, Clozaril and Risperdal. The chemical and brand names of these two drugs, and their dosages are contained in Figure 3.4. Each of these drugs is described below.

### Clozaril

Clozaril is an atypical antipsychotic drug that has recently become available in the United States, although it has been used in Europe for

| Atypical Antipsychotics | | |
| --- | --- | --- |
| Brand Name | Chemical Name | Average Oral Dosage (mg/day) |
| Clozaril | clozapine | 200–900 |
| Risperdal | risperidone | 1–8 |

Figure 3.4

over 20 years. Clozaril is unique compared to traditional antipsychotic medications, for several reasons. Some research indicates that Clozaril is an especially effective medication for patients whose symptoms are less responsive to traditional antipsychotics ("treatment-refractory" patients). In several research studies, patients with schizophrenia who had not benefited substantially from traditional antipsychotics showed significant improvements after receiving Clozaril for a number of months. Improvements occurred both in the positive symptoms of the disorder (hallucinations and delusions) as well as the negative symptoms (social withdrawal). Despite the benefits of Clozaril, conservative estimates suggest that only between 10 and 30 percent of patients with treatment-refractory schizophrenia benefit from Clozaril.

Another remarkable feature of Clozaril is that, unlike the traditional antipsychotics, it does not appear to cause tardive dyskinesia. At the same time, when Clozaril is given to a person with tardive dyskinesia, it tends to improve (or *mask*) the condition. Clozaril is not a cure for tardive dyskinesia, because it cannot eliminate the syndrome; that is, the tardive dyskinesia will reappear in a patient who previously had the condition and stops taking Clozaril.

Clozaril does cause side effects, but different ones from those caused by the traditional antipsychotics. In particular, Clozaril does not have the extrapyramidal side effects of traditional antipsychotics, such as tremors and akathisia. Some of the side effects of Clozaril include fatigue, increased salivation, changes in blood pressure, dizziness, constipation, stiffness, and headache. Clozaril also causes one very serious side effect in a small minority of patients who take the drug (about 1 in 100 or 1 percent), a reduction in number of white blood cells, called *agranulocytosis*. If this side effect begins to develop, the person must be taken off Clozaril and switched to another antipsychotic, because white blood cells are necessary to fight diseases. In order to make sure that agranulocytosis is not developing, the patient's blood must be checked weekly with a simple blood test. With this weekly monitoring, Clozaril is a very safe drug. It is possible that in the future blood monitoring may be required less frequently.

### Risperdal

Risperdal was introduced to the United States market in early 1994, so that its use up until now has been limited to clinical drug trials. Risperdal differs from both the traditional antipsychotics and Clozaril. The results of carefully conducted drug studies indicate that a major advantage of Risperdal is that it causes significantly fewer and less problematic side effects than traditional antipsychotics, although it can cause mild sedation and dizziness. In addition, Risperdal poses no significant risk for agranulocytosis, unlike Clozaril, and thus blood tests are not required for patients taking this medication. The clinical effects of Risperdal appear to be comparable to that of traditional antipsychotics. However, Risperdal has not been available long enough to judge whether it produces different clinical effects from other antipsychotics.

It is unknown whether Risperdal causes tardive dyskinesia. Although Risperdal produces significantly fewer side effects than other antipsychotics, it can cause mild side effects similar to those caused by the traditional antipsychotics.

## The Future of Research on Antipsychotic Medications

The pharmaceutical industry is currently testing a wide range of new antipsychotic medications, and it is likely that over the next several years more atypical antipsychotics will become available. As these new drugs are developed, they usually represent small but significant steps forward in the pharmacological treatment of schizophrenia. Since accumulating evidence from research indicates that schizophrenia is heterogeneous with respect to both symptoms and cause, we believe it is unlikely that any single medication in the future will prove to be a cure for schizophrenia. However, we are optimistic about the advances that have been made in recent years, and expect that continued progress in this area will result in further improvements in our ability to treat this disorder.

## How Do Antipsychotic Medications Work?

Scientists do not have a full understanding of why antipsychotic medications are effective. However, there is evidence that these medications have important effects on the action of a particular neurotransmitter in the brain, dopamine. Research conducted on laboratory animals has shown that the clinical potency of different antipsychotic medications can be almost perfectly explained by the amount of dopamine in the brain that is reduced by that drug. In other words, a certain amount of a high potency antipsychotic medication (such as Haldol) will cause more reduction in dopamine than the same amount of a lower potency medication (such as Thorazine). Drugs that increase dopamine, such as stimulants (for example, cocaine or amphetamine) or L-Dopa, tend to worsen the symptoms of schizophrenia, whereas drugs with no effect on dopamine tend not to affect the symptoms of the disorder.

The role of dopamine in the regulation of mood, thinking, and behavior is extremely complex, and more is being discovered about it every day. For example, there is more than one kind of dopamine ($DA_1$, $DA_2$, and so on) and different medications tend to have different effects on each type of dopamine. Furthermore, dopamine serves different functions in different parts of the brain. Some theories suggest that people with schizophrenia have too little dopamine in the *prefrontal cortex,* a part of the brain involved in attention and processing information and too much in the *mesolimbic area* of the brain (involved in imagery, perception, and emotion). To make matters even more complicated, the atypical antipsychotics tend to also influence another important neurotransmitter, serotonin, in addition to dopamine. Every day scientists are learning more about how the brain works (both in nonpatients and people with schizophrenia) and this knowledge is gradually being translated into better treatments for persons with schizophrenia.

# Other Medical Treatments for Schizophrenia

In the history of modern medicine, a great many different medical treatments have been tried in an effort to help persons with schizophrenia. Although many reports of successful treatments exist, often they are not based on carefully conducted scientific studies. Even when positive results from a new treatment are found in a rigorously conducted scientific study, other scientists may have difficulty replicating the results in follow-up research.

In this section we provide a concise review of other medical treatments for schizophrenia. We begin the review with a discussion of medications other than antipsychotics that are sometimes used to treat schizophrenia. Then we discuss other medical procedures for treating schizophrenia. Our primary goal in this review is to provide you with a summary of the scientific evidence supporting other medical treatments for schizophrenia.

## Antianxiety and Sedative Medications

Anxiety is one of the most common and debilitating symptoms of schizophrenia. Patients may experience anxiety due to symptoms such as hearing voices yelling at them or delusions that others can read their minds or want to hurt them. Some patients experience "free floating" anxiety and depression that is not a result of any other specific symptoms. Occasionally, antianxiety and sedative medications are given to reduce the anxiety and improve sleep. The most commonly prescribed type of antianxiety medication is a drug class called *benzodiazepines.* Little controlled research supports the benefits of antianxiety medications for patients with schizophrenia, but some patients seem to find these medications helpful.

The side effects of benzodiazepines are generally mild and not very disturbing. Sometimes they may have an effect on *psychomotor performance* (muscular coordination), especially early in treatment. However, these medications must be used cautiously because they can be addictive. Patients can develop tolerance to benzodiazepines (requiring higher doses to achieve the same effects) or abuse them (use higher doses than prescribed in order to get "high"). Nevertheless, most patients who take these medications do not become addicted to them. Figure 3.5 contains a list of the most commonly prescribed antianxiety and sedative medications and their dosage ranges. Figure 3.6 contains common side effects of these medications.

## Antianxiety and Sedative Medications

| Type of Drug | Brand Name | Chemical Name | Average Dosage (mg/day) |
|---|---|---|---|
| Benzodiazepines | Ativan | lorazepam | 0.5–6 |
| | Centrax | prazepam | 20–60 |
| | Dalmane | flurazepam | 15–30 |
| | Halcion | triazolam | 0.125–0.5 |
| | Klonopin | clonazepam | 0.5–20 |
| | Librium | chlordiazepoxide | 15–100 |
| | Restoril | temazepam | 7.5–60 |
| | Serax | oxazepam | 30–120 |
| | Valium | diazepam | 2–60 |
| | Xanax | alprazolam | 0.5–6 |
| Antihistamines | Benadryl | diphenhydramine | 25–300 |
| Others | BuSpar | buspirone | 20–60 |
| | Noctec | chloral hydrate | 500–2000 |

Figure 3.5

## Side Effects of Antianxiety and Sedative Medications

| Drug Class | Side Effects |
|---|---|
| Benzodiazepines | Drowsiness, decreased fine motor skill |
| Antihistamines | Drowsiness, dry mouth and mucus membranes |
| Others | Drowsiness |

Figure 3.6

## Antidepressant Medications

Depression is a very common symptom in schizophrenia. A wide range of antidepressant drugs have been found to improve depression in people with major depression (a different psychiatric disorder). However, in most scientific studies in which antidepressant medication has been provided in addition to antipsychotics to patients with schizophrenia little or no improvement in their depression was found. Even worse, in some studies of antidepressant medication for schizophrenia, the drugs led to *increases* in positive symptoms. For these reasons, antidepressant medications are usually not prescribed for patients with schizophrenia.

**Antidepressant Medications**

| Type of Drug | Brand Name | Chemical Name | Average Dosage (mg/day) |
|---|---|---|---|
| Tricyclic anti-depressants (TCAs) | Anafranil | clomipramine | 25–250 |
| | Asendin | amoxapine | 150–400 |
| | Elavil | amitriptyline | 100–300 |
| | Norpramin | desipramine | 100–300 |
| | Pamelor, Aventyl | nortriptyline | 50–150 |
| | Sinequan, Adapin | doxepin | 75–300 |
| | Tofranil | imipramine | 100–300 |
| | Vivactil | protriptyline | 10–60 |
| Monoamine oxidase inhibitors (MAOIs) | Marplan | isocarboxazid | 10–50 |
| | Nardil | phenelzine | 45–90 |
| Selective serotonin reuptake inhibitors (SSRIs) | Paxil | paroxetine | 20–50 |
| | Prozac | fluoxetine | 20–80 |
| | Zoloft | sertraline | 50–200 |
| Other compounds | Desyrel | trazodone | 150–600 |
| | Ludiomil | maprotiline | 75–225 |
| | Wellbutrin | bupropion | 75–450 |

Figure 3.7

## Side Effects of Antidepressants

| Drug Class | Side Effects |
| --- | --- |
| TCAs | Dry mouth, dizziness, sedation or agitation, weight gain, constipation, heart palpitations, cardiac abnormalities |
| MAOIs | Insomnia, dizziness, weight gain, sexual difficulties, confusion or memory problems, overstimulation, hypertensive crisis |
| SSRIs | Nausea, vomiting, excitement, agitation |
| Other compounds | Sedation or agitation |

Figure 3.8

In recent years, some research has suggested that some patients who are depressed and have a schizoaffective disorder may benefit from antidepressant medications in addition to their antipsychotic medication. However, these findings are still too preliminary to be accepted as fact. Research on other uses of antidepressant medication for schizophrenia continues (for example, on whether these medications are helpful for patients with treatment-refractory symptoms), but their benefits remain to be established.

Despite the absence of compelling evidence supporting the use of antidepressants for schizophrenia, these medications are occasionally prescribed, and some patients appear to benefit from them. Figure 3.7 contains the names of commonly prescribed antidepressant medications and their dosages. Figure 3.8 identifies side effects of these medications.

## Mood Stabilizing Medications

Mood stabilizing medications are named for clinical effects on persons with a bipolar (manic-depressive) disorder. These medications tend to reduce both manic symptoms (such as grandiosity and decreased need for sleep) and symptoms of depression in patients with this disorder. Three mood stabilizing medications are used most often: lithium, Tegretol, and Depakote (or Depakene). Little systematic research supports the effects of Tegretol or Depakote on schizophrenia. Similarly, the results of research on lithium suggest that it has little benefit for patients with schizophrenia or schizoaffective disorder.

Even though research has not provided support for the effects of mood stabilizing medications on schizophrenia, these medications are occasionally prescribed. Of course, it is possible that some of these medications benefit some patients. However, it is not known which medications help whom. Because your relative may be prescribed these medications, the names of the medications and their dosage ranges are listed in Figure 3.9, and their side effects are listed in Figure 3.10.

## Mood Stabilizing Medications

| Type of Drug | Brand Name | Chemical Name | Average Dosage (mg/day) |
|---|---|---|---|
| Anticonvulsant | Depakene, Depakote | valproic acid | 125–2000 |
| | Tegretol | carbamazepine | 100–2000 |
| Lithium | Eskalith (also available in a controlled-release form) | lithium carbonate | 900–3600 |

Figure 3.9

## Side Effects of Mood Stabilizing Medications

| Drug Class | Side Effects |
|---|---|
| Lithium | Minor: nausea, stomach cramps, thirst, fatigue, headache, tremor<br>Serious:[a] vomiting, diarrhea, extreme thirst, muscle twitching, slurred speech, confusion, stupor |
| Anticonvulsants | Minor: fatigue, muscle ache, skin rash, headache, dizziness, constipation or diarrhea, loss of appetite<br>Serious:[a] fever, jaundice, confusion, swelling of lymph glands, vomiting, vision problems (such as seeing double) |

[a] Consult physician immediately if any of these side effects are noted.

Figure 3.10

## Electroconvulsive Therapy

Electroconvulsive Therapy (ECT) is a treatment in which a mild electrical shock is given to a person's brain in an effort to improve symptoms. It is used primarily for the treatment of persons with major depression, especially when they have experienced little benefit from antidepressant medications. For these individuals, ECT can be very effective. It is used much less frequently for schizophrenia, but there are occasions when it can be helpful. Electroconvulsive Therapy can improve movement in patients with schizophrenia who have *catatonia* (stuporousness or rigidly maintaining a particular position). In addition, ECT can be useful in calming patients with schizophrenia who are in a state of severe, uncontrolled agitation or excitement. Fortunately, such cases tend to be rare. Finally, ECT is occasionally given when a patient with schizophrenia experiences severe, unremitting depression and suicidality that is unresponsive to conventional pharmacological treatment. In such cases, ECT is used as a "last resort" and is sometimes effective.

## Other Strategies

Many other medications and medical treatments for schizophrenia have been tried. Sometimes a new treatment is discovered, preliminary trials are promising, and it is rapidly touted as a miracle cure for schizophrenia. Invariably, subsequent controlled research on such new strategies proves disappointing, and in most cases the "miracle cures" are not even as good as conventional treatments. It would be impossible to list here the hundreds of "new treatments" over the years that have failed to meet expectations. A few of the strategies you might have heard about include orthomolecular approaches (such as megavitamins), hemodialysis (kidney dialysis), psychosurgery (surgery on parts of the brain), and insulin shock (giving a person high doses of insulin to induce a temporary state of coma). We advise you to remain skeptical about new, unorthodox treatments of schizophrenia until they have been objectively evaluated in scientific studies.

# Medication Compliance

Antipsychotic medications are the most potent treatment currently available for schizophrenia, but they are only effective if taken on a regular basis. Irregular compliance with medication can be a problem because the drug fails to maintain a stable level in the blood, which is necessary to reduce symptoms and prevent relapses. The issue of medication compliance in patients with schizophrenia is an important one. Estimates are that 50 to 75 percent of patients with schizophrenia are noncompliant with their medication at some time over the course of their illness.

If you are concerned that your relative may not be compliant with his or her medication, it is important first to understand some of the reasons people with schizophrenia find it difficult to take medication. After discussing reasons for noncompliance, we will suggest some methods you can use to evaluate and monitor your relative's medication compliance. Then, we will provide you with some strategies for enhancing medication compliance in your relative.

## Reasons for Medication Noncompliance in Schizophrenia

Problems with adhering to medication regimens are not limited to people with schizophrenia or psychiatric patients; they are also common in many other types of medical disorders. For example, people with essential hypertension who are prescribed medications that lower their blood pressure often don't take their medication for two reasons: the medications have unpleasant side effects, such as causing sexual dysfunction, and essential hypertension causes few noticeable symptoms (although it does increase the risk of heart attack or stroke), so that people forget easily to take their medication.

People with schizophrenia can be noncompliant with medication for the same reasons as people with hypertension. As we discussed previously, antipsychotic medications can cause troubling side effects, which may lead to noncompliance in patients who see this as the easiest solution. Some patients also deny that they have schizophrenia or even that they have any problems at all. For these patients, this denial may help them not think of themselves as failures in society or their family. However, the denial can also interfere with their ability to participate in their own treatment by taking medication regularly, because they see no need for medication.

A less common obstacle occurs when patients acknowledge they have a disorder, but fail to see the benefits of medication or argue that it does not help them. It is true that in a small percentage of patients with schizophrenia, medication is not helpful. More often, relatives and others can see the benefits of medication more readily than the patient.

For patients who have insight into their illness, or at least some awareness of the difficulties they experience, taking medication regularly can be an unpleasant reminder of their disorder or problems. Forgetting to take medication means avoiding the negative thoughts associated with the illness and the limits it imposes.

A very common reason patients do not take their medication is simply that they forget. Even people who do not have schizophrenia forget to take their medications. In schizophrenia, however, this problem is magnified because of the pervasive cognitive deficits, including memory im-

pairment, that are characteristic of the illness. Other symptoms of schizophrenia can result in patients refusing to take medications. *Negativity* refers to a sense of defeat, hopelessness, and unwillingness to try to change
in patients with schizophrenia. Patients who are extremely negativistic
often believe that change is not worth the effort or is impossible, and
they may resist attempts to get them to take medication. Sometimes these
patients even resent efforts to engage them interpersonally, preferring instead to be left alone. Improving medication compliance can be very difficult with these patients, because any interaction with them seems like
an intrusion into their world.

Other symptoms that can interfere with taking medication are suspiciousness, hostility, and psychotic symptoms. Suspiciousness and hostility are often related to psychotic symptoms, such as paranoid delusions
or critical auditory hallucinations, even when those psychotic symptoms
are not outwardly apparent or the patient denies them. Efforts to persuade the patient to take medication may be viewed as attempts to control
him or her, or may even be interpreted as attempts to hurt. For example,
we have known patients who believed that their parents were trying to
"poison" them by convincing them to take antipsychotic medications.
These beliefs can be difficult to counter, because often there is a grain of
truth to them. Relatives and mental health professionals *are* trying to control patients (or at least the symptoms of their illness) with antipsychotic
medications, and these medications *can* produce unpleasant side effects
and subjective states. Most people use the word **poison** to refer to substances that kill people or have toxic effects without any benefits. If your
relative does not acknowledge any benefits of medication and is aware
only of its negative side effects, viewing it as poison may not seem so
farfetched. Thus, the symptoms of schizophrenia can also interfere with
medication compliance.

## Clues to Medication Noncompliance

You may already know whether your relative is compliant with his
or her medication. For example, you may observe him or her take medication regularly, or you may have had arguments about medication in
which your relative has adamantly refused to take it. On the other hand,
you, like many other people with a relative who has schizophrenia, may
be unsure whether he or she is taking medication. It is not always obvious when a patient is taking medication, so that collecting information
on this issue is often necessary.

One especially important clue to your relative's medication compliance can be his or her symptoms. The symptoms of schizophrenia vary
in severity over time, but usually they will be relatively stable if he orshe
is taking the medication and there are no other major changes or stress.
If you notice a worsening in your relative's condition but cannot think

---

## Common Reasons for Medication Noncompliance

- Unpleasant medication side effects
- Denial of the illness or need for medication
- Reminder of the illness
- Suspiciousness, hostility, or psychotic symptoms
- Cognitive impairments
- Extreme negativity

---

of any recent stressors he or she has faced (such as beginning a new job, increasing time at work, or changing residence), it is possible that medication noncompliance has become a problem. It is critical to detect increases in the symptoms of schizophrenia, such as social withdrawal, talking to oneself (auditory hallucinations), or preoccupation with delusions, as soon as possible, to take corrective action. Sometimes medication noncompliance leads to unique changes in behavior, thinking, or feeling before a major relapse of symptoms occurs. Recognizing these subtle changes quickly and addressing problems with medication noncompliance can prevent relapses and rehospitalizations. These changes are called *early warning signs*. The next chapter is devoted to teaching you how to recognize and monitor these precursors of relapse.

One easy, but often overlooked way of finding out whether your relative is taking medication is to ask him or her. Many patients will honestly and directly answer this question, even when they are not taking their medication as prescribed. If your relative says that he or she is not taking medication regularly, chances are it is true and you can begin to take steps to deal with that situation. If your relative assures you that he or she is taking medication, it is not necessarily true, but it may be.

Another way of evaluating whether your relative is taking medication is to do "pill counts": count the number of pills in the bottle at intervals (such as every day or weekly) to determine whether the correct number of pills is missing since the last count. If too few pills are missing (or too many), your relative has not taken the correct number of pills. This technique is often used by health professionals who must supervise patients taking their own medication. The method is not foolproof, because patients can remove pills from the bottle and throw them away, especially if they are aware the pills are being counted. However, it is a useful method for surreptitiously evaluating whether your relative is taking medication when you cannot ask directly.

Observing your relative taking medication often provides very accurate information about his or her compliance. Although it is possible for a patient to pretend to take medication by holding it in the cheek instead of swallowing it ("cheeking it") and then spitting it out later, this does not happen often. However, you may not find it convenient to consistently observe your relative taking medication, and he or she may only take it when you watch.

Figure 3.11 provides an overview of the different methods you can use to evaluate whether your relative is taking his or her medication. As you can see, each method has its advantages and disadvantages. Since no method is perfect, it is best not to rely too much on any one method and to use a combination of strategies instead. This will maximize the

## Strategies for Evaluating Medication Compliance

| Strategy | Advantages | Disadvantages |
| --- | --- | --- |
| Observing an unexplained worsening of symptoms | Can be very sensitive to medication changes | Other factors can cause worsening of symptoms, such as stress |
| Asking the patient | Convenient and sometimes accurate; especially useful when patient acknowledges not taking medications | Often inaccurate |
| Observing the patient take medications | Very accurate | Inconvenient to do regularly: patient may "cheek" medication; requires access to the patient; may engender resentment in the patient |
| Pill counts | Fairly accurate | Takes time and must be done regularly; patient may throw away medication; requires access to patient's medication |

Figure 3.11

accuracy of the information you get concerning your relative's compliance with medication.

## Enhancing Medication Compliance

There are a number of different strategies available to you if your relative does not consistently take medication. However, before you attempt to change your relative's behavior, it is crucial to try to establish a dialogue that may provide a forum for dealing with the problem. During this discussion, strive to maintain an open, nonthreatening atmosphere. Explain your concerns to your relative, but try to avoid blaming him or her. Listen to your relative and try to understand the situation from his or her perspective. Then attempt to find a common ground that incorporates both your concerns and your relative's viewpoint. This is not always possible, but you will never know if you don't try.

Some specific strategies for improving compliance with medications are described below. If medication compliance is a problem for your relative, be open to trying several different strategies and working on it over a period of time. In addition, even when you develop some strategies that work, you will need to continue to monitor your relative's compliance in case he or she becomes noncompliant again.

### Highlight the Benefits of Medication

Your relative may not be fully aware of the benefits of medication. By helping him or her understand the effects of medication, you can enable your relative to become a more active member of his or her own treatment team. In our experience, patients respond most positively to the message that antipsychotic medications prevent rehospitalizations. Most patients don't like being hospitalized, and this can serve as a motivating factor in medication compliance. Some patients also respond to the notion that medication can facilitate their ability to achieve goals, such as more independent living or work. Although medication itself will not achieve those goals, most of the long-term goals that patients have are difficult to achieve if their symptoms are not sufficiently controlled or they have frequent relapses.

Depending on your relationship with your relative, you might be the best person to discuss the advantages of medication. Sometimes just being a relative decreases the credibility of what you have to say, however, and this may be especially true if you are trying to provide medical information, such as regarding the effects of medication. If you feel that you are not the best person to talk with your relative about this or your attempts have not been successful, try to find someone else. This other person should be someone that your relative respects or with whom he or she enjoys a positive relationship. A psychiatrist or another person involved in your relative's treatment are possible candidates, as are friends and other relatives.

### Address Issues Related to Side Effects

By this time you are familiar with the side effects of antipsychotic medications and the possibility that these problems can contribute to non-compliance. If your relative has experienced medication side effects that lead to noncompliance or inconsistent compliance, you may be in a good position to help. In general, there are two different ways of helping your relative deal with medication side effects: encouraging him or her to discuss medication side effects with the psychiatrist and helping him or her develop coping strategies to manage the side effects.

*Discussing medication side effects with the psychiatrist.* Neither you nor your relative is an expert on the side effects of antipsychotic medications, but your relative's psychiatrist is. Therefore, one of the best ways of helping your relative deal with side effects is to facilitate his or her ability to talk these issues over with the psychiatrist. The psychiatrist has many possible options for decreasing side effects, such as lowering the medication dosage, prescribing side effect medications, or switching to another type of antipsychotic.

For your relative's conversation with the psychiatrist to be as effective as possible, he or she needs to be prepared to describe the specific side effect, how often it occurs, how long the side effect has been a problem, the degree of discomfort it causes, and any strategies used to try to cope with it, including not taking medication. Many patients feel anxious when talking to their psychiatrist. Your relative may find it helpful to practice the conversation with you first before talking with the doctor. He or she may also benefit from writing down some of his or her concerns about medication side effects and using this list as a reminder during the conversation with the doctor.

Some patients find it very difficult to effectively advocate for themselves. Lack of assertiveness is one of the greatest interpersonal difficulties of people with schizophrenia. Although one way of dealing with this problem is to help your relative practice, another strategy is to join the meeting with your relative and the psychiatrist. If this appears to be a viable option for you, talk it over with your relative to see if he or she agrees. If you both agree it is worth pursuing, set up an appointment for you and your relative to meet with the psychiatrist. It is best if your relative can arrange this appointment, so that it is clear to the psychiatrist that he or she supports the plan. This meeting can focus on a review of the problematic side effects, including how it has contributed to medication noncompliance, and can lead to a discussion of options for decreasing or managing the problem.

*Developing coping strategies for side effects.* The easiest way to develop coping strategies for side effects is to review with your relative the specific strategies described earlier in this chapter and to pick one or two to work on. For each particular strategy, first talk it over, then practice it, and then make a plan to put the strategy into action. You may need to be involved in prompting your relative to use the coping strategy or in identifying other ways that he or she can be reminded to use it. After you and your relative have arrived at a plan, arrange to follow it up at a specific time (such as the following week) to see how it is going and how it may need to be modified.

For example, Sarah's son, Bill, had a terrible time with akathisia, even when his psychiatrist prescribed him the lowest possible dosage. He said, "Sometimes I feel like jumping out of my skin." He was often restless and paced frequently. Because of his akathisia, Bill began skipping doses of his medication, and some of his symptoms of schizophrenia began to worsen. After Sarah talked over her concerns with Bill, they decided to explore some coping strategies. Bill came up with the idea of taking a walk every day to relieve some of the tension and feelings of restlessness. Sarah also thought this would be a good idea. She suggested that they take a walk around the block together to see how it went. They did this and Bill reported that it helped him relax a little. They agreed on a plan that Bill would take a walk every day around 3:00 PM. Bill and Sarah decided to meet the following week to see how the plan was going. At this meeting, both Bill and Sarah felt his akathisia had decreased, and Bill had resumed taking his medication. Bill said that he still sometimes felt restless during the day, and he and Sarah began to explore other strategies that he could use in addition to taking daily walks.

## Build Medication Compliance into the Daily Routine

Helping your relative incorporate taking medication into his or her daily routine minimizes the chances that doses will be forgotten. For most people, daily living activities such as brushing teeth, showering, and going to work are done so routinely that they become automatic, and need not be planned or thought about. Patients with schizophrenia may experience difficulty establishing daily routines, but with help such routines can be developed. Rather than attempting to establish a new, potentially complicated daily routine for your relative, try to understand what his or her current routine actually *is*, and consider how taking medication can be incorporated into that schedule.

Depending on whether your relative takes medication in the morning, the evening, or both, look for convenient times to add medication to his or her daily activities. In the morning, at breakfast is a good time to take medication, because of easy access to beverages. In the evening, many patients find it convenient to take medication at dinner time (if dinner is eaten at a regular time), before brushing teeth, or just before going to bed. Discuss the different options with your relative to decide when routine medication can be most easily included in his or her daily routine.

In addition to planning on how to integrate medication into your relative's routine, you may need to consider how he or she will remember to take the medication. Get your relative involved in coming up with an answer to this problem, so that he or she will be invested in the solution. The less you can be involved in actually reminding your relative to take medication the better, although it may be necessary at times. Posting notes in prominent places (such as on the bathroom mirror or toothpaste tube) can be helpful reminders. You may need to periodically change the location of these notes if your relative gets used to them or begins to avoid them.

### Simplify the Medication Regimen

Simplicity is golden when it comes to medication regimens. The fewer medications that must be taken and the fewer times per day, the easier it will be for your relative to comply. Taking medication more than once per day requires more effort and provides more opportunities for missed doses. Many medications prescribed for schizophrenia can be taken once per day, in the morning or evening. Your relative can consult his or her psychiatrist about this.

### Use Contingencies to Promote Medication Compliance

The word *contingencies* refers to the consequences of behaviors. Everyone is aware that their behavior is shaped by naturally occurring consequences in the environment. When you are late to work, your boss may glare at you or your pay may be docked, which may make you be more punctual next time. When you cook a nice meal, family members or guests may smile and compliment your cooking, which encourages you to do it again. By systematically providing positive consequences for taking medication, or by removing privileges for not taking it, you can improve your relative's compliance with medication.

Compliance can be promoted most effectively when contingencies are provided both for taking and not taking medication. The best consequences to select are those that are readily available, you have control over, and your relative values. Examples of positive consequences for medication compliance include spending money, taking a trip or outing, renting a video, having a special meal cooked, using the family car, spending time with someone special, or engaging in a recreational activity. The negative consequences of not taking medication can include the loss of those same positive activities.

If your relative lives in your home and is noncompliant with medication, the ultimate contingency that you may need to use is his or her privilege of continuing to live at home. As the person who pays the bills, you have the right to live in a peaceful, safe environment and to insist that your relative meet certain reasonable standards of behavior. You may choose to include medication compliance as one of those standards of behavior. However, we encourage you to use this strong contingency *only* if you are willing to follow through on it and insist that your relative live elsewhere if he or she is noncompliant. Otherwise, you are establishing contingencies you are unable to or unwilling to enforce and your credibility will be reduced.

In order to use contingencies to enhance compliance with medication, the specific consequences need to be written down, discussed with your relative, and posted somewhere. You also have to decide how you will evaluate your relative's compliance with medication (for example, observing him or her take it, pill counts). Establishing clear, meaningful, and enforceable contingencies can be a very potent strategy for enhancing medication compliance. However, it takes time to work, and you need to be open to modifying the specific contingencies you have set, depending on their effect (or lack of effect) on your relative's medication compliance.

### Consider Injectable Medications

Antipsychotic medications that can be taken in the form of long-acting injections (such as Prolixin or Haldol) have several advantages over oral medication. The most obvious advantage is that as long as your relative attends his or her appointments, you need not worry about compliance. Injectable medications bypass the need to remember to take medications, and the patient is reminded less often about his or her illness. Injectable medications also have the advantage of producing a very steady blood level of the medication (more so than oral medication), which can result in better symptom reduction. This means that if your relative needs to reschedule a doctor's appointment when he or she is due for a shot, it can be done without the medication in the body falling below therapeutic levels.

Many patients readily agree to take injectable medications when the option is presented to them. Others object, usually for one of two reasons. First, they may have experienced problematic side effects from injectable medications in the past, and therefore are reluctant to try again. Second, they may dislike or be afraid of needles.

The side effects of injectable medications are the same as when the same medications are taken orally. However, sometimes a patient is given too high a dosage the first time he or she is given injectable medication, and this leads to unpleasant side effects, such as muscle spasms (acute dystonia). Since the medication is in the body for an extended period of time, severe side effects must sometimes be treated with injectable side effect medication. If your relative has had this experience in the past, he or she is still a candidate for injectable medication.

These medications should be started at very low doses and supplemented with oral medication. The dosage of injectable medication should be increased very gradually, while tapering off the oral medication, until a therapeutic level of the injectable medication has been achieved. This process may take several months. In our experience, the vast majority of patients who have previously had negative experiences with injectable medications can be treated successfully with this type of medication, provided that very low dosage levels are used in the beginning.

Patients who dislike or are afraid of needles may be more difficult to persuade to try injectable medications. Your relative may be relieved to learn that the size of the needles used to inject medication is quite small and causes little pain. The *idea* of injectable medications may be scary to your relative. As patients learn more about it, such as by having a conversation with a psychiatrist or nurse, they sometimes warm to it. When talking over this option with your relative, it may be helpful to encourage him or her to *try* it and see how it goes. Many patients who are reluctant to try injectable medications soon find out that they are not as bad as expected, and agree to continue taking the medications.

## Evaluating the Quality of Pharmacological Treatment

How do you know if your relative is receiving the best pharmacological treatment possible? This is one of the most important questions to ask and one of the more difficult ones to answer. Because medications usually do not eliminate all symptoms, you cannot judge whether your relative is receiving the best treatment strictly by the severity of his or her symptoms. Nevertheless, there are some guidelines for judging your relative's care, which may be helpful in determining whether steps need to be taken to try to improve it.

As a first step toward evaluating your relative's care, we encourage you to begin a log of the different medications your relative is receiving, their dosage levels, and the reasons for each medication. When changes are made in your relative's pharmacological treatment, note these changes and the reasons in the log. This will provide you with an ongoing record of your relative's medications. Feel free to make copies of the Medication Log provided here.

We will now describe a number of different criteria you can use to evaluate your relative's treatment. No one criterion is absolutely essential, but in combination they will provide you with the information you need to make informed decisions.

## Medication Log

*Instructions:* Complete this log for all medications your relative is currently prescribed. When a change is made, note the change, date, and reason for changing. When a prescription is stopped by the doctor, carefully draw a single line through the name of that medication. (*Note*: When photocopying this form, you may want to enlarge it, to allow more room for writing.)

| Medication Name | Date | Dosage | Purpose | Date Changed | Reason for Change |
|---|---|---|---|---|---|
| | | | | | |
| | | | | | |
| | | | | | |
| | | | | | |
| | | | | | |
| | | | | | |
| | | | | | |
| | | | | | |
| | | | | | |
| | | | | | |

## Polypharmacy

*Polypharmacy* refers to prescribing multiple classes of medications. Of course, many patients with schizophrenia take two different types of medication: an antipsychotic and a side effect medication. However, sometimes patients are prescribed three, four, five, even six different types of medication. Taking multiple types of drugs increases the number of possible side effects, complicates the medication regimen, and is more expensive. Most research on the pharmacological treatment of schizophrenia indicates that multiple types of medication do not provide added clinical benefits.

In particular, combining different types of antipsychotic medication has not been found to be helpful. Some psychiatrists prescribe a traditional antipsychotic in addition to Clozaril, but this has not yet been shown to be more effective than Clozaril alone. Patients who receive antidepressant and mood stabilizing drugs in addition to their antipsychotics rarely benefit from this triple combination.

Polypharmacy is often practiced because the psychiatrist may prescribe additional medications to treat symptoms without evaluating whether some medications are unnecessary. As a consequence, the number of different drugs a patient receives gradually increases. In most cases of polypharmacy, patients can be gradually taken off different medications and monitored to evaluate changes in symptoms.

## Overmedication

Over the past decade a wealth of information has emerged indicating that patients with schizophrenia can be effectively treated with much lower doses of antipsychotic medication than previously thought. Most psychiatrists are aware of this, but it is still possible that your relative is receiving higher than the optimal dosage. One reason overmedication can be a problem is that the dosage of antipsychotic medication required to treat acute symptoms is usually higher than the dosage required during a period of stabilization. If your relative has been maintained on the same amount of medication for a long period of time since his or her last hospitalization, it is possible that he or she would benefit from a reduction in dosage.

Overmedication often results in more severe side effects and lethargy. It is almost impossible to know for certain that a patient is being overmedicated without changing his or her dosage level. If a decision is made to reduce dosage level, it is best if it is decreased very gradually over several weeks or months and the patient's symptoms are monitored closely for any worsening.

## Frequency of Evaluations

Your relative needs to see his or her psychiatrist (or nurse) regularly to have symptoms and dosage levels checked. There is no absolute rule for how frequent such visits need to be, but in general, more frequent appointments are preferable to less frequent ones, to detect changes in your relative's condition more rapidly. The optimal frequency of doctor visits may depend on the stability of your relative's symptoms. If your relative has recently had a relapse or has been rehospitalized within the past six months, more frequent doctor's visits are preferable.

Our recommendation is that patients see their doctor (or nurse) every two weeks for at least six months to a year after their last relapse or rehospitalization. If symptoms are severe, especially immediately after discharge, weekly appointments may be called for. Even after a year it is preferable for many patients to continue to have medication visits every two weeks. Some patients with stable symptoms can be seen less often, such as monthly. Occasionally, patients can go even longer periods between appointments (such as six to eight weeks), although we have found those patients to be rare. If a patient is seen less often than every two weeks, it is best if he or she is in contact with someone who can monitor symptoms and alert the doctor in the event of a change. We believe that patients with schizophrenia need to see a psychiatrist or nurse more often than once every three months to receive optimal pharmacological treatment.

## Duration of Medication Visits

As with the frequency of medication visits, there is no hard and fast rule for how long a visit should be. However, in most cases more than five minutes are required. The purpose of regular medication checks is to monitor symptoms and side effects. This simply cannot be accomplished with most patients in a very brief meeting. If a psychiatrist has never met your relative, he or she will need to spend at least a half hour or an hour getting acquainted, especially if a careful diagnostic interview is conducted. After initial meetings it is best if checkups take at least 15 minutes. Not every checkup needs to be with the doctor; often a nurse will be more familiar with the patient's symptoms and functioning.

## Availability and Responsiveness

The episodic nature of schizophrenia mandates that rapid action be taken when changes in symptoms are detected. An important element in the quality of your relative's pharmacological treatment is whether the psychiatrist is responsive to concerns raised about symptoms and is available for special appointments if necessary. It is preferable if the psychiatrist is responsive to concerns raised by either your relative or you. If your relative lives with you or you have weekly contact, chances are you are more aware of changes in his or her symptoms than the psychiatrist. If your relative's psychiatrist is not receptive to you and does not value your observations, this limits your ability to work together and may compromise your relative's overall treatment.

Doctors do have the responsibility of dealing with issues of patient confidentiality. Therefore, in order for there to be open communication between you and your relative's psychiatrist, your relative needs to give permission. Once permission is granted, you will be able to evaluate whether the psychiatrist is interested in your observations and appears responsive to your concerns. If your relative refuses to give permission for you to talk with the psychiatrist, your contact will naturally be quite limited.

---

### Criteria for Evaluating the Quality of Pharmacological Treatment

- Polypharmacy—Prescribing multiple classes of drugs is avoided.

- Overmedication—Lowest possible antipsychotic dosage level is prescribed.

- Frequency of Evaluations—Patient's symptoms are evaluated frequently (usually every 2–4 weeks).

- Duration of Medication Visits—Patient meets with doctor or nurse at least 15 minutes.

- Availability and Responsiveness—Doctor is available for special appointments. He or she is interested in your relative's concerns and is responsive in addressing them.

---

# Advocating for Better Pharmacological Treatment

We have identified above a number of different criteria to use for evaluating the quality of your relative's pharmacological treatment. You should not be surprised to find that your relative's treatment does not meet all of these criteria. In particular, if your relative receives pharmacological treatment at a local community mental health center, chances are higher that he or she is seen infrequently and for only brief periods of time. The major reason for this is not that the psychiatrist doesn't care, but rather that public funding for mental health care is typically low, and as a result psychiatrists often have very large case loads.

Thus, if your relative receives pharmacological treatment at the local community mental health center, you will probably not be able to increase the frequency or duration of his or her medication evaluations. One strategy to compensate for this limitation, while your relative continues to receive treatment in the public sector, is to supplement the evaluation conducted by the doctor with your own evaluation. Chapter 4 ("Early Warning Signs of Relapse") is devoted to this topic. In addition, if your relative is involved in other activities at the mental health center, such as a day treatment or vocational program, his or her symptoms can also be monitored by other staff members there. You and your relative can meet with program staff to discuss whether this is already being done.

Concerns that you and your relative may have about polypharmacy and overmedication can be raised directly with the psychiatrist in a concerned, up-front manner. When discussing these concerns, it is advisable to avoid sounding accusatory, so that the psychiatrist is not put on the defensive. It is also better not to provide a specific solution unless asked, so that it does not appear that you and your relative are trying to do the psychiatrist's job. Rather, describe the basis of the your concern as specifically as possible, and let the psychiatrist suggest a solution. For example, if you are concerned about the number of different medications your relative is taking, you may want to focus on the complexity of the medication regimen. If you are concerned about overmedication, focus on the possible signs of overmedication, such as side effects. Above all, it is desirable to communicate to the psychiatrist a cooperative spirit regarding pharmacological treatment, so that you and your relative are seen as allies in the overall treatment process.

If the psychiatrist is not responsive or is under-responsive to concerns raised by you and your relative, and you continue to be dissatisfied with treatment, your choices will depend upon where the treatment is provided. If treatment is provided at a community mental health center and private treatment is not an option, you may need to work within the system to try and get your concerns addressed. This may involve talking with other professionals at the center to get ideas about how to approach the problem. Sometimes these professionals can act as advocates for your relative in a manner in which you cannot. Another possible option is to explore other treatment providers who accept your relative's insurance. Many university hospitals provide high-quality pharmacological treatment and accept commonly available insurance. Similarly, some private organizations provide mental health treatment and accept insurance.

When seeking a private-practice psychiatrist, it is best to look for someone who works regularly with patients with schizophrenia and, if possible, has a reputation for working collaboratively with family members. Referrals can be obtained from mental health professionals, other families, and the telephone book, and local affliates of the National Alliance for the Mentally Ill (see Resources appendix). When selecting a psychiatrist, you will need to strike a balance between "shopping around" to get the best care and striving for the continuity that can be established by working with one person over an extended period of time.

## Common Questions About Antipsychotic Medications

We provide here the answers to some of the most common questions about antipsychotics raised by relatives and patients.

*Are antipsychotic medications addictive?* Antipsychotics are *not* addictive. Some common properties of addictive drugs are that they cause pleasurable feelings, can lead to physical tolerance, and can cause withdrawal effects if the drug is stopped. Antipsychotic medications share none of these properties. Addictive drugs include alcohol, nicotine, stimulants (for example, cocaine), or opiates (such as heroin). However, if your relative stops taking antipsychotics, his or her risk of relapse will increase.

*Do antipsychotics interact with other drugs?* It is safe to take antipsychotic medications with other medications used to treat physical conditions such as allergies, diabetes, epilepsy, or bacterial infections. The physician should be consulted if you or your relative has questions about the safety of taking specific drugs. Alcohol should be used only in moderation (not more than two drinks per week), because it can interfere with the effects of antipsychotics. Street drugs, such as marijuana or cocaine, should be avoided.

*What should be done if a dose of antipsychotic medication is missed?* Consult your relative's psychiatrist regarding this question, since the answer varies from patient to patient. In some cases the doctor will inform the patient to simply take the next dose at the recommended time (not to double the dose); in other cases the patient will be instructed to take the missed dose as soon as he or she remembers.

*How long must antipsychotics be taken?* The consensus among experts is that most patients with schizophrenia or schizoaffective disorder need to take antipsychotics throughout their lives. Research has been done to evaluate whether patients can take medications only when their symptoms begin to worsen, and not between episodes. The results of these studies suggest that this is *not* as effective a strategy for preventing relapses as taking regular, low doses of medication between episodes.

On some occasions, a person may be diagnosed with a schizophreniform disorder. This disorder is just like schizophrenia, but the patient has been ill for less than six months (see Chapter 2). When this is recognized quickly and treated with antipsychotic medications, the patient's symptoms may be completely eliminated by the medication. It is still recommended, however, that he or she remain on antipsychotic medications for an extended period of time as a preventative measure (usually at least one to two years). If this time period passes without a relapse *and* the patient wants to stop medication, many psychiatrists will agree to gradually taper off the dose to explore whether the patient can remain off the medication. If symptoms begin to reappear, the medication is started again. This is common clinical practice. However, little research has addressed the question of whether people who have developed a schizophreniform disorder that does not progress into schizophrenia can be taken off antipsychotic medication.

# 4

# Early Warning Signs
of Relapse

As you know from reading Chapter 1, the course of schizophrenia is usually episodic, with symptoms varying in intensity over time. When symptoms significantly worsen or when old symptoms reappear, this is usually referred to as an *episode of the illness* or a *relapse*. Some relapses require the patient to be rehospitalized for the treatment of severe symptoms, which can be disruptive to both the patient and his or her family members. Many people feel that a relapse and rehospitalization is a setback for patients, because it may take several weeks or even months to regain their prior level of functioning.

A major goal of current treatment programs for schizophrenia is the prevention of relapses and rehospitalizations. One way of avoiding relapses is for patients to take medications on a regular basis, as discussed in Chapter 3, "Medication." There are also other steps that you and your ill relative can take to prevent relapses. One of the most successful strategies involves developing an awareness of the *early warning signs* of the illness, subtle changes in a patient's behavior and symptoms that occur in the days and weeks before a relapse occurs. By carefully monitoring early warning signs, you, your relative, and treatment providers work together as the "relapse-prevention team," helping to improve the course of the illness and minimize setbacks (see Figure 4.1). In this chapter, we focus on how you can detect the early warning signs of a relapse and the steps you can take to prevent a full-blown episode from happening.

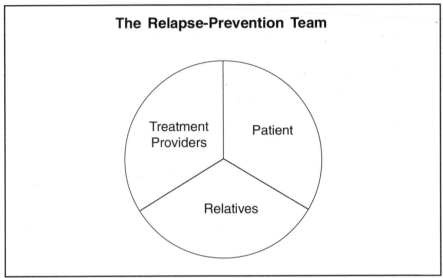

Figure 4.1

# Recognizing the Early Warning Signs of a Relapse

Symptom relapses usually develop gradually over time, not in just one or two days. Often it is many weeks from the time a patient's symptoms first begin to worsen to the time a major relapse occurs. The early changes in behavior, mood, and thought processes tend to be rather small. At first sight, these early signs may seem too insignificant to pay attention to. Recognizing and responding to these subtle, apparently minor changes, however, *can* prevent relapses and rehospitalizations.

There are a number of early warning signs that have been found to precede relapses in many people with schizophrenia. Among the most frequently reported signs are increased depression, social withdrawal, and irritability. Although some early warning signs are common in people with schizophrenia, just as some symptoms are common, each patient has a *unique* pattern of early warning signs that predict when a relapse will occur. Therefore, in order to detect the signs of a relapse in your relative and take steps accordingly, you need to become aware of his or her individual set of early warning signs.

## Common Early Warning Signs

The following are descriptions of early warning signs that are often present in patients with schizophrenia before they experience a relapse. We use examples to illustrate how these signs can vary from person to person.

*Tension and nervousness.* Jack reported feeling so nervous the week before he had a relapse that he couldn't spend time with his five-year-old nephew, an activity he usually enjoyed. He said his nephew's movements seemed too quick and his voice was too loud, and that he couldn't relax around him. Linda reported feeling so tense that she was unable to sit still, and she kept pacing back and forth during the day.

*Eating less or eating more.* One family noticed that three weeks before their daughter Annie's relapse she stopped eating breakfast and lunch. She ate only a very small amount at dinner and reported having no appetite. She lost over ten pounds before she was admitted to the hospital for treatment. In contrast, Bob found himself eating constantly and gaining weight in the month before he had a relapse.

*Trouble sleeping or sleeping too much.* One family noticed several days before Tom had a relapse that his bed had not been slept in. When they asked him about this, he said that he had been having trouble sleeping recently, and that he had been spending his nights watching television or looking out the window. Andy had a similar problem. His wife noticed that he was up all night pacing, sleeping little or not at all. (Sometimes increased difficulty in sleeping is readily apparent to the family by changes in the patient's behavior such as pacing in the middle of the night or playing the stereo loudly late at night.) Janice had the opposite problem before she had a relapse. Although usually an early riser, she couldn't get up in the morning. She stayed in bed until her mother insisted she get up for lunch.

*Depression.* Patients frequently report feeling sad, discouraged, and helpless in the weeks before a relapse. They may appear "down" or unin-

---

## Common Early Warning Signs of Relapse

- Tension or agitation
- Eating problems
- Concentration problems
- Sleeping too little or too much
- Depression
- Social withdrawal
- Irritability
- Decreased compliance with treatment
- Anxiety

---

interested in their usual pastimes. Some may have a feeling that life is not worth living and may contemplate, or even attempt, suicide. Two weeks before relapsing, Elise said she had difficulty facing the day and felt like crying much of the time. Joe wondered out loud, "What's the point in living?" Jennifer managed to perform her daily activities, but got no pleasure from them. Before having a relapse, Samuel would become preoccupied with thoughts of killing himself, and several times in the past he had been rehospitalized after attempting suicide. All these patients experienced depression before their relapse.

*Social withdrawal.* Before some patients relapse, they start to pull back from social situations. This social withdrawal may be in response to small increases in psychotic symptoms or because they find it more difficult to handle social interactions. In the most extreme examples, the patient might refuse to leave his or her room, even to eat. One patient, Dan, usually went out for coffee and donuts with a friend twice a week. One month prior to relapse he found that he did not want to spend time with anyone and refused to go out for coffee. Bernice usually enjoyed eating dinner with her parents. Two weeks before she relapsed she started asking to take a tray of food up to her room at dinner.

*Irritability.* Some patients describe feeling touchy, impatient, or "on edge" in the weeks before a relapse. A few weeks prior to Michelle's relapse, her husband noticed that she would "fly off the handle" at things that would not ordinarily make her angry. For example, she got angry if someone rattled the dishes while loading the dishwasher, and she slammed the door if anyone asked where she was going when she left the apartment. Ted usually enjoyed listening to the radio, but when he started to relapse, he found that he "couldn't stand" music.

*Decreased compliance with treatment.* When some people are about to experience a relapse, they stop following through with treatment recommendations. Patients sometimes stop taking their medications, refuse to see the doctor, or skip their day treatment or vocational program. One of Eleanor's early warning signs was throwing away her bottles of medicine. Jerome stopped going to his day program three weeks before he had a relapse and had to go back to the hospital.

The early warning signs that are commonly observed by family members and reported by patients are listed in the Early Warning Signs Questionnaire, later in this chapter.

## Early Warning Signs in Very Symptomatic Patients

Some patients have persistent symptoms, even when they are receiving optimal doses of medication. For example, some patients hear voices all the time. Often they can learn to ignore the voices and accomplish tasks in spite of them. Other patients have delusions, such as believing that people are plotting against them, which are present nearly all the time. For these patients, a relapse is a dramatic increase in the severity of symptoms or a decrease in their ability to control their behavior in response to the symptoms. Early warning signs of relapse are therefore signaled by changes in symptom severity or lapses in the patient's ability to control his or her behavior.

For example, Steven was generally suspicious of people around him, but a week before his relapse he became more paranoid. He believed that neighbors were talking about him and plotting to kidnap him. Another patient, Alice, always heard voices but was able to ignore these voices. Prior to her relapse she began to obey commands that her voices made of her, for instance, following a stranger home from the video store. Both these patients were able to avoid rehospitalization when their relatives sought help as soon as their symptoms and behaviors showed signs of change.

## Unique Early Warning Signs of Relapse

Some patients have a tendency to experience early warning signs that are *not* common. These are called *idiosyncratic signs*. You and the patient are in the best position to recognize these signs. Examples of such idiosyncratic signs that preceded relapses include dressing all in black, buying lots of lottery tickets, collecting weapons, whistling constantly, suddenly getting a close-cropped haircut.

To determine which, if any, idiosyncratic early warning signs your relative with schizophrenia might have, it can be helpful to ask the following questions:

- Did any unusual changes in the patient's behavior occur in the weeks before his or her last relapse?
- Did he or she do things that seemed "out of character" before a relapse?
- Have the same behaviors preceded other relapses in the past?

These questions can help family members pinpoint the critical signs of an impending relapse. The Early Warning Signs Questionnaire has space at the end for you to record your relative's unique warning signs.

## Responding to Early Warning Signs

The primary goal of monitoring early warning signs is to be able to act quickly to prevent relapses. The earlier an intervention is made, the more likely it is that a relapse can be averted. Even if a relapse does occur, early intervention can decrease the severity of the episode and can increase the chances of being able to manage the problem without hospitalization. When hospitalization is necessary, if the family has been able to recognize and respond quickly to the early warning signs of relapse, a brief hospitalization is often sufficient to stabilize the patient's symptoms.

For example, Samuel had a history of feeling depressed and suicidal before relapsing, and had several times been hospitalized after suicide attempts. After he and his wife learned his early warning signs, they were able to prevent several relapses by alerting his treatment providers when his depression worsened. On one occasion when Samuel felt suicidal, he was hospitalized for eight days, which was much shorter than his previous hospital stays. Most important, actual suicide attempts were avoided by Samuel and his wife's awareness of his early warning signs.

Most relapses in schizophrenia occur when the patient experiences more stress, the patient stops taking medication, or the amount of medication taken becomes insufficient to control the level of symptoms. When early warning signs are noted, the major strategies to take to avoid a relapse are to lower the level of stress, evaluate medication compliance, and assess the need for an increase in medication. The following are specific steps to take when you suspect that the early warning signs of a relapse are occurring. The critical steps of responding to early warning signs are summarized in Figure 4.2.

***Meet to discuss the concern as soon as possible.*** Either you or the patient can call a meeting to discuss concerns about early warning signs. If at all possible, this meeting should include the patient as well as any other family members involved. It is essential that you strive to create an open, nonjudgmental atmosphere for this discussion. Your primary goal in calling this meeting is to discuss your concerns with the patient and other family members about a possible impending relapse. The more patient involvement and open communication that can take place in this discussion, the easier it will be to determine whether a relapse is likely and how it can be prevented.

Do not immediately assume that a relapse is about to happen when early warning signs are detected. Many early signs are subtle changes in behavior that could also occur for reasons other than an impending relapse. The purpose of this step is to evaluate whether particular changes in behavior actually *are* early warning signs of a relapse.

In the discussion calmly explain to your ill relative why you are concerned. Describe what specific changes in behavior you have observed, for how long you have noticed these changes, and how the behavior is different from his or her usual pattern. Explain your concern that these changes preceded relapses in the past. Consider whether there are alternative explanations for your relative's behavior.

For example, Bill was spending more time in his room because he was listening to music on several new compact discs he had recently received as a gift. In this case, Bill's social withdrawal was not an early warning sign of a relapse. On the other hand, when Ben began to withdraw by sleeping most of the morning, not coming down to meals, and not participating in family activities, he could not explain his behavior except to say that he was tired. Ben's psychiatrist agreed with his relatives that his excessive sleeping was an early warning sign and his medication dosage was increased for several weeks. As a result of this, Ben did not have a relapse at that time.

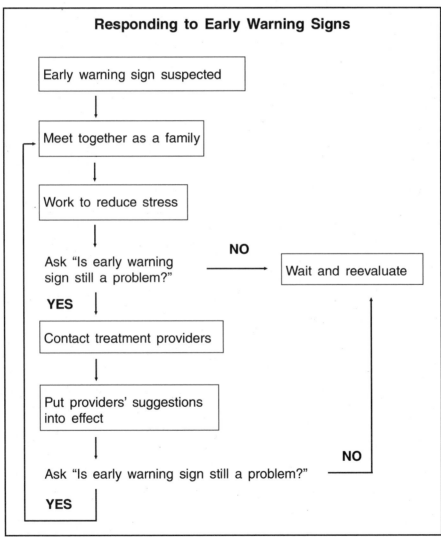

Figure 4.2

By the end of the meeting try to reach a consensus with your familiy members about whether or not early warning signs of a relapse have appeared. If you decide that the signs have *not* occurred, you can stop at this point, and check again later to make sure the problem has not worsened. If you decide that your relative *has* shown early warning signs of a relapse, proceed to the next step.

*Evaluate the patient's medication compliance.* Early warning signs and relapses can follow soon after the patient stops taking medication. If you do not already closely monitor your relative's medication compliance, try to evaluate his or her medication routine as soon as early warning signs appear. This can be accomplished by asking your relative directly whether he or she has been taking medication or by checking how much medication is left in the bottle. If medication noncompliance is confirmed, you need to discuss with your family how to increase compliance, such as through improved monitoring, reminders, and rewards for compliance (see Chapter 3). If medication noncompliance is not a problem, proceed to the next step.

*Evaluate stress experienced by the patient and plan how to deal with it.* In modern society, everyone experiences stress, which comes from a variety of sources. Stress is an especially important factor for schizophrenia because it can lead to symptom relapses. In addition, people with schizophrenia tend to be highly sensitive to the effects of stressors such as arguments, criticism, and sudden increased responsibilities.

For example, when Ellie increased her volunteer time from 10 to 15 hours per week, her auditory hallucinations worsened and she experienced more difficulty concentrating. To find out whether your relative has had a recent increase in stress, ask yourself some of the following questions:

- Has the patient experienced a recent life event, such as the loss of a job, illness, reduced income, or death of someone close?

- Has there been a significant change in the patient's routine over the past two weeks? Was there a change in the patient's treatment program or place of residence?

- Have there been arguments, conflicts or strong disagreements between the patient and other family members?

- Did the patient have a change in an important relationship? Breaking up with a boyfriend or a girlfriend? Starting a new relationship? Seeing a different therapist, psychiatrist, or case manager?

- Has the patient had an increase in responsibilities, such as more time at work?

- Did the patient stop participating in some leisure activities he or she usually enjoyed?

These questions point to common areas of stress for persons with schizophrenia. Remember, however, that what is stressful for one person is not necessarily stressful to another. It is important, therefore, to check with your relative whether something was experienced as stressful before you assume that it is a problem. Evaluating stress can be especially difficult because not everyone (ill or not) is aware of experiencing stress; some always deny it. In addition, bear in mind that not *all* relapses are precipitated by stress.

If you and your relative have been able to identify sources of stress, everyone involved needs to put their heads together to figure out how to deal with the stress. There are two basic ways of responding to stress: you can try to *reduce* the source of the stress itself, or you can help your relative *cope* better with the stress that exists. Reducing stress involves such things as cutting back on responsibilities, looking for new leisure activities, getting a temporary loan to reduce financial distress, or resolving a pressing conflict. Coping includes strategies such as using relaxation techniques, talking to a counselor, and engaging in recreational activities. Other strategies are included in Chapter 8, "Managing Stress." Later in the chapter a worksheet is presented to help you identify your relative's stressors and methods of dealing with them.

*Consult the treatment providers to evaluate the need for a change in medication.* Sometimes the patient's usual dose of medication is not enough to keep his or her symptoms under control, even when efforts are made to reduce stress. His or her psychiatrist can evaluate whether increasing the dose of medication is needed to prevent a relapse. The psychiatrist usually needs to see the patient in order to determine whether additional medication is required.

If early warning signs have developed that you are quite confident indicate an impending relapse, it may be necessary to arrange a special appointment for your relative before the next one that is scheduled. Providing additional medication during the first few weeks after early warning signs have been detected is a powerful strategy for preventing relapses and rehospitalizations. We have provided a Contacts with Treatment Providers Log for you to use to record the phone numbers of treatment providers and their advice.

*Monitor the early warning signs until the situation is resolved.* Once you have noticed early warning signs and have taken steps to address the problem, it is important to keep an eye on those signs until you see clear improvement. This will provide you with information about whether you have been successful in averting a relapse. Useful questions for you and your relative to ask include:

- Is the sign (or symptom) still the same?
- Has it gotten worse or better?
- Is it still a problem?

While you are monitoring early warning signs, it is best that your relative not feel that he or she is being spied upon or that other family members are "walking on eggs" around them. Try to keep your family routines normal and include relaxing activities each day. Plan to follow up with a family meeting every week (or more often) until the problem is resolved. The Early Warning Signs Follow-Up Log is provided for keeping track of family meetings held to discuss early warning signs. An example describing how one family used this and the other worksheets in this chapter appears later. All worksheets referred to fall at the end of the chapter.

# Developing a Personal Plan for Dealing with Early Warning Signs

Up to now in this chapter, we have focused on providing suggestions on how to prevent relapses in your relative by monitoring early warning signs. In addition to following these general suggestions, it can be helpful to formulate a specific plan for how you can respond to these signs. Just as each patient has his or her own unique early warning signs, each family also has it's own unique combination of resources. By developing a plan in advance, by being proactive rather than reactive, you will be prepared to respond to early warning signs quickly, effectively, and with a minimum of stress and confusion for everyone.

## Discuss Past Relapses

To develop a plan for responding to early warning signs, it is best if you first talk with the patient and other family members about relapses that have happened in the past. (If you live alone with your ill relative or have the major responsibility for managing his or her care, you can still benefit from reading the rest of this chapter. See especially the section toward the end entitled "If You Live Alone with the Patient.") Ask questions such as:

- What early signs of relapse did your relative show?
- What were the earliest cues that a relapse was about to occur?

The Early Warning Signs Questionnaire is a standardized form for assessing common early warning signs of relapse. It also includes space to note signs of relapse that are unique to your relative. Complete this questionnaire with the help of the patient (if he or she is willing) and other family members who are in close contact with the patient.

Those items on the questionnaire that you score "very" or "extremely" are important early warning signs for your relative that you should make special note of. It is just these special signs that you need to monitor in your relative on a regular basis, not the entire list of early warning signs. As an aid to remembering which of your relative's signs are most important to track, use the Early Warning Signs Memo to list the three to five early warning signs that you need to monitor. Do not write down more than five signs, because it will be too difficult to monitor them all.

## Discuss Past Stressors on the Patient

You also need to talk about which types of situations have been stressful for your relative in the past and what has helped to reduce stress. This discussion lays the groundwork for managing stress in the future by making it easier to identify possible sources of stress and to generate strategies for dealing with the stress.

Discussion about what is stressful for the patient needs to include input from each family member starting with your relative who has schizophrenia. Sometimes patients can provide valuable information concerning situations they have experienced as stressful that other family members could not know about. It is also possible that you have noticed that your relative's symptoms worsened or a relapse occurred following a particular event or problem, but he or she reports that this situation was not stressful. There is no right or wrong answer to the question of what is stressful, so it is important that you listen to everyone's point of view.

The Stressors and Strategies for Coping worksheet can be used to record sources of stress to the patient and possible strategies for reducing each type of stress. This form can then be used in a family meeting when you are deciding how to respond to early warning signs in the patient.

## Decide How to Conduct a Family Meeting

For most families, having a family meeting is an important step in responding to early warning signs of relapse. It is at these meetings that the signs are discussed and plans are made for what to do next. Part of establishing your own personal plan is determining the following:

- Who will be present at the family meeting?
- Will the patient be included in the initial meeting?
- Where will the meeting be held?

- How can everyone be contacted?

- Would a chairperson be useful?

- Can any obstacles be anticipated?

Settling the logistical questions involved in having a family meeting will help you call a meeting when early warning signs are suspected. The more advance planning you put into how you and your family will meet to respond to early warning signs, the more prepared you will be when it actually happens.

## Putting Your Plan into Action

After you and your family have identified the patient's unique pattern of early warning signs, discussed past stresses and strategies to overcome them, and resolved logistical questions about family meetings, you are prepared to put your personal plan into action. The core ingredients of the plan should be discussed by everyone in advance, to be sure that everyone is familiar with it. As discussed in the previous section of this chapter, these steps include:

- Meeting to discuss the concern about the patient's early warning signs

- Evaluating medication compliance and (if necessary) how to deal with it

- Evaluating stress and (if necessary) plan how to deal with it

- If the signs are still a concern, contacting the treatment providers

- Monitoring the early warning signs until the problem is resolved

The following is an example of how one family developed a personal plan and responded to early warning signs.

During a period when Ed's symptoms were under control, he and his family held a meeting to talk about what to do if he experienced early warning signs in the future. The meeting was attended by Ed, his mother, father, brother, sister, and brother-in-law.

First they discussed Ed's previous early warning signs and completed the Early Warning Signs Questionnaire. Everyone agreed that before his last relapse, Ed had become more tense (question 23) and had difficulty sleeping (question 20). Several family members also noted that on two occasions before having relapses, Ed had become very preoccupied with talking about a girlfriend he'd had in high school more than ten years ago. This unique early warning sign, along with the other two signs from the questionnaire, were selected as the three most important signs of a possible relapse for Ed, and were recorded on the Early Warning Signs Memo.

Next the family reviewed what had caused stress for Ed in the past. Ed noted that "changes" were stressful. His family reported noticing that Ed "flew off the handle" easily when he became involved in a family argument. Ed agreed that arguments were upsetting. He said it helped to first cool off and then to tell his mother how he felt. They recorded this information on the Stressors and Strategies for Coping worksheet.

In terms of a family meeting, they decided that Ed's mother would be the most likely person to call a meeting because she had the most contact with Ed. They decided that they did not need a chairperson. The family agreed to meet at the parents' house, since Ed and his brother lived at home. They also decided to include Aunt Helen in the family meeting, because Ed feels close to her. The family kept all information in a folder marked "Early Warning Signs Plan," along with extra blank copies of the Contracts with Treatment Providers Log and the Early Warning Signs Follow-Up Log.

Six months later, Ed started having difficulty sleeping. After Ed reported that he only slept two hours per night for three nights in a row, Ed's mother called a family meeting. When they discussed Ed's two other early warning signs (irritability and preoccupation with his past girlfriend), Ed and his family agreed that there were slight increases in these signs as well.

Evaluation of Ed's medication compliance indicated that he had continued to take his medication as prescribed. When the family discussed what stressors Ed might be experiencing, he reminded them that he was taking a new course at a community college. His family added that he had to take the bus to class; sitting or standing on crowded buses made Ed feel nervous. Ed's brother suggested that he could give Ed a ride to class on Tuesdays and Thursdays. Ed felt that this would be helpful. He also agreed to talk with the teacher about postponing some of the class deadlines. The family meeting and plans were noted on the Early Warning Signs Follow-Up Log.

One week after the meeting was held and the suggestions were followed through, another family meeting was held. Ed said he was feeling somewhat better, but was still having difficulty sleeping. He called his doctor and described his early warning signs. The doctor set up an appointment for him to come in early. Once again, the results of this family meeting were recorded on the Early Warning Signs Follow-Up Log.

Ed's doctor increased his antipsychotic medicine slightly; he was told to take an extra dosage of medication a few hours before going to bed at night. This meeting with the doctor and the doctor's advice was recorded on the Contacts with Treatment Providers Log. The following week another family meeting was held. Ed reported feeling much better. His sleep had returned to normal. One more follow-up meeting was held, and Ed said that the sleep problem was still resolved. The results of both of these meetings were recorded on the appropriate worksheets.

Both Ed and his family agreed that no more family meetings were needed at this time. Ed continued to take an extra dosage of medication for one month, after which point his doctor reduced his medication to its previous level. By addressing early warning signs promptly and having follow-up meetings, Ed and his family were able to help prevent a relapse.

## If You Live Alone with the Patient

If you have the major responsibility for caring for your relative with schizophrenia, or if you feel alone because you lack support from other members of your family, coping with your ill relative can be even more difficult. It is stressful to make decisions alone, and you may worry about whether you are making the right choices when it comes to matters like responding to early warning signs of a relapse. This stress can be compounded if it is hard to talk to your relative about the possibility of an impending relapse because he or she lacks insight into the symptoms of the illness. Despite the difficulties of living alone with your relative, there are reasons to be optimistic that you can learn to recognize his or her early warning signs and take prompt corrective action. There are also a number of things you can do ahead of time to make it easier to head off a relapse when one threatens.

First, it can be very helpful to find someone who can support you in your efforts to cope with your relative, someone you can bounce ideas off of. Relatives who are not living at home, friends, clergy, and counselors can all be helpful people to talk with in times of need. Even if someone lives far away, talking to the person on the phone can give you perspective on your observations and help you to arrive at a decision about what to do next. When you have identified someone (or several people) who can be supportive to you in managing your relative's illness, you can use this person to help you develop your personal plan for dealing with your relative's particular early warning signs. Working out a plan in advance is especially important when you live alone. When your relative's symptoms worsen and you are under stress you can turn to it automatically.

Second, it may be useful to consider developing a stronger relationship with your relative's treatment providers. These people can become part of your support network for dealing with your relative. When you are concerned that your relative may be facing an impending relapse, you can contact the treatment providers and discuss your observations with them. Explore in advance who the best people are to discuss with you your concerns about your relative. The most likely possibilities are your relative's psychiatrist, social worker, case manager, or counselor. Whoever the person is, it is critical that you feel comfortable talking with him or her and that you are confident that your concerns will be heeded and responded to.

Third, you may need to monitor your relative's compliance with medication more carefully, so that you can respond as early as possible to noncompliance (see Chapter 3 on medication for further discussion of medication monitoring). If the stress associated with increased monitoring becomes too burdensome, consult your team about long-lasting injectable (depot) medications, which can be easier for both patients and relatives.

Finally, if you are not already a member of a self-help advocacy organization, seeking out support groups through organizations such as the National Alliance for the Mentally Ill (NAMI) can provide you with much needed social support for planning on how to cope with your relative's early warning signs. (Addresses of such organizations are listed in the Resources appendix at the end of the book.) Most people find it reassuring to meet others who are coping in similar situations. Establishing supportive relationships with other relatives of the mentally ill can help you take steps toward preventing relapses in your ill relative.

# Early Warning Signs Questionnaire*

*Instructions*: Below is a list of common early warning signs that other patients and family members have observed the week before a relapse. For each early warning sign, please indicate how much of a problem that particular sign was before your relative's most recent relapse. Talk over each sign and try to agree whether it was "not" a problem, "slightly" a problem, "somewhat" a problem, "very much" a problem, or "extremely" a problem. Check the space that corresponds to your answer. If there is a disagreement about a sign, try to compromise in your answer.

|  | No | Slightly | Somewhat | Very | Extremely |
|---|---|---|---|---|---|
| 1. Did the patient's mood shift back and forth? | — | — | — | — | — |
| 2. Was the patient's energy level high? | — | — | — | — | — |
| 3. Was the patient's energy level low? | — | — | — | — | — |
| 4. Did the patient lose interest in doing things? | — | — | — | — | — |
| 5. Did the patient lose interest in the way he or she looked or dressed? | — | — | — | — | — |
| 6. Did the patient feel discouraged about the future? | — | — | — | — | — |
| 7. Did the patient have trouble concentrating or thinking straight? | — | — | — | — | — |
| 8. Were the patient's thoughts so fast that he or she couldn't keep up with them? | — | — | — | — | — |
| 9. Was the patient afraid he or she would lose control or "go crazy"? | — | — | — | — | — |
| 10. Was the patient puzzled or confused about what was going on around him or her? | — | — | — | — | — |
| 11. Did the patient feel distant from family and friends? | — | — | — | — | — |
| 12. Did the patient have the feeling that he or she didn't fit in? | — | — | — | — | — |
| 13. Did religion become more meaningful to the patient than before? | — | — | — | — | — |
| 14. Did the patient feel afraid that something bad was going to happen? | — | — | — | — | — |
| 15. Did you have difficulty understanding what the patient was saying? | — | — | — | — | — |
| 16. Did the patient feel lonely? | — | — | — | — | — |

* Adapted from Herz and Melville, 1992

17. Was the patient bothered by thoughts he or she couldn't get rid of?

— — — — —

18. Did the patient feel overwhelmed by demands or feel that too much was being asked of him or her?

— — — — —

19. Did the patient feel bored?

— — — — —

20. Was the patient having trouble sleeping?

— — — — —

21. Was the patient feeling bad for no reason?

— — — — —

22. Was the patient worrying that he or she had physical problems?

— — — — —

23. Did the patient feel tense and nervous?

— — — — —

24. Was the patient getting angry at little things?

— — — — —

25. Did the patient have trouble sitting still and so had to keep moving or pacing?

— — — — —

26. Did the patient feel depressed or worthless?

— — — — —

27. Did the patient have trouble remembering things?

— — — — —

28. Was the patient eating less than usual?

— — — — —

29. Was the patient hearing voices or seeing things that others didn't see or hear?

— — — — —

30. Did the patient feel that other people were staring at or talking about him or her?

— — — — —

31. Was the patient aware that he or she was getting ill again?

— — — — —

32. Had the patient been cooperative about keeping appointments with treatment providers?

— — — — —

33. Had the patient been taking his or her medications as prescribed?

— — — — —

34. Did the patient display any other unusual feelings or behaviors before the relapse? If so, list them in the space below and rate how much they affected the patient. _____

— — — — —

_____   — — — — —

_____   — — — — —

_____   — — — — —

35. Were there any particular life events that had occurred recently before the patient became ill? If so, describe them below.

_____

_____

_____

_____

36. How many days elapsed between the time you noticed changes in the patient's feelings, thoughts, or behaviors and the time of his or her relapse?

_____

## Early Warning Signs Memo

*Instructions:* List the three to five most important early warning signs of relapse for your relative. Consider both signs listed in the Early Warning Signs Questionnaire as well as changes in positive symptoms (such as hallucinations or delusions).

1. _____

2. _____

3. _____

4. _____

5. _____

## Stressors and Strategies for Coping

*Instructions:* Copy this page and use it to list events and situations that have been stressful in the past and what helped your relative to reduce the stress or cope with it.

| Areas of Stress | What Helped? |
|---|---|
|  |  |
|  |  |
|  |  |
|  |  |
|  |  |
|  |  |
|  |  |

## Early Warning Signs Follow-Up Log

| Follow-Up Dates | Meeting Held? | Still a Problem? | Plan | Tasks (Who and What) |
|---|---|---|---|---|
|  |  |  |  |  |
|  |  |  |  |  |
|  |  |  |  |  |
|  |  |  |  |  |
|  |  |  |  |  |

## Contacts with Treatment Providers Log

| Treatment Provider | Phone Number | Date Contacted | Advice or Strategy |
|---|---|---|---|
| Psychiatrist: | | | |
| Nurse: | | | |
| Case manager: | | | |
| Therapist: | | | |
| Social worker: | | | |
| Others: | | | |

# 5

# Community Resources

Medication is very helpful in controlling the major symptoms of schizo-phrenia, but for most patients some symptoms and impairments persist. For example, problems with concentration, social withdrawal, unemploy-ment, and low levels of educational attainment are common even in pa-tients who take medication on a regular basis. There are a variety of out-patient services that can help patients who live in the community manage their illness and achieve personal goals. Identifying which services are most important for your relative is a critical step toward helping him or her develop a comprehensive treatment plan.

It is best for you and your relative both to be actively involved in identifying and obtaining the necessary community services. By working together you can ensure that your relative's needs and interests are met. Occasionally family members meet with resistance when trying to work with certain mental health professionals, who sometimes view involved and caring family members as a nuisance or as threats to treatment. How-ever, professionals increasingly are becoming aware of the importance of family members as a support to the patient and as members of the treat-ment team itself. It is usually possible to form a positive, collaborative relationship between mental health professionals, relatives, and the pa-tient.

The purpose of this chapter is to describe the different types of out-patient mental health services that can be obtained in most communities. We also provide some suggestions about how to advocate for your family member. Each state, city, and county has different types of the services described, so you will need to investigate what your specific community has to offer. In addition, during this time of national health care reform, there are many changes under consideration that could influence the types of psychiatric treatment available to your relative. Keeping informed about the services your relative is eligible for will enable you to make sure that he or she gets the best treatment possible. Information about new developments in mental health services can be obtained by contacting your relative's case manager, your local community mental health center, social workers at a local psychiatric hospital, or your local chapter of the Alliance for the Mentally Ill (see Resources appendix).

## Community Mental Health Centers

When psychotropic medications were discovered, it enabled the majority of chronically ill patients to be discharged from the state hospitals and treated in the community. In 1963, President Kennedy's administration passed the Community Mental Health Centers Act, which established a network of local mental health centers to provide services to persons near their homes. These centers were created for the purpose of helping recently discharged psychiatric patients to cope more effectively outside the hospital and to get back on their feet. As a result of this initiative, every major city in the United States was mandated by federal law to maintain local community mental health facilities available to everyone who lived in the area. The services are not restricted to any particular income group or diagnostic group.

Since 1963, about 800 Community Mental Health Centers (CMHCs) have been funded to serve as the major focal point for the provision of outpatient mental health services in their area. Each center provides services based on geographic divisions, usually referred to as "catchment areas." The CMHC in your catchment area is required to provide services to you and your family member. Fees are determined based on insurance coverage, eligibility for medical assistance, and the person's ability to pay.

Community Mental Health Centers provide a wide range of services to fill the different needs of clients. These services usually include evaluations, case management, pharmacological treatment, outpatient therapy, day treatment programs, emergency services, occupational therapy, recreational therapy, and referrals to other facilities (such as vocational programs). Many centers are also affiliated with community residences, transportation, and vocational and educational programs. These services will be described in more detail later in this chapter.

### Contacting a CMHC

When a patient is hospitalized, part of the discharge plan usually includes a referral to the appropriate CMHC. An appointment at the local

CMHC is often scheduled before discharge. If this was not arranged, the patient or a family member can call to arrange an interview. Phone numbers can usually be found in the government listings pages of the phone book under "Mental Health."

The first appointment, sometimes referred to as the *intake interview,* is for the purpose of evaluating which services are most appropriate for the patient. Your relative will need to be prepared to answer questions about the history of his or her illness, dates of hospitalizations, living situation, social supports, and finances. It is helpful for your relative to bring to the intake interview insurance cards, medical assistance cards, Social Security information, and any other available documents.

The intake interview is an excellent opportunity for your relative to learn about the services that are available through the CMHC. Some examples of questions to ask include:

- What kind of therapy is offered?
- How frequently would I have to attend?
- Is transportation provided?
- How long do I stay in a particular program?
- Are vocational rehabilitation services or placement programs available?
- What opportunities are there for continuing my education?
- Will I have an individual therapist?
- May I have a tour of the facility?

## Services Available at CMHCs

### Case Management

After the intake interview, the patient is usually assigned a *case manager.* The case manager has the responsibility of establishing clear treatment goals in conjunction with the patient, addressing social and financial needs, and coordinating and monitoring overall treatment. Thus, the case manager works with both the patient and various other members of the treatment team, such as a psychiatrist, therapist, and vocational specialist.

If your relative needs services that are not available at your local CMHC, the case manager makes appropriate referrals to outside programs. He or she also assists patients in applying for financial benefits such as Social Security Administration (SSA) benefits (disability insurance and Supplemental Security Income), public assistance, medicare, and medical assistance. To make referrals and complete applications, the case manager often needs to coordinate with the patient, family, psychiatrist, and other mental health treatment providers.

The case manager is the first person for your relative to contact if he or she is not getting the services he or she needs. You can assist your relative by initiating phone calls or helping him or her practice what to say. Once your relative has established a relationship with his or her case manager, they will meet on a regular basis to monitor progress toward goals. If your relative agrees, you can also maintain contact with the case manager. This type of ongoing contact can be beneficial to your relative by ensuring that information is shared among the patient, relatives, and professionals on the treatment team.

### Pharmacological Treatment

Community Mental Health Centers have psychiatrists on staff who are available to evaluate a patient's medication needs and prescribe the proper medication and dosage. These psychiatrists see patients regularly, usually once every month or two. In some centers nurses are available to talk with patients about medication, or psychiatrists may conduct medication groups, where they meet with several patients at once. Patients or family members can contact the psychiatrist if they have questions about medication or concerns about side effects (see Chapter 3).

### Partial Hospital or Day Treatment Programs

Partial hospital (day treatment) programs are designed to provide a structured therapeutic environment on an outpatient basis. These programs are usually available daily for about six hours, but some people attend for fewer hours per day. Day treatment programs have a daily routine that usually includes group therapy and activities, such as arts and crafts, relaxation, and cooking. They also provide important opportunities to socialize with others on a regular basis. The following are examples of the variety of services available at day treatment programs:

- Psychiatric evaluations and medication monitoring
- Individual and group psychotherapy
- Art therapy, movement therapy, and music therapy
- Arts and crafts, music, and social activities
- Education for independent living (cooking, shopping)
- Social skills training
- Self-help and support groups
- Prevocational training
- Groups on men's and women's issues, current events
- Relaxation training

## Therapy and Counseling

Some CMHCs offer psychotherapy. Your relative might benefit from talking to a therapist on a regular basis, although the benefits of individual therapy for persons with schizophrenia have not yet been clearly established. There are many different schools of individual therapy that have been explored for people with schizophrenia. In general, psychodynamic or insight oriented approaches to therapy have not been found to be helpful to patients with schizophrenia and may even be stressful for some people. Therapy approaches that are geared toward the practical and attempt to teach patients how to cope more effectively with their illness are most helpful; these include cognitive behavioral approaches.

Psychotherapists come from a variety of different disciplines—social work, clinical psychology or counseling, nursing, and psychiatry. Some therapists have bachelor's-level degrees, but most have master's degrees or doctorates. Regardless of the therapist's degree, the most important factors are whether he or she can address problems in a reality-based way and can develop a trusting relationship with your relative.

Group therapy is often offered at CMHCs to address areas such as assertiveness or substance abuse problems. Social skills training may be provided to systematically teach patients more effective methods of interacting with others and getting their needs met. Social skills training is discussed in more detail in Chapter 14.

In addition, some CMHCs also offer programs aimed at educating families about schizophrenia and reducing tension among family members. Several controlled research studies have shown that family interventions are beneficial both to patients with schizophrenia and to their relatives. In some CMHCs, family therapy is held in multiple family groups in which several families meet with a therapist together. Other CMHCs may provide family therapy to individual families. Usually patients are included in family sessions, although sometimes they are not.

Although outpatient therapy is usually available at CMHCs, the specific types of therapy offered (such as behavior therapy and family therapy) are often limited. Furthermore, when therapy is available, there may be a long waiting list. Psychotherapy can also be obtained by exploring in the private sector.

## Housing Options

Many CMHCs have established community residences for persons with mental illness (or contracts with such residences), which provide housing, supervision, supportive services, and training in skills for daily living. This type of housing is often considered transitional because there may be a limit on how long a resident can stay. Levels of structure and supervision differ between community residences, but most have a formal admission process, specific rules, and a requirement that residents be involved in a treatment program or activity during the day. The supervision is provided by experienced staff members and often includes training in skills such as cooking, grooming, and money management. Some CMHCs also have supervised apartment programs for patients who are more independent.

Other housing options may also be available in your state, either through the CMHC or another agency. Different states refer to these options by different names, including domiciliary care ("dom care"), personal care, board and care, and halfway houses. There are also privately operated boarding homes, which are not required to provide supervision or supportive services. Other residential programs are available in many states for outpatients with special problems, such as seriously ill patients, (including those previously in state hospitals), patients with substance abuse problems, and patients who are single parents of a young child.

Some regions have special respite homes where patients can spend a few days in the community under close supervision while a crisis abates, thereby avoiding hospitalization. When patients who do not require close supervision need emergency housing, city agencies or a private agency such as the Salvation Army can be helpful.

### Vocational Programs

Some CMHCs have vocational programs to help prepare people to enter or reenter the volunteer or paid workforce. The case manager can also tell you about other programs that are not run by the center. For example, many vocational programs are conducted under the auspices of the state. There are also programs operated by consumers (such as the Fountain House model; see Resources appendix), which may provide volunteer and paid work opportunities, both inside and outside their agency. See Chapter 14 for further details on vocational programs and helping your relative find employment.

### Educational Programs

Most CMHCs offer programs to help people work on their high school equivalency diplomas. When these programs are not available directly through the CMHC, the case manager can refer patients to such programs in the community. For example, many school districts offer special education programs and evening high school classes for older students. Similarly, the case manager can refer patients to programs in their community that provide technical training in areas such as computer programming and automotive repair.

If your relative has graduated from high school and is interested in taking college courses, we recommend that he or she start by first taking one course at a community college or university, and then gradually increasing the number of courses, if desired. Taking too many courses at once, especially at the beginning, can be stressful and can compromise your relative's ability to do as well as he or she possibly could, resulting in a discouraging experience. Some colleges have special programs, run in conjunction with state or local mental health agencies, that provide extra support and counseling to psychiatric patients who are trying to complete college degrees.

### Transportation

Some CMHCs provide transportation to their programs. If your local CMHC cannot provide transportation, it is possible that there is a transportation program available through the city, state, or county for patients who receive medical assistance. Advance registration is required to participate in these programs. Information about such transportation programs can be obtained through your relative's caseworker or by looking in the government listings of the telephone directory.

Some bus and subway companies have reduced fare programs for people with mental illness. These fare reductions may only be available to people who are receiving other mental health benefits, such as medicare or SSI. Consulting regional transportation companies, your relative's case worker, or other families with a mentally ill relative can give you information about special fares.

## Private Service Providers

Alternatives to the publicly funded treatment programs at CMHCs are also available. These include private agencies, local hospitals, teaching hospitals affiliated with a medical school, individual therapists, and some vocational and day treatment programs. Your relative's insurance and your financial resources are the major factors determining whether your relative will be eligible. It is a good idea to ask directly about costs and payment procedures when you inquire about services from a private agency.

Do not assume that you or your relative cannot afford treatment from a private agency, even if you have few resources. Some private agencies, such as teaching hospitals at medical schools, accept insurance and do not charge extra for mental health services. Similarly, some private day treatment programs or partial hospitalization programs accept the standard insurance available to most patients. Therefore, investigating private treatment agencies may be worthwhile, even if you cannot afford to pay for services for your relative.

Self-help (consumer) groups and advocacy groups can also be a source of assistance. Some of these groups provide volunteer programs for patients to gain work experience that may eventually lead to employment. Others provide support groups that encourage patients in the recovery process or help relatives cope with an ill family member. Some groups also work to change legislation to better serve people with mental illness. Each state has different organizations available. The National Alliance for the Mentally Ill (NAMI), however, has chapters in every state. This organization provides information, support and advocacy to persons with mental illness and their families. Other national organizations include the National Mental Health Consumers' Association and the National Mental Health Association. The Resources appendix lists such organizations and how to contact them.

## Financial and Insurance Benefits

Your relative with schizophrenia is probably eligible for some monetary and insurance benefits. The extent of the benefits depends on the severity of his or her illness and on his or her economic resources. Patients and relatives often find the procedures for applying for benefits to be quite confusing and time-consuming. A social worker can be especially helpful in assisting you understand the different benefits available and how to apply for them.

When applying for benefits it is helpful to be as organized as possible and to maintain records. Keeping all of your relative's documents in one place and recording dates and the names of people you talk to during the application process will facilitate you in obtaining the benefits your relative is entitled to. Maintaining records is also necessary because sometimes a benefit must be applied for more than once before it is granted.

Most major financial benefits are provided by local (state or county) and federal government. Financial benefits provided by a state have different titles and eligibility requirements depending on which state you live in, but they are often referred to as *public assistance* or *welfare*. In order to be eligible for public assistance, your relative must have insufficient income from other sources and, in some cases, show that he or she is unable to work because of illness. Financial support from public assistance provided by states is usually quite modest.

The federal financial benefits are Social Security Disability Insurance (SSDI) and Supplemental Security Income (SSI). Both SSDI and SSI are given to individuals with a disability, such as a psychiatric illness, that prevents the patient from working. In order to be eligible for SSDI, your relative must have worked in the past and contributed money to Social Security, but be currently unable to work. SSDI is provided to people independently of whether they have other (nonwork-related) sources of income. SSI is given to patients who are currently unable to work because of their psychiatric disorder, regardless of their past work history. However, to be eligible for SSI, your relative's income must not exceed a certain amount (this does not include financial support you give to your relative). An evaluation by a psychiatrist or psychologist is usually necessary in order to document that your relative is unable to work because of his or her psychiatric disorder.

Figure 5.1 summarizes the major financial benefits for people with mental illness. The specific eligibility criteria and the amount of the financial award may vary from year to year. Call the appropriate state office (look in the phone book under "Public Assistance" or "Public Welfare") or federal office (under "Social Security Administration") to get current application information, or ask your relative's caseworker.

The major types of health care benefits for people with mental illness are provided by local government (state or county) and federal govern-

| Major Monetary Benefits for People with Mental Illness | | | | | |
|---|---|---|---|---|---|
| Benefit | Who Is Eligible? | Based on Disability? | Based on Financial Need? | Medical Insurance Provided? | Where to Apply |
| Social Security Disability Insurance (SSDI) | Persons who are now disabled, but worked in the past and contributed to Social Security (or, in some cases, whose parents (contributed) | Yes | No | After two years of receiving SSDI, people are eligible for Medicare | Social Security Administration office |
| Supplemental Security (SSI) | Persons who are disabled who do not qualify for SSDI (or only small amount of SSDI) and have limited income and assets | Yes | Yes | Medicaid | Social Security Administration office |
| Public assistance or welfare | Low-income adults who have serious mental health problems and meet state criteria | Yes, but criteria are not as stringent as SSA programs | Yes | Usually medical assistance is provided | Office of public assistance or welfare |

Figure 5.1

ment. Health insurance provided by the state is usually called *medical assistance* or *medicaid*. In order to be eligible for this type of insurance, your relative must have insufficient income from personal resources. In some cases, the patient must also show that he or she is disabled by illness. The specific types of health care expenses (such as inpatient bills, outpatient bills, and prescriptions) covered by medical assistance vary from state to state and depend upon the severity of the patient's illness.

Whereas the state or county government provides medical assistance, health insurance is provided by the federal government in the Medicare program. Patients are eligible for Medicare if they have been disabled by a psychiatric illness and have been receiving SSDI for more than two years. Similar to SSDI, Medicare is provided independent of the patient's nonemployment income. If your relative receives SSI and is not eligible for SSDI, his or her medical assistance will probably cover most routine medical expenses incurred by the illness. Figure 5.2 summarizes health care benefits available to persons with mental illness.

Other monetary and health care benefits may be available through the Veterans Administration (VA) if your relative served in the military. Low-income individuals may be eligible for food stamps or Aid to Families with Dependent Children (AFDC). Contact your state's public assistance or welfare office for details on who is eligible for specific programs.

### Major Health Care Benefits for People with Mental Illness

| Benefit | Who Is Eligible? | Based on Disability? | Based on Financial Need? | What Is Usually Covered? | Where to Apply |
|---|---|---|---|---|---|
| Medicare | Disabled persons who have been entitled to SSDI for more than two years | Yes | No | Inpatient and outpatient bills, subject to deductibles, copayments and "ceilings" for certain services | Social Security Administration office |
| Medicaid, also known as medical assistance | Low-income persons who meet state or county criteria | Yes | Yes | Inpatient and outpatient bill, subject to small copayments and restrictions on reimbursements | Office of public assistance or welfare |

Figure 5.2

# Getting What You Need
# from the Mental Health System

Patients and their relatives often report that although they are satisfied by many services provided by the mental health system, they also feel frustrated by the system. They describe confusion about who to contact in the bureaucracy, misunderstandings about what their relative is eligible for, and difficulty evaluating whether their relative benefits from the treatment provided. Some common questions of family members include:

- Is day treatment really helping?

- What can be done about medication side effects?

- What kind of educational programs are available to help me and my relative learn about schizophrenia?

- How can we find an appropriate community residence?

- How can my relative get a job?

- Why is there such a long wait for an individual therapist?

- Are there any other medications available at the clinic, such as Clozaril or Risperdal?

- Why doesn't my relative qualify for vocational rehabilitation?

One of the things that will help you most in getting what you need from the mental health system is developing a good relationship and open communication with key members of your relative's treatment team. If this type of relationship can be established before major concerns arise, it will be easier to talk about problems when they come up. Staff members usually appreciate hearing from caring family members. If possible, identify a staff member who might be helpful as an advocate or spokesperson for your concerns. It is reassuring to feel that someone understands your point of view and shares your desire to help your relative.

When problems do come up, the following guidelines may help you address your concerns.

*Talk over the problems with the treatment provider who is most directly involved.* For example: If you need a referral, speak to the case manager. If you have questions about the rules of a community residence, consult with the residence director. If you feel that more therapy sessions would be helpful, talk to the therapist. If you are concerned with symptoms worsening or with medication side effects, speak to the psychiatrist. Keep in mind that it is generally not helpful to complain about clinical issues to the secretary or other office staff, because they are not involved with your relative's treatment.

*Communicate your concerns calmly and clearly.* It is helpful to be as well-informed and organized as possible in your interactions with mental health professionals. You may find it useful to make notes of your concerns before raising them with a mental health professional. When speaking, be assertive, but try to listen to the other person's point of view. Stay focused on the problem and be persistent in seeking a solution.

*Take additional action if you are not satisfied after speaking with a staff person.* Sometimes it is necessary to speak with more than one person to get your relative's needs met. If you have trouble getting somewhere, trying talking over your concerns with another staff member. This person may be able to intercede on your behalf and help address your needs. In some cases it may be necessary to talk with the supervisor of the person with whom you first spoke. Let the supervisor know your specific concerns.

*Follow through promptly on suggestions made by staff members that require some action on your part.* Professionals may make some suggestions that you choose not to follow through on. However, if the suggestion seems reasonable, act on it as quickly as possible so that you will know the results. If it does not work, the professional may be able to make another suggestion. It also helps to check back with others to see if they have followed up on what they agreed to do. Being persistent often leads to a solution, even if the problem initially seems overwhelming.

*Let people know that you appreciate their efforts.* This makes them more likely to want to continue helping and creates a positive atmosphere.

*If your attempts to find a solution fail, contact the "designated problem solver" at the agency.* Most CMHCs have a consumer relations staff member who is assigned to help patients and relatives solve problems with receiving services. You can also call the director of the agency. In addition, organizations such as the Alliance for the Mentally Ill will help advocate for families.

*Keep trying, even in the face of obstacles.* You may not be able to get every need fully met. However, persisting in an assertive, nonhostile manner usually results in important improvements.

# PART III

# Creating a Supportive Environment

# 6

# Communicating Effectively

Many families with a mentally ill relative experience difficulties in communication. Frequent arguments can erupt, there may be long periods of time when family members do not talk among themselves, misunderstandings lead to hurt feelings. Of course, problems in communication also happen in families where no one has a psychiatric disorder. Indeed, communication problems seem to be almost universal.

However, communication in the family is disrupted even more easily when one member has schizophrenia, because of the interference caused by symptoms. In addition to the difficulties your relative may have communicating with you, if you are under high levels of stress due to having to cope with your relative's illness, such stress can further worsen communication. In this chapter we explain how symptoms and stress can interfere with communication and then give specific suggestions for how you can interact more effectively with your relative.

Before reading this chapter, it is a good idea to evaluate how well you are currently doing when it comes to communicating with your ill family member. Everyone has strengths and weaknesses in this area, and it can be helpful to determine where you could use the most improvement. The Communication Quiz will help you assess your own communication skills.

## Why Communication Is Often a Problem

### Symptoms of the Illness

Many of the communication problems you experience with your relative may be directly linked to his or her symptoms of schizophrenia.

## Communication Quiz

*Instructions:* Answer each statement, regarding how you communicate with your ill relative. For each statement, mark whether it is "rarely" true, "sometimes" true, or "often" true. Focus on your current communication style, rather than long ago. When you have completed the quiz, you can consult the scoring key at the end of the chapter.

| | *Rarely True* | *Sometimes True* | *Often True* |
|---|---|---|---|
| 1. I get to the point quickly. | _____ | _____ | _____ |
| 2. I postpone addressing conflicts. | _____ | _____ | _____ |
| 3. I am clear and refer to specifics. | _____ | _____ | _____ |
| 4. I raise my voice to make a point. | _____ | _____ | _____ |
| 5. I ask questions to see if I understand. | _____ | _____ | _____ |
| 6. I see no need to praise an adult. | _____ | _____ | _____ |
| 7. If someone knows me well they should know what I think and feel. | _____ | _____ | _____ |
| 8. I usually know the solution to problems without needing to discuss them. | _____ | _____ | _____ |
| 9. When something goes wrong I try to figure out who is to blame. | _____ | _____ | _____ |
| 10. I try to focus on behaviors when communicating. | _____ | _____ | _____ |
| 11. I often know what my relative is feeling without needing to ask. | _____ | _____ | _____ |
| 12. I use a calm voice. | _____ | _____ | _____ |

|  | Rarely True | Sometimes True | Often True |
|---|---|---|---|
| 13. I tell my relative what he or she should do. | _____ | _____ | _____ |
| 14. When I'm upset I try not to let my feelings show. | _____ | _____ | _____ |
| 15. When I say something, I expect the other person to understand it. | _____ | _____ | _____ |
| 16. I express my feelings and opinions using the word *I* whenever possible. | _____ | _____ | _____ |

Cognitive deficits are a common problem for patients with schizophrenia. These deficits are reflected in areas such as impaired concentration, difficulties reaching conclusions (deductive reasoning), and memory problems. For example, Ed found it very difficult to stay focused on the topic of a conversation. He sometimes became distracted by irrelevant stimuli; other times he found it difficult to follow the other person's line of reasoning. Ed's father sometimes found it frustrating to try to communicate with him, because he didn't seem to pay attention and had trouble "getting the point." It seemed to Ed's father that if only Ed tried a little harder he would be able to concentrate better and hear what others had to say.

Delusions and hallucinations can also interfere with communication. Linda heard voices much of the time and found it hard to ignore her hallucinations when she was talking with someone. Sometimes Linda's voices actually told her not to listen to the real person. Alice also felt very distracted when she heard auditory hallucinations while she was trying to converse with someone. She described the experience as being "like too many tennis balls coming over the net at once—I don't know which one to hit." Randy had delusions that FBI agents were recording his conversations, which made him reluctant to express his true feelings to anyone for fear that it would be used as evidence against him.

Negative symptoms of schizophrenia pose a special set of problems when it comes to communicating. Negative symptoms include blunted affect (the person's face does not indicate the emotion he or she is feeling), poverty of speech (not having much to say), anhedonia (not being able to experience pleasure), and apathy (not caring about what happens). These negative symptoms can make it difficult for you to get an accurate "reading" of how your relative is feeling. Not knowing how he or she

---

### Symptoms of Schizophrenia That Interfere with Communication

- Delusions

- Hallucinations

- Cognitive deficits

- Blunted affect

- Poverty of speech

- Anhedonia

- Apathy

---

feels can make conversations more difficult. For example, Ed's mother felt frustrated trying to communicate with him. She said, "I don't know where Ed stands on so many things. Sometimes he says one thing, but then his facial expression suggests something different. At other times he hardly wants to talk at all. I want to help him, but I don't know what he wants."

You may have also found it difficult to communicate with your relative because he or she is demoralized and seems to have given up. It may seem like nothing you say to your relative makes a difference. For example, Kate's mother described feeling discouraged because her daughter would not engage in conversations aimed at improving specific problem areas. Whenever Kate's mother tried to talk with her, Kate would put her off by saying, "It's hopeless anyway—what's the point of talking about it?" Kate's unwillingness to talk about making changes affected her mother, who began to feel that the situation actually *was* hopeless.

## Stress of Coping with a Psychiatric Illness in the Family

Difficulties interacting with a relative who has schizophrenia are not only a byproduct of the symptoms of the illness, they can also arise from the stress you may be under from coping with your relative. In the past, family members often blamed themselves for problems in communicating and even felt guilty. One mother said, "Every time we had an argument I would cry and blame myself—why couldn't we understand each other?" When people are living under a strain, regardless of the source of the stress (financial, medical, legal, emotional), communication can break down. Coping with schizophrenia in the family can be a major strain on everyone, especially when the majority of care falls on the family.

The stress you may have experienced can be worsened if your relative is unable to express appreciation to you for efforts you have made to help. For example, one mother said, "Linda is a lovely person, but sometimes it's so hard to talk to her and I don't know if she even notices what I do for her. I don't expect a lot of thanks, but a little would be nice every once in a while."

You may have also found it frustrating to try to distinguish which problem behaviors in your relative are caused by his or her illness, and which are not. For example, Jerry's brother said, "When he doesn't want to talk to me, I don't know if it's because of his symptoms or because he's mad at me." Family members often wonder whether it is their relative's personality or symptoms that are responsible for certain behaviors. As a consequence of this ambiguity, the communication skills of family members may suffer because they are unsure how responsible their relative is for his or her behavior.

## How Improving Communication Can Help

Improving your skills at communicating with your relative may reduce his or her risk of relapse and improve symptoms. The stress-vulnerability model of schizophrenia (Chapter 1) indicates that stress puts a strain on the patient's biological vulnerability and can lead to increases in symptoms and relapses. Better communication can lower the amount of conflict and stress in the family, improving your relative's long-term outcome. Good communication can also reduce the burden you bear in caring for your ill relative.

In addition, improved communication between family members can help the overall quality of relationships in the family. Patients benefit from hearing praise from relatives for following treatment plans and making steps toward greater independence. Similarly, relatives appreciate knowing that they are not taken for granted. Effective communication can prevent some conflicts from developing and can resolve others with a minimum of stress. As stress is related to many health problems, such as high blood pressure and heart disease, it is helpful to all family members to reduce stress through improved communication skills.

## Skills for Communicating Effectively with Your Ill Relative

The communication skills we discuss in this chapter may be helpful for your interactions with many different people. However, these skills are especially important to use when communicating with your ill relative, so that you can learn to compensate for problems related to the symptoms of schizophrenia.

*Get to the point.* People with schizophrenia often have difficulty "tracking" (focusing on) information and drawing conclusions from conversations with others. Therefore, when communicating with your relative it is helpful to be brief and stick to one topic at a time. Keep communications simple and direct, and avoid complex language and roundabout introductions to a topic. Getting to the point quickly will result in fewer misunderstandings between you and your relative.

To get to the point, remember to:

- Clearly state your topic or concern

- Use direct, simple language

- Keep it brief

*Express your feelings directly.* One way of being clear about your feelings is to use statements using the word *I*, such as, "I was really pleased when you set the table tonight," or "I am upset that you have not taken medication for two days." Using "I" statements lets your relative know directly how you feel. Taking responsibility for your own thoughts and feelings is more effective than referring to a third party or generalizing, such as, "Uncle John thinks you're doing better" or "Some people should do more chores around the house."

People with schizophrenia often find it difficult to recognize feelings in others. They may miss subtle cues about others' emotions, such as changes in facial expression or tone of voice. Verbally expressing your feelings to your relative, including both positive and negative feelings, will reduce the amount of guessing your relative must do to understand what you are feeling. Using direct, verbal feeling statements will result in less confusion and less tension, even when you are upset about something.

To express your feelings directly, remember to:

- Use "I" statements

- Make a verbal "feeling" statement ("I feel *relieved* when you take your medicine" or "I get *worried* when you come home late")

- Speak in a calm voice

- Don't assume your relative will know how you feel if you don't tell him or her

*Use praise effectively.* People with schizophrenia often feel demoralized and think that they can't do anything well. It helps them to know when they have done something that pleased you or when they have done something "right." By praising your relative for specific behaviors, you encourage him or her to do more of the things that please you. Praise can be particularly helpful when it comes to encouraging your relative to follow through with treatment plans and increase independent behavior.

Your relative may be painfully aware of his or her own limitations. Praise will help your relative become more aware of his or her strengths. People with schizophrenia tend to make progress toward better functioning in small steps. Recognizing and encouraging your relative when he or she has achieved these small accomplishments can help him or her see that true progress is possible and that effort is rewarded.

To use praise effectively, remember to:

- Make eye contact with your relative

- Tell him or her specifically what he or she did that pleased you

- Use an "I" statement to say how it makes you feel

*Check out what the other person thinks or feels.* If your relative has blunted affect (not much vocal or facial expressiveness) or poverty of speech (not talking much), you may feel that you often have to guess at what he or she thinks or feels. Although some of your guesses may be correct, many will be wrong, leading to misunderstandings and frustration. Rather than guessing what your relative is thinking or feeling, listen carefully to what he or she has to say, ask questions when you don't understand or something is unclear, and check out what you have heard to make sure you understood correctly. One way of checking out your understanding is to paraphrase what you heard and to ask your relative if that was what he or she meant.

To check out your understanding, remember to:

- Listen carefully; don't rush your relative

- Ask questions when you don't understand

- Repeat back what you heard and ask if that is what your relative meant

- Ask more questions, if necessary

*Be clear and specific.* As previously noted, your relative may have difficulty focusing and extracting important points during a conversation. You can help your relative by being as specific as possible and focusing on *behaviors*, which are easily observed, rather than *attitudes* or *personality traits*, which are subjective and difficult to define. Being specific can help you communicate to your relative which behaviors you like and which you would like to change. Your relative will understand you better and is more likely to follow through on suggestions and requests if you are specific.

To speak clearly and specifically, remember to:

- Avoid long sentences and "introductions" to topics

- Focus on behaviors, not attitudes or personality traits

- Make direct requests that specify exactly what you would like

- Concentrate on one topic at a time

## Managing Conflict

When any group of people live together or spend significant time together, conflicts are inevitable. No one agrees all the time! When one family member has schizophrenia, conflict in the household is even more likely because of the symptoms of the illness.

Your relative's cognitive problems may make it difficult for him or her to anticipate problem situations or to recognize the negative repercussions of some of his or her behavior. For example, Ed failed to think ahead about the consequences of leaving leftover food in his room (ants). Your relative may also have difficulty coming up with possible solutions to problems or may find it hard to express his or her point of view. These types of limitations, which are common in patients with schizophrenia, can lead to misunderstandings and conflicts.

This problem is compounded by the fact that your relative is also especially vulnerable to the negative effects of unresolved conflict because of his or her illness. Frequent or intense conflict can increase the stress on your relative, resulting in a worsening of symptoms. Therefore, rapidly resolving conflicts through good communication can have beneficial effects for both you and your relative.

## Strategies for Managing Conflict

In general, it is best to address a conflict as soon as it is recognized. Do not be reluctant to take the initiative and address the conflict in a conversation with your relative. Conflicts involving your relative's behavior are usually easier to resolve before the situation has resulted in negative consequences or the behavior has become entrenched. For example, when Lisa stopped taking her medications, her mother raised the problem with her as soon as possible, before the lack of medication led to a worsening of symptoms and a reduction in Lisa's ability to respond to logical reasons for resuming medication.

When discussing a disagreement or concern, try to stay calm and in control of your temper, express yourself clearly, and attend to your relative's perspective. Lisa's mother spoke to her about her medication in a calm manner, which made Lisa receptive to listening and talking about the issue. It is best to approach conflicts with your mind as open as possible. Rather than trying to convince your relative that he or she is wrong, express your views and then listen to what your relative has to say. Then think of solutions that take into account both your concerns and your relative's. In Lisa's example, her mother approached Lisa with her concerns, but was willing to listen when Lisa told her about the uncomfortable side effects of the medication. They came up with the solution of setting up a special doctor's appointment for Lisa to explain her concerns about the medication side effects. By attending to Lisa's concerns about side effects, a potentially volatile conflict was avoided, and her medication noncompliance was successfully addressed.

Resolving conflicts requires using the same communication skills described earlier in this chapter. In addition, the following strategies may be helpful in dealing with conflict situations with your relative:

*Avoid blaming.* People often feel criticized or guilty when they are blamed for something. Rather than blaming your relative, describe the problem situation or behavior, and explain how it makes you feel. If you focus on finding solutions instead of placing blame, you will have a more constructive dialogue with your relative.

*Speak in a calm voice.* People tend to be more receptive to hearing a calm tone of voice than one that is harsh, loud, or angry. A gentle manner of speaking is easier both to hear and to comprehend. Some patients with schizophrenia are particularly sensitive to harsh, critical tones. A negative tone of voice or shouting can put your relative on the defensive, making it difficult for him or her to hear what you say and less likely to come up with a solution to the situation.

*Use short, clear statements to highlight the main points.* When discussing a point of conflict, it is vital that you help your relative focus on the major topic. Short, clear, and specific statements are easier to understand and respond to than lengthy statements. Avoid talking about things that do not relate to the problem at hand, and pause frequently to review what has already been said.

*Elicit your relative's point of view.* One-sided discussions of conflicts do not lead to lasting resolutions. Since your relative may have trouble expressing him- or herself, you may need to actively ask for his or her perspective. When seeking your relative's opinion about something, be sure to allow enough time for him or her to answer. If you solicit your relative's point of view, the chances are good that he or she will have some ideas about how to resolve the problem. On the other hand, if you do not seek out your relative's opinion about a conflict, he or she may feel frustrated and less invested in resolving the problem.

*Focus on specific behaviors.* Personality, attitudes, and feelings can be very difficult to change. In contrast, people often find it easier to change their behavior. Patients with schizophrenia are easily discouraged by criticism. For example, comments about being lazy or slow can be upsetting and may distract your relative from attending to the problem at hand.

## An Example of Conflict

The following example illustrates what happens when good communication skills are *not* used in a conflict.

Joe has schizophrenia and lives at home with his mother and two sisters. Each person in the household is expected to do some housework. Joe was assigned the task of setting the table for dinner. At first he did this on a regular basis. As the weeks went on, however, he stayed in his room more and two or three times a week neglected to set the table. At first his mother did not want confront Joe about this, hoping that the lapse would be temporary. The problem persisted, however, until Joe ceased setting the table altogether. One evening, Joe's mother and one of his sisters were sitting around talking about how resentful they felt that he wasn't helping out anymore. When Joe came down for dinner, his sister yelled at him, "You're making Mom upset. You never do anything around this house. You're lazy!" When Joe did not answer, his mother said in an angry tone, "She's right, you should do a lot more around here. We're not your slaves." Joe looked confused and retreated to his room saying, "I'm not hungry." Tension continued to mount in the family as the conflict remained unresolved.

Perhaps this particular conflict could have been resolved if certain communication skills had been used. First, it would have been helpful for Joe to hear right away that he had forgotten to set the table. At that point a gentle reminder could have been given. By the time Joe heard about his mother's and sister's concerns, their feelings had already become very strong and the conflict had escalated. Even at that point, however, it would have been easier for Joe to listen to his mother and sister if they had not yelled at him. Their communication would have been more effective if they had spoken to him calmly, been specific about which behaviors they wanted changed, and made clear feeling statements about how they felt. Although it was probably clear to Joe that his mother and sister were angry with him, they did not explain the exact reason for their anger. Referring specifically to Joe's failure to set the table could have helped him understand the basis of their concern.

Sometimes situations are mishandled, such as this one. But, even when conflicts develop into misunderstandings and arguments, all is not lost. You can always "start over" and address the disagreement again. Try to be honest about having made some mistakes in past discussions, and use your communication skills to deal with the conflict. For example, Joe's mother could apologize for yelling at him and calmly reintroduce the problem of Joe not setting the table anymore.

## Common Pitfalls to Effective Communication

Thus far we have focused primarily on the communication skills that we recommend you use. There are also some common problems we advise you to avoid. These "pitfalls to effective communication" are summarized in Figure 6.1. It is not always easy to avoid these common problems in communication, but as you become aware of them you will be rewarded by fewer arguments and a calmer atmosphere in your home.

Nonetheless, conflicts are inevitable in any household, and certain conflicts may be especially difficult to resolve. Communication skills can be helpful in resolving some of these conflicts. Chapter 7, "Solving Problems," offers additional strategies.

## Common Pitfalls to Effective Communication

| Communication Problem | Example of Problem Statement | Alternative Statement |
|---|---|---|
| Coercive statements ("shoulds" and "musts") | "You should know when to put out the trash." | "I would appreciate it if you would take out the trash every night after dinner." |
| Mixing positive and negative statements | "You look nice today, but why did you wear those silly shoes?" | "I really like the dress you're wearing today." |
| Speaking for others ("we" statements) | "We are concerned that you have been sleeping a lot lately." | "I am concerned that you have been sleeping a lot lately." |
| Mind-reading | "You're angry at me for forgetting our movie date." | "You look angry. Are you feeling that way?" |
| Name-calling and put-downs | "You're so inconsiderate." | "I get upset when I see your clothes laying all around the living room. I would appreciate it if you would pick them up." |
| Dwelling on the past | "You didn't visit me in the hospital this time, just like the first time I was in the hospital two years ago." | "I was disappointed that you didn't visit me in the hospital this last time." |
| Giving inconsistent verbal and nonverbal signals | "It's OK with me if you want to do that," (while sighing and rolling eyes). | "I don't feel good about you doing that." |

Figure 6.1

## Key to Communication Quiz

Questions 1, 3, 5, 10, 12, and 16 on the quiz represent strengths in communication. That is, an answer of "sometimes" or "often" indicates that you are communicating in a way that is likely to reduce stress and conflict. Questions 2, 4, 6, 7, 8, 9, 11, 13, 14, and 15 represent areas where communication could be improved. For these questions, note which ones receive an answer of "sometimes" or "often" and concentrate on corresponding sections of this chapter to see how to improve your communication in these areas.

# 7

# Solving Problems

Problems are inevitable in life. Each day, family members may confront any number of life challenges, ranging from relatively minor (such as a broken washing machine or a traffic jam) to profoundly life-changing (a career change, major illness, or a birth or death in the family). Furthermore, as discussed in the preceding chapter, whenever people live together or spend time together, conflicts and disagreements come up that can lead to problems. Having different opinions, goals, and expectations is just a natural part of being human. Making decisions is also a part of life, including everyday decisions (like what to wear) and more consequential ones (such as whether one's grandmother can continue to live at home independently).

Some people find it stressful to make even simple decisions. They may be racked with doubts, wondering, "Did we really know all the facts?" "Did we make the right choice?" "Were we being too emotional?" The decision-making process is difficult enough when the consequences of our decisions involve only ourselves, but it becomes even more complicated when our decisions affect others. This is often the case when a family member has a disability.

Having a relative with schizophrenia can add to the burden of problem solving and decision making in several ways. First, the symptoms of the illness may create specific problems for other family members, who must then either try to change the behavior or learn to cope with it. Second, the cognitive deficits associated with schizophrenia make it difficult for some patients to actively participate in a discussion about a problem. Third, relatives of the patient must assume extra responsibilities for managing the illness, a task which is fraught with many problems, such as medication noncompliance.

Figure 7.1 lists some of the most common problems in families with a member with schizophrenia. These problems usually originate with the patient, but have a "ripple effect" on other members of the family. How many of the problems on this list have you encountered?

Given all the possible problems you might encounter in coping with your relative's illness, it would be impossible to tell you how to solve each one specifically. The goal of this chapter is to provide you with some

---

### Common Problems Related to Schizophrenia

- Poor self-esteem
- Lack of friends
- Unemployment
- Persistent auditory hallucinations
- Depression
- Suicidal thoughts
- Substance abuse
- Persistent delusions
- Irregular sleeping patterns
- Medication side effects
- Getting up late
- Medication noncompliance
- Arguments related to symptoms
- Violent behavior
- Insufficient income
- Difficulty managing money
- Not knowing how to plan for the future
- Arguments over household tasks
- Division of household chores
- Finding a supportive living situation
- Planning enjoyable family outings
- Finding enjoyable leisure activities
- Insufficient community services
- Applying for public assistance
- Encountering prejudice about the illness

---

Figure 7.1

strategies for solving problems effectively. The strategies we focus on here have been found to be helpful by other families with a mentally ill relative. By developing your problem solving *skills,* you will be more able to solve both current problems and problems that will arise in the future.

## Styles of Problem Solving

Each person has his or her own way of solving problems. Some people are satisfied with their approach to solving problems and feel that they consistently arrive at the best solutions. Others are less content and would like to improve their ability to solve difficult problems. Although each person is unique, the problem solving style of most people falls into one of five general categories. Each style can be characterized by the person's attitude toward problems and by the consequences of the decisions that are made. As you read about each of these styles, consider which one is closest to yours.

*Avoidance Style.* The predominant attitude of this style can be summed up as, "If I don't see the problem, it's not there." Sometimes problems do improve on their own, but usually the longer one waits the worse the situation gets. Another problem with the Avoidance Style is that certain solutions that might have been effective in the early stages of a problem can no longer be used.

*Discouraged Style.* The discouraged attitude is reflected by thinking such as, "I can't do anything about this problem anyway, so why try? It won't make any difference." This attitude is understandable, especially when someone has encountered very tough problems or has been disappointed on many occasions by how things turned out. However, giving up and not trying to solve problems is an ineffective style that invariably leads to worse problems and more discouragement. This unwillingness to try to improve the status quo is often accompanied by feelings of depression, hopelessness, and inadequacy.

*Takeover Style.* The attitude of this style is "I'm in charge around here" and "People should do what I tell them." Inherent in this style is the belief that the person, and no one else, knows the answers to all problems. Although other people involved in a problem may initially go along with a plan generated by this style of problem solver, they tend to feel resentful and end up doing something different. People with this style often feel a great deal of stress because they believe they are personally responsible for solving every problem and convincing everyone that their solutions are the right ones.

*Talking Style.* "If I talk about the problem long enough it will get solved," is the attitude of this style of problem solver. Notably absent from this style is any inclination to take action toward solving the problem. This attitude has both positive and negative features. On one hand, by talking about it the person gets the opportunity to express his or her feelings, which sometimes results in another person taking action to solve the problem. On the other hand, if no one else takes the initiative, the problem remains unchanged.

*Active Style.* People with this style have the attitude, "If there is a problem, there must be a solution." Usually the person recognizes problems quickly, gets others involved as much as possible, and takes steps toward putting plans into action. This style tends to be the most effective one for solving problems.

The Active Style has also been called the Problem-Solving Coping Style by Thomas J. d'Zurilla, Ph.D., an expert on problem solving, at the State University of New York at Stony Brook. According to Dr. d'Zurilla, people who develop the Problem Solving Coping Style are more able to adapt to stressors in their environment and are less vulnerable to negative feelings such as depression and anxiety. The positive outlook of people with an Active Style is reflected by their attitudes about problems and how to approach them, summarized in Figure 7.2. If you don't currently use the Active Style, you can begin to change by reviewing the attitudes in this list before tackling a problem, in order to foster a positive, coping-oriented frame of mind.

## Guidelines for Effective Problem Solving

There are many effective ways of solving problems. You probably know people who have developed their own strategies over the years and have found them to work quite well. You may be one of those people

---

### Attitudes of People with an Active Style of Solving Problems

- Problems are inevitable. I don't blame myself for having problems.
- A problem is a challenge to be confronted, not a threat to be avoided.
- It is better to try to solve a problem and fail than to never try to solve the problem at all.
- There is a solution to every problem, or at least every problem situation can be improved upon. If I set my mind to it, I can find a solution and carry it out.
- Solving most problems takes time and effort.

Figure 7.2

yourself. Regardless of your personal approach to solving problems, the following guidelines could help improve your ability to attack difficult problems:

*Develop a positive, optimistic mood when dealing with the problem.* Research has shown that when people are in a good mood they are more creative and better able to solve problems than when they are anxious, angry, or depressed. Having an upbeat, positive attitude when thinking about a problem or discussing it with other family members can improve your chances of coming up with good solutions. Choose a time to work on a problem when you feel calm and able to concentrate. Focus on how to improve things for the future, and avoid dwelling on the past, to create a positive outlook.

*Respect everyone's point of view.* Try to talk directly to the people affected by the problem. If they are not available, think about what the situation looks like from their perspective. If you don't take other people's opinions into consideration, they will not feel invested in carrying out solutions and may undermine your attempts to solve the problem.

*Avoid blaming and fault-finding.* People tend to blame each other when there is a disagreement or conflict. Blaming often puts people on the defensive, which can lead to either denial of the problem (or responsibility) or counterattack. Blaming can interfere with effective problem solving by focusing the discussion on who is at fault, rather than how the situation can be improved.

*Identify as many solutions as possible.* The greater the number of possible solutions you can think of, the more likely it is that an effective solution will be among them. Try not to limit yourself to "usual" solutions; be as creative and spontaneous as you can. An unusual solution may turn out to be the one that solves the problem.

*Be willing to compromise.* Being willing to "give and take" when it comes to solving problems can result in solutions that are more acceptable to everyone. When people feel they have something to gain from a solution, they will actively work with others toward achieving it. Even when you are solving problems alone, it helps to be flexible and to explore how different solutions can be combined and to avoid getting stuck in a single viewpoint.

*Formulate a plan of action.* A solution is only effective if it is followed through on. All the talk in the world won't help if you don't try to *do* something about the problem. A plan that breaks down the solution into manageable steps is helpful in putting the solution into action. Many solutions sound good, but you can't know if they work until you try them out. If the plan of action doesn't work, then at least you know you've tried one possible solution and you can move on to others.

## Examples of Problem Solving

We provide below three examples of how families and individuals have used these problem solving guidelines to address specific problems. The first example illustrates how family members, including the patient, worked together to solve a problem. The second example describes how one parent working alone solved a problem involving her daughter, who refused to participate in problem solving. The third example shows how a couple worked together to change problematic smoking behavior in their daughter, who was not motivated to change her behavior.

### Example 1

David was a 22-year-old man diagnosed with schizoaffective disorder. He lived at home with his parents and three younger siblings: Alex, age 20; Deborah, age 17; and Tanya, age 15. David took his medication regularly and attended a day treatment program during the week. On weekends, however, he developed the habit of sleeping until lunchtime and napping throughout much of the afternoon. His parents became concerned with David's excessive sleeping and asked everyone in the family, including David, to get together to discuss the problem. The parents picked Monday evening after dinner for the meeting. They arranged to have pizza for dinner that night so there would be a relaxed atmosphere and time would be freed up from cooking and washing dishes.

The father started the meeting on a positive note by saying that he was pleased by how things were going in the family, pointing out that everyone was getting along well and helping out in the household. He then said that he was concerned that David was spending so much of the weekend sleeping and that he would like to explore how this situation could be changed. He asked everyone to give their point of view about the problem. David spoke up right away, saying that he would like to be more active over the weekend, but found this difficult to do. Deborah said that she often felt tired over the weekend, and asked David whether the same was true for him. David said that he didn't really feel tired when he slept late, but he did feel kind of bored. After further discussion, the family concluded that David was sleeping so much over weekends because he had few interesting activities to do. This prompted family members to try to find enjoyable activities to do over the weekend that David would be willing to get up for.

Several family outings were suggested, including:

- The zoo
- A local library
- The shopping mall
- A sporting event

- A movie

- Disneyland

Tanya's suggestion of going to Disneyland was accepted with humor by the other family members. Although there was some disagreement about the best place to go, they compromised by choosing the zoo for their first outing and the mall for the next one. They made a plan to carry out their solution by going to the zoo the following Saturday morning at 10:00 to avoid the crowds. Father agreed to drive, and Alex agreed to pack a lunch for everyone. David said that he would call the zoo to ask about admission costs and to inquire about special family rates. David also asked his mother to wake him at 9:00 so that he would have time to get ready. The family decided to stay for a maximum of three hours. A follow-up meeting was planned for the following Monday.

At the follow-up meeting, the family members discussed what they had liked about the outing and what they had not liked. First they noted that David had woken up on time and had not napped all day Saturday. This was a big improvement. Everyone seemed to enjoy the zoo, but David found that three hours was too long. They planned the next outing for the mall to be two hours long.

### Example 2

Kathy was a 30-year-old woman with schizophrenia who lived in a community residence. She had phone contact several times a week with her mother, who was a single parent with no other children. Her mother also tried to visit her at least once a week. Kathy looked forward to these visits. Although Kathy's mother cared deeply about her, she often felt uncomfortable spending time with her because of her poor grooming and hygiene. She felt especially embarrassed by Kathy's appearance when they went out into the neighborhood together. Previous attempts to get Kathy to take better care of her appearance had failed and she now refused to discuss the situation with her mother, insisting "I look fine."

Kathy's mother decided she would have to solve the problem by herself, without Kathy's help, although she would try to take Kathy's point of view into consideration. After consulting with the staff at the community residence, Kathy's mother made a list of strategies for dealing with the problem. Her list included:

- Try not to care about Kathy's appearance

- Suspend visits until staff members report that Kathy is well groomed

- Point out Kathy's shortcomings in grooming at every visit

- Reward Kathy for good grooming by spending more time with her when she is clean and neat

Her mother decided that rewarding Kathy for good grooming was the best solution. She formulated a specific plan, which she shared with Kathy and the staff members of the residence. The plan can be summarized as follows: If Kathy was appropriately groomed when her mother arrived, she would praise her for this and then take her out to the local coffee shop. If Kathy was not appropriately groomed, she would comment on this, spend about 15 minutes visiting with her at the community residence, and leave. Kathy's mother explained to her that "appropriate grooming" means a clean body, unsoiled clothes, and combed hair. Her mother decided to evaluate this solution after six weeks.

At first, Kathy did not take her mother's plan seriously and expected that she would be taken out regardless of her appearance. Her mother was clear and firm about following through, however, and Kathy began to spend more time on her hygiene before her mother arrived. At the end of six weeks Kathy had been neat and clean for three of her mother's visits. Her mother was very pleased and praised Kathy for the improvement. She planned to keep her plan in place for the next six months.

### Example 3

Melinda was a 40-year-old patient who lived at home with her two parents. In spite of taking her medication regularly, she was troubled by persistent hallucinations and delusions. The parents were comfortable with Melinda living at home, although they were bothered by her incessant smoking. She smoked two packs of cigarettes per day, which caused an odor in the house and aggravated her mother's asthma. Melinda had agreed on numerous occasions to smoke only on the enclosed porch or in her own room, but she did not follow through on her promise. Her parents tried to praise Melinda when she smoked in appropriate places, but this happened so rarely it seemed to have little effect on her behavior. In fact, Melinda continued her smoking habits and became agitated whenever the topic of smoking was raised. The parents decided to discuss between the two of them the problem of Melinda disobeying the household rules about smoking. Their potential solutions included:

- Do not allow smoking anywhere in the house
- Take away some of Melinda's spending money
- Hold Melinda's cigarettes and give them out one at a time
- Use a spray bottle to put out any cigarettes smoked in rooms other than her bedroom or the enclosed porch
- Praise Melinda for smoking in the designated rooms

After considering the different solutions, Melinda's parents decided to combine two solutions: praising Melinda when she smoked in the designated rooms *and* fining her 25 cents each time she smoked in an off-limits room. This money would be put away in a special fund that would be reserved for paying for housecleaning. They chose this purpose for the fund, because the cigarette smoke caused grime and odor that required extra cleaning.

Melinda's parents carried out their decision by first writing down the rules about smoking and posting them in several rooms of the house. They then sat down with Melinda and explained the consequences of not following these rules. They made a bank out of a coffee can and labeled it "Housekeeping" to show that it would contain the money forfeited for disobeying the smoking rules. They explained this all to Melinda in a very calm, matter-of-fact way. Although Melinda objected and initially resented her parents' attempts to control her smoking, she listened as they explained their plan.

At first they found it difficult to follow through with their plan. But as they became more consistent in taking away quarters for smoking infractions, they found that Melinda was following the rules more. They decided to continue this plan indefinitely.

# A Step-by-Step Method of Solving Problems

Some people find a structured approach to solving problems is more effective than having a less formal discussion. We describe here a six-step method of solving problems. This method was adapted for families by Ian R. H. Falloon, M.D. and his colleagues, and has been found to be helpful in families with a mentally ill relative. We refer to this method as Step-by-Step Problem Solving. Remember that regardless of which method of problem solving you use, it is best to start with a positive frame of mind (see Figure 7.2).

## *Steps for Solving Problems*

The step-by-step method can be used by individuals or groups of people. We recommend you keep written records of your problem solving efforts. Maintaining written records helps you keep on track when working on a problem. These records can also be referred to later if the initial plan does not solve the problem. We have provided a Problem Solving Worksheet, which you may photocopy. It lists the six steps of problem solving and provides spaces for recording important points. If you are solving problems as part of a family, it is helpful to have a chairperson who guides everyone systematically through the steps. The chairperson can also keep the written record, or you may want to have a different member act as secretary and complete the worksheet. The primary role of the chairperson is to keep family members focused on the task, to remind them of the steps of problem solving, to get all family members involved in the discussion, and to prevent the discussion from deteriorating into arguments. The six steps of the Step-by-Step Problem Solving Method are described below.

*Step 1: Define the problem.* This step is perhaps the most important of all. Defining a problem as specifically as possible sets the stage for the most effective problem solving. If you are meeting together as a family, it is crucial to talk about how the situation is a problem for each person. When each person has expressed his or her point of view, the chairperson helps the group arrive at a common definition of the problem. It is essential that each person agree with the definition to ensure that everyone will be invested in solving the problem. This may require family members to compromise with one another when defining the problem. Reframing the problem as a goal to be accomplished or a situation that needs improvement sometimes helps family members agree on a definition. If you are solving the problem on your own, you will still need to begin by defining the problem, although you may find it helpful to consider how others (mainly your ill relative) perceive the problem.

It can be helpful to practice defining problems. We have provided the Defining-Problems Exercise to give you some practice.

*Step 2: Generate possible solutions.* The goal of this step is to brainstorm as many solutions to the problem as possible. The more alternative solutions generated the better. If you are working as a family, it is important for each family member to express at least one idea of how the problem might be solved. If you are solving the problem alone, think of as many solutions as you can. Don't evaluate or criticize the solutions at this point—be as creative as possible. Even outlandish solutions are welcome. These outrageous solutions can help loosen people up and may even lead to a creative idea that actually solves the problem. To get some practice, do the Generating-Solutions Exercise provided here.

*Step 3: Evaluate the advantages and disadvantages of each solution.* After you have come up with five or six possible solutions for a problem, it is time to discuss the advantages and disadvantages of each. This can be done briefly by highlighting the main strengths and weaknesses of each solution.

*Step 4: Choose the best solution.* When choosing a solution, consider its practicality, the probable impact on the defined problem, and the resources needed to implement it. Sometimes after evaluating the solutions, one solution clearly stands out as the best. Other times, two or more solutions have merit. Solutions can be modified or combined to arrive at a "best" one.

When solving problems as a family, it is necessary to agree on a solution. Sometimes a compromise between two or three solutions is the

## Defining-Problems Exercise

*Instructions:* As you read the following description, imagine that you are involved in a problem solving discussion. How many different problems can you define? Write down the different problems you identify in the space provided

Ellen is a 27-year-old woman with schizophrenia. She lives with her sister Lana and Lana's sons, ages 3 and 7. Ellen does not do any chores, although she contributes money to running the household. Mornings have become extremely hectic at home, and everyone is beginning to feel the strain. The children get up at 6:30 and need help getting ready for daycare and school. Lana must also prepare to go to her part-time job. When Lana gets up she usually finds the kitchen a mess, with dirty dishes and food left out from the night before. She must work in the kitchen to prepare breakfast and the children's lunches. The children have a lot of energy in the morning and require her attention. Sometimes Lana is late for her job and has her pay docked, which makes her feel tense. Ellen does not wake until after Lana and the children are gone. The house is empty and cluttered from Lana's last-minute preparations to leave. Ellen feels depressed by being alone and often goes back to bed after a cup of coffee. She is eligible for a job training program, but has not been able to attend consistently.

*List of Problems*

1.
2.
3.
4.
5.
6.
7.
8.
9.
10.

A list of the problems we identified appears at the end of this chapter.

## Generating-Solutions Exercise

*Instructions:* Read the following description and think about possible solutions to the Smith family's problem. Be as creative as possible. Write down your ideas in the space provided below.

The Smith family consists of two parents and three children over the age of 20. Two of the children, Anne and Lois, live with their parents. Their brother Joe has schizophrenia and lives in an apartment with a roommate. He has a monthly income of $270. The last week of each month he usually runs out of funds and asks his parents and sisters for money. The family members do not have much money to spare. The family (including Joe) defined the problem as "How can Joe avoid asking family members for money each month?"

Possible Solutions

1.

2.

3.

4.

5.

6.

7.

8.

9.

10.

A list of our ideas for possible solutions can be found at the end of this chapter.

best solution. If it is extremely hard to agree on a solution, it can be useful to select one option to try first, with the understanding that another idea will be tried if the first is not successful.

*Step 5: Plan how to carry out the best solution.* Sometimes people think that problem solving is over once a solution has been selected. However, without an explicit plan, many solutions are never implemented. The best plans break down a solution into several specific steps and assign someone to carry out each step. If you are solving problems as a family, individual members can divide up the tasks based on ability and time available. It is also helpful to specify when each task will be completed and set a date to follow up on the plan.

Although the Problem Solving Worksheet contains a space for planning, a larger planning sheet can be helpful. Consequently, we have provided the Action Planning Worksheet. Many people find it helpful to post the completed sheet on the refrigerator or somewhere else in the house where everyone involved is likely to see it.

*Step 6: Evaluate whether the solution was implemented and if the problem was solved.* Set a date to evaluate your progress. If you are meeting as a family, discuss the steps that were accomplished and praise all efforts that were made. If you are on your own, make sure to give yourself credit for what you have accomplished. The evaluation process involves determining which steps of the plan were carried out, how effective each step was, and whether the overall problem has been solved. Sometimes plans are only partially carried out. When this happens, further plans must be made to complete the steps. Other times the steps were carried out, but the problem remains. When this happens alternate solutions must be considered. The Problem Solving Worksheet completed during the first attempt can help remind you of other solutions that were considered.

The more you practice the step-by-step approach to problem solving, the more efficient you will become and the less time the process will take. Often, a problem can be discussed, solutions generated and selected, and a plan of action agreed upon in just 10 to 15 minutes. This method can be used for new problems or for reviewing old problems. Many families report that using this approach helps them make decisions about many types of problems, ranging from crisis situations to long-term planning.

## Solving Problems With or Without Other Family Members

In general, problem solving is most effective when it includes everyone affected by the problem, including the patient. Some patients' symptoms are well controlled and they are excellent problem solvers. However, not all patients are able to actively participate in solving problems with

## Problem Solving Worksheet*

### Step 1: What is the problem or what do you want to achieve?

Talk about the problem or goal, listen carefully, ask questions, get everybody's opinion. Then write down *exactly* what the problem or goal is.

### Step 2: List all possible solutions.

Write down *all* ideas, even bad ones. Get everybody to come up with at least one possible solution. List the solutions *without discussion* at this stage.

1.
2.
3.
4.
5.
6.

### Step 3: Discuss each possible solution.

*Quickly* go down the list of possible solutions and discuss the *main* advantages and disadvantages of each one.

### Step 4: Choose the "best" solution.

Choose the solution that can be carried out most easily to solve the problem.

### Step 5: Plan how to carry out the best solution.

List the resources needed and major obstacles to overcome. Assign tasks and set time table.

Step 1.

Step 2.

Step 3.

Step 4.

### Step 6: Review implementation and praise *all* efforts.

First focus on what you have accomplished. Then review whether the plan was successful and revise it as necessary.

* Adapted from J. Falloon, K. Mueser, S. Gingerich, S. Rappaport, C. McGill, and V. Hole. *Behavioral family therapy: A workbook.* Buckingham, England: Buckingham Mental Health Service, 1988.

## Action-Planning Worksheet

Problem or goal: _____

_____

Date for follow-up: _____

_____

| Task to Be Done | Person Assigned | Date to Be Done | Completed? |
|---|---|---|---|
| 1. | | | |
| 2. | | | |
| 3. | | | |
| 4. | | | |
| 5. | | | |
| 6. | | | |
| 7. | | | |
| 8. | | | |
| 9. | | | |
| 10. | | | |

others. Some patients have persistent auditory hallucinations or delusions, impaired attention, poor concentration, or chronic apathy; they may find participating in problem solving meetings to be very stressful and nonproductive.

If a symptomatic patient can be reoriented easily and guided to focus on the problem, it is worthwhile trying to include him or her. However, it is sometimes more effective for family members (or a single family member) to solve problems alone. It is also possible for patients to participate in some steps of problem solving, such as defining the problem and suggesting solutions, but not others, such as evaluating solutions and developing a plan of action.

## Examples of Step-By-Step Problem Solving

The following examples describe how one individual and one family used Step-by-Step Problem Solving.

### Example 1

Jennifer was a 24-year-old woman with schizophrenia who lived at home with her mother, who was divorced. Her brother, Bob, was supportive, but lived several hundred miles away. When Jennifer was last discharged from the hospital, her social worker suggested that she apply for financial assistance. She refused this suggestion, and responded to her mother's repeated requests to apply for assistance by saying, "I don't want to go to any office. I'm afraid of the people there." Her mother was unsuccessful in trying to engage Jennifer in conversation about this topic. When her mother began experiencing financial difficulty, she decided it was necessary to pursue this problem on her own.

First she called the social worker at the hospital to talk over the situation. The social worker was able to tell her which entitlements Jennifer was eligible for, the addresses of the agencies she needed to apply to, and the necessary documentation. She also told Jennifer's mother that in their state the person applying for assistance could complete the initial application at home, but needed to be present for an interview at the second stage of the process. The social worker said that Jennifer's reaction was not uncommon, that patients were often apprehensive about applying for help.

Jennifer's mother decided that she would go to the office and get the application form. She decided that the major problem was getting Jennifer to go to an interview. She tried to think of possible solutions to this problem, including:

- Offering Jennifer money to go to the interview

- "Tricking" Jennifer into thinking she was going somewhere else

- Arranging for another patient to talk to Jennifer about what the interview was like so that she would be less apprehensive

- Waiting until Bob visited at Thanksgiving so that he could accompany her to the interview

- Telling Jennifer she could not live at home unless she applied for financial help

After evaluating the possible solutions, Jennifer's mother decided to combine two solutions: She would ask a friend of Jennifer's to talk to her about her successful experience with applying for financial assistance, and she would wait a few more weeks until Bob came home so that he could help her with the interview process.

When planning how to implement the solution, Jennifer's mother identified the following steps:

1. Talk to Jennifer about her decision and explain the reasons for it.

2. Complete the written application for Jennifer's financial assistance (within one week).

3. Contact Jennifer's friend and arrange for her to come over and talk to Jennifer (within two weeks).

4. Call Bob and explain the need for his support (within two weeks).

5. Arrange for Jennifer to have the interview when Bob is home for the holidays (within three weeks).

6. Call the social worker for suggestions (as needed).

7. Evaluate how the solution worked during Bob's visit.

### Example 2

Len was a 26-year-old man with schizophrenia who lived at home with his parents and younger sister, Linda. Although Len usually got along with his sister, he had begun getting into frequent arguments with her. Linda was very upset by this and started spending more and more time away from home. Len's parents became aware of the situation and called the family together to discuss it. Although Len was initially reluctant to participate, saying, "People will only pick on me," his parents quietly persisted. They arranged to meet after dinner one evening when everyone was feeling relatively calm and in a good mood.

Len's parents started the discussion by saying that they had noticed more arguments recently and that they would like to hear everyone's point of view. They avoided blaming Len or Linda and they maintained a positive tone in the discussion, focusing on how to improve the situation. In the process of getting each person's point of view, Len revealed that he had been hearing more voices recently. After being gently questioned further, Len said that the voices were warning him that Linda was stealing his possessions and wanted to hurt him. He himself was quite troubled by the increase in voices.

Family members brainstormed several ideas about what Len could do in response to the voices:

- Ignore them

- Play music to drown the voices out

- Avoid Linda

- Consult his doctor about a medication adjustment

Although the rest of the family wanted Len to call the doctor immediately, Len was opposed to this solution because he thought the doctor would automatically increase his medication, which would increase his side effects. After more discussion, everyone agreed to a compromise. Len would try playing music to see if he could distract himself from the voices when they became intrusive. If this did not work, Len could call his doctor.

The family planned to implement the ideas as follows:

1. Len would play music to distract himself from the voices for three days.

2. Len would post a sign in his room reminding himself to listen to music when the voices bothered him.

3. If, after the three days, he was still troubled by the voices, Len would call the doctor on the morning of the fourth day.

4. Len's father would give him a ride to the doctor for the appointment.

5. The family would meet again in one week to evaluate how the plan worked.

As you have seen, there is no magic formula for solving problems. However, with teamwork and determination it is possible to find solutions that will lead to improvement in many situations.

---

## Key to Defining-Problems Exercise

1. Ellen does not help with the household chores.
2. The kitchen is not cleaned up at night.
3. Lana needs help with the children in the morning.
4. Lana is sometimes late for work.
5. Ellen feels depressed in the morning.
6. Ellen often misses her job training program.

---

## Key to Generating-Solutions Exercise

1. Joe could plan a monthly budget, with help from family members.
2. Joe's parents could manage his money for him.
3. Each family member could contribute a small amount to Joe's expenses.
4. Joe could get a part-time job.
5. Joe could ask his roommate for money.
6. Joe could consult with a social worker about his eligibility for more financial assistance.
7. Family members could refuse to give Joe money at the end of the month.

# 8

# Managing Stress

As you recall from Chapter 1, the stress-vulnerability model of schizo-phrenia suggests that the severity and course of symptoms are deter-mined by three different factors: biological vulnerability, stress, and cop-ing skill. Comprehensive treatment of the illness requires that each of these factors be addressed. First, biological vulnerability can be reduced by antipsychotic medication, which corrects the imbalance of brain chem-istry, and by limiting the use of substances such as street drugs and al-cohol. Second, stress from the patient's environment can be reduced in a variety of ways. Third, patients can be taught more effective coping skills so that they are better able to handle everyday types of stress.

As family members, you can influence each of these three factors, such as by encouraging your relative to take his or her medication, re-ducing stress, and helping your relative develop better skills for coping with it. The focus of this chapter is on improving skills for coping effec-tively with stress. As your relative becomes increasingly able to manage stress, he or she will be less vulnerable to symptom relapses and will be able to enjoy life more fully.

Reducing the effects of stress is important not only to your relative, but to everyone else as well. It is difficult to enjoy yourself if you're constantly feeling tense and pressured. Furthermore, when you experi-ence stress, some of this tension may be passed on to your relative. There-fore, when stress on one family member is reduced, or if that person learns how to cope more effectively with tension, it will tend to lower the stress on the rest of the family. Consequently, this chapter will describe strategies both for coping with stress and for lowering stress in *all* family members.

# Identifying Sources of Stress

*Stress* is the term used to describe a feeling of strain, pressure, or tension. People are said to be "under stress" when they are forced to adjust their behavior to cope with a difficult circumstance or event. Stressful events can be thought of as threats or challenges from the environment. The environmental challenge or event is referred to as a stressor. People differ markedly with respect to what they find stressful; what is stressful to one person may be exciting to another. For example, rock climbing, taking a trip, and going to a party are activities that some people find enjoyable and others find stressful. Similarly, some people look forward to challenges as opportunities for change, while others see the challenges as threats to their control and experience them as stressful.

To cope effectively with stress, you need to be able to identify the sources of stress in your life. Stressors can be divided into two broad categories: *life events* and *daily hassles.*

## Life Events

Although each person is unique in how he or she perceives stress, there are certain events most people find stressful—life events. *Life events* refers to major life occurrences, such as moving, having a baby, starting a new job, being ill, experiencing a death in the family, and getting a divorce. Even when these events are the source of happiness (for example, getting married), they can be stressful. Some stressors are more severe than others; for example, divorce is generally more stressful than a traffic ticket. Regardless of the severity of stressors, recognizing that a life event is likely to be stressful for your relative will enable you to be prepared to help him or her cope.

The Stressful Life Events Checklist can help you get an idea of how much stress you and your relative have experienced over the past year. Although there are many other possible stressors you or your relative might have experienced, this checklist provides a general summary of some of the most common stressors that people experience.

## Daily Hassles

In addition to life events, most people are faced with daily stressors, or "hassles." Hassles are usually of smaller magnitude, but they can add up if they occur on a regular basis. Some examples of daily hassles are financial difficulties, crowded or noisy living conditions, minor medical problems, arguments or conflicts, frequent criticism or intrusions, a long commute, and unpleasant household chores. The cumulative effects of unrelenting daily hassles can be as stressful as major life events—in some cases, even more stressful. For example, ongoing stress from a tense

# Stressful Life Events Checklist

*Instructions:* Check each life event that you or your relative has experienced over the past year. Use two checkmarks for any event that you or your relative found especially stressful. Count up the total number of checkmarks to find out how much stress you and your relative have experienced in the last year.

0–3 events = mild stress    4–6 events = moderate stress
7 or more = high stress

| *Event* | *Experienced by Your Relative* | *Experienced by You* |
|---|---|---|
| 1. Moving | _____ | _____ |
| 2. Family vacation | _____ | _____ |
| 3. New baby | _____ | _____ |
| 4. Marriage | _____ | _____ |
| 5. Family holiday at your house | _____ | _____ |
| 6. Family member moves out | _____ | _____ |
| 7. Family member moves in | _____ | _____ |
| 8. Financial problems | _____ | _____ |
| 9. Buying a house | _____ | _____ |
| 10. Inheriting or winning money | _____ | _____ |
| 11. Physical illness | _____ | _____ |
| 12. Physical injury | _____ | _____ |
| 13. Caring for an ill relative | _____ | _____ |
| 14. Hospitalization | _____ | _____ |
| 15. Hospitalization of a relative | _____ | _____ |
| 16. Death of someone close | _____ | _____ |
| 17. Victim of a crime | _____ | _____ |
| 18. Retirement | _____ | _____ |
| 19. New job (paid or volunteer) | _____ | _____ |
| 20. Loss of job | _____ | _____ |
| 21. Reduction in income | _____ | _____ |
| 22. Conflict at work | _____ | _____ |
| 23. Separation/Divorce | _____ | _____ |
| 24. Change in time spent with friends | _____ | _____ |
| 25. New boy/girlfriend | _____ | _____ |
| 26. Reduction in leisure activities | _____ | _____ |
| 27. Starting a diet | _____ | _____ |
| 28. Stopping smoking | _____ | _____ |
| 29. Legal problems | _____ | _____ |
| 30. Car accident | _____ | _____ |

## Daily Hassles Worksheet

*Instructions:* Write down the most stressful daily hassles you have experienced over the past year. Discuss with your relative what he or she finds stressful and include these daily hassles on the list.

*Your Hassles*                           *Your Relative's Hassles*

1.                                        1.

2.                                        2.

3.                                        3.

4.                                        4.

5.                                        5.

6.                                        6.

7.                                        7.

8.                                        8.

family atmosphere can have effects just as negative as stress from a life event, such as starting a new job or someone close to you dying. The Daily Hassles Worksheet is a form for you to list the day-to-day difficulties experienced by you and your ill relative. You may find it helpful to talk to your relative to find out what type of daily hassles he or she finds troublesome. Your lists may overlap, or you may be surprised at the differences.

## Recognizing Signs of Stress

Stress can have a wide range of effects on people, including changes in physical state, thinking, mood, and behavior. Just as people differ in what they find stressful, their responses to stress are also different. Some show only physical signs, such as headaches or indigestion. Others have difficulty with their thinking and concentration or have mood changes, such as irritability or anxiousness. Still others may show their stress through behaviors such as nailbiting or restlessness. Most people respond to stress with a combination of physical, thinking, mood, and behavior changes.

Understanding how your relative responds to stress can enable you to recognize when he or she is under stress. Similarly, recognizing your own stress-response pattern will help you know when you are under stress, so that you can take action to reduce the stress. The Signs of Stress Checklist can help you identify individual signs of stress. Complete this checklist for yourself. Then consult your relative and complete the checklist (working together if possible) for him or her.

## Managing Stress

Now that you are familiar with your own and your relative's sources and signs of stress, let's turn to how to manage stress. Some reactions to stress tend to make the situation worse, such as yelling, blaming yourself, or withdrawing. Other ways of responding to stress are more adaptive, such as when the stressor itself is reduced or the negative effects of the stressor are minimized. We discuss below both strategies for reducing the sources of stress and for managing its negative effects. As you read the following sections, consider which strategies you or your relative currently use and which ones could be used more often.

### Reducing the Sources of Stress

Whenever possible, it is helpful to avoid stress by eliminating its source. Putting energy into prevention can pay off. The following strategies can be used to help you and your relative reduce exposure to stress in your lives.

*Avoid situations that caused stress in the past.* If a situation was stressful before, there is a high chance that it will cause problems again. For example, if your relative became tense and agitated during the last big family Christmas celebration, consider letting him or her stay home this year or abbreviating the visit to make it more manageable. If you find it stressful to drive at rush hour, try scheduling your car trips at other times of the day.

*Set reasonable expectations.* It is important not to expect too much from ourselves or from others. Setting realistic goals can help to reduce stress. Try to develop a meaningful but not overdemanding schedule for your relative, with expectations that he or she can comfortably meet. Patients with schizophrenia tend to benefit from moderate, but not excessive structure.

Patients also benefit from activities that are meaningful to them. Depending on your relative, meaningful activity may be a day program, a volunteer job, part-time employment, or spending a few hours at the library each day.

Problems result when the environment is either overstimulating or understimulating. Helping your relative find the right balance of stimulation and reasonable expectations will minimize his or her stress. For example, for some patients a volunteer job once a week may be preferable to a day program three days a week.

*Maintain good health habits.* Eating right and getting enough sleep can help buffer the effects of stress. Being well-nourished and well-rested usually fortifies people to deal with hassles and crises. Scheduling regular physical exercise can also help decrease stress and increase one's sense of well-being. Taking a walk, riding a bicycle, swimming, bowling, tennis, and jogging are examples of exercise that people often enjoy. If possible, schedule some form of exercise two to three times per week.

*Schedule frequent leisure activities.* Most people find that taking a break from their normal routine is refreshing. For example, going to a movie, walking in the park or eating out can all help to reduce stress. Having a hobby such as sewing, coin collecting, or drawing can be an enjoyable way of spending leisure time. It is especially helpful to plan leisure activities on a regular basis; this gives you something to look forward to and prevents stressors from building up.

For your relative, you may need to help him or her think of leisure activities, perhaps the ones that were enjoyed before the illness. In Chapter 10, the section "Coping with Negative Symptoms" has some suggestions for identifying activities your relative might enjoy. For yourself, schedule leisure activities that you find relaxing and enjoyable. It will help you "recharge" your energy.

# Signs of Stress Checklist

*Instructions:* Place a checkmark next to each physical, thinking, mood, or behavioral change experienced by you or your relative when under stress.

| *Physical Changes* | *Your Relative* | *Yourself* |
|---|---|---|
| 1. Increased heart rate and blood pressure | _____ | _____ |
| 2. Heart palpitations | _____ | _____ |
| 3. Perspiration | _____ | _____ |
| 4. Headache | _____ | _____ |
| 5. Back or neck pain | _____ | _____ |
| 6. Loss of appetite or increased appetite | _____ | _____ |
| 7. Sleep disturbance | _____ | _____ |
| 8. Diarrhea, indigestion, or nausea | _____ | _____ |
| 9. Shakiness | _____ | _____ |
| 10. Frequent need to urinate | _____ | _____ |
| 11. Fatigue | _____ | _____ |
| 12. Dry mouth | _____ | _____ |
| 13. Muscular tension | _____ | _____ |

*Changes in Thinking*

| | | |
|---|---|---|
| 14. Worry | _____ | _____ |
| 15. Problems with concentration | _____ | _____ |
| 16. Confusion, inattentiveness | _____ | _____ |
| 17. "Catastrophizing" about what will happen | _____ | _____ |
| 18. Rigidness | _____ | _____ |
| 19. Hypervigilance | _____ | _____ |
| 20. Feelings of unreality | _____ | _____ |

*continued on next page*

| Mood Changes | Your Relative | Yourself |
|---|---|---|
| 21. Depression | _____ | _____ |
| 22. Anger or irritability | _____ | _____ |
| 23. Apathy | _____ | _____ |
| 24. Anxiety | _____ | _____ |
| 25. Tearfulness or the urge to cry | _____ | _____ |
| 26. Feeling "keyed up" or agitated | _____ | _____ |

| Behavioral Changes | | |
|---|---|---|
| 27. Difficulty communicating | _____ | _____ |
| 28. Teeth grinding | _____ | _____ |
| 29. Nervous laughter | _____ | _____ |
| 30. Stuttering | _____ | _____ |
| 31. Accident proneness | _____ | _____ |
| 32. Drug or alcohol abuse | _____ | _____ |
| 33. Trembling, nervous tics | _____ | _____ |
| 34. Aggressive or violent behavior | _____ | _____ |

## Coping with Unavoidable Stress

Nobody can lead a stress-free life. When the inevitable stressors occur, it helps to have coping strategies for dealing with their negative effects. Several strategies are discussed below.

*Communicate directly about stress.* Talking about feelings can help prevent stress from building up once it occurs. If you let someone know how you are feeling, it often provides some immediate relief. Furthermore, sometimes other people have ideas about how to deal with a stressor that can be helpful to you. It is especially important that your relative tell someone when he or she is feeling under stress, because these feelings can indicate an early warning sign of relapse. If your relative can talk to you or someone else during times of stress, he or she may be able to get some help that will prevent a relapse. For yourself, talking to someone who understands can help you feel under less pressure and more able to cope with a difficult situation.

*Engage family members in a problem-solving discussion.* If just talking to someone does not help, it may be a good idea to meet with family members (including your ill relative, when possible) to discuss the situation and explore possible solutions to the problem that is causing the stress. Openly discussing the problem with others and trying to resolve it can reduce stress.

*Use relaxation techniques.* Certain methods of reducing the effects of stress require learning and practicing specific techniques. Some examples are deep breathing exercises, biofeedback, meditation, imagery, progressive muscle relaxation, and self-hypnosis. These methods can be learned from books, classes, or sessions with trained therapists. At the end of this chapter is a list of books and tapes about relaxation and stress reduction, which may be useful to both you and your relative.

One example of a relaxation technique that you or your relative can try on your own is deep breathing. The Deep Breathing Exercise worksheet lists eight steps you can use to reduce tension. It doesn't take a lot of time and can even be done in fairly public places without attracting attention, so you may want to copy the worksheet and carry it with you until you have the steps memorized.

*Use positive self-talk.* In general, the more negatively you view a particular situation, the more stress you will experience from it. In truth, many situations that people encounter are very tough, and they often respond with negative, self-defeating thoughts, such as "This is awful," "I can't stand it," or "I'm a nervous wreck." These self-defeating thoughts can be replaced with more positive "self-talk." Positive self-talk includes saying coping-oriented things to yourself, such as "This is a challenge, but I can handle it," "I'm going to do the best that I can do," and "It's too bad this happened, but I am capable of dealing with it."

## Deep Breathing Exercise

1. Sit in a comfortable chair, with your back fully supported.

2. Take ten deep, slow breaths, breathing in through your nose and out from your mouth.

3. Notice the feeling of your diaphragm filling with air, then emptying.

4. Concentrate on the air traveling through the air passageways.

5. Next, each time you exhale, silently repeat the word *relax*. Do this approximately 30 times. Do not worry about counting exactly.

6. Feel yourself letting go of tension in your body. Think of standing under a shower or waterfall, the water washing away the feelings of tension.

7. Now, gradually begin to breathe normally. Concentrate on your breathing. Allow your mind to wander, but gently steer it back to your breathing.

8. Sit quietly for a minute or two and concentrate on your natural breathing.

For example, instead of saying to yourself, "I shouldn't have to wait in a long line like this—it just isn't fair," try saying "I really wish I didn't have to wait in this long line—is there an alternative?" You can use this strategy in a variety of circumstances, and you can help your relative by suggesting different ways for him or her to think about a stressful situation. Further information about positive self-talk is provided in Chapter 11, under "Correcting Maladaptive Thinking."

*Maintain your sense of humor.* The old saying that laughter is the best medicine also applies to the management of stress. Granted, many times there seems to be nothing to laugh about. However, if you can manage to see the lighter side of a stressful situation, you may be able to keep from being totally overwhelmed by it. For example, an argument with someone can sometimes be derailed by a humorous remark, particularly if you poke fun at yourself and not the other person. Many people with schizophrenia have a good sense of humor and respond well to a good-natured joke.

*Use religion or other spiritual inspiration.* For thousands of years people have been comforted and guided by religious beliefs, which helped give meaning to their lives. These spiritual beliefs can help people cope with stress arising from difficult circumstances. For some people, prayer or other religious activities (going to church or synagogue) may substantially reduce stress. For less religious people, communion with nature is a source of inspiration that can lower stress. Religious organizations can also be a source of social support, which can reduce feelings of isolation and stress.

*Make a plan to increase your coping ability.* It can be very helpful to assess how you and your relative currently cope with stress and whether there is room for improvement. The Coping Method Checklist will guide you in determining which methods you and your relative currently use and which ones might be worth exploring. After completing the checklist, the Implementing a New Coping Method worksheet can be used to help you develop a plan for trying out a new method of handling stress, including any of the strategies described here, as well as others you may have heard of or read about. The following are books and tapes that provide information and instructions for specific strategies that you might like to try:

*Applied Relaxation Training* (audiocassette), by M. McKay, P. Fanning, and N. Sonenberg. Oakland, Calif: New Harbinger Publications, 1991.

*Body Awareness and Imagination* (audiocassette), by M. McKay and P. Fanning. Oakland, Calif: New Harbinger Publications, 1987.

*Body Relaxed—Mind at Ease* (audiocassette), by H. Sanders. Oakland, Calif: New Harbinger Publications, 1993.

*Creative Visualization,* by R. Shone. Rochester, Vt: Destiny Books, 1988.

*The Doctors' Guide to Instant Stress Relief,* by R. G. Nathan, T. E. Staats, and P. Rosch. New York: Ballantine Books, 1987.

*Dusk: The Piano Music of Jim Chappell* (audiocassette), by J. Chappell. Music West Records and Cassettes, 1987.

*In the Mind's Eye,* by A. A. Lazarus. New York: Rawson, 1978.

*Letting Go of Stress* (audiocassette), by E. E. Miller and S. Halpern. 1980. Available from Source, P.O. Box W, Stanford, Calif. 94309.

*Life's Little Relaxation Book,* by S. M. Selzer. New York: S.P.I. Books, 1994

*The New Three Minute Meditator,* by D. Harp with N. Feldman. Oakland, Calif: New Harbinger Publications, 1990.

*Progressive Relaxation and Breathing* (audiocassette), by M. McKay and P. Fanning. Oakland, Calif: New Harbinger Publications, 1987.

*The Relaxation and Stress Reduction Workbook,* 3rd edition, by M. Davis, E. R. Eshelman, and M. McKay. Oakland, Calif.: New Harbinger Publications, 1988.

*The Relaxation Response,* by H. Benson. New York: Avon Books, 1975.

*Stress Management: A Comprehensive Guide to Wellness,* by E. Charlesworth and R. Nathan. New York: Ballantine Books, 1984.

*The Stress Solution: An Action Plan to Manage the Stress in Your Life,* by L. H. Miller, A. D. Smith, and L. Rothstein. New York: Pocket Books, 1993.

*Time Out from Stress,* vol. 1 by P. Fanning and M. McKay. Oakland, Calif: New Harbinger Publications, 1993.

*Visualization for Change,* by P. Fanning. Oakland, Calif: New Harbinger Publications, 1988.

# Coping Method Checklist

*Instructions:* Check off the methods currently used by you or your relative to cope with stress. Then check off the methods you and your relative would like to explore. The Implementing a New Coping Method worksheet will help you make specific plans for trying out new methods.

| Coping Method | You Currently Use | You Would Like to Try | Your Relative Currently Uses | Your Relative Would Like to Try |
|---|---|---|---|---|
| Communicating directly about stress | _____ | _____ | _____ | _____ |
| Engaging in family problem-solving | _____ | _____ | _____ | _____ |
| Using specific relaxation techniques (meditation, imagery, deep breathing) | _____ | _____ | _____ | _____ |
| Using positive self-talk | _____ | _____ | _____ | _____ |
| Maintaining sense of humor | _____ | _____ | _____ | _____ |
| Practicing religion or other spiritual inspiration | _____ | _____ | _____ | _____ |
| Others: | _____ | _____ | _____ | _____ |
| _____ | _____ | _____ | _____ | _____ |
| _____ | _____ | _____ | _____ | _____ |

## Implementing a New Coping Method

*Instructions:* Review your Coping Method Checklist and select a method for coping with stress that you or your relative would like to try. Think about the steps you need to take to implement the method, and list them in the space provided below. Keep in mind any materials you might need and people who might be able to help, and choose appropriate locations and times to practice the new method. Bear in mind that any method will take some time to be effective, so be sure to give whatever technique you choose an adequate trial period.

Coping method I would like to try: _____

Length of time I will commit to trying the technique: _____

Steps necessary to implement this method:

1.

2.

3.

4.

5.

6.


Coping method that my relative would like to try: _____
_____

Length of time my relative commits to trying the technique: ___
_____

Steps necessary to implement this method:

1.

2.

3.

4.

5.

6.

# 9

# Establishing
# Household Rules

Every home needs a set of rules that family members are expected to follow. These rules can be informal; they don't always have to be spelled out. However, as we will discuss, making household rules explicit can improve the chances that your ill relative will follow the rules, leading to a more cooperative family environment. An example of a common household rule is the expectation that family members will settle disagreements without resorting to physical violence or threats. Another rule is that all family members will help in the running of the household: chores, cooking, errands.

Establishing specific rules in your family can ensure that no one's personal rights are intruded upon and that everyone has something to contribute to the household. You have the fundamental right to live in a home in which you feel safe and comfortable, your privacy is respected, and all family members contribute at least something to the ongoing operation. This chapter focuses on helping you achieve this basic right by describing how to develop household rules for your relative that will clarify expectations for his or her behavior. If you feel unsafe, tense, or uncomfortable in your home, or if you are resentful or feel "taken advantage of" by your relative's behavior, this chapter can help you assert your right to live in a positive, supportive home environment.

## The Value of Explicit Rules

There are a number of reasons you should consider establishing *explicit* household rules for your ill relative, rather than leaving these rules as unspoken expectations.

## Patients Often Lack Knowledge About Common Social Norms

Research has shown that people with schizophrenia often lack an understanding of the unwritten rules that govern much social behavior, including how to live with and get along with others. In addition, patients may find it difficult to judge other people's feelings by their tone of voice and facial expression. The result is that many people with schizophrenia are somewhat isolated from the world around them, and they have difficulty taking into consideration the needs and feelings of their relatives.

For example, Bernice would play the stereo at high volume late into the night. Her sleeping pattern was disrupted by the illness and she was "out of sync" with the rest of the household, sleeping much of the day and staying up through the night. She preferred to listen to loud music, and it didn't occur to her that it would disturb other family members. When her relatives asked her to turn down her music, she would often agree, but would later forget about their request and increase the volume again.

Spelling out explicit household rules can help compensate for your relative's lack of social judgment by making it clear what is expected and what is not allowed.

## Symptoms Can Be a Problem

Many of the symptoms of schizophrenia can interfere with your relative's ability to follow conventional rules for living with others, such as picking up after oneself, contributing to the household, or following simple requests. People with schizophrenia often suffer from low energy and have little motivation (negative symptoms), resulting in a lack of initiative. Other symptoms, such as paranoid delusions or auditory hallucinations (positive symptoms), can also interfere with your relative's ability to live cooperatively with you, and may necessitate that you establish clear household rules.

For example, Ed's negative symptoms make it difficult for him to get up in the morning and do chores, such as washing the breakfast dishes. Ed also has persistent positive symptoms. He has delusions that the CIA is trying to kidnap him and at times he believes that his parents are in cahoots with the CIA. As a result of these delusions, Ed is sometimes suspicious of his parents and does not comply with their requests.

## Clear Household Rules Reduce Stress

People with schizophrenia have difficulties living with other people, which can result in high levels of stress on everyone in the home. The unpredictable behavior of your relative, coupled with his or her insensitivity to the needs of others, may cause you to experience feelings of anxiety, annoyance, and frustration, since you must do extra work to make up for your relative. You may deal with these feelings by openly criticizing your relative or by simply bearing the added responsibilities silently, resentfully. In either case, you experience stress from living with your relative if he or she cannot follow basic rules of communal living. Furthermore, this stress pervades the family atmosphere, increasing the stress on your ill relative as well.

Establishing clear household rules will help to create a more peaceful family environment for everyone living at home. By clarifying what is expected of your ill relative, you will help yourself develop realistic expectations for your relative's behavior, taking into consideration his or her level of symptoms. Setting realistic expectations can also help improve the self-esteem of patients, because they will have the satisfaction of meeting expectations and contributing to the household without being constantly "nagged" by their relatives. In short, specifying household rules is beneficial to all family members.

## Who Should Establish Household Rules?

The family members who bear the primary responsibility for maintaining the home have the right to establish the household rules. These people include the owner of the home, persons who pay the majority of the expenses, and persons with the role of coordinating home maintenance activities, such as cooking, cleaning, and shopping. You alone might have the major responsibility for determining rules, or you may share it with one or more other family members.

If you are a parent and have a child with schizophrenia who lives at home, then you (and other family members who share major responsibilities) are the person who must establish the household rules. Similarly, if your sibling, niece, nephew, or grandchild has schizophrenia and lives in your home, then you, along with other members of your household who also share the major responsibilities, will set the rules for living at home. In most families, the person with schizophrenia does not have the primary responsibility for running the household. However, in families in which the patient *does* have an important role—for example—if your spouse has schizophrenia, rules need to be established jointly, with the patient actively participating in the process.

## Fundamental Rules for All Families

You and your family must decide what specific household rules you feel most comfortable living with. There are five rules that we recommend to *all* families, because they are related to ensuring the safety of people and property and preventing disruptive, socially unacceptable, or illegal behavior:

### Fundamental Household Rules

- No violence to people or property
- No inappropriate sexual behavior (for example, walking around naked, masturbating in front of others)
- No smoking in bed
- Everyone must bathe or shower regularly
- No illegal drug use

## Special Problem Areas

In addition to the five fundamental rules for all families, there are often other rules that need to be made to address the difficulties of living with a relative who has schizophrenia. Three problem areas are especially common: compliance with medication, failure to do household chores, and disturbing behavior. You can establish specific household rules to deal with each of these problems, as described below.

### Medication Noncompliance

Most people with schizophrenia have difficulty complying with their antipsychotic medication at some point during their illness. It has been estimated that during the first year after diagnosis of the illness, 50 percent of all patients are noncompliant with their prescribed medications, and this figure climbs to over 80 percent during the first two years. Although patients often gradually become more compliant with their medication over time, problems with medication compliance in schizophrenia are widespread and need to be overcome if the illness is to be successfully managed at home.

As discussed in Chapter 3, there are many possible reasons your relative may be noncompliant with his or her medication. However, regardless of the specific reason for noncompliance, you have the right to insist that your relative take medication on a regular basis and see his or her doctor. Medication is an integral part of your relative's psychiatric treatment and is vital to minimizing symptoms and rehospitalizations. If your relative refuses to take medication and you allow him or her to continue living at home, you could actually contribute to a *worse* prognosis or outcome of the illness. To avoid this problem, you can establish medication compliance as a condition of your relative's continuing to live at home—in other words, you can make it a household rule. Specific strategies for monitoring and enhancing medication compliance are described in Chapter 3. However, your first step toward ensuring compliance with medication is to establish this as a clear rule for your relative, and follow up to make sure the rule is followed.

## Disturbing Behavior

People with schizophrenia can behave in ways that are upsetting, annoying, or anxiety provoking. Some symptoms, such as impaired thought processes, can interfere with the ability to judge social appropriateness. Positive symptoms (delusions or hallucinations) may cause patients to act in ways that are disturbing to others. Negative symptoms, such as apathy, can be so severe that they are upsetting to relatives.

For example, Jessica hears voices that threaten her. In response, she sometimes shouts "Stop that! Don't come near me!" in the middle of a quiet dinner. Allen has paranoid delusions that others can read his mind. He has repeatedly unplugged the refrigerator because he believes it is a listening device used to eavesdrop on his thoughts. Paula sleeps so much of the day she doesn't get out of bed until 4:00 PM.

Some upsetting behaviors may be beyond your relative's control. However, there are many disturbing behaviors that can be managed through the use of household rules. Remember, your goal is to limit the disturbing effect your relative's behavior has on you, not to actually change the symptoms that cause the behavior. Thus, you can make the rule, "There will be no shouting in the home," but not, "You will not listen to auditory hallucinations." Figure 9.1 lists upsetting behaviors that are common in people with schizophrenia. For each behavior we suggest one household rule that other families have found helpful in dealing with problem behaviors.

## Failure to Do Household Chores

Chores are commonly a problem because patients often lack the initiative to help out on their own and have difficulties following a routine. You may have negative feelings if your relative does not contribute to the running of your household. It is reasonable for you to expect your ill relative to do something useful around the house. Even if your relative is quite impaired and can only do a few minor chores, chances are you will feel better if you know he or she is trying to help. In addition, once chores have been agreed upon, your relative will probably feel better. Everyone likes to have something useful to do and to feel appreciated for the efforts they make.

In determining what chores your relative should do, it is important to select chores based on his or her ability. You need to consider four factors that are related to your relative's ability to do a chore: complexity, judgment, timing, and the amount of social contact required.

## Household Rules Regarding Upsetting Behaviors

| Common Upsetting Behaviors | Suggested Household Rules |
|---|---|
| Staying in bed most of the day | Get out of bed by 10:00 AM on weekdays and 12:00 noon on weekends |
| Shouting | No raising your voice |
| Offensive language | No swearing or insulting people |
| Watching TV most of the day | TV watching to be no more than three hours per day |
| Refusing day treatment | Go to day treatment at least three days per week |
| Bad manners during eating | Don't talk with your mouth full; take small bites; clean up after yourself if you spill something |
| Smoking in the house | Smoke outside the house (or in a designated room) |

Figure 9.1

*Complexity.* One way of gauging the complexity of a chore is to evaluate how many steps are required to complete it and the difficulty of each step. People often underestimate the number of steps required to complete chores because they have done them so often that the task becomes automatic. However, many people with schizophrenia have to learn or relearn chores, and it may take a long time before the steps become automatic.

*Judgment.* "Judgment" refers to your relative's ability to make spontaneous decisions based on the specific circumstances of the situation. For example, when cooking, the person must often experiment with the amount of seasoning used, adjust the heat of the range or oven, and determine when the dish is done. The amount of judgment required for different chores varies considerably. Chores need to be selected according to your relative's ability to make such judgments. Some chores involve very little judgment, such as taking out the trash or setting the table. Other chores require more judgment, such as cooking.

*Timing.* Some chores need to be done at certain times of the day, while others are more flexible. For example, in most families cleaning up the dishes takes place right after each meal. Shopping or taking out the garbage, on the other hand, can be done at any time of the day or evening. If your relative sleeps late or is unable to do chores at certain times of the day, these limitations should be taken into account when deciding which chores he or she will be expected to do.

*Social contact.* Your relative may find it difficult to be around large groups of people or to interact with strangers. For example, it is hard for some patients to shop because they dislike going to a crowded grocery store or having to interact with the cashier. Some chores require more social contact than others, and you should consider your relative's comfort during social interactions when identifying the right jobs for him or her.

## Selecting the Right Chores for Your Relative

To help you choose which chores are best for your relative with schizophrenia, we have summarized some of the most common household chores in Figure 9.2. This table provides a breakdown of each chore into smaller steps. For each chore, we also provide estimates of the amounts of judgment required, time pressure involved, and social contact required. These ratings reflect how difficult chores are for a person with schizophrenia, based on our experience working with many families. Your own evaluation may differ slightly from ours, depending upon the nature of the chores in your own home. Also, there may be chores you need done but that we have not included in our list. You can evaluate these chores yourself by breaking them down into small steps and then assessing each of the dimensions included in Figure 9.2.

Make a list of the regular chores and additional jobs you need performed routinely in your household, bearing in mind your relative's limitations in judgment, time pressure, and so on. Select one or two simple chores for your relative to perform on a regular basis. At the beginning stages of establishing household rules, it is preferable to err on the side of too few expectations, rather than making too many. If you start out with fewer expectations, your relative is more likely to experience success and the positive feelings that come with doing a job right. After your relative has shown some consistency in doing the assigned chores, you can gradually add more responsibilities over time. This approach will build up your relative's confidence that he or she *can* play an important role in maintaining the home.

# Establishing Household Rules for Your Family

Each family is different, and each person with schizophrenia has a unique pattern of symptoms. In addition to the five fundamental rules we recommend for everyone, your family will probably benefit from establishing a few other rules to address specific problem areas. This section

## Common Household Chores

| Chore and Basic Steps | Judgment Required | Time Pressure | Social Interaction Required |
|---|---|---|---|
| *Shopping for groceries* | | | |
| • Make out list | Moderate | Minimal | Moderate |
| • Get to/from store | to high | | to high |
| • Pick out items from store | | | |
| • Pay | | | |
| • Put away groceries | | | |
| *Meal preparation* | | | |
| • Choose menu | Moderate | High | Minimal |
| • Plan timing | to high | | |
| • Ensure ingredients are available | | | |
| • Follow recipe | | | |
| • Prepare ingredients | | | |
| • Use stove or burner | | | |
| • Cook ingredients or assemble | | | |
| *Setting table* | | | |
| • Choose appropriate number of dishes, utensils | Minimal | Moderate to high | Minimal |
| • Place dishes and utensils around table | | | |
| • Place condiments on table | | | |
| *Clearing table* | | | |
| • Scrape plates | Minimal | Minimal | Minimal |
| • Put away leftovers | | | |
| • Clear table of dishes and utensils | | | |
| • Put dirty dishes in sink or dishwasher | | | |
| *Washing dishes by hand* | | | |
| • Fill dishpan with soap and water | Minimal | Moderate | Minimal |
| • Wash and rinse each dish | | | |

Figure 9.2

## Common Household Chores

| Chore and Basic Steps | Judgment Required | Time Pressure | Social Interaction Required |
|---|---|---|---|
| *Washing dishes by hand (continued)* <br> • Dry each dish or put in drainer to dry <br> • Put away clean, dry dishes <br> • Wipe counters and wash sink | | | |
| *Taking out garbage* <br> • Make sure all garbage is in container <br> • Tie up garbage bag <br> • Take bag to outdoor can <br> • Put a bag in the container | Minimal | Moderate | Minimal |
| *Laundry* <br> • Gather dirty laundry <br> • Sort, if necessary <br> • Load machine and add detergent <br> • Select setting and turn on washer <br> • Move washed clothes to dryer <br> • Select setting and turn on dryer <br> • Fold clean clothes <br> • Put away clean clothes | Minimal to moderate | Minimal | Minimal |
| *General cleaning* <br> • Straighten up (put each thing where it belongs) <br> • Vacuum floor and carpet <br> • Wash floors | Minimal to moderate | Minimal | Minimal |
| *Cleaning the bathroom* <br> • Scrub toilet <br> • Scrub sink and bathtub or shower <br> • Wash floor | Minimal | Minimal | Minimal |

Figure 9.2

guides you in setting up additional household rules for your ill relative living at home.

## Characteristics of Good Rules

There are three characteristics of good household rules that increase their chances of being followed.

*Good rules are behaviorally specific.* When rules focus on behavior, rather than personality or "attitude," it is easier for your relative to be clear about what is expected or prohibited. When rules are behaviorally specific, it is also easier for you to evaluate which rules are being followed and which are not.

*Good rules are realistic.* Good, effective household rules should be attainable, and therefore must take into consideration the limitations that schizophrenia imposes. Part of developing realistic expectations for your relative involves starting out small and gradually building up, always trying to make sure that your relative is capable of meeting your expectations.

*Good rules are rational.* Nobody likes to follow rules that seem arbitrary or without a basis. If you want a rule to be followed, it is important that you explain the reason for the rule to your relative. Your relative may not agree with you, but when you explain why it is important to you, it is more likely that the rule will be followed, for example: "Stereos should be played very softly after 11:00 PM because Mom can't sleep with the stereo on loud and she has to get up at 6:00 AM for work."

## Steps for Establishing Your Own Rules

There are several steps you can use to effectively establish your own family rules, described below.

*Step 1: Meet as a "committee."* Arrange a meeting of all the family members who share the responsibility for running the household (often the parents). Find out at this meeting what each person thinks is important to maintaining a low-stress environment and order in your home. You should have this meeting at a time when there is a minimum of tension. Rules made in the heat of an argument tend to be overly rigid and punitive. Setting rules before tension builds, on the other hand, can help to avoid arguments and stress.

*Step 2: Work on selected problems.* Select a few of the most important problem areas and agree on a tentative rule for each one. Limit the number of rules (not including the five fundamental rules) to five or less, and give priority to the problems that most upset your family's equilibrium. To decide which behaviors are most important, first determine which of your relative's behaviors are intolerable to family members and which are simply annoying or bothersome. Work on the intolerable behaviors first.

*Step 3: Set penalties.* Establish consequences for violating the rules, including the five fundamental rules. If your relative knows the consequences in advance, he or she will be more likely to follow the rules.

When determining the penalties for breaking a rule, we recommend that you consider two factors. First, breaking more serious rules should result in more severe consequences. For example, smoking in bed or destroying property are more serious infractions and should have greater penalties attached than forgetting to take out the garbage. Second, you must be willing (and able!) to enforce any consequences that you establish. If rules are not enforced, they will rapidly lose their meaning, and the purpose of establishing household rules will be undermined. For example, do not establish a consequence of requiring your relative to move out of your home unless you are truly willing to follow through on it.

Determining the appropriate consequences for violating household rules is an individual matter that you and your family must decide on your own. The most natural consequences available to you may include limiting privileges that you have control over, such as use of the car, spending money, cigarettes, special foods, movie rentals, and so on. In most families, the people with the major household responsibilities ultimately have the right to insist that the patient not live at home if he or she does not follow basic rules, although some families may not choose this possible consequence. Figure 9.3 provides some examples of household rules and the consequences for breaking them.

*Step 4: Meet as a family.* Meet with the entire family, including your ill relative, to discuss the rules that have been decided upon. Be willing to compromise about some of the rules, but do not agree to a compromise that you will feel uncomfortable with. For example, a smoking rule could be modified to include a more acceptable smoking area, but it would be best not to allow smoking in bed.

*Step 5: Record your decisions.* Write down the rules that are agreed upon, beginning with the five fundamental rules and adding other rules that were chosen. Check to make sure that all the rules are behaviorally specific, realistic, and based on a clear rationale. We have provided the Household Rules Worksheet for you to use to record your complete list of rules. After you have completed your list, give a copy to each member in the household and post one copy in a prominent location in your home, such as on your refrigerator.

## When the Patient Doesn't Live at Home

Household rules can also be established for your relative if he or she does not live at home but visits on a regular basis. In such instances,

## Examples of Household Rules and the Consequences for Breaking Them

| Rule | Consequences for Violating the Rule |
|---|---|
| No violence to people or property | • Violence to others will receive one warning; if it happens again, the person may no longer live at home<br>• Destroyed property must be replaced |
| No inappropriate sexual behavior | • The person must go to his or her room for at least an hour |
| No smoking in bed or other fire hazards | • Cigarettes will be rationed on a schedule.<br>• No cigarettes given out after 9:00 PM |
| Everyone must bathe or shower regularly | • Video rentals (or another specific recreational activity) are not permitted until bath or shower is taken |
| No illegal drugs may be used | • Money will be managed by another person for one month |
| Patient will take medication as prescribed | • Spending money is withheld until patient takes medication |
| Patient will take out the garbage by 9:00 PM each day | • No cigarettes until the garbage is taken out |
| Patient will set the table for dinner by 5:30 PM each evening | • Patient may not eat with the family; after the others have finished eating, patient may set a place and eat |
| The stereo will be turned off by 11:00 PM each night | • Decrease spending money by $5 per week each time it happens |
| Everyone will get up by 10:00 AM on weekdays and 12:00 noon on weekends | • Regular family outing will be canceled for one week |

Figure 9.3

## Household Rules Worksheet

*Household Rule*                         *Consequence for Not*
                                          *Following Rule*

1. No violence to people or property    _____

2. No inappropriate sexual behavior     _____

3. No smoking in bed or other fire      _____
   hazards

4. Bathe or shower regularly            _____

5. No illegal drugs may be used         _____

6. _____      _____

7. _____      _____

8. _____      _____

9. _____      _____

10. _____     _____

the five fundamental rules apply during visits home, and you can develop additional rules to address specific problems that arise surrounding these visits. For example, special rules can be made concerning phone calls home, surprise visits, smoking in the home, requests for money, and helping out around mealtime.

### When a Spouse Has Schizophrenia

If your spouse or partner has schizophrenia, it may still be important to agree on specific rules for living together. In a process similar to the one described above, you first need to identify for yourself which problem areas are most critical, and then formulate some tentative rules for each area. When you have an idea of the rules you would like to establish, have a meeting with your spouse to talk it over.

During your meeting, explain to your spouse that you would feel more comfortable if the two of you could agree on some basic rules for sharing a home. Discuss with your spouse the five fundamental rules and the other rules you have identified. Be open to establishing some additional rules concerning *your own* behavior, so that your spouse will be able to have some of his or her specific concerns addressed. The process of negotiating household rules with your mate can help clarify expectations for both persons, improving the overall quality of your relationship.

## Following Through on Household Rules

### Providing Encouragement

The most powerful tool for helping your ill relative (and other family members as well) follow household rules is *praise*. Positive feedback acknowledges effort and helps build a cooperative spirit in the household. Family members can praise each other regularly for following the rules. For example, a mother might tell her son, "I'm really pleased to see you did your laundry today without my reminding you."

After your rules have been set, meet regularly as a family to discuss how the new system is working. One way to get these meetings off to a good start is to begin the meeting by pointing out what is going well. For example, Lisa might tell her brother, "I like the way you've been turning off your stereo at 11:00 PM. I can go to sleep a lot easier." As you discuss all the rules, you may need to make some modifications, such as making a rule more specific or lowering the expectation to something more realistic. Establishing household rules that work requires ongoing monitoring to ensure that the rules are reasonable and helpful, and are abided by.

Providing specific rewards can also help your relative follow household rules. People with schizophrenia often lack motivation. By giving your relative the opportunity to earn special privileges or other known reinforcers by following rules, you are able to provide additional motivation and send the message that his or her efforts are appreciated. *Rewarding* your relative for following household rules should not be confused with *bribing*. A reward is a positive reinforcement that is given to the person *after* they perform a desirable behavior, whereas a bribe is an incentive that is given *before* the person has done the behavior. Examples of rewards for complying with rules are contained in Figure 9.4.

## What to Do When Rules Are Not Followed

Do not panic when rules aren't immediately successful. You can expect that some violations of rules will occur at first. It will take time for your family to learn the rules and get used to following them on a day-to-day basis. Your relative may need to find out whether you really "mean business" by testing the rules. That is, he or she may need to find out what happens when the rules are not followed. Testing new rules is natural, and you can respond to these challenges calmly but firmly.

A good first response to a rule violation is to immediately remind the person of the rule that he or she has broken. A rule may be broken because your relative forgot it or did not fully understand the rule. An-

---

**Suggested Rewards for Following Household Rules**

- Special outing (amusement park, video arcade, park, swimming pool, picnic)
- More spending money
- Going out to eat
- New clothes
- Spending time alone with a family member
- Ride in the car (instead of public transportation)
- Playing a sport together
- Decoration for own room
- Tape or CD
- Concert
- Choosing video
- Extra cigarettes (use sparingly)
- Choosing special menu at home

Figure 9.4

swer any questions that he or she has about the rule, but try to be clear and brief. Inform your relative that you expect the rule to be followed in the future and remind him or her of the consequences of not abiding by the rule.

If your relative still does not follow the rule, despite experiencing the negative consequences, review the rule itself. Ask the following questions again:

- Is the rule defined in terms of behavior?

- Is your relative capable of following the rule?

- Is the reason for the rule clear?

You may need to modify the rule based on your answers to these questions. If you do modify the rule, call a family meeting to review the change and alter your list of rules accordingly.

When rules are broken, it can be helpful to further consider the use of rewards to encourage compliance. Additional motivation may provide the necessary impetus for following the rules. If you have already tried to reinforce your relative, but it does not seem to have worked, consider trying more or different rewards. Talk directly with your relative to learn what obstacles interfere with complying with the rule, and what rewards he or she would be interested in earning.

If your relative continues to disobey certain rules, you may need to reexamine the consequences for the violation. First, consequences are effective only if they are applied consistently. Second, for consequences to be effective deterrents to noncompliance with rules, they need to be provided immediately after the rule is broken, and they must involve a loss or penalty that is genuinely felt by the person. You may need to explore other possible consequences in order to enforce compliance with your rules.

If your relative consistently disobeys certain household rules, despite experiencing the consequences of the behavior, one (or more) of three explanations is likely:

- Your expectations for your relative's behavior may be unrealistic.

- There may not be enough positive reinforcement for complying with the rule.

- The consequences of breaking the rule may be insufficient.

You need to weigh each of these factors to evaluate how to improve your relative's ability to meet your expectations for his or her living at home.

# The Basic Rights of Caregivers

You and other caregivers have the right to live in a peaceful home and to expect your family members to behave in an acceptable manner. In some families, in spite of vigorous attempts to establish basic rules for a person with schizophrenia living at home, the stress and burden on the relatives become too great. In such circumstances, you may decide that it is best if your relative lives elsewhere, such as in a community residence, boarding home, shared apartment, or individual apartment.

It is not a failure on anyone's part if the choice is made that your ill relative must move out. You can still remain in regular contact with your relative and continue to be an important person in his or her social support system. For many people with a psychiatric illness, leaving their home of origin is an important step toward more independent living. If such a transition can be made smoothly and with the support of you and other family members, the result can be a reduction of stress on everyone. An additional consideration is that your relative's capacity for independent living may increase when he or she moves into a different living situation which is supervised by a nonfamily member. Changing living arrangements is not something that is done lightly, but there are a number of positive consequences for both you and your relative that can follow such a transition.

# PART IV

## Specific Problems

# 10

# Persistent Positive and Negative Symptoms

Pharmacological advances over the past several decades have greatly improved the outlook for persons with schizophrenia, enabling most patients to be treated in the community with only occasional hospitalizations required to manage acute exacerbations. Despite these advances, even with optimal pharmacological treatment most patients continue to experience symptoms. The characteristic symptoms of schizophrenia, both positive and negative, present special challenges to patients and relatives alike. As described in Chapter 2, positive symptoms include hallucinations, delusions, and bizarre behavior; negative symptoms include apathy, anhedonia (loss of pleasure), alogia (diminished thought or amount of speech), blunted affect, and attention problems. Unlike problems such as depression, anxiety, and substance abuse, which are relatively common in the general population, positive and negative symptoms are rarely found in people who do not have schizophrenia or another major psychiatric disorder (such as bipolar disorder or major depression).

Learning how to cope effectively with these unique symptoms requires special knowledge and effort. There are no magical solutions for curing persistent symptoms of schizophrenia in your relative. However, there are good reasons to be optimistic that your family, like many others with similar experiences, can learn to manage these symptoms effectively, thereby improving the quality of all your lives. This chapter will provide you with guidelines and suggestions for minimizing the effect of positive and negative symptoms on you and your family and for helping your relative cope as well as possible with these troubling symptoms.

# Coping with Positive Symptoms

It is almost a certainty that your relative with schizophrenia has had positive symptoms at some time during his or her illness. When these symptoms worsen and become a threat to the safety of your relative or others, or when they result in a significant deterioration in self-care or the ability to fulfill previously met obligations (such as work or attending a day program), short-term hospitalization may be necessary. If your relative only experiences positive symptoms during such a relapse, your need to cope with these symptoms is limited to monitoring and recognizing the emergence of positive symptoms, so that you can take immediate action to prevent a major relapse, as described in Chapter 4.

On the other hand, your relative may not be so fortunate. About half of people with schizophrenia experience positive symptoms between relapses, when they are "stable" and living in the community. Your relative may experience mild positive symptoms between episodes, such as occasionally hearing voices or sometimes believing that others are talking about him or her (delusions of reference). Alternatively, it is possible that his or her symptoms are more chronic and severe, such as relentless auditory hallucinations, pervasive beliefs that others can read his or her mind, or stable paranoid delusions. If your relative has persistent positive symptoms, they probably cause at least some distress. Furthermore, when these behaviors lead to offensive, threatening, or other unpredictable behaviors, they can have a negative effect on you. Coping effectively with positive symptoms, therefore, reduces stress on both your relative and you. Before considering how to help your relative cope more effectively with positive symptoms, we first review some other factors that can contribute to the severity of these symptoms.

## Considering Other Factors

The stress-vulnerability model of schizophrenia points to three possible factors that could contribute to more severe positive symptoms: inadequate pharmacological treatment, substance abuse, and high levels of unmitigated stress. Is your relative receiving optimal doses of medication? This is not an easy question to answer. One indication that your relative has received appropriate pharmacological treatment is that he or she has received trials of different antipsychotic medications and different dosages of each medication when symptoms were unremitting. Also, if your relative is still bothered by persistent symptoms and has not yet had a trial of Clozaril, which tends to be more effective than other anti-psychotics for positive symptoms, this should be considered. Another indication that your relative is receiving adequate pharmacological treatment is if his or her positive symptoms have been fairly constant in recent years, and there have not been times when the symptoms were significantly better.

As discussed in more detail in Chapter 12, drug and alcohol abuse can undermine the effects of medication and worsen positive symptoms. If substance abuse is a problem for your relative, you will need to address it in order to reduce his or her positive symptoms. When drug or alcohol abuse occurs as an attempt to cope with, or "self-medicate," persistent positive symptoms, you can combine the strategies described in this chapter with those strategies covered in Chapter 12 for dealing with substance abuse.

High levels of stress can worsen positive symptoms, but this is a less common source of persistent symptoms. If stress is playing a role in your relative's positive symptoms, it is usually because he or she is exposed to *chronic* stressors, such as an extremely demanding, hostile, or unsupportive environment. Efforts to make the environment more supportive, such as establishing more realistic expectations, reinforcing small steps of improvement, and communicating in a more positive and constructive manner, may result in improved positive symptoms for your relative.

Although it is important to evaluate these possible factors as contributors to your relative's positive symptoms, many patients have persistent symptoms even when their medication is well managed, they do not use alcohol or drugs, and their families are supportive. The coping strategies described below may be useful for such patients.

## Listening Empathically

The key to many useful strategies for helping your relative deal with persistent positive symptoms is being able to talk with him or her about those symptoms. In beginning a fruitful dialogue, avoid trying to convince your relative that certain delusional beliefs are not true. Patients are not capable of participating in a logical debate about the reality of their delusions, except in the rare instances when they themselves question their beliefs and ask others for feedback. The nature of delusions is that patients cling to them in spite of overwhelming evidence against them. For this reason, you are not likely to be successful in talking your relative out of believing a delusion, and you may inadvertently increase tension between the two of you. In fact, there is even some evidence that challenging patients about a delusion can actually *increase* their belief in the delusion.

Rather than trying to convince your relative that his or her beliefs are false, listening carefully and showing your concern can lay the groundwork for talking about the problem. To your relative, the delusion seems totally real, and if it causes feelings of anxiety or frustration, those feelings are also quite real. You can validate your relative's feelings about delusional beliefs without reinforcing the actual beliefs. To validate your relative's feelings, use empathic listening skills (good eye contact, paraphrasing, asking clarifying questions) to reflect back what you understand about his or her feelings. By focusing on *feelings*, rather than *beliefs*, you avoid unnecessarily challenging him or her. Here is an example:

| | |
|---|---|
| *Patient:* | I can't go to my day treatment program. |
| *Relative:* | What seems to be the problem? |
| *Patient:* | Everybody can read my mind there. And they talk about me. |
| *Relative:* | Does that make you feel uncomfortable? |
| *Patient:* | Sure it does! I feel scared. |
| *Relative:* | It sounds like when you're at the program you feel scared when you think other people can read your thoughts or are talking about you. |
| *Patient:* | Yes. It makes me want to hide. |
| *Relative:* | I can understand that. Those feelings must be difficult for you to cope with. |
| *Patient:* | They are. |
| *Relative:* | I can see how worried you are. Maybe we could see if there are some ways of helping you deal with this situation, feeling frightened that others can read your thoughts. |

By reflecting back your relative's feelings, you are communicating that you are on his or her side and that you want to help. If your relative is willing to talk about these feelings, the discussion can then turn to strategies for dealing with the feelings and the delusions associated with them. Specific strategies are described in the following section.

Unlike delusions, which patients lack insight into, hallucinations are sometimes recognized as not being real. However, emphasizing to your relative that the hallucinations are not real serves little purpose, since real or not they cause distress. Talking about the feelings associated with hallucinations is more productive and can convey your concern more effectively. It can also be a starting point for working with your relative to improve his or her ability to cope with the hallucinations.

Some patients are very reluctant to talk about positive symptoms and their effects. Your relative may be suspicious of you or may have learned from past experience that others often react negatively when he or she talks about delusions or hallucinations. Your relative may have a strong sense of privacy which makes him or her reluctant to talk about these symptoms. If your relative does not want to talk about these symptoms, respect his or her wishes. You may still be able to help address some of the feelings associated with positive symptoms without talking about the symptoms themselves.

## Specific Coping Strategies

Even if your relative is willing to talk about his or her symptoms, he or she might not be interested in developing strategies to deal with them more effectively. Not all positive symptoms cause feelings of distress, and in the absence of distress there is little motivation to work on coping with them. For example, a minority of patients have voices that are kind, encouraging, or interesting. If positive symptoms cause distress, but your relative prefers not to talk about the symptoms themselves, work together on developing strategies for managing the depression or anxiety that results from the symptoms (see Chapter 11).

If your relative is interested in developing strategies that deal more directly with positive symptoms and their associated feelings, you can work together to identify these strategies, plan how to try them out, and follow up and evaluate their success. *Coping strategies* refers to specific methods that can be used to reduce symptoms, negative feelings related to symptoms, or both. A wide range of different coping strategies can be used to cope with positive symptoms. In general, these coping strategies involve changes in arousal level, behavior, or cognition (thinking). Specific strategies are summarized in Figure 10.1; examples are provided below.

### Strategies Involving a Change in Arousal Level

Either increasing or decreasing stimulation from the environment can have beneficial effects on positive symptoms. Physical exercise or listening to loud, stimulating music are examples of strategies for increasing arousal. Relaxation exercises, deep breathing, imagery, closing one's eyes, or blocking ones ears are ways of decreasing arousal.

### Behavioral Strategies

Positive symptoms often can be decreased by increasing participation in activities, either social or nonsocial. Taking a walk, doing a puzzle, reading, engaging in a conversation, and playing a game with someone are all examples of changes in behavior than can reduce the disruptive effects of positive symptoms. Some patients with persistent auditory hallucinations experience relief when they hum to themselves. Some patients with frequent ideas of reference (such as thoughts that others might be talking about them) benefit from reality-testing; that is, checking out with another person whether their thoughts seem realistic. When selecting behavioral coping strategies for dealing with positive symptoms, focus on those behaviors that are most readily available to your relative and can most easily be done.

### Strategies for Coping with Persistent Positive Symptoms

| Strategies | Examples |
|---|---|
| *Arousal Level* | |
| Decreasing arousal | Relaxing, deep breathing, blocking ears, closing eyes |
| Increasing arousal | Getting physical exercise, listening to loud and stimulating music |
| *Behavior* | |
| Increasing nonsocial activity | Walking, doing puzzles, reading, pursuing hobby |
| Increasing interpersonal contact | Initiating conversation, playing a game with someone else |
| Reality testing | Seeking opinions from others |
| *Cognition* | |
| Shifting attention | Thinking about something pleasant, listening to the radio |
| Fighting back | Telling voices to stop |
| Positive self-talk | Telling yourself "Take it easy," "you can handle it" |
| Problem solving | Asking oneself, "What is the problem?" "What can I do about it?" "What else can I do?" etc. |
| Ignoring the symptom | Paying as little attention to the symptom as possible |
| Acceptance | Accepting that the symptom is not going to go away and deciding to get on with other goals |
| Prayer | Asking for help in coping from a higher power |

Figure 10.1

### Cognitive Strategies

A variety of different cognitive strategies can be useful for coping with positive symptoms.

*Shifting attention.* This strategy involves engaging in some mental activity that competes with the positive symptom, thus drawing attention away from that symptom. Thinking about something pleasant is one strategy for shifting attention, although most patients find this difficult. Passive diversions such as watching TV or listening to music can be helpful. Sometimes patients with chronic auditory hallucinations find music to be a particularly useful diversion, especially listening with earphones.

*Fighting back.* In contrast to shifting the focus of attention, fighting back involves taking an assertive (or aggressive) approach to these symptoms. For example, a patient who hears voices yelling at him might think back to the voices, "Stop! I'm not listening to you! I don't care what you say!" Sometimes patients fight back by speaking out loud to voices, which may have positive effects but can also be socially disruptive.

*Positive self-talk.* As opposed to directly fighting against the positive symptoms, positive self-talk involves thinking in ways that praise one's own efforts. For example, a patient with many paranoid feelings may say to himself or herself, "I'm afraid, but I can handle it. I'll be all-right." A patient with frequent hallucinations can say, "Take it easy, I'm *not* going to let these voices get to me. Stay cool."

Almost everyone engages in positive self-talk at some time, and tuning into your own can help you identify positive self-statements that can be adapted for your relative to use. Some patients are able to adopt positive self-talk as a coping strategy, but patients with many cognitive impairments may have more difficulty.

*Problem solving.* Taking a problem-solving approach to positive symptoms means that the patient explores ways of overcoming the problems associated with the symptom. Asking questions such as "What is the problem?" "What can I do about it?" "What else can I do?" and "How could I try this idea out?" can promote a positive, task-oriented approach to the problem. As with positive self-talk, many patients find this strategy difficult to use, although some are able to.

*Ignoring the symptom.* Paying as little attention as possible to a persistent symptom is a useful strategy for some patients. This can be combined with positive self-talk, such as saying to oneself, "I'm not going to let these voices run my life!"

*Acceptance.* Some patients find that attending calmly to a symptom and accepting it is quite effective. This strategy may be useful for your relative if the symptom is not too threatening and if acceptance of it can help him or her get on with life. For example, Juan had prominent delusions of reference and believed that others frequently talked about him on the bus, in stores, and at work. He was eventually able to accept and expect these beliefs. This enabled him to make more progress toward important goals, such as working part-time. It also helped him realize that the best type of job for him was one that did not involve very much contact with other people.

Kathy had a delusion that she designed a building that she never received credit for. After years of frustration with trying to get credit and compensation for her "stolen" idea, she began to accept the fact that she would never get the recognition she deserved. Although she continued to believe that she had designed the building, she no longer devoted most of her efforts to proving this and started to pursue other, more realistic goals.

Geoff heard auditory hallucinations almost continuously, and eventually was able to accept that these voices were not going to go away.

*Prayer.* For some people, prayer provides hope, understanding, and acceptance of difficult situations. It is a powerful strategy that enables some patients to cope better with persistent positive symptoms.

## Helping Your Relative Develop Coping Strategies

It is clear from the preceding discussion that there are many possible strategies your relative can use to cope more effectively with persistent positive symptoms. However, most strategies take time and effort to plan and implement. Therefore, it is best if you can adopt a team approach to working with your relative on developing coping strategies. There are good reasons to be optimistic about being able to help your relative cope with these symptoms. Controlled research conducted by Professor Nicholas Tarrier at the University of Manchester in England has shown that systematically working with patients to develop coping strategies for positive symptoms can reduce symptom severity and distress.

The following are guidelines for helping your relative develop effective coping strategies.

*Step 1: Select one positive symptom at a time to work on.* It may be tempting to work on many different symptoms at once, but the more you take on, the slower the progress will be. It is vital that your relative experience some success with coping strategies as soon as possible. The more specific the symptom that you are trying to address, the more rapid change will be. Examples of specific positive symptoms include auditory hallucinations, beliefs that others are talking about you (delusions of reference), and paranoid thinking.

*Step 2: Gather information about the symptom.* Determine what the symptom is like, how it affects your relative, how frequently it occurs and under what circumstances and at what time, and how long it lasts.

Find out how your relative currently deals with the symptom, including what things he or she does that appear to help and what seems to make it worse. Explore whether there are any consequences that might "reinforce" the positive symptom, such as avoidance of certain responsibilities. Learning as much as possible about the symptom and how your relative currently manages it will be helpful when it comes to planning specific coping strategies. The Persistent Positive Symptoms Coping Assessment is provided to help you do this.

For example, Anna Marie was troubled by persistent auditory hallucinations. These hallucinations usually involved one male voice talking to her, telling her she was "a no-good slut" and that she had "no reason to keep on living." Sometimes she heard more than one voice. The hallucinations caused her to feel anxious and depressed. She heard the voices almost all the time. However, they were worst in the late afternoon, when she was sitting around the house after her program. She responded to the voices sometimes by retreating to her room and relaxing, but it didn't seem to help much. She noticed that when she could get out of the house in the late afternoon the voices were less problematic. Sometimes Anna Marie skipped her evening chore of setting the table before dinner because the voices were bothering her.

*Step 3: Modify potentially reinforcing consequences of the symptom.* Sometimes there are positive consequences of a symptom, such as in the example above of Anna Marie, who occasionally skipped setting the table when her voices bothered her. This does not mean that the patient is deliberately *trying* to have the symptom in order to achieve special treatment or that the symptom is an attempt to "manipulate" others. However, the positive consequences can make the symptom more likely to happen. Trying to reduce possibly rewarding effects for a symptom serves to reduce the symptom.

Continuing with the example of Anna Marie, her mother decided to encourage her to set the table, even when her hallucinations bothered her. Anna Marie's mother expressed sympathy to her about the voices she heard, but also stressed the importance of Anna Marie meeting her responsibility of setting the table, even when she was troubled by the voices. Anna Marie agreed to try to be consistent about doing this chore.

*Step 4: Select a coping strategy to work on.* Several hints may prove useful when helping your relative select a coping strategy to work on. Your relative's previous experience with different coping strategies is a good place to start. If your relative has had positive experiences in the past using certain strategies to cope with the symptom, or if he or she is currently employing a strategy that seems to work, one of these strategies can be selected. Starting with a strategy that your relative has used already has an advantage in that he or she does not have to learn that strategy, although it may need to be adapted. However, if your relative

## Persistent Positive Symptoms Coping Assessment

*Instructions:* Complete a separate copy of this form for each positive symptom that you and your relative agree to work on.

1. Describe the symptom. Be as specific as possible._____
_____

2. What is your relative's reaction to symptom? What feelings does the symptom cause? _____
_____

3. a. At what time of day does the symptom occur most often or when is it most severe? _____
_____

   b. At what time of day does the symptom occur least often or is least severe? _____
_____

4. a. In what situations is the symptom most likely to occur or is worst? _____
_____

   b. In what situations is the symptom least likely to occur or is least troubling? _____
_____

5. a. What strategies has the patient tried in the past to cope with the symptom? _____
_____

   b. Which of these strategies has worked? Which have not? ___
_____

6. a. What strategies is the patient currently using to cope with the symptom? _____
_____

   b. Which of these strategies are helpful? Which are not? _____
_____

   c. How often are the helpful coping strategies used? _____
_____

7. Are there any positive consequences of having the symptom, such as avoiding unpleasant tasks or situations? _____
_____

8. Are there any negative consequences, such as not being able to enjoy a movie? _____
_____

frequently uses a certain strategy but continues to experience distress, select a different strategy.

A new strategy can be selected from the list in Figure 10.1 or by identifying other coping strategies. Talk over with your relative which strategy seems most promising. If your relative already uses one strategy and you want to try another, consider a strategy that is in a different category from the first one. For example, Sandra found that listening to music distracted her from her auditory hallucinations (a cognitive strategy), and decided to try another coping strategy for this symptom, engaging her mother in a conversation when the voices became worse (a behavioral strategy).

Your relative may not be convinced that any particular strategy will be helpful. Encourage him or her to try a strategy by saying that if one doesn't work, another can always be tried ("Nothing ventured, nothing gained"). Empathize with your relative that it is hard to try to cope with symptoms, but that by the two of you working together you believe that he or she may benefit and be less troubled.

Returning to the example of Anna Marie, she selected going out for a walk in the afternoon as the first coping strategy to use for dealing with her hallucinations. Anna Marie had used this strategy in the past, but only very infrequently.

*Step 5: Practice the coping strategy.* Helping your relative practice the coping strategy can make a critical difference in whether he or she is able to use the strategy in the most difficult situations. The best way to help your relative practice the strategy is for you to observe while he or she practices it. If your relative is not experiencing the symptom at the time, he or she can practice the coping strategy by pretending that the symptom is present.

When auditory hallucinations are the problem, but your relative is not currently hearing them, you can play the role of the hallucinations, verbalizing the voices out loud while your relative practices the coping strategy. If your strategy involves social activity, the help of a third person can be enlisted so that one person plays the role of the voices and the other is the person involved in the social interaction.

The easiest way for your relative to practice coping strategies in the thinking category is for him or her to first verbalize the thoughts out loud. Plan out what adaptive thoughts will be used before practicing them. Because many patients are not used to employing thinking strategies to cope with symptoms, it may be helpful for you to demonstrate the strategy first, by thinking out loud, followed by your relative trying the strategy, also by thinking out loud. As your relative becomes more familiar with the strategy, he or she can practice it by thinking silently. You may find that your relative needs to practice the strategy many times on different occasions before it starts to feel natural.

Anna Marie did not need much practice for her coping strategy of going out for a walk. For practice, she and her mother did a few role plays in which Anna Marie prepared to go on her walk and headed out the door, while her mother played the role of the hallucinations.

***Step 6: Formulate a plan to implement the coping strategy.*** Once your relative has had some practice with the coping strategy, you can devise a plan to put it into effect. The information you gathered about when and where the symptom is most problematic can be useful in planning how to implement the strategy. Rather than trying the coping strategy every time the symptom occurs, identify one or two of the situations where it occurs most frequently, and focus initially on coping in just those situations. This will make it easier to know whether the strategy is helpful.

When planning, consider how your relative will remember to use the strategy in the specified situation. You may be able to help by prompting your relative, or he or she can use written reminders or other cues. It can also be useful for your relative to rate how helpful the coping strategy was for dealing with the symptom each time it is used in an actual situation. This can be done by making up a record sheet that includes the date, time, and effectiveness of the coping strategy (ratings can be made along the lines of: 1 = not helpful, 2 = somewhat helpful, 3 = very helpful). This record sheet can be tailored to the specific plan that you and your relative agree upon, and modified as the plan is changed.

Sometimes setting a goal for implementing a plan, and identifying a "reward" for following through on the plan, is helpful. This reward can be something that you provide, such as a trip to the video store, or that your relative provides him or herself, such as listening to music. Following up on and troubleshooting the plan on a regular basis is also necessary to evaluate whether your relative is trying the strategy and how it is working.

Anna Marie and her mother agreed upon a plan in which Anna Marie would take a 15-minute walk each afternoon at 4:00 PM, a time at which her voices were often more intense. To help her remember, they posted a reminder sign in the living room, above the TV, where Anna Marie spent much of her time in the afternoon. Each day after the walk Anna Marie agreed to record her walk on a sheet that she and her mother devised, including a rating of how helpful the walk was. Her mother agreed to remind Anna Marie to complete the sheet if she forgot. She and her mother also reached an agreement that if Anna Marie succeeded in going out six of the next seven days, her mother would buy her a new pair of running shoes.

***Step 7: Evaluate the success of the plan.*** A strategy often needs to be used for a while (several days or weeks) before it is effective at reducing the targeted symptom. Therefore, your first concern when following up on a plan is whether the strategy is being implemented, not how effective it is. You may need to encourage and support your relative to keep trying if he or she is following through on the plan but not experiencing any relief. Try to meet with your relative regularly (at least weekly) to evaluate whether the plan is helping and, when success is apparent, to expand the situations in which the coping strategy is used. Be positive about even small improvements, and encourage your relative's continued use of strategies that seem to produce any benefit.

Anna Marie and her mother agreed to meet each week to discuss how the plan was working. After one week there was some success, which became more apparent after two more weeks. At this time, Anna Marie and her mother agreed that an even longer walk might be helpful, so they arrived at plan of slowly working up to 30 minutes per day, by increasing her daily walk by 5 minutes each week.

*Step 8: Develop additional coping strategies.* If little or no improvement occurs after a month or more, it is best to consider alternative strategies. However, even if your relative has experienced success with the new coping strategy, it is preferable to help him or her develop at least one more strategy. Surveys conducted of patients with schizophrenia have found that those who cope most effectively with their symptoms tend to use many different coping strategies. Therefore, a good goal is to help your relative develop multiple coping strategies for each problematic symptom.

Despite Anna Marie's improved ability to cope with her auditory hallucinations, they continued to disturb her. Because Anna Marie already used a behavioral coping strategy, she and her mother decided to explore a strategy that involved changes in thinking. Anna Marie was particularly interested in developing more positive self-talk, which she thought might also help with her tendency to become depressed. Therefore, she and her mother began to work on developing this additional strategy, practicing it, planning its implementation, and following it up. Eventually, Anna Marie developed several other strategies for coping with her hallucinations, which resulted in lowering her distress.

## Tailoring Coping Strategies to Your Relative

The method described above is one general approach to helping a relative develop coping strategies for persistent positive symptoms. These symptoms are not easily changed, and much work may be needed on the parts of both you and your relative. However, the method described here is not the only way to help your relative. You may find a more informal approach easier to manage, such as suggesting different strategies to your relative, posting a list of strategies somewhere your relative will see it, or engaging him or her in a conversation focused on exploring ways of dealing with troubling symptoms.

Our most fundamental message to you is that if your relative is willing to talk about his or her persistent positive symptoms, and experiences some distress due to them, you can help him or her cope more effectively with them.

## Dealing with the Effects of Positive Symptoms on You

Persistent positive symptoms in your relative can have negative effects on you, especially if he or she has little insight into these symptoms. Patients sometimes "talk crazy," are difficult to understand, or falsely accuse others of plotting against them or stealing their thoughts. Sometimes these symptoms lead to verbal or physical aggression or acting on delusions, such as unplugging the refrigerator because the patient believes it is "bugged," staying up late at night talking out loud to voices, or acting inappropriately in public. All of these behaviors can be disruptive to your and your family's routine, leading to tension, anxiety, and frustration. We describe some strategies for handling disruptive behaviors caused by persistent positive symptoms. To a large extent, these strategies involve using methods described elsewhere in this book for setting expectations, reducing tension, and dealing with behavior problems.

### Setting Realistic Expectations

High levels of stress and tension will be present if your expectations for your relative's behavior differ radically from his or her actual behavior. Setting realistic expectations involves anticipating what your relative is *capable* of, given that he or she has schizophrenia. Your relative's past behavior is one indication of what he or she is likely to do in the future. Although improvements in behavior are possible, they tend to occur slowly, over long periods of time, and with much family support and encouragement. For your current expectations of your relative to be realistic, it is best if they do not involve major behavioral changes. For example, if for years your relative has responded to auditory hallucinations by loudly talking back, it is probably not realistic to expect him or her to simply stop talking back. A more realistic expectation or goal might be for him or her not to *shout* back at the voices, to confine his or her talking back to a particular room in the house, or to whisper to the voices after 11:00 PM.

Other factors to consider in setting realistic expectations for your relative include whether or not he or she is responsive to requests you make and whether he or she can be motivated to work toward particular goals. If your relative is not responsive or is difficult to motivate, these limitations need to be taken into account when setting expectations.

### Enforcing Household Rules

In the previous chapter we stressed the importance of establishing household rules if your relative lives at home. Setting such rules helps structure patients' time at home, lowers the resentment of other family members, builds self-esteem for patients who follow the rules, sets limits on disruptive or dangerous behavior, and reduces your and other relatives' anxiety due to unpredictable behavior. Although you cannot set a household rule that your relative will not have a particular symptom (such as hearing voices), you can establish rules regarding disruptive behaviors that are a response to the symptom (such as shouting back at the voices).

Two general considerations are involved in setting rules concerning your relative's responses to his or her positive symptoms: Which rules can you realistically expect your relative to be able to follow? And which behaviors are you willing to put up with and which not? Using the example of a patient who often shouts back at voices, upsetting other family members and awakening people at night, rules can be aimed at lowering the loudness of the patient's talking back or limiting the rooms in the house where he or she talks to voices (such as only in the patient's room). Your relative may respond to hallucinations by punching walls or destroying property. These behaviors are more often the result of frustration with the symptom than anger toward other family members, but they can be very disruptive to the family, and costly as well. Establishing rules that address the destruction of property may be helpful in this respect. Your relative may be paranoid and may have threatened you or other family members, or actually tried to injure you. Once again, deciding what rules you want family members to live by can have an effect on these behaviors.

A vital part of establishing household rules is determining and enforcing the consequences of following and not following the rules. The essentials of using contingencies to change your relative's behavior are described in the preceding chapter. Ultimately, if your relative's behavior in response to his or her persistent positive symptoms is very disruptive, you will need to decide which behaviors you do not feel comfortable living with and how far you are willing to go to prevent the disruptive effects of certain behaviors. If your relative lives at home, the ultimate contingency you have to work with is his or her privilege of continuing to live at home. This contingency can be used, however, only if you are willing to enforce it, which could mean requiring your relative to live elsewhere if he or she does not follow certain rules.

Severe, persistent positive symptoms can have a profound impact on some patients' behavior that is difficult or impossible for family members to control at home, even when setting clear expectations and consequences for the behavior. In our experience, some patients respond to positive symptoms in ways that are so disruptive or threatening that living at home presents an overwhelming burden on other family members or actual risk. Often these patients do better and even experience some relief from their symptoms if they move to another, more structured, supervised living arrangement. Relatives can continue to be supportive, and tension in family relationships often improves when the patient lives elsewhere.

### Using Communication and Problem Solving Skills

As reviewed in Chapters 6 and 7, using good communication skills and taking a problem-solving approach to problem behaviors in your relative can be very helpful. The essence of good communication with your relative about his or her behaviors is being brief and to the point, making good eye contact, being specific about the behaviors you would like changed, and avoiding harsh and overly critical statements. Often a simple communication about a problem behavior can be quite effective, for example, "It really bothers me when you talk to yourself in the living room. I would appreciate it if you would go to your room when you want to talk to yourself."

Similarly, using problem solving can help generate a variety of solutions to problem behaviors. For example, family members may find it disruptive when the patient talks about a certain fixed delusion (such as being in league with the Devil), and may get together to plan how to handle the situation. Possible solutions that the family might consider include ignoring such talk, asking the patient to stop, listening sympathetically, switching the topic, and refocusing the patient on another activity.

### Providing Structure

There is strong evidence that the more structured activity a patient is engaged in, the less severe his or her psychotic symptoms will be and the less likely disruptive or bizarre behavior will occur. It appears that engaging in a meaningful but not overly demanding structure draws the attention of patients with persistent positive symptoms away from those symptoms and toward the activity. Therefore, attempting to increase the structure of your relative's day can have beneficial effects on his or her positive symptoms. Structure can be increased by helping him or her develop a routine, both around the house and also outside of the home. Out-of-home activities, such as day treatment, drop-in social programs, volunteer work, and paid employment, can result in reductions in positive symptoms and their associated behaviors. However, all attempts at increasing structure need to be gradual. Too much change at once might be too stressful for your relative.

## Coping with Negative Symptoms

Negative symptoms, such as apathy, social avoidance, and blunted affect (diminished emotional expressiveness) are the true hallmark of schizophrenia. Although negative symptoms are sometimes present in other disorders, such as depression, they are much more prominent in schizophrenia. Negative symptoms tend to be more stable over time than positive symptoms, and mild negative symptoms (such as having few friends or interests) often precede by many years the development of positive symptoms and the full syndrome of schizophrenia. Thus, you may have noticed early signs of negative symptoms several years before your relative developed schizophrenia.

In addition to the fact that negative symptoms are common and stable over time, these symptoms are important for several other reasons. Patients with more negative symptoms tend to experience greater difficulties meeting role expectations and enjoying social relationships. Furthermore, patients with more severe negative symptoms may be more prone to experiencing positive symptoms and relapses.

Aside from the effects negative symptoms have on your relative, they can also affect you. Many family members find problems such as avoidance, apathy, and lack of follow-through to be even more frustrating than the positive symptoms. Learning how to cope more effectively with negative symptoms, including how *you* cope with it as well as how your relative does, can improve both your relationship and your relative's adjustment to his or her illness. We describe below how to evaluate negative symptoms in your relative and then offer coping strategies for helping you and your relative manage these symptoms.

### Evaluating Negative Symptoms in Your Relative

Negative symptoms are described in detail in Chapter 2. Basically, these symptoms are characterized by the patient *not* doing, thinking, or feeling things that other people ordinarily do, think, and feel. For example, not laughing at something most people think is funny (blunted affect) or not enjoying close relationships with others (anhedonia) are negative symptoms.

There are many different ways of categorizing negative symptoms. One of the most widely used approaches was developed by Nancy Andreasen, M.D., Ph.D. at the University of Iowa, who identified five different types of negative symptoms: blunted affect (diminished facial or vocal expressiveness), alogia (diminished speech or thought), apathy (difficulty initiating or carrying out plans), anhedonia (lack of pleasure), and

## Negative Symptoms Checklist*

*Instructions:* Place a check next to each negative symptom which you have observed in your relative over the past month.

*Blunted Affect*

1. Diminished or absent facial expressiveness      _____
   during interactions with others
2. Unchanging, monotonous, or inexpressive         _____
   voice tone when conversing
3. Lack of gestures when conversing                _____

*Alogia*

4. Little said during interactions                 _____
5. What is said in conversation doesn't add        _____
   up to much
6. Stopping in the middle of a sentence and        _____
   forgetting what was to be said

*Apathy*

7. Difficulty initiating or following through on   _____
   activities
8. Lack of interest in doing things                _____
9. Sitting around doing little or engaged in       _____
   activities requiring little effort (such as
   watching TV)

*Anhedonia*

10. Lack of enjoyment from recreational activities _____
11. Inability to feel close to others, such as     _____
    friends or relatives
12. Difficulty experiencing pleasure from anything _____

*Inattention*

13. Becoming easily distracted during             _____
    conversations
14. Difficulty focusing attention on a task, such  _____
    as reading a magazine article or getting
    dressed
15. Stopping midway through something, such        _____
    as a task or conversation

* Adapted from N. C. Andreasen, "Modified Scale for the Assessment of Negative Symptoms" Department of Health and Human Services, 1985

inattention (difficulty paying attention). Some clues to determine which negative symptoms your relative is experiencing are contained in the Negative Symptoms Checklist.

## Distinguishing Negative Symptoms from Other Problems

William T. Carpenter, M.D. at the University of Maryland, has pointed out that negative symptoms can be either primary or secondary. *Secondary* negative symptoms may be caused by factors such as depression, anxiety, medication side effects, or even the positive symptoms of schizophrenia. *Primary* negative symptoms are not related to or caused by any of these factors. Trying to distinguish between primary and secondary negative symptoms can provide you with clues about how to help your relative with these symptoms.

Negative symptoms can overlap with the symptoms of depression. For example, lack of enjoyment from activities (anhedonia) can occur because it is a negative symptom or because of depression. Similarly, anxiety can lead to social avoidance or lack of enjoyment. The primary distinction between negative symptoms and depression or anxiety is your relative's mood. If your relative's mood is low and he or she talks about feeling sad or down, depression may be a problem. If he or she says he or she is anxious, then anxiety may be a problem. If your relative has a number of the symptoms listed in the Negative Symptoms Checklist, but does not report feeling sad or anxious, negative symptoms may be the primary problem. Further information on assessing depression and anxiety is provided in Chapter 11.

Medication side effects can also be mistaken for negative symptoms. As discussed in Chapter 3, one common side effect of antipsychotic medication is akinesia, which is reflected by diminished expressiveness. Akinesia and blunted affect can be difficult to distinguish from one another without altering the patient's dosage or type of medication. High levels of medication can also cause side effects of drowsiness, lethargy, and low energy levels, making the patient appear apathetic and uninterested. If you are concerned that your relative may have these side effects, consult his or her psychiatrist.

Positive symptoms can also contribute to negative symptoms. For example, if your relative avoids contact with others when auditory hallucinations become more severe, or if persistent delusions of reference interfere with your relative's ability to enjoy him or herself, these positive symptoms could cause negative symptoms such as social withdrawal and anhedonia. This does not mean that if your relative has both positive and negative symptoms (which most patients with schizophrenia do) that the negative symptoms are *caused* by the positive symptoms, although it is a possibility. It is also possible that both types of symptoms are independent, or even that the negative symptoms are leading to the positive symptoms. For example, if your relative tends to avoid people and is engaged in few structured activities (negative symptoms), this lack of meaningful stimulation can increase his or her vulnerability to positive symptoms, such as hallucinations.

The factors that can contribute to negative symptoms, and questions for determining whether they might be contributing to your relative's negative symptoms, are listed in Figure 10.2. If you think that some of your relative's negative symptoms may be secondary to one of these factors, one way of helping him or her deal with these symptoms is to address the underlying problem. Thus, strategies for reducing depression and anxiety (Chapter 11), medication side effects (Chapter 3), or distress caused by positive symptoms (this chapter), may have beneficial effects on these secondary negative symptoms. If you think that your relative's negative symptoms are primary, or if negative symptoms persist despite your attempts to address other underlying factors (such as depression), strategies for coping with specific negative symptoms can be helpful.

## Coping with Specific Symptoms

Negative symptoms pose somewhat different problems than positive symptoms. Positive symptoms usually cause distress to the patient, who may or may not be willing to talk about the symptoms and work toward developing better coping strategies. Positive symptoms are a problem to the family when they lead to behaviors that are disruptive, offensive, or

### Factors That Can Contribute to Negative Symptoms

| Factor | Questions to Ask |
| --- | --- |
| Depression and anxiety | Is my relative's mood depressed? Is my relative anxious or fearful? |
| Medication side effects | Have increases in medication led to worse negative symptoms? Does my relative appear more sedated than he or she used to? |
| Positive symptoms | Did my relative's positive symptoms get worse *before* his or her negative symptoms? Does my relative say that positive symptoms interfere with initiating or enjoying activities? |

Figure 10.2

frightening. Negative symptoms, on the other hand, tend to be less distressing to patients. Patients may have a vague awareness of their negative symptoms, but often these symptoms don't bother them very much. Although patients may not be distressed by negative symptoms, relatives frequently are, which can lead to tensions in the home. In many families, the strains caused by negative symptoms are greater than the stress of positive symptoms. Thus, the best strategies for coping with negative symptoms are those that both reduce your own distress and help your relative compensate or overcome the limitations imposed by his or her symptoms.

### Blunted Affect

Most patients with blunted affect are surprisingly unaware of their lack of emotional expressiveness. Thus, if your relative has blunted affect, it probably is not a source of significant distress to him or her. However, it can lead to misunderstandings between you and your relative.

With most people, facial expression and tone of voice are a good indication of their feelings. However, this is not so for patients with schizophrenia who have blunted affect. These patients' lack of expressiveness can be misleading. Patients with blunted affect often experience emotions just as strongly as other people, they simply do not convey these feelings in their facial expressions or tone of voice. For example, just because your relative does not appear interested when you are conversing with him or her, or does not appear to enjoy watching a movie, doesn't mean that he or she isn't actually interested in you or isn't enjoying the movie.

The best way to avoid misunderstandings that arise from blunted affect is to get in the habit of checking with your relative about how he or she feels and to avoid assuming you know his or her feelings without asking.

### Alogia

The most common problem associated with alogia is poverty of speech (not talking much). A less common problem is that when the patient talks what he or she says doesn't add up to much (poverty of speech content). If your relative says little, he or she is probably aware of this, but not distressed by it. You, on the other hand, may have found it frustrating to communicate with your relative when he or she has so little to say.

The most important first step toward coping effectively with alogia is to realize that this symptom is not your relative's fault. Many patients with schizophrenia have this problem, which may be related to the cognitive deficits associated with the illness. Accepting this symptom as a part of the illness involves not blaming your relative for having difficulty holding up his or her end of a conversation. Acceptance also means not taking your relative's lack of communication personally; poverty of speech is not an indication that your relative doesn't like you or care about you, it is just a symptom of schizophrenia.

Although alogia is a symptom, there are ways of making conversations with your relative easier and more comfortable. One strategy that some families find helpful is to make a special point of doing activities together, such as taking shopping trips, going to the movies, or going on nature walks. Doing things together provides a way of being with each other that puts less pressure on your relative to maintain a conversation. It allows your relative to talk at a pace that is less taxing and permits many breaks, making the overall experience more enjoyable for both of you. In addition, doing activities together provides good topics for later conversation. For example, after going somewhere together, you can later bring up the trip and exchange views about the experience.

### Apathy and Anhedonia

Although apathy and anhedonia are not the same, most patients who have one symptom also have the other. Furthermore, the same coping strategies tend to be effective for both symptoms. Therefore, strategies for managing these two symptoms are considered together.

Of all the symptoms of schizophrenia, relatives often find apathy the most frustrating. One of the reasons you may find it hard to cope with your relative's apathy is that it may seem to be more under his or her control than other symptoms, such as hallucinations. For example, we have heard many family members express the same sentiment as Bob's father, "I know Bob has schizophrenia and can't help that, but if only he could go to his program regularly or work at a part-time job!" However, apathy is not directly under your relative's control; like hallucinations, delusions, or alogia, apathy is a symptom of schizophrenia.

Just as the first step toward coping effectively with alogia is acceptance, so is it also the first step toward coping with apathy. Realizing that apathy is part of your relative's illness will help you avoid blaming him or her for this symptom, and may enable you to more firmly establish realistic expectations for what he or she can accomplish. Family members who cope effectively with apathy often have developed a positive mental attitude that enables them to maintain a good relationship with their relative. Examples of positive self-statements family members have used to help them accept their relative's apathy are these:

- I know he or she is doing the best that he or she can.

- I understand that his or her difficulty doing things and following through is a part of his or her illness.

- He or she is not lazy, this is just a symptom of schizophrenia.

- I can't change his or her behavior, but maybe I can help a little.

- We both have to keep living our own lives.

Accepting apathy as a part of your relative's illness does not mean that there is nothing you can do to help him or her with this symptom. There are a number of different strategies you can explore that may help to reduce your relative's apathy and increase his or her enjoyment (reduce anhedonia). Many families have found these strategies to be helpful, although usually some apathy and anhedonia continues to persist.

*Automatically include the patient in activities with family members.* Left alone, patients with apathy and anhedonia may just sit around the house doing nothing. By trying to include your relative in activities that other family members are doing, you can often engage him or her in conversation and sometimes stimulate some of his or her interest. These activities can include day-to-day tasks such as shopping, and taking a trip to the bank or dry cleaner, as well as enjoyable activities, such as spontaneously going out for pizza, a trip to the museum, or the movies.

When inviting your relative to join you doing something, avoid placing expectations on his or her behavior. Simply invite your relative to come along, and allow him or her to participate to the extent he or she desires. By not placing demands on your relative's behavior, you may make him or her more willing to join you in activities. Patients often have trouble anticipating what it will be like to do a particular activity, so they have little interest and expect not to enjoy it. Getting your relative involved in actual activities circumvents his or her negative expectations and provides experiences that sometimes turn out to be more fun or interesting than expected.

*Regularly schedule enjoyable activities.* As previously described, apathy and anhedonia often involve having negative expectations about how enjoyable an activity will be. Patients may think they know how they will feel when they do something, but these expectations are not necessarily correct. When patients get into the habit of doing a recreational activity on a regular basis, their enjoyment of the activity gradually grows. By scheduling specific recreational activities each week, you can help your relative learn how to anticipate and enjoy activities such as going to the movies, going out to eat, bowling, visiting art galleries, and walking in the park.

At first, you may need to do most of the work in selecting an activity that you think your relative may enjoy. You may also need to convince him or her to participate in it with you. Once your relative agrees to come along, place as few expectations on his or her behavior as possible, and after it is over check in to find out what the experience was like. Do not expect your relative to report after the first time that he or she found the activity very enjoyable; it may take many occasions before he or she feels real pleasure. However, if you are able to stick with doing an activity together over a period of time, chances are good that your relative will begin to enjoy it and become able to anticipate these positive feelings. If one activity doesn't seem to work over a period of time, try another.

For example, one patient, Selma, was interested in practically nothing and reported being unable to enjoy anything. Selma's parents decided to try scheduling a regular activity that would involve her to see whether they could improve her apathy and anhedonia. After discussing it together, they agreed to eat dinner out once a week. They chose Wednesday as the night each week they ate out. Selma was not very interested in coming out to dinner with her parents, but with some encouragement she agreed to come. At first, they went to the same restaurant each week, so that Selma could become familiar with it. For the first six weeks, Selma ordered the same meal each week, a cheeseburger and fries. After the first time, she seemed to find the dinners a little more enjoyable. Gradu-

---

### Strategies for Helping Your Relative Cope with Apathy and Anhedonia

*Automatically include your relative in activities with other family members:*

- Make a habit of inviting him or her to join you when going somewhere.

- Include your relative in routine errands (such as shopping) and simple pleasures (such as taking a walk).

- Don't place expectations on his or her behavior.

- Talk about the event with your relative later in the day.

*Regularly schedule enjoyable activities that include your relative:*

- Choose an activity that will not require much effort at first.

- Try hard to convince your relative to join you.

- Select a specific time each week to do the activity.

- Do the same activity each week; stick to it for at least several weeks.

- Talk with your relative about the activity later in the day or the next day.

- After a few weeks, begin mentioning the activity to your relative and anticipating what it will be like.

---

ally, Selma began to try different selections from the menu. One week, after a few months of eating out, she indicated to her mother on Tuesday that she was thinking of trying a chicken dish the next night they went to the restaurant. Selma had begun to look forward to their night out. Eventually, the family agreed to begin trying different restaurants on their night out to expand the range of their experience.

*Identify recreational activities that were formerly enjoyed.* At the core of apathy and anhedonia is the expectation that activities will not be enjoyable. Identifying potentially pleasurable activities can be difficult, because your relative may give you little help. One key to finding activities that your relative might enjoy is to explore activities he or she used to do previously but no longer does. Patients sometimes give up hobbies, sports, or interests because of the disruption caused by their schizophrenia (positive symptoms, hospitalizations, family conflicts) rather than out

---

## Strategies for Helping Your Relative Cope with Apathy and Anhedonia

*Identify recreational activities that your relative formerly enjoyed:*

- Think of things your relative used to do (such as hobbies, sports, interests).
- Consider how to engage your relative in this interest again in a small step that takes little effort.

*Break down big goals into small steps:*

- Talk with your relative about how he or she would like things to be different.
- Identify a first small step toward that goal.
- Use problem solving to plan how to work toward the goal.

*Increase daily structure:*

- Build some structure into every day.
- Plan recreational activities for the weekend.

*Focus on the future, not the past:*

- Avoid comparisons with how your relative used to be.
- Convey optimism for improving the future.
- Strategize together about how to make changes.

---

of a lack of enjoyment from the activity. They may not have positive expectations for these activities because it has been so long since they tried them or because it reminds them of the time before they were ill. By helping your relative identify these activities and form a plan to try them again, you can help him or her experience some unanticipated enjoyment. Bear in mind that it may be necessary for your relative to become familiar with the activity over a period of time before it truly becomes enjoyable again.

For example, Pedro had been an avid sports enthusiast as an adolescent before he developed schizophrenia. He had been an excellent baseball player, attended many games, and followed several sports on TV and in the papers. These interests seemed to fall by the wayside after he developed schizophrenia; he didn't even know how his favorite baseball team had done the previous year and showed no interest in anything. His mother and brother remembered his love of sports and decided to try to see if this interest could be revived. After talking it over, Pedro agreed to try watching some baseball games on the TV with his brother. The first several times he couldn't watch the whole game, although he admitted some enjoyment in watching part of it. Over time, he became able to watch an entire game on TV, and he and his brother went to a local minor league game. Later that year, Pedro's mother gave him a subscription to a sports magazine and he began reading occasional articles from the magazine.

*Break down big goals into small steps.* Your relative may have vague ideas of how he or she would like things to be different, but not of how to achieve these goals. Apathy and anhedonia may result from this difficulty in pursuing goals. By talking about these goals with your relative, you can help him or her identify small steps that can be taken toward the goal, without applying pressure to take those steps. With each step, you can praise and encourage your relative for the progress, while reminding him or her of how the step contributes to the longer-term goal. Strategies for solving problems can be useful in helping your relative make progress toward goals (see Chapter 7).

*Increase daily structure.* Just as increased structure can have beneficial effects on positive symptoms, it can also be helpful for apathy and anhedonia. Apathy and anhedonia can be a byproduct of inactivity. Doing nothing can lead to caring about nothing, which can worsen the tendency to do nothing. This vicious circle can be broken by ensuring that your relative is engaged in at least some daily structured activities, such as a day or vocational program, volunteer work or a job. Planning specific activities to do over the weekend can help to structure this time, such as taking a walk, going to the store, doing chores, or visiting a museum.

*Focus on the future, not the past.* For some patients, apathy and anhedonia are partially caused by their own awareness of how they have changed. They may feel discouraged, that trying is not worth the effort. Reminding your relative of how he or she used to be different can contribute to this feeling of being a "failure." Focusing instead on the future and strategizing with your relative about how to make changes avoids unnecessary and discouraging comparisons with the past.

### Inattention

Problems with attention are very common in schizophrenia. Not only are these difficulties quite apparent to family members, but patients themselves are frequently aware of them, and sometimes find them quite upsetting. You may have experienced some problems communicating with your relative because of his or her impairments in attention. Your relative may also have told you about feeling frustrated when his or her poor attention has interfered with activities such as working, reading, or following directions. Fortunately, there are a variety of strategies you can use to compensate for your relative's problems with attention when communicating with him or her, and other strategies you can suggest to help him or her cope with and improve on these limitations. However, it is also important for you to adjust your expectations of your relative's capabilities based on your understanding of his or her difficulty with attention.

*Adopt strategies for improved communication.* Many of the communication skills outlined in Chapter 6 can be useful in compensating for attentional impairments when talking with your relative. Using good eye contact can ensure that your relative is paying attention to you when you are talking. Speaking in short sentences, not talking too quickly, and pausing often can help compensate for the slower rate at which your relative processes information. Asking your relative questions to find out what he or she understood can help you evaluate whether you are getting your point across. Avoid asking yes-or-no questions, since these are easy to respond to without understanding. Instead, try asking open-ended questions, such as "What was your understanding of what I just said?" and "What did I just say I was concerned about?"

Your relative's problems with attention may be a bigger obstacle to communication at some times than at others. For example, he or she may walk away while you are talking in the middle of a sentence, or seem very preoccupied or "out of it" and have great difficulty staying on the topic, even with frequent reminders. An alternative to strenuously trying to get your relative to attend during these conversations is to come back at a different time, when your relative's attention is better. If your relative always has severe problems with attention, it is important to keep your interactions with him or her as brief and to the point as possible.

*Develop organizing skills.* One of the biggest problems that poor attention causes is that it is difficult for the patient to get organized. Dis-

## Strategies for Improving Communication

- Establish good eye contact

- Speak slowly, in short sentences, taking frequent pauses

- Keep interactions brief and to the point

- Ask questions to check on his or her understanding of the conversation

- If communication is very difficult, try again at a different time

organization is a natural byproduct of problems with attention because in order to organize and develop a plan, you need to be able to attend to many details. If you can only attend to a few details at a time, organization will suffer.

Teaching your relative better organizing skills is an excellent strategy for helping him or her compensate for poor attention. Some organizing skills that patients find helpful include keeping a pocket calendar (to record appointments, telephone numbers, notes), making lists, and holding a regular planning meeting (such as a weekly session to plan for the upcoming week). These skills take time to teach and require some motivation on your relative's part. However, if you break each of these skills into small steps, as described below, your relative will be able to learn them and overcome some of his or her attentional limitations.

*Break down tasks into manageable steps.* Breaking down tasks into small component steps can help your relative compensate for problems with attention. Your relative may find that he or she easily becomes lost when working on a big task, such as losing track of where he or she was, or has trouble resuming a task after a break. Breaking the job into several smaller pieces and focusing on only one piece at a time decreases the load on your relative's attention and makes it easier to keep track of what needs to be done next.

Dividing up a task into smaller parts is a general strategy that can be used to do jobs or chores, to work toward personal goals, or even to develop recreational interests. For example, Hank really wanted to be able to read mystery novels, but he couldn't keep his attention on the reading for more than a few minutes. He and his father talked about this, and his father suggested Hank start with some brief articles from a detective magazine. They bought a magazine, and his father identified some articles for him to start with. Even these articles were too long for Hank to read in one sitting, so they agreed that reading two paragraphs at a time would be a good first step. After reading two paragraphs, he would summarize what he had read to his father, and then take a break. After some success with this plan, they increased the reading to three paragraphs at a time, and so forth. Over a period of time, Hank was able to read some articles in the magazine without any breaks, and others with one or two breaks. He began to work on reading short mystery novels, and found that his ability to attend had improved substantially.

*Improve attention through practice.* To some extent, you can help your relative improve his or her attention through practice, providing that he or she is interested. The example above of how Hank improved his ability to concentrate on reading illustrates one way of accomplishing this. Many other strategies are possible. The basic idea is to choose an interesting activity that requires attention, but in which the time spent on the activity can be controlled by you and your relative. Then your relative starts out by spending a brief time on the activity, and gradually increases the amount of time. Your relative may find it especially helpful if you join him or her in the activity. Some examples of activities that families have used to help their relatives improve attention include:

- Working out with an exercise tape
- Watching a game show and trying to beat the contestants by saying the answers first
- Playing word games or puzzles from the newspaper or game books
- Playing video games, cards, board games

*Look for tasks your relative can do at his or her own pace.* The frustrations of a limited attention span are often related to the tasks that patients are expected to perform, at home, at work, or at a day treatment program. Instead of trying to improve your relative's ability to attend, an alternative is to identify tasks that your relative can do at his or her pace and that allow him or her to take frequent breaks. For example, doing the dishes can be done at one's own pace, whereas cooking or setting the table require more timing. The closer the match you achieve between your relative's attentional capacity and the demands of his or her environment (at home and elsewhere), the better everyone is going to feel.

# 11

# Depression and Anxiety

Problems with depression and anxiety are among the most common reasons people in the general population seek psychological and psychiatric help. Indeed, surveys of psychiatric problems indicate that about 10 percent of all people suffer from significant depression at some time during their lives and 15 percent have an anxiety disorder. Considering how common it is for people with no other psychiatric disorders to experience difficulties with their mood, it is no surprise that these problems are even more prominent among patients with schizophrenia. Although estimates vary as to how common these problems are among people with schizophrenia, it is safe to assume that the vast majority of all patients experience depression, anxiety, or both. For a significant number of patients, these painful emotions interfere with social and vocational adjustment, day-to-day functioning, and the quality of life.

Despite the prominence of anxiety and depression in patients with schizophrenia, there are ways that you can help your relative. In this chapter we discuss the nature of depression and anxiety problems in patients with schizophrenia, how to evaluate whether your relative experiences difficulties with these emotions, and strategies for coping with or overcoming them. As someone who is faced with managing the serious illness of schizophrenia, you too may be no stranger to depression and anxiety. Therefore, we will also address how you can deal with these feelings when they arise in yourself.

# Depression in Schizophrenia

Patients with schizophrenia are especially prone to depression. Almost all people with this disorder report feelings of sadness and hopelessness at some time. There are a variety of different reasons your relative may be especially susceptible to depression. Many patients experience auditory hallucinations of voices that criticize them, call them derogatory names, or exhort them to hurt themselves. When these voices are chronic and there is no escape, depression may be a natural response. Some patients are acutely aware of how their illness has affected them, including the limitations it places on their ability to achieve personal goals and the differences that exist between themselves and their peers who do not have schizophrenia. If your relative has insight into his or her illness, it may have the disadvantage of making him or her more aware of the social stigma associated with mental illness. Patients with better social functioning and with friends who are not psychiatric patients may also be vulnerable to depression because they understand that they are "different."

Some of the problems of depression in schizophrenia are reflected in patients thinking thoughts about hurting or killing themselves (*suicidal ideation*) and attempting suicide. About half (50 percent) of all patients with schizophrenia make a suicide attempt at some time during their life, and about one in every ten patients dies from suicide. This risk of suicide is much higher than in the general population. Most patients who have suicidal ideation or who make suicide attempts have problems with depression. Sometimes patients make suicide attempts because they have hallucinations that command them to do so, even though they do not feel depressed; however, this does not appear to happen often. In Chapter 13, "Responding to Crises," we describe strategies for evaluating your relative's risk for suicide, taking steps to prevent suicide attempts, and responding to an imminent threat of suicide.

Partially as a consequence of depression, many patients find it difficult to pursue employment or improve their social relationships; their hopelessness makes them give up and renders them unable to enjoy even the simple pleasures of life. Helping your relative cope effectively with depression involves creating a sense of optimism, a belief that the future can be better and a willingness to try. Instilling a more positive mental attitude can improve both the quality of your relative's day-to-day experiences and the course and long-term prognosis of his or her illness. Strategies described in this chapter for coping with depression are aimed at helping to create feelings of optimism and hope.

To assist you in helping your relative, we describe the symptoms of depression, followed by how to distinguish depression from other common problems in schizophrenia, such as negative symptoms and medication side effects. The role of depression as a precursor to relapse is also discussed. Then we review a number of strategies that we have found useful in improving depression in patients with schizophrenia.

## Symptoms of Depression

There are many different symptoms of depression. The most common symptoms can be divided into three broad categories: mood disturbances, negative thoughts, and physical and behavioral changes. Examples of symptoms in each of these categories are provided below.

### Mood Disturbances

A variety of different negative moods are often present in depression. The most common mood is a feeling of sadness, a sense of loss or hurt that may be constant over time. Sad feelings are often reflected in the patient's facial expressions and voice tone. Sometimes, however, the sad feelings are present but are not apparent in the voice or facial expression. This feeling of sadness may be accompanied by feelings of guilt; your relative may excessively ruminate over mistakes he or she has made in the past or assume blame for things he or she did not do. If your relative has severe depression, he or she may experience feelings of dread, a unique and horrible feeling that is difficult to describe but contains elements of pain, fear, and despair. These feelings can make it difficult for patients to face the day each morning. Patients with depression may also have feelings of anger (directed at themselves or others) and irritability, although some feelings of sadness usually are also present.

### Negative Thoughts

Negative thinking and mood problems go hand in hand. Some of the most common negative thoughts in patients with depression include hopelessness, helplessness, and worthlessness. Your relative may be overly self-critical and perfectionistic, which results in his or her becoming easily discouraged and giving up. Your relative may ruminate or brood excessively about negative topics, including death, or have suicidal ideation.

### Physical and Behavioral Changes

A very common sign of depression is loss of appetite. Your relative may also have difficulty sleeping, either sleeping too much or too little. Patients often report a loss of energy, which may be accompanied by slowed activity and social withdrawal. You may have observed some of these signs of depression in your relative (such as eating less), and your relative may have described other signs. Sometimes depression is reflected by an *increase* in activity level, such as agitation.

## Distinguishing Depression from Other Common Problems in Schizophrenia

Evaluating whether your relative is experiencing depression can be complicated by a number of other factors, including the presence of negative symptoms, medication side effects, and physical problems.

### Negative Symptoms

Negative symptoms are easily mistaken for depression. For example, if your relative has blunted affect (flattened facial expression, inexpressive tone of voice), talking with him or her may leave you with the impression that he or she is depressed because of the apparent lack of enjoyment or engagement in the conversation. Similarly, if your relative experiences less enjoyment from recreational activities or social relationships (anhedonia), you might conclude that this is due to an underlying depression. In both of these cases, it is possible that your relative is experiencing negative symptoms, depression, or both. The confusion arises from the fact that these two types of symptoms overlap. People with depression do experience less enjoyment from activities and relationships, and are often less expressive when interacting with others. However, lack of enjoyment or expressiveness in a person with schizophrenia does not necessarily imply the presence of depression and may be due solely to negative symptoms.

The best way to clarify what your relative is feeling is to ask him or her. Your relative's reports of sadness, guilt, hopelessness, helplessness, and self-blame are the most important indicators as to whether he or she is depressed.

### Medication Side Effects

In addition to negative symptoms, two side effects of antipsychotic medications can easily be mistaken for depression. These side effects need to be recognized before they can be successfully treated. (See Chapter 3 for further information about treating these side effects.)

Akinesia causes the patient to show a reduction in spontaneous movements, such as facial expression and gestures, as well as difficulty in initiating usual activities. Akinesia is very difficult to distinguish from blunted affect. However, akinesia can be improved by altering the dosage or type of antipsychotic medication or side effect medication. Just as it may be easy to mistake blunted affect for depression, akinesia may be mistaken for depression. Talking with your relative about how he or she feels is the best strategy for assessing depression. If you are concerned that your relative may have akinesia, consult his or her physician.

Akathisia causes feelings of restlessness, usually accompanied by such behaviors as pacing or rocking from foot to foot. Akathisia is a very upsetting side effect for many patients, and it can make the patient appear unusually agitated. The primary distinction between akathisia and depression is that in akathisia, the patient's distress is mainly due to the feeling of restlessness, whereas in depression distress stems from feelings of sadness, hopelessness, and so forth. Once again, talking with your relative is the key to understanding whether he or she has depression. Akathisia can be effectively treated by modifying the dosage or type of antipsychotic medication. If you are concerned that your relative may have akathisia, consult his or her physician.

### Physical Problems

Symptoms of depression can also occur as a result of physical conditions such as anemia, thyroid gland malfunction, and diabetes. Furthermore, certain medications used to treat heart disease and hypertension can produce mild symptoms of depression. One type of medication for heart disease, beta blockers (such as Inderal), can produce some symptoms of depression. Beta blockers are also occasionally used in the treatment of schizophrenia and antipsychotic medication side effects. Encouraging your relative to get a physical exam can help to determine whether his or her symptoms of depression are the result of a physical condition.

## Assessing Depression in Your Relative

It is clear that there are many different symptoms of depression, and that these symptoms can overlap with other symptoms of schizophrenia, medication side effects, or physical problems. Two worksheets, the Symptoms of Depression Checklist and the Complicating Factors Checklist (of factors that resemble, overlap with depression, or actually cause depression), can help you get a better idea of whether depression is a problem. You will need to complete these checklists working together with your relative. There is no set number of symptoms that must be present to conclude that your relative has depression, although some mood problems are usually present, particularly feelings of sadness or dread. The more symptoms that are present, the more likely it is that depression is a problem.

### Depression and Relapse

Research on the course of schizophrenia over time has found that increases in symptoms of depression frequently take place several weeks before a major relapse of psychotic symptoms. Often the changes in mood are subtle, but to family members who know the patient well, these changes can be quite apparent. Therefore, it is important to recognize that a recent increase in depressive symptoms in your relative may be an early warning sign of relapse. This is a cue to put into action the plan you developed for responding to early warning signs (see Chapter 4). This chapter focuses on strategies for helping your relative cope with persistent depression, that is not simply an early warning sign of relapse.

# Symptoms of Depression Checklist

*Instructions:* Place a check next to each symptom that your relative has had over the past month.

*Mood Symptoms*

Sadness _____

Guilt _____

Dread _____

Irritability _____

Anger _____

*Negative Thoughts*

Hopelessness _____

Helplessness _____

Worthlessness _____

Thoughts about death _____

Suicidal thoughts _____

*Physical and Behavioral Changes*

Loss of appetite _____

Sleep problems _____

Slowed activity level _____

Agitation _____

## Complicating Factors Checklist

*Instructions:* Place a check next to each factor that you think might have been present in your relative over the past month.

*Negative Symptoms*

Blunted affect                                          _____

Anhedonia                                               _____

*Antipsychotic Side Effects*

Akinesia (reduced facial                                _____
expression and
movements)

Akathisia (restlessness)                                _____

*Physical Problems*

Anemia                                                  _____

Thyroid malfunction                                     _____

Diabetes                                                _____

Side effects from other                                 _____
medications

## Helping Your Relative Cope with Depression

There are many different ways of helping your relative cope with and overcome feelings of depression. No single strategy is best, and patients often benefit from trying a number of different methods. What is most important is to help your relative identify which strategies are most effective at improving his or her mood and coping with specific symptoms.

Before this can be accomplished, you need to talk over the matter with your relative and see whether he or she views depression as a problem and can be motivated to work toward improving his or her mood. People with depression often lack energy and motivation. Therefore, it is best to try small steps and establish modest goals at the beginning, to avoid overwhelming your relative and expecting more effort than he or she can muster. In your discussions with your relative about depression, you can be of greatest help by showing him or her that you understand and are concerned with his or her feelings and by instilling some hope that change for the better is possible.

## Specific Coping Strategies

The strategies described below are drawn from research on the treatment of depression, as well as our own clinical experience working with patients who have schizophrenia. We offer as many strategies as possible, to enable you to pick and choose those strategies that appear to be most promising.

### Scheduling Pleasant Events

When people are depressed they often cease to engage in activities they used to enjoy. A stressful life event or a difficult situation can interfere with a person's usual routine, including recreational activities, and often the person does not resume these activities. Patients with schizophrenia are especially prone to developing depression for this reason, because of the chaotic effects of their disorder. For example, the daily routine of patients is greatly disrupted every time a relapse and psychiatric hospitalization takes place, and it is not surprising that patients have difficulty reestablishing their routines following discharge from the hospital. Indeed, for many years clinicians have noted that depression sometimes arises after the patient has recovered from a psychotic episode (called *postpsychotic depression*), and some of this depression may reflect the disruptive effects of a relapse on the patient's routine.

Assisting your relative in making plans to engage in enjoyable activities, including scheduling specific times, can help lift him or her out of depression. Planning to take a one-hour walk in the park on Thursday afternoon or going out to a movie on a Friday night are examples of scheduling specific times for pleasant activities. Your relative may find it difficult to schedule and follow through on pleasant activities on his or her own. If you meet regularly with your relative to talk over and schedule possible activities, you will facilitate his or her ability to plan activities and help in evaluating the success of previous plans.

If your relative has been depressed for a long time, he or she may be unsure of which activities would be enjoyable or may be pessimistic that anything could be fun. In this situation your best bet is to encourage your relative to experiment with different activities to find out what is enjoyable. Helping your relative evaluate, choose, and follow through on possible options will improve the chances that enjoyable activities can be identified. If your relative has had a long-standing depression, bear in mind that his or her energy and motivation to change may be low. To accommodate this, select activities that do not require great amounts of energy and that you can do with your relative, to provide added encouragement. We recommend you start out by helping your relative schedule at least one pleasant activity per week and gradually increase the number of activities over time.

### Increasing Activity Level

People often become inactive and lethargic when they are depressed. Furthermore, feelings of lethargy can worsen a state of depression. People with schizophrenia may be especially vulnerable to depression that arises from inactivity because they have limited amounts of stamina and are prone to lethargy, even when they are not depressed. Helping your relative increase his or her activity level, such as by walking, jogging, bicycling, or aerobics, can have a marked effect on improving his or her mood. Even less strenuous types of exercise, such as walking up the stairs instead of taking the elevator, can help.

Engaging in exercise regularly or modifying daily habits can be hard, even for people who do not have a psychiatric disorder. Naturally, these difficulties are even greater for a person with schizophrenia. The following are a few pointers for helping your relative increase his or her activity level.

*Set small, attainable goals.* By helping your relative set manageable goals that he or she is likely to achieve, you "program in success" and your relative's efforts to change are encouraged. For example, the two of you might set a goal of taking a ten-minute walk once per week.

*Work very gradually toward long-term goals.* After your relative achieves success with the first small goal, think of a new one that is one small step closer to the long-term goal. For example, after a few weeks of taking one ten-minute walk per week, take two walks per week, working toward the long-term goal of walking or jogging daily.

*Build in rewards for following through.* Talk over with your relative ideas for a reward for following through on his or her plan regularly. Rewards can be either administered by your relative him- or herself (for example, watching a favorite TV show, taking a nap) or by you (cooking a special meal, renting a movie to watch together).

*Record progress on a regular basis.* Encouraging your relative to mark down on a calendar, a record book, or a notebook every time he or she engages in the planned activity can show progress over time. These records can be reviewed routinely to point out increases in activity and to troubleshoot when the activity has been missed.

*Consider including others in the activity.* Explore with your relative whether doing the activity with others would make it more enjoyable or easier to do. Your relative can consider asking you, a friend, or another relative to come along or could do the activity with an organized group (such as the YMCA) or in a public place (such as a park).

### Correcting Maladaptive Thinking

How and what people think about the world around them has a tremendous bearing on their mood. For example, if someone thinks that the world is a cruel, cold, unforgiving place, these thoughts will contribute to unpleasant feelings. Certain thinking styles may be self-defeating because the person only sees the bad side of things or gives up, leading to or perpetuating feelings of depression. By challenging and correcting these maladaptive thoughts, improvements in depression are possible. In fact, there is now a great deal of evidence from research that helping people recognize and change their thinking styles has a beneficial effect on the symptoms of depression.

If your relative has problems with depression, the chances are high that he or she has some maladaptive thinking patterns, aside from any delusions he or she may have. Trying to help your relative change his or her thinking may improve his or her depression. Some patients with schizophrenia are more amenable to this approach than others. If your relative has many cognitive impairments, such as very poor memory, problems with comprehension, or mild levels of confusion, modifying his or her thinking style may not be feasible. However, you will never know unless you try. We describe below two approaches that can be used to correct maladaptive thinking: challenging self-defeating beliefs and correcting cognitive distortions.

*Recognize and challenge self-defeating beliefs.* Patients who hold strong beliefs and think in absolute terms about the way the world "ought" to be are more vulnerable to depression or anger when the world fails to meet their expectations. Thus, beliefs involving "shoulds" and "musts" tend to be self-defeating, because they do not fit the real world, which is not always fair or just. People with schizophrenia can be especially prone to these types of beliefs, because they are saddled with the burden of a severe illness that occurs quite randomly and is not "fair."

Helping your relative recognize and challenge self-defeating beliefs can improve his or her mood by providing a more realistic and adaptive way of thinking about the world and his or her circumstances. The key to recognizing self-defeating beliefs in your relative is to look for statements or actions that suggest a refusal to accept the world as it is or an insistence on things working out a certain way (such as getting a job, living independently). Examples of self-defeating beliefs and more adaptive alternatives are provided in Figure 11.1. Once you have identified what appears to be a self-defeating belief in your relative, try following these four steps:

1. *Clarify whether your relative has the belief.* You can observe statements and behaviors that suggest that your relative has a self-defeating belief, but the belief itself can only be confirmed by talking about it. Make a guess at what your relative believes, ask him or her about it, and tell him or her why you made that guess, for example, "I noticed that you seemed pretty down since Ellen didn't want to go out for coffee a few days ago. Was that what you were upset about?" If the answer is yes, say, "Are you still upset now because you think that *everybody* should like you?"

---

### Self-Defeating Beliefs Versus Adaptive Thoughts

| *Self-Defeating Belief* | *Adaptive Alternative Thought* |
|---|---|
| I *must* be liked by everyone. | It would be nice if everyone liked me, but I know that's not possible. |
| My relative *shouldn't* give me such a hard time. | I would prefer it if my relative didn't give me such as hard time. What can I do to change this problem? |
| I *have to* get this job. | I would like to get this job and I'll try my best to get it. If I can't, I can always try getting another job, or even work up to it with a volunteer job. |
| It's *unfair* that I have to suffer like this when I don't deserve it. | I don't like having to suffer this way, nobody likes to suffer. Is there something I can do to improve this situation? |

Figure 11.1

2. *Empathize with your relative's feelings.* Show your relative you understand how he or she feels, for example, "I understand how it can be upsetting when someone doesn't seem to like you."

3. *Suggest to your relative how his or her belief might not be realistic.* Gently point out why the belief may not be true, for example, "I think it is really hard to go through life with everyone liking you. I'm not sure it's even possible. What do you think?"

4. *Suggest a more adaptive way of thinking about the situation.* Identify a more realistic alternative that acknowledges your relative's basic concern, for example, "Maybe a different way of thinking about it is to think that you want other people to like you, but you know that not everybody will. How does that sound?"

Do not try to force your relative to confront these self-defeating beliefs if he or she is unwilling or rejects the idea. You will know fairly soon after trying whether your relative is open to talking about these beliefs.

For more information about correcting self-defeating or irrational beliefs, consult books by Albert Ellis, Ph.D., who pioneered this approach, for example, A. Ellis and R.A. Harper, *A New Guide to Rational Living* (Hollywood, Calif.: Wilshire Book Company, 1975). You might also want to contact the Institute for Rational Living, 212-535-0822.

**Correct cognitive distortions.** *Cognitive distortions* refers to thinking problems that lead people to reach incorrect conclusions about specific events. Irrational beliefs and cognitive distortions are quite similar, since both are self-defeating and both can be replaced by more adaptive thinking styles. Cognitive distortions differ in that they reflect ways that people often distort specific information, as opposed to more general beliefs. Examples of common cognitive distortions are provided in Figure 11.2.

You can help your relative correct his or her cognitive distortions by using a method similar to the one discussed for challenging self-defeating beliefs. First you identify the thinking pattern and empathize with your relative about the feelings associated with it. Then you can talk about why the thinking pattern is a distortion and suggest a more adaptive way of thinking about the situation.

For example, Bob was depressed about being recently turned down for a part-time job. When he talked it over with his mother, he revealed that he believed that he would never be able to get a job, which was a depressing prospect. His mother empathized with his disappointment about not getting the job, and then raised the question of whether he really had enough information to *know* that he would never get a job. When they explored this together, Bob admitted that he had looked for only one other job in the past few months and agreed that he might be "jumping to conclusions" when he thought he would never get a job. By correcting this distortion, Bob felt better about his employment prospects.

More information about correcting cognitive distortions can be found in books such as David D. Burns's *Feeling Good: The New Mood Therapy* (New York: William Morrow, 1980) and Arthur Freeman and Rosa DeWolf's *Woulda, Coulda, Shoulda: Overcoming Regrets, Mistakes, and Missed Opportunities* (New York: William Morrow, 1989).

---

## Examples of Cognitive Distortions*

| Cognitive Distortion | Example |
|---|---|
| All-or-nothing thinking | Seeing things in "black-and-white," for example, "If I can't get the job I really want, it's not even worth looking at something else." |
| Overgeneralization | Viewing a single negative event as indicating a never-ending pattern of defeat, for example, "I'm a failure because I was just hospitalized again." |
| Mental filter | Focusing only on the negative and ignoring the positive, for example, "I don't think I'm getting anywhere; I still don't have a job" (despite having stayed out of the hospital six months and having improved self-care skills). |
| Overpersonalizing events | Interpreting an event as personal when it is not, for example, "I don't like to ride the bus because the bus driver doesn't like me; he scowls at me" (when the bus driver scowls at everybody). |
| Jumping to conclusions | Reaching conclusions based on inadequate information, for example, "I know you think I'm lazy when I don't get up on time," or "If I call up one of my old friends she won't be interested in getting together with me because it's been so long since we've seen each other." |

* Adapted from D. D. Burns, *Feeling Good: The New Mood Therapy.* New York: William Morrow, 1980.

Figure 11.2

## Coping Strategies for Specific Symptoms

Some symptoms of depression can be very troubling and persist over long periods of time. You can help your relative manage these symp-

---

**Strategies for Coping with Specific
Symptoms of Depression**

| *Symptom* | *Coping Strategies* |
|---|---|
| Loss of interest, lack of energy, slowed activity level | Set goals for daily activities |
| | Take small steps to structure a full program of constructive activity |
| | Pinpoint small areas of remaining interest that you can pursue easily and build upon them |
| | Avoid comparing your current interest or energy level with the past |
| Loss of appetite | Eat small portions of food that you like Take your time |
| | Avoid eating with others if you feel pressure to finish |
| | Drink plenty of fluids, especially fruit juices, milkshakes |
| Sleep disturbance | Go to bed at your usual time |
| | Avoid sleeping during the day |
| | Reduce caffeine intake (coffee, tea, colas) to not more than two or three per day and not for several hours before going to bed |
| | Don't lie awake in bed for more than 30 minutes—get up and find something to do |
| | Try relaxation exercises (see Chapter 8) |

Figure 11.3

toms by encouraging him or her to try specific coping strategies. Strategies for coping with several common symptoms of depression are provided in Figure 11.3.

## Dealing with Your Own Depression

Depression can be contagious. If your relative has problems with depression these feelings can also affect you, leading to similar feelings. You may also experience depression because of your struggle to cope with your relative's illness. If your mood is depressed and you have some of the other symptoms of depression described earlier in this chapter, it is important to try to deal with this problem. Depression can sap your energy, dampen your ability to solve problems, make you irritable, and interfere with your ability to help your relative.

Some of the strategies described in the previous section for coping with depression may be helpful for you. Scheduling pleasant events and increasing activity level may be useful strategies for you to consider. For many relatives, the strain of having a close family member with schizophrenia is so great that they stop taking care of their own needs, including recreational and health pursuits, and focus all of their attention on trying to help their relative. The upshot is that depression ensues, often mixed with feelings of resentment. You can combat this depression by setting aside time for yourself to pursue activities that are enjoyable, self-improving, or both—for example, art lessons, a fitness program, needlework, or fishing.

Just as cognitive distortions and self-defeating beliefs can play a role in depression in your relative, they may also influence your own mood. Becoming attuned to your thoughts and beliefs about your relative's illness may help you identify maladaptive thoughts that may contribute to your depression. By challenging these thoughts, you can take control of your own thinking and thereby improve your mood. One common cognitive distortion in family members with an ill relative is "all-or-nothing thinking," for example, "My relative has no life because he or she has schizophrenia." This is a distortion of reality because, although the relative's life is greatly affected by the illness, he or she nevertheless *has* a life and is capable of feelings and accomplishments. Another common distortion in relatives is "overgeneralization," for example, "My relative has nothing going for him or her," when he or she works part-time at a volunteer job and helps out around the house. In each case, the cognitive distortion reflects a grain of truth that is then exaggerated to a maladaptive degree.

Similarly, self-defeating beliefs about your relative's illness can contribute to depression. For example, you may often think, "It's unfair my relative has schizophrenia, we didn't do anything to deserve this!" It is true that neither you nor anyone else caused your relative's illness, and it's not "fair" for anyone to suffer with such a problem. However, this is a world in which bad things sometimes happen to people who don't deserve it, as exhibited by poverty, starvation, war, natural disasters and crime. Dwelling on the unfairness of the world doesn't get you or your relative anywhere, and may even interfere with your ability to cope more effectively with the illness.

Another example of a common irrational belief is the thought "My relative should show his or her love for me; I can't stand it if he or she doesn't." It is true that it would be nice if your relative showed more love for you, and it is disappointing if he or she does not, but you can live with this situation and even maintain a decent, sometimes rewarding relationship with him or her. Challenging these types of irrational beliefs can enable you to develop a more adaptive way of thinking about your relative's illness and to see it as something you can deal with.

The shock and disruption caused by the development of schizophrenia in a relative frequently results in family members keeping more to themselves and seeing friends less often. This can stem from either the social embarrassment felt by some family members, the amount of time devoted to caring for the relative, or both. Social relationships are an important source of well-being and support for most people, and without these relationships you are more vulnerable to depression. Increasing the time you spend with close friends or making new friends can strengthen your social-support network, reducing symptoms of depression.

If you have been avoiding people for a long time because of your relative's illness, you may need to explore different ways of meeting new people, such as attending public events or joining a group of people with a similar interest. Joining a local chapter of the Alliance for the Mentally Ill (see Resources appendix) can provide you with much needed social support for coping with your relative's illness and social contacts that may lead to rewarding friendships.

For some families the experience of having a close relative develop schizophrenia can seem devastating, especially if the person has substantial impairments due to the illness. Parents often find that they need to adjust their expectations for their child's future, including career options, independent living, and marriage and children. Many family members have told us that having a relative develop schizophrenia is like experiencing the loss or even death of someone close to them. This is an understandable reaction, but we believe that by learning strategies to better manage the illness and improve its course, family members can find reasons to be more optimistic. When they focus on improving their relative's strengths and abilities, family members often feel less overwhelmed by the limitations imposed by the illness.

Even with improved coping, however, some family members may continue to grieve over the effects of schizophrenia on their relative. If you experience strong, persistent feelings of depression that are difficult to escape, you may have unresolved grief about the loss of your relative—a common reaction. "Unresolved grief" is usually a mixture of persistent feelings of sadness, anger, and frustration, which the person has not fully expressed and which weighs him or her down. The best way to deal with this grief and to get on with your life is to talk about it with someone who can be supportive to you. This person can be a close friend, a relative, a group of other relatives with similar experiences, or a psychotherapist. The grieving process takes time, and you may need to talk about your feelings many times before you feel ready to move on. Recognizing your need to grieve, and allowing yourself the time to do it, can enable you to get over your depression and help you to accept your relative and his or her illness.

## Coping with Your Own Depression

| Source of Depression | Solutions |
| --- | --- |
| Lack of time spent in enjoyable activities | Set aside regular time for recreation or self-improvement |
| Cognitive distortions and irrational beliefs about your relative's illness | Identify and challenge distortions and beliefs, using self-help books if necessary |
| Lack of social support | Increase time with friends; look for ways to meet new people; join Alliance for the Mentally Ill (AMI) |
| Unresolved grief | Talk with relatives and close friends; psychotherapy |

# Anxiety in Schizophrenia

Anxiety is a very common problem for patients with schizophrenia, and can be just as debilitating as depression. There are a number of different factors that can contribute to your relative's anxiety. As discussed in Chapter 10, patients often experience anxiety due to the positive symptoms of their illness. Auditory hallucinations can cause anxiety when the voices are insulting or order the person what to do (*command hallucinations*). These voices are unpredictable and may get worse if the patient tries to combat them. Patients who experience command hallucinations are often in a special bind; they may feel anxious about the consequences of either ignoring these voices *or* complying with the orders. Delusions can be equally anxiety-provoking; imagine how *you* would feel if you thought that someone else was trying to hurt you, others could read your mind, or people could put thoughts into your head.

A different reason your relative may feel anxious is that he or she may be haunted by memories of psychotic symptoms in the past that currently are not present. These memories may create a sense of vulnerability in your relative, who may be afraid it can happen again. This fear can result in your relative avoiding situations associated with those memories or being afraid to make any changes, thus effectively immobilizing him or her. Anxiety based on memories of past psychotic experiences is similar to post-traumatic stress disorder, in which people develop anxiety and other symptoms after exposure to a traumatic life event, such as an accident, war, or natural disaster.

Another source of anxiety for your relative may be the uncertainty of his or her future. By its very nature, schizophrenia involves episodes of loss of control over one's thinking and feeling and even one's own future. The unpredictability of relapses and rehospitalizations, and the difficulties most patients have with employment and self-care, can make them very dependent upon others to support their day-to-day functioning. This dependency contributes to anxiety, especially if the patient lives with his or her parents, who will not be able to provide care indefinitely.

Helping your relative manage anxiety effectively, and overcome it when possible, can have many benefits. The most obvious one is reducing distress. Another benefit is the ability to deal with potentially anxiety-provoking situations, rather than avoiding them, which may be important in achieving long-term goals (such as work or closer personal relationships). A final benefit is your relationship with your relative may improve if he or she is less anxious, since anxiety often makes people irritable and difficult to get along with.

## Symptoms of Anxiety

The symptoms of anxiety can be divided into three broad groups: mood and thinking, behavior, and increased arousal. Milder levels of anxiety tend to be associated with thoughts of worry or concern, whereas with more severe anxiety the predominant mood is one of fear or terror. The behavior that is the hallmark of anxiety is avoidance of situations, people, or thoughts that cause (or are expected to cause) anxiety. This avoidance may be so great that your relative is afraid to do almost anything. Exposure to fearful situations, people, or thoughts results in increased arousal, such as greater perspiration, heart palpitations, and muscular tension, as well as behavioral changes, such as trembling and agitation.

## Assessing Anxiety in Your Relative

If you have observed possible symptoms of anxiety in your relative, but are unsure of his or her feelings, talking with your relative about

## Symptoms of Anxiety Checklist

*Instructions:* Place a check mark next to each symptom that your relative has had over the past month.

*Mood and Thinking*

Worry or concern                                    _____

Fear                                                _____

Irritability                                        _____

Difficulty concentrating                            _____

*Behavior*

Avoidance of feared                                 _____
situations

Escape from unpleasant                              _____
situations

Trembling                                           _____

Agitation (for example,                             _____
pacing)

*Increased Arousal*

Perspiration                                        _____

Heart palpitations                                  _____

Muscular tension                                    _____

"Butterflies" in stomach                            _____

Mild nausea                                         _____

Dizziness                                           _____

Shortness of breath                                 _____

these feelings can be helpful. It is easy to mistake behaviors such as social avoidance or agitation for anxiety, when other possible explanations exist (such as an increase in positive symptoms). Therefore, talking with your relative is critical to knowing whether he or she has a problem with anxiety. When talking with him or her, it may be useful to use a number of different words to refer to anxiety, such as *scary, afraid, worried,* or *concerned*. The Symptoms of Anxiety Checklist may also be helpful.

Once you know that your relative has problems with anxiety, you can proceed to gather more information about the basis of those fears. When talking with your relative, focus on being as empathic as possible (using reflective listening skills), avoid making judgments (such as implying that a fear or concern is not valid), and try to get specific information about the sources of the anxiety (such as specific situations, persons, or beliefs). It is preferable to start by asking open-ended questions (such as, "What concerns you about going to the day treatment program?"), rather than closed-ended questions ("Are you afraid to ride the bus to the day treatment program?"), because the latter tend to be more leading. Your principal goal is to understand under what circumstances your relative feels anxious. Such an understanding will guide you in helping your relative develop strategies for managing the anxiety.

## Helping Your Relative Cope with Anxiety

A variety of different strategies can be used to help your relative cope with anxiety. The specific methods you can use depend on the source of your relative's fears. We discuss below strategies for handling anxiety that arises from four common sources in patients with schizophrenia: psychotic symptoms, specific situations, memories of past psychotic symptoms, and the future.

### Anxiety Related to Psychotic Symptoms

You may have already experienced the difficulties of trying to deal with your relative's anxiety if it is secondary to psychotic symptoms. This is a common problem for many family members. The initial reaction of most family members to a relative's anxiety about a delusion or hallucination is to try to persuade their relative that the belief or perception is not real. This effort invariably fails because the very nature of delusions and hallucinations is that they seem real to patients. If they didn't seem so real, or if patients could be easily talked out of their beliefs, they wouldn't have the many problems associated with these symptoms.

Rather than attempting to convince your relative that he or she shouldn't be anxious about a psychotic symptom, you will be more helpful if you try to understand and empathize with his or her feelings, and then explore ways of reducing those unpleasant feelings. This will put you in the position of being a sympathetic helper to your relative instead of an adversary. The best way of showing that you are concerned and understand your relative's feelings is to first listen to him or her and then imagine how you would feel if you had those same experiences. After you have tried to understand what your relative's experience is like, let him or her know what you heard by reflecting back, for example, "I can understand, it must be very upsetting to hear these voices yelling at you all the time," or, "I can see why you feel anxious, thinking that people can read your mind."

By reflecting back your relative's concerns you validate his or her feelings, help him or her feel understood, and avoid unnecessary judgments about the sources of the concerns themselves (the delusions or hallucinations). If your relative is fearful about delusions, you may find it helpful to view these beliefs as being similar to phobias that many people have. Objectively, it doesn't make sense to be terrified of being in a high building, in a closed space, or most snakes and spiders. Yet to people with these phobias, the anxiety is quite real and the "groundlessness" of their fears doesn't really matter.

---

### Guidelines for Helping Your Relative Cope with Anxiety Related to Psychotic Symptoms

Listen to your relative's description of his or her feelings and what causes them:

- Avoid being judgmental or trying to talk your relative out of his or her beliefs or feelings.
- Imagine how *you* would feel if you experienced what your relative is experiencing.
- Reflect back what you have heard to validate your relative's feelings.

Show your empathy and concern to your relative and offer to help:

- Let him or her know you understand those feelings.
- Don't force your help upon him or her.

If your relative is willing, explore strategies with him or her for reducing the anxiety, such as:

- Improving coping with psychotic symptoms.
- Using relaxation and other stress-reduction techniques.
- Making plans to handle difficult situations.

---

Just showing your relative that you understand and are concerned about his or her feelings can help. You can then explore with him or her whether there are ways of reducing this anxiety. Some patients reject such offers of help, while others readily accept. Patients often do not want help with anxiety about psychotic symptoms because of a strong sense of privacy. If your relative accepts your help, you can talk together about how to deal with this anxiety. The following three general strategies are useful for coping with this type of anxiety.

*Improve coping with the psychotic symptoms.* Helping your relative develop strategies for minimizing the disruptive effects of psychotic symptoms can decrease the anxiety associated with those symptoms. For example, use of distraction techniques, self-talk, and social engagement can reduce the intensity of auditory hallucinations. (See Chapter 10 for more detailed information on helping your relative cope with persistent psychotic symptoms.)

*Use relaxation and other stress-reduction techniques.* Relaxation techniques, such as progressive muscle relaxation, breathing exercises, and pleasant imagery, often have a direct effect on reducing anxiety. Methods for reducing stress that may have beneficial effects on anxiety are described in Chapter 8.

*Identify ways to manage difficult situations.* The anxiety related to psychotic symptoms may be worse in some situations than others. By identifying problematic situations you can help your relative develop a plan for minimizing the stress of that specific situation. For example, a family gathering involving many relatives might be hard for a patient with paranoid thoughts. This situation could be handled by the patient spending a half-hour at a time at the gathering, and taking breaks to rest and relax before returning. Taking a problem-solving approach to helping your relative manage these problematic situations can be quite effective (see Chapter 7).

### Anxiety Related to Specific Situations

Your relative may find certain situations anxiety provoking and consequently avoids these situations whenever possible. The fear associated with these situations can actually grow each time your relative successfully avoids one. As your relative becomes increasingly avoidant, it becomes more and more difficult for him or her to function adequately or to pursue long-term goals. Sometimes this fear of situations is related to a past negative experience; other times it is less clear where the anxiety came from.

You can help your relative cope with anxiety about specific situations by encouraging him or her to gradually expose himself or herself to those situations, thus overcoming the fear associated with them. Talk over the idea with your relative to make sure he or she is in agreement with you about the advantages of conquering the fear. Then work together to identify related situations. Using that list, you can rate the situations by how much anxiety each situation causes.

The idea is for your relative to start with the situation that causes the lowest level of fear, and to repeatedly confront this situation until he or she no longer feels anxious. Then he or she moves onto the next situation, which is only a little more anxiety-provoking than the first. Once again, repeated exposures to the situation will result in a decrease in anxiety, at which point your relative can go on to a slightly more anxiety-provoking situation. Over a period of time, this exposure to situations will result in a gradual reduction in your relative's fear. This approach has been successfully used by many people to overcome anxiety related to phobias, public speaking, and so on.

For example, Duane felt very anxious about riding on public transportation and over the past year he had refused to go on any buses or subways at all. As a consequence of Duane's anxiety his mother had to drive him to his day treatment program a few miles away, and he was unable to participate in a vocational program across town. After Duane and his mother talked it over, Duane agreed to try to work with his mother on decreasing his anxiety about riding public transportation. Even the *idea* of riding public transportation caused Duane to feel anxious, so they agreed to start on some situations that wouldn't involve actually getting on the bus or subway. Then they began to work on more challenging situations. Duane's mother agreed to accompany him in some of these situations to make them less anxiety provoking. The situations that they started working on included (in the following order):

- Waiting at the bus stop closest to home with his mother and watching three buses go by.

- Waiting at another bus stop with his mother and watching three buses go by.

- Waiting at the bus stop closest to home alone and watching three buses go by.

- Waiting at another bus stop alone and watching three buses go by.

- Riding one stop with his mother on the bus closest to home, and then one stop back home.

- Riding three stops with his mother on the bus closest to home, and then three stops back home.

- Riding one stop and back alone.

- Riding three stops and back alone.

When these situations were mastered and Duane could use the bus for short trips close to home, they began to work on traveling farther away from home and decreasing his anxiety to riding the subway. Gradually, over several months, Duane overcame most of his anxiety to riding on public transportation, and began to be able to take advantage of opportunities he had previously avoided because of his anxiety.

### Anxiety Related to Past Psychotic Symptoms

If your relative experiences prominent psychotic symptoms only during acute episodes of his or her illness, but not between these episodes, he or she may be troubled by intrusive, unpleasant memories of these symptoms or problems associated with them. These memories often create feelings of anxiety. Sometimes the anxiety is related to a particular situation in which the psychotic symptoms occurred, resulting in fear of that situation.

For example, one patient, Don, went to a baseball game while he was experiencing a relapse of psychotic symptoms and became terrified that other fans were looking at and talking about him. Family members were alert to Don's early warning signs of relapse, and were able to arrange a special appointment with his psychiatrist, who adjusted his medication and averted a relapse. However, Don continued to remember his experience at the baseball game after his psychotic symptoms had abated, and he no longer wanted to go to games because of the anxiety he felt about them. This anxiety even spread to riding the subway line that he had taken the day he had trouble with his psychotic symptoms.

At other times the anxiety may be due to memories of losing control, being frightened by bizarre thoughts, or being intruded upon by upsetting hallucinations. These fears are more general and are not focused on particular situations. Rather, the anxiety reflects the patient's emotions about the memory of the disturbing symptoms and his or her concern over whether the symptoms will return. This concern can be so great that your relative is afraid to do almost anything for fear of "rocking the boat" and risking a relapse. The avoidance itself can lead to a relapse if your relative fails to become involved in any meaningful activities.

There are several ways of helping your relative overcome anxiety related to past psychotic symptoms. If your relative is anxious about a specific situation, the strategy described in the previous section can be applied. In the example of Don, he and his family were able to work towards gradually helping him overcome his fear of the subway and baseball games, so that he was able once again to enjoy going to games. If your relative feels anxious that his or her psychotic symptoms will return, you can help by talking about how the chances of a relapse can be minimized. Taking medication on a regular basis, participating in some type of daily structured activity, being alert to stress and how to handle it effectively, and monitoring early warning signs of relapse can all greatly reduce the possibility of a symptom relapse. Understanding how these steps can prevent future relapses will increase your relative's feeling of control, thus decreasing feelings of vulnerability and anxiety.

When anxiety stems from intrusive memories of past psychotic symptoms, gently encouraging your relative to talk with you about the memories can be very beneficial. These memories are a particularly common problem for patients who have had only one or two previous episodes of psychotic symptoms. If your relative is willing to talk, be as supportive and empathic as possible, let him or her talk as long as he or she wishes, and avoid jumping in too quickly and trying to "solve" the problem. Just the process of talking about the unpleasant memories with someone who is supportive can reduce anxiety and make it easier to live with the memories. Your relative may need to talk about the memories more than once before the anxiety is sufficiently under control.

### Anxiety About the Future

Many patients are concerned about their future, including where they are going to live, how they can support themselves, and who is going

---

## Dealing with Anxiety Not Due to Current Psychotic Symptoms

| Source of Anxiety | Coping Strategies |
|---|---|
| Specific situations | Encourage gradual exposure to feared situations |
| | Use relaxation techniques to handle anxiety in those situations |
| Past psychotic symptoms | Discuss how future symptom relapses can be prevented (such as by medication compliance, monitoring early warning signs of relapse) |
| | Encourage your relative to talk about the specific negative experiences with the symptoms and his or her feelings; be an empathic listener |
| The future | Begin to make plans for your relative's care in the future |
| | Talk over future plans and involve your relative in making plans whenever possible |

---

to be there to help them. Considering how dependent patients with schizophrenia can be on others to help them get their basic needs met, anxiety about the future can almost be expected. However, each patient's perception of the future is unique, and some patients have great difficulty looking ahead. Therefore, if you think this concern may be contributing to your relative's anxiety, check it out with him or her.

Anxiety about what is going to happen in your relative's future is best allayed by beginning the difficult process of planning for his or her future, involving your relative in this process whenever possible. Even if you can't be precise about all the future plans, the more you talk about it and the more information you get, the less anxiety your relative is going to feel. This important topic is addressed in the last chapter of this book.

## Dealing with Your Own Anxiety

Living with or having a close relationship with someone who has schizophrenia can result in anxiety, for several reasons. The sheer unpredictability of your relative's disorder can be a major contributing factor to your anxiety. Symptoms vary in severity over time, including changes in mood, thinking, and behavior. There is often little consistency between what patients say and what they do, further lowering predictability. Treatments for schizophrenia are not completely effective, which limits everyone's ability to control the disorder. In fact, the only predictable thing about schizophrenia is that it probably will not suddenly go away. And your difficulty predicting the future course of your relative's disorder may be compounded by concern about his or her future. Dealing effectively with these anxious feelings is crucial to improving your own satisfaction with life, and may also have beneficial effects on your relationship with your ill relative, as well as with other family members.

By reading this book, you are already taking the most important step you can toward overcoming your anxiety about your relative. At the core of most anxiety are worries about the unpredictability and uncontrollability of the events surrounding you. By becoming informed about schizophrenia, including its symptoms, course, and treatment, and by developing strategies for handling common problems, such as stress, communication problems, and specific symptoms, you are increasing your ability to anticipate and modify your relative's behavior. This will pay off in the long run by reducing your anxiety. In the meanwhile, you can also use short-term strategies for reducing anxiety, such as the methods described in Chapter 8 for managing stress.

# 12

# Alcohol and Drug Abuse

Our society pays a high price for the destructive effects of substance abuse. Almost everyone knows someone who has problems with alcohol or drugs. The illegal drug trade has left an increasingly violent trail of destruction in our inner cities, and alcohol or drug abuse is frequently implicated in all kinds of accidents, including motor vehicle, pedestrian, and industrial accidents. Many of the problems associated with substance abuse are magnified in patients with schizophrenia, whose biological vulnerabilities make them even more sensitive to the effects of alcohol and drugs. If your relative with schizophrenia drinks excessively or uses drugs, you may already know how this complicates the treatment of his or her disorder.

In this chapter we provide you with the information you will need to cope more effectively with a relative who has a substance abuse problem. We begin with a discussion of how common alcohol and drug abuse is in persons with schizophrenia, and review the effects on the symptoms and course of the disorder. Then we discuss the different types of commonly abused substances, their specific effects, and some of the characteristics of patients who abuse. We provide you with some strategies for evaluating whether your relative has a drug or alcohol problem. Finally, we present guidelines for handling your relative's substance abuse problem and minimizing its effects on both the illness and the well-being of all the members of your family.

Substance use disorders in patients with schizophrenia can be quite severe, and for some patients the struggle is a very long one. However, by becoming more informed about the problem, available treatment options, and strategies for managing it, you can play an important role in helping your relative regain more control over his or her life and begin to escape from the clutches of alcohol and drug abuse.

# The Scope of the Problem

Problems related to the use of alcohol and drugs are some of the most common difficulties encountered by people throughout their lives. When excessive substance use interferes with an individual's ability to work effectively, his or her social relationships or health, or brings him or her into contact with the law, that person has an *alcohol or drug abuse disorder* (according to the psychiatric diagnostic system *DSM-IV*). If these problems are compounded by a physical dependence upon the substance, he or she has an *alcohol or drug dependence disorder*. Physical dependence is present if a person experiences withdrawal symptoms (such as headaches, nausea, tremors) when the substance is not taken or if the person develops tolerance to the substance (larger amounts must be taken to achieve the same effects).

Surveys indicate that alcohol and drug use disorders are actually the most common type of psychiatric disorder that exists in the general population. In the largest survey ever conducted of psychiatric disorders in the United States by the National Institute of Mental Health, a staggering 13.5 percent of the people were found to have had an alcohol use disorder at some time during their lives, and 6.1 percent had a drug use disorder during their lives. A total of 16.7 percent of people had experienced an alcohol or drug use disorder (this number is less than the combined percentages because some people had both alcohol and drug use disorders). Thus, almost 17 out of every 100 persons had experienced a substance use disorder. This same survey found that almost 15 out of every 100 persons had an anxiety disorder (such as phobia or panic disorder), 8 to 9 persons had an affective disorder (such as depression or bipolar disorder), and 1 to 2 persons out of 100 had schizophrenia.

It is clear that alcohol and drug use disorders are indeed a major problem in our society. This problem, however, is even greater for persons with schizophrenia. Research on substance use disorders has consistently found that patients with another psychiatric disorder are even more prone to developing substance use problems than people who don't have another disorder. This increased vulnerability to drug and alcohol-related problems is dramatically higher for persons with schizophrenia than for other disorders, such as depression or anxiety. Most surveys indicate that as many as 30 to 60 percent of patients with schizophrenia experience problems with drugs or alcohol at some time during their lives. The National Institute of Mental Health survey described above found that 47 percent of patients with schizophrenia had a history of a substance use disorder. Some of the findings from this survey are summarized in Figure 12.1.

What this means for you is that the chances are high (about 50 percent) that your relative with schizophrenia has had a problem with alcohol or drugs. This does not mean necessarily that he or she has been abusing alcohol or drugs recently. The chances that your relative *currently* has a problem with substance abuse are somewhat lower, about 25 percent, but nevertheless these chances are quite high. In short, substance abuse is a problem that plagues many patients with schizophrenia.

## The Effects of Substance Abuse on Schizophrenia

Alcohol and drug abuse have a variety of different negative effects on patients with schizophrenia. At the most basic level, substance abuse can worsen symptoms, increasing patients' vulnerability to relapses and rehospitalizations. Patients with schizophrenia have extremely sensitive nervous systems, due to their biological vulnerability to the disorder. As a result of their vulnerability, even small amounts of substances can counter the protective effects of antipsychotic medication, leading to a deterioration in functioning. Another factor that can complicate the treatment of patients with substance abuse problems is that they are often more difficult to engage in treatment, refusing to attend day programs, vocational programs, or therapy.

Substance abuse also has harmful effects on the functioning of persons with schizophrenia, similar to its effects on persons who do not have another psychiatric disorder. Substance use disorders frequently have a harmful effect on the quality of interpersonal relationships and the ability to work. Furthermore, patients with a substance use disorder are more prone to legal problems (for example, being arrested for possession of illegal drugs, arrest for driving under the influence of alcohol), housing instability (for example, being evicted from a group home), health problems arising from chronic substance abuse, and money problems. Patients with a severe substance use disorder often spend all of their available

---

### Lifetime Alcohol and Drug Use Disorders in the General Population and Psychiatric Patients
(percentages)

| Population | Alcohol Use Disorder | Drug Use Disorder | Alcohol or Drug Disorder |
|---|---|---|---|
| General population | 13.5 | 6.1 | 16.7 |
| Any anxiety disorder | 17.9 | 11.9 | 23.7 |
| Any mood disorder | 21.8 | 19.4 | 32.0 |
| Schizophrenia | 33.7 | 25.7 | 47.0 |

Source: D. A. Regier, M. E. Farmer, D. S. Rae, B. Z. Locke, S. J. Keith, L. L. Judd, and F. K. Goodwin. 1990. Comorbidity of mental disorders with alcohol and other drug abuse. *Journal of the American Medical Association.*

Figure 12.1

money on drugs or alcohol, and may even steal to support a drug habit. These problems can be compounded by substance-abusing peers, who may pressure or encourage them to spend any available money on drugs or alcohol.

## The Effects of Substance Abuse on Other Family Members

If you are familiar with the multiple effects of substance abuse on your relative with schizophrenia, you probably also know its impact on you and other family members. Frustration is one of the most common reactions of family members with a relative who has a substance use disorder. Family members often understand that having the illness of schizophrenia is beyond the patient's control, but they have more difficulty viewing excessive drug or alcohol use as also beyond control. The frustration of many family members in seeing a close relative with schizophrenia continue to abuse substances, threatening "self-destruction," is made worse when the abuse occurs in flagrant violation of household rules and disrupts an otherwise peaceful atmosphere at home.

Another common reaction among family members is anxiety and fear. Substance abuse makes some patients more unpredictable; these patients may be more prone to hostile or angry outbursts, social withdrawal, or suicide attempts. Considering how unpredictable schizophrenia can be, this increased unpredictability can be quite nerve-wracking. The fear associated with the lack of a predictable pattern of behavior in the patients can be even greater if the patient steals from family members or has a history of violence.

Substance abuse in a patient with schizophrenia can produce other negative reactions in family members, such as feelings of anger, helplessness, and despair. Some family members may become disengaged, while others get involved in frequent arguments. When the patient lives at home, these feelings can result in a tense family atmosphere that is unpleasant for all.

If your relative currently has a substance use disorder, or has recently had one, it is clear why you need to take steps to address this problem: Substance abuse has a negative effect on the course of the illness and adjustment, as well as on the lives of other concerned family members. Helping your relative decrease his or her need for drugs or alcohol will improve the outlook of his or her illness, and may reduce tension among family members.

## Patterns of Substance Abuse in Schizophrenia

There are many different substances that people use to alter their mood, some of which are legal and others not. When considering the types of substances people with schizophrenia are most likely to abuse, we focus here on those which can have a negative impact on the illness. Many patients with schizophrenia smoke cigarettes and drink coffee, sometimes to excess. However, because neither nicotine nor caffeine has been consistently found to influence the symptoms of schizophrenia, smoking and coffee drinking are not discussed further here (see Chapter 9, "Household Rules," for strategies for regulating smoking).

## Types of Abused Substances

The most commonly abused substances can be grouped into the following categories: alcohol, cannabis (marijuana), stimulants (such as cocaine), hallucinogens (such as LSD), sedatives (such as Valium), and narcotics (such as heroin). Figure 12.2 provides examples of specific drugs within each of these categories and their effects on persons who take them. Within each category, the effects of different types of drugs are quite similar.

Patients with schizophrenia are most likely to abuse alcohol, followed by marijuana and cocaine. Many patients have experimented with hallucinogens, especially when they were young, but chronic hallucinogen abuse is rare. Sedative and narcotics abuse occurs less frequently in patients with schizophrenia. The majority of patients who have a substance use disorder abuse more than one type of drug. Many family members wonder why their relative uses specific drugs and not others. The key to understanding which substances your relative abuses lies in their availability. This is why alcohol is the most commonly abused substance. Where you live and who your relative spends time with are the major determinants of which types of substances he or she abuses.

Schizophrenia is a biological illness that is quite sensitive to the effects of mind altering substances. Even relatively small amounts of drugs or alcohol can worsen your relative's illness. As a result of this, your relative may have a substance use disorder even though he or she does not use large quantities of drugs or alcohol. Patients with schizophrenia do not often become physically dependent upon alcohol or drugs, although psychological dependence is quite common.

## Social Situations

Substance abuse can occur in both social and nonsocial situations. There is a tendency for drug abuse to take place more often in social settings, because illegal drugs are usually obtained from other people. Alcohol, on the other hand, can be readily obtained and consumed alone; about half of all alcohol abuse by patients with schizophrenia occurs alone and half in social situations.

## Commonly Abused Substances and Their Effects

| Type of Substance | Effects |
| --- | --- |
| Alcohol—Beer, wine, "hard" liquor | Drowsiness, slurred speech, loss of motor coordination, slowed reaction time, relaxation, depression |
| Cannabis—Marijuana, hash, THC | Mild euphoria, relaxation, anxiety or panic, perceptual distortions, racing or paranoid thoughts |
| Stimulants—Cocaine, "speed" (amphetamine) | Alertness, energy, feeling "high," anxiety, nervousness, psychotic symptoms |
| Hallucinogens—LSD, PCP, MDA, mescaline, peyote | Perceptual distortions or hallucinations, impaired judgment, feelings of unreality |
| Sedatives—Valium, Librium, Seconal | Drowsiness, slurred speech, loss of motor coordination, slowed reaction time, relaxation, depression |
| Narcotics—Heroin, morphine, codeine | Euphoria, drowsiness, relaxation, "high" or "spacey" feelings, slowed reflexes |

Figure 12.2

## Characteristics of Patients with Substance Abuse Problems

Men with schizophrenia are more prone to substance abuse than women (just as in the general population), and younger patients are more vulnerable than older ones. Patients with a substance use disorder often used drugs and alcohol before they became ill with schizophrenia, and for these patients substance abuse may be a long-standing problem. For many patients, an early experience with substance abuse interferes with completing their education (such as graduating from high school). Another factor that is related to substance abuse in schizophrenia is whether the patient has any relatives with a substance use disorder (such as a parent or uncle with alcoholism). Research studies indicate that, similar to schizophrenia, vulnerability to substance abuse can be partly due to genetic factors.

Characteristics of patients with schizophrenia who are more prone to substance use disorders include the following:

- Male

- Young

- Single or divorced

- Lower educational level

- Good social functioning before onset of schizophrenia

- Substance abuse before onset of schizophrenia

- Frequent relapses and rehospitalizations

- Depression and suicidality

## Assessing Your Relative's Substance Use

Sometimes family members know that their relative has a substance abuse problem. This is the case when the patient does not attempt to conceal his or her abuse, or gets into legal trouble because of it (for example, a driving accident under the influence of alcohol or drugs, arrest for drunken driving, arrest for selling or possessing drugs). Other times, however, it may be less clear to you whether your relative is currently using alcohol or drugs. Many patients will admit to substance abuse in the past, but deny current abuse, even though the problem continues. We discuss here some of the ways that you can evaluate whether your relative is abusing drugs or alcohol. It is especially important to explore your relative's current substance use if you know that he or she has had problems with substance abuse in the past, since past behavior is the strongest predictor of current behavior.

At the most basic level, simply talking with your relative about his or her substance use may be very informative. As with the assessment of medication compliance (Chapter 3), patients often volunteer accurate information about their substance use if they are asked in a straight forward, matter-of-fact way. When talking with your relative, it is best to take a nonthreatening approach that avoids putting him or her on the defensive. If your relative acknowledges current alcohol or drug abuse, it is likely that the problem is present. Denial of current substance abuse, on the other hand, is no guarantee that your relative is not abusing.

One important clue that your relative may be secretly using drugs or alcohol is a worsening of symptoms that cannot be accounted for by medication noncompliance or identifiable life stressors. Similarly, failing to meet expectations that were formerly met (such as oversleeping and being late for a job or program, not doing agreed-upon household chores)

252 Coping with Schizophrenia

can be an indication that your relative is using alcohol or drugs. If you observe any of these signs, you can begin to gather other information that will help you determine whether current substance abuse is a problem. If you conclude that your relative is *not* using drugs or alcohol, these changes may be early warning signs of a relapse.

Another helpful source of information about your relative's use of alcohol or drugs might be mental health professionals who know and work with your relative. Patients sometimes tell their case manager, psychiatrist, or therapist about alcohol or drug abuse without talking about it with family members. If you have a good relationship with any of these professionals and your relative has given permission for you to be in contact with them, talking this matter over with them may be beneficial.

There are other signs of possible substance abuse that you can be alert to. Empty bottles of alcohol or drug paraphernalia may be carelessly left laying around, such as pipes (marijuana, crack cocaine), rolling papers (marijuana), cut plastic tubes (for snorting cocaine, speed, or heroin), vials or small bags (for storing drugs), or (rarely) needles. You may smell marijuana or crack cocaine smoke from your relative's room or notice alcohol missing from your supply. Your relative's appearance may have recently deteriorated (for example, appearing disheveled, tired, anxious), he or she may have become more withdrawn, or more agitated and irritable. Alternatively, your relative may have begun associating with a different crowd, including people who seem "tough," who always want to "party," who don't work, or who appear interested in your relative's money. Your relative may have experienced recent health problems, such as a bad cough, severe headaches, stomach pain, or "the shakes."

Another possible sign of covert substance abuse is a worsening in your relative's ability to manage money or missing money or valuables in your home. Since most patients with schizophrenia have very limited funds, those who develop a serious substance abuse problem may steal to support their habit, including stealing from their own families. For example, we worked with a family in which the 25-year-old son with schizophrenia repeatedly sold his relatives' possessions (such as their TV set) in order to support his crack cocaine addiction. Sometimes patients will borrow money from people, or owe money to a dealer, and may be fearful of the consequences of not paying the money back.

If your relative denies abusing drugs or alcohol, but you are concerned that he or she may be doing so, look for a combination of the clues described above. Usually, you will want to find more than one sign before concluding that he or she has a current problem. Whenever possible, collaborate with professionals involved in your relative's treatment in determining whether your relative is currently abusing substances. After you have gathered all the available information about your relative's alcohol and drug use, complete the Substance Abuse Effects Checklist to identify the effect that substance abuse is having on your relative.

# Understanding Your Relative's Substance Use

Why are patients with schizophrenia so prone to alcohol and drug abuse? What motives does your relative have for using these substances? You, like other relatives and professionals, may be puzzled about why someone with a psychobiological disorder such as schizophrenia would be tempted to use substances that are known to worsen symptoms and result in rehospitalizations. When you consider the effects of alcohol and drug abuse on schizophrenia, the behavior just doesn't seem to make sense. On the other hand, if you try to understand your relative's behavior from his or her perspective, including the role that substance use may play in coping with the illness, you will probably find the behavior more comprehensible. Furthermore, understanding your relative's specific motives for using drugs or alcohol may provide you with important clues about how to help him or her overcome this difficult problem.

Everybody with a substance use disorder, whether or not they also have another psychiatric disorder, can provide an explanation for why they use drugs or alcohol to excess. However, these explanations or motives are not necessarily an accurate reflection of the effects of those particular substances on that person. For example, many people explain that they drink alcohol excessively because they are depressed, yet research has shown that alcohol tends to increase, not decrease depression. Despite the questionable accuracy of patients' accounts for why they use substances, these explanations provide valuable insights into the patient's perspective. If you are going to be successful in helping your relative with this problem, it will be important to show that you want to understand some of his or her reasons for drinking or using drugs.

There are many different motives that patients with schizophrenia may have for using substances. Most of these motives can be grouped into three broad categories: socialization, coping with symptoms, and pleasure enhancement. Your relative's substance abuse may be related to any of these reasons or may be a combination of two or all three reasons. The chances are high that at least one of these motives fits your relative's pattern of abuse.

## Socialization

Most patients with schizophrenia have fewer social outlets than nonpatients, and thus they have fewer opportunities for getting their social needs met. Since a great deal of substance abuse takes place in social settings, using drugs or alcohol with others may be a convenient outlet for meeting these social needs. Furthermore, many patients began using these substances with friends before they became ill with schizophrenia, and continuing to use them is a part of maintaining these friendships.

## Substance Abuse Effects Checklist

*Instructions:* Place a check next to each problem area that your relative has experienced *due to alcohol or drug abuse* within the past three months.

Increase in symptoms                                          _____

Relapse or rehospitalization                                  _____

Increase in depression or suicidality                         _____

Treatment noncompliance                                       _____

Social problems (more arguments, withdrawal)                  _____

Not meeting work or program expectations                      _____

Not meeting household responsibilities                        _____

Legal problems                                                _____

Health problems (including accidents)                         _____

Money problems                                                _____

Housing instability                                           _____

By drinking and using drugs with others, patients may feel more "normal" and less stigmatized by their illness; this may result in a feeling of being accepted by others, a positive sense of belonging to a group, and better self-esteem. If your relative has friends who use drugs or alcohol, and prefers to spend at least some time with others, socialization motives for his or her substance abuse may be especially important.

## Coping with Symptoms

As you are already aware, patients with schizophrenia experience a wide range of symptoms, many of which can be extremely distressing. For some patients, substance abuse is motivated by attempts to cope with these symptoms. For example, patients with chronic auditory hallucinations sometimes use alcohol excessively, even to the point of drinking until they pass out, as a temporary escape from the voices. Patients with negative symptoms may abuse stimulants to increase their arousal and energy level. Any substance may be used by patients to temporarily alleviate feelings of anxiety, depression, or irritability. Of course, the long-term effect of substance abuse is usually a worsening of symptoms. However, many people with substance abuse problems do not make decisions based on the long-range outlook, but rather based on immediate consequences; in the eyes of many patients, the short-term benefits of substance abuse on symptom relief may be difficult to resist. If your relative experiences persistent symptoms that are distressing, he may be especially vulnerable to substance abuse as an attempt at self-medication.

Some patients use drugs or alcohol as a strategy for coping with medication side effects, such as akathisia (restlessness) or sedation. This motive appears to be less common than substance use aimed at coping with symptoms. If this appears to be a motive for your relative, developing alternative strategies for coping with side effects may be helpful (see Chapter 3).

## Pleasure Enhancement

If alcohol or drugs did not cause pleasurable feelings (or at least greatly reduce unpleasant feelings), these substances would not be addictive. Indeed, patients who do not like the effects of commonly abused substances avoid them and the problems associated with their abuse. Patients with schizophrenia are particularly prone to using alcohol or drugs for these pleasurable effects, because they tend to have limited alternative activities that are enjoyable and they suffer from boredom. Many patients engage in few recreational or leisure activities, either because they lack the required resources or because the effort to initiate the activities is too great. They often lack close interpersonal relationships, including romantic or sexual relationships, because of poor social skills. Furthermore, patients often do not have the positive experiences associated with working, such as extra money and self-esteem. Alcohol and drug use provides a convenient, immediate source of pleasure to many patients. If your relative engages in few enjoyable activities other than substance use, pleasure enhancement may be one of his or her motives.

### Other Motives

Although most patients with a substance use disorder will admit to at least one of the three motives described above, other motives are also possible. Patients who abuse large amounts of alcohol or drugs and develop a strong physical or psychological dependence may continue use in order to prevent withdrawal effects or because of cravings. Some patients continue to use substances because they have used them for so long it has become a part of their lifestyle; the habit develops a life of its own.

### Evaluating Your Relative's Motives

We have identified a variety of different motives that patients with schizophrenia often have for using drugs or alcohol. You may already know some of the reasons your relative uses substances from things he or she has said in the past. You may also find it helpful to broach the topic with your relative to find out what his or her perceptions are. When raising the issue with your relative, remember that your goal is to *understand* some of the reasons he or she uses substances, not to pass judgment or change behavior (this will come next). By communicating that you are interested and care about why your relative uses alcohol or drugs, you will be taking an important step toward beginning to deal with this problem.

When you have collected all the information available to you about possible motives for your relative's substance abuse, you can complete the Motives for Substance Abuse Checklist.

## How You Can Help

Your special relationship with your relative puts you in a unique position to help him or her deal with the problem of substance abuse. If your relative lives with you or you see each other often, you are familiar with his or her symptoms and level of functioning, and you may be privy to his or her pattern of substance abuse. You also know your relative better than anyone else, and your closeness and shared history together may enable you to motivate him or her to begin the long road to recovery. Your optimism and willingness to make a concerted effort to address the

## Motives for Substance Abuse Checklist

*Instructions:* Check off the motives for substance abuse that your relative has demonstrated or expressed to you.

*Socialization*

Substance use in social situations                    _____

Substance use with peers before onset of illness    _____

Desire to be with other people                        _____

Limited other social opportunities                    _____

*Coping with Symptoms or Side Effects*

Substance use when alone                              _____

Persistent, distressing symptoms                      _____

Severe depression or anxiety                          _____

Medication side effects                               _____

*Pleasure Enhancement*

Limited other leisure activities                      _____

Lack of close relationships                           _____

Boredom                                               _____

Not working                                           _____

*Other Motives*

Prevent withdrawal symptoms                           _____

Craving                                               _____

Habit                                                 _____

substance abuse disorder may be the single most critical factor in helping your relative toward a better future.

In this section, we describe strategies you can use to handle a substance abuse disorder in your relative. For most families, these strategies are helpful, but not sufficient in and of themselves, to overcome a substance abuse problem. Substance abuse is a long-standing problem in many patients with schizophrenia, and may require years to overcome. Therefore, professional, long-term intervention is often needed to successfully treat substance abuse in schizophrenia. Your involvement may be an important bridge for your relative's engagement (or reengagement) in professional treatment.

## Keeping Channels of Communication Open

Talking with your relative about his or her substance abuse is the first and most important step toward dealing with the problem. If you can't talk about it, your ability to directly help him or her will be limited. You need to be willing to talk about it and to continue talking about it, probably for a long time. Most patients who abuse alcohol or drugs deny or minimize their problem, whether or not they also have schizophrenia. Before patients are willing to work toward reducing their drug or alcohol use, they must be persuaded that it is a problem. Your best chance of doing this is by keeping channels of communication open with your relative.

If you have not talked about the problem with your relative, or if you tried long ago but gave up because it seemed useless, prepare yourself to talk again. If you have been talking, keep it up, and follow some of the guidelines we provide here. Above all, do not lose hope and give up.

Some of the key points in talking with your relative about his or her substance abuse problem are summarized in Figure 12.3.

Your immediate goals when talking to your relative are to open up the channels of communication, to express your concerns, and to understand your relative's perspective. Your longer-term goals, which will require much talking over a lengthy period, are to persuade your relative that he or she has a problem and to begin to develop a plan for dealing with this problem. When talking, express your concerns directly—use "I" statements and "feeling" statements and be specific. Try to understand your relative's perspective by being a good listener, using reflective listening skills (see Chapter 6). Be firm rather than meek, but avoid being judgmental or expressing outrage or strong feelings of anger. Anger with your relative about his or her drug or alcohol abuse may reflect a blaming attitude for something that is not completely under his or her control. It is natural to feel angry when one is in a situation that is difficult to control. However, expressing this anger may discourage your relative from

# Key Points in Talking with Your Relative About Substance Abuse

*Short-Term Goals*

- Keep communication open (or open communication channels)
- Express your concerns
- Understand your relative's perspective

*Long-Term Goals*

- Persuade your relative that he or she has a substance abuse problem
- Motivate your relative to work on the problem
- Plan steps that can be taken to deal with the problem

*Communication Skills*

- Be firm, specific, use "I" and "feeling" statements
- Use reflective listening skills—paraphrasing what your relative says, asking relevant questions
- Avoid statements that are angry, blaming, threatening, or judgmental

*Basic Facts to Remember*
*About Substance Abuse*

- Drug and alcohol abuse problems are very common in schizophrenia
- It is important to reduce substance abuse in order to improve the course of schizophrenia
- Substance abuse is not completely under patients' voluntary control
- Repeated efforts and long-term treatment are needed to solve substance abuse problems
- Optimism and determination are key ingredients for successful treatment

Figure 12.3

talking with you further about the problem, thereby reducing your ability to change the situation. Instead, communicating your feelings of being upset or frustrated to your relative, which avoid the onus of blame, may be more helpful.

If you find it difficult to engage your relative in a discussion, or he or she avoids you, communicate up front that it is important for you to talk together and that you don't blame him or her for anything. It may be helpful to set aside a particular time to talk, or to talk during some other enjoyable activity (such as on an outing), when your relative is in a good mood. Gentle persistence will pay off in the long run.

## Sticking Together

Substance abuse in a relative can have an extremely divisive effect on the rest of the family, at times pitting one family member against another. When the family member with schizophrenia is the offspring, conflicts often arise between the parents about how to handle a problem. To avoid the divisive effects of substance abuse in your family, you need to stick together and adopt a team approach to the problem. A team approach requires family members to reach a consensus about the problem and what needs to be done, and for them to decide on a plan for how to deal with the problem. It is important to iron out major disagreements between you and other family members *before* you include the patient in discussions about how to handle the problem. If this is done, you will be able to present a unified front between family members in discussions with the patient, and will avoid sending conflicting messages. Since continued efforts are most often required to make an impact on substance abuse, discussions between family members need to be held on a regular basis.

## Identifying Advantages and Disadvantages of Substance Abuse

Patients with a substance use disorder typically deny or downplay the negative consequences of their alcohol or drug use. One strategy for persuading your relative that he or she has a problem and for building motivation to work on it is to help him or her recognize the consequences of substance abuse. It may be tempting to try to do this by pointing out to your relative the disadvantages of his or her substance abuse. However, this often fails because people tend to reject or deny disadvantages suggested by other people.

A more effective alternative is to help your relative construct a list of the advantages and disadvantages of his or her substance use. Disadvantages that are identified by your relative carry more weight than those identified by others, so it is best if you contribute as few disadvantages as possible. When constructing this list, you can provide hints or ask your relative general questions about areas that he or she may have overlooked, for example, "Can you think of any effects your drinking has on your money situation?" It is helpful to identify both advantages *and* disadvantages of substance use, to provide a more balanced picture of the effects of substance abuse. If a comprehensive list is drawn up, the disadvantages will usually outweigh the advantages. We recommend that this list be written down, preferably by the patient. We have provided a form that can be copied and used for this purpose: the Advantages and Disadvantages of Using Drugs or Alcohol Worksheet. When the list has been completed, it can be posted in a prominent location (such as on the refrigerator), and added to when further advantages and disadvantages are identified.

For example, Tom had had problems with drinking and smoking marijuana for several years. With the prompting of his parents, he constructed a list of the advantages and disadvantages of his substance use. The *advantages* he identified included:

1. It relaxes me

2. It is fun to do with friends

3. It reduces boredom

4. I sleep better after drinking

5. Smoking pot makes me feel "high"

The list of *disadvantages* included:

1. I often run out of money before the end of the month

2. Smoking pot sometimes makes me paranoid

3. I feel groggy the day after I have been drinking

4. Sometimes it makes the voices worse

5. It causes tension between me and my parents

6. I still feel depressed after drinking or smoking pot

## Developing Alternatives to Substance Use

Recognizing the disadvantages of using drugs or alcohol may make your relative more inclined to work on this problem. However, to decrease his or her substance use, you will also need to address the positive effects of alcohol and drug use. Helping your relative construct a list of advantages and disadvantages will also provide you with additional information about why your relative uses drugs or alcohol. It is not practical (and often not possible) to try to reduce the positive effects of substance use. A better strategy is to identify alternative ways that your relative

## Advantages and Disadvantages of Using Drugs or Alcohol

*Instructions:* Write down all of the advantages you can identify for using drugs or alcohol and all of the disadvantages. Try to think of every possible advantage and disadvantage.

| Advantages | Disadvantages |
|---|---|
| 1. | 1. |
| 2. | 2. |
| 3. | 3. |
| 4. | 4. |
| 5. | 5. |
| 6. | 6. |
| 7. | 7. |
| 8. | 8. |
| 9. | 9. |
| 10. | 10. |
| 11. | 11. |
| 12. | 12. |
| 13. | 13. |
| 14. | 14. |
| 15. | 15. |

can get his or her needs met, so that these alternative activities can begin to take the place of substance abuse.

Helping your relative develop alternatives to substance abuse is not an easy task. For most patients, using drugs or alcohol is a habit that requires little planning or effort and that produces rapid results. Alternative activities will not be as convenient or have such immediate effects until they are practiced and become a part of the patient's usual routine. The challenge is to identify possible alternatives and to begin to help your relative explore those alternatives that appear to have the greatest promise. Clearly, identifying and trying out alternatives to substance use requires time and effort. Your relative will probably not be willing to put the energy into developing alternatives until he or she has at least partial insight into his or her problem. However, once your relative is willing to work on this, it can have profound effects on his or her substance abuse problem because it involves a change in lifestyle.

Developing alternatives to drug or alcohol abuse involves using a combination of strategies described in this book. Problem-solving methods (Chapter 7) can be especially helpful—family members working collaboratively toward the goal of finding and implementing alternatives to substance use. Potential solutions are brainstormed, then evaluated, and a plan is formulated to try out different alternatives. Follow-up discussions focus on evaluating the success of the plan, modifying plans when necessary, and generating additional alternatives.

As discussed earlier in this chapter, most of the positive effects of alcohol or drug use involve either socialization, pleasure enhancement, or coping with symptoms. Chapter 14 ("Improving Quality of Life") describes strategies for helping your relative improve his or her social functioning and enjoyment of life. These strategies can serve as alternatives to substance use when the motives involve either socialization or pleasure enhancement. Chapter 10 ("Persistent Positive and Negative Symptoms") and 11 ("Depression and Anxiety") discuss ways of helping patients cope with troubling symptoms that do not involve substance use. Read these chapters for specific details about how to help your relative enhance his or her socialization and leisure activities and how to cope better with symptoms. The following sections provide some pointers to consider when helping your relative develop alternatives to substance use.

### Socialization

Developing alternatives for socialization is perhaps your most difficult task, but it's also one of the most important ones. If your relative uses alcohol or drugs with friends, he or she will have to learn how to socialize with these friends without using substances or will need to make new friends who don't abuse drugs or alcohol. In either case, your relative needs to be motivated not to use substances with friends. Learning how to refuse offers from friends to use alcohol or drugs requires assertiveness skills, such as good eye contact, speaking in a firm tone of voice, and repeatedly saying "no" if the other person persists. If your relative is motivated, you can help improve his or her assertiveness by doing brief role plays of simulated social encounters (see examples of social skills training in Chapter 14). In the role plays, you or other family members can play the role of friends offering or pressuring your relative to use substances. After each role play, provide your relative with specific feedback about what he or she did well and how his or her performance could be improved. Check out how the skills worked by talking to your relative after he or she has used them in a real situation, and then fine tune them as necessary.

The feasibility of helping your relative develop alternative friendships depends on several factors. If your relative has close and long-standing relationships with many friends who use alcohol and drugs, and knows few people who do not use substances, it may not be realistic to try to develop alternative friendships unless other major changes are undertaken. Examples of such changes would be your relative moving to a structured living situation or beginning work. On the other hand, if some of your relative's friends use drugs and alcohol and others do not, efforts can focus on decreasing contact with some friends and increasing it with others. If your relative's relationships are not very close or long-standing, developing other friends may be a viable option. You may wish to consider whether helping your relative improve his or her social skills will facilitate making new friends.

### Pleasure Enhancement

Your relative may engage in fewer leisure activities than before partly because of his or her substance use problem. Using alcohol and drugs is a form of recreation that often supplants other leisure pursuits. It may be helpful to point out to your relative that he or she *has* enjoyed other activities in the past and to begin to explore which of these activities might be worth trying again. An important consideration when trying to help your relative develop alternative sources of pleasure is the time factor. Drugs or alcohol produce rapid, positive effects on your relative, whereas more time is required to find other sources of enjoyment. For your relative to continue to be motivated to work toward alternative leisure activities, he or she will need help dealing with the temptation or craving for alcohol or drugs. A problem-solving approach—involving generating, evaluating, and selecting various options—can be helpful in deciding how to deal with the immediate need for substances.

### Coping with Symptoms

Most of the issues pertinent to the development of alternative leisure activities also apply to helping your relative develop better strategies for coping with troublesome symptoms. Developing these strategies takes time, and you will need to consider additional methods for dealing with your relative's immediate temptations to use drugs or alcohol. If your relative's symptoms are directly related to the negative effects of his or her substance abuse, developing alternative coping strategies may not be possible (nor fruitful) until the substance use is reduced or stopped. For example, stimulant abuse (cocaine or "amphetamine") can worsen psychotic symptoms such as hallucinations or delusions, whereas alcohol abuse often worsens depression. In either case, developing coping strategies for these symptoms is unlikely to pay off as long as the patient continues to use those substances.

## Encouraging Participation in Structured Activities

Drug and alcohol abuse is usually linked to an excess of unstructured time, both in the general population and among persons with schizophrenia. Patients with schizophrenia often have little structured time, such as specific household responsibilities, regular attendance at a day treatment or vocational program, or work. Consequently, they may have more time for hanging out and using alcohol or drugs. If your relative does not have a regular routine and is engaged in few structured activities, it will be helpful to work toward structuring his or her time. Increasing the time your relative spends engaged in structured activities can add more meaning and purpose to his or her life, as well as reduce the opportunities for using alcohol and drugs.

The chances are high that your relative will resist efforts to increase the structure of his or her day. After all, your relative is doing what seems natural to him or her and may see little reason to change. You may be successful in motivating your relative by discussing how certain structured activities are related to his or her longer-term goals (for example, day treatment is related to making friends, employment to more independent functioning). However, other steps may also be necessary. In the next section, we discuss how to use contingencies (positive and negative consequences) to reduce substance abuse and encourage more adaptive behaviors.

## Establishing Contingencies

Many of the strategies we describe for how you can help your relative deal with a substance abuse problem require him or her to cooperate or show some willingness to change. An important goal to work toward with your relative is the development of insight into the problem and a desire to change. However, these are not absolute requirements for changing his or her substance use behavior. By establishing specific rewards for abstinence and costs for substance use (contingencies), and systematically following through, you may be able to alter your relative's use of alcohol or drugs. The same basic principles apply to encouraging your relative to become engaged in structured activities or in professional treatment for his or her substance abuse disorder.

Your ability to use contingencies to modify your relative's substance abuse behavior depends upon the extent of your contact with him or her, chiefly, whether he or she lives at home. If your relative does not live in your home, unless you provide significant financial support you will not be able to use contingencies to modify his or her substance use. Setting contingencies is most effective if your relative lives with you.

We describe how to set contingencies in Chapter 9 and also briefly refer to this topic in Chapter 3 as a strategy for enhancing medication compliance. The steps of establishing contingencies are summarized in Figure 12.4. This approach capitalizes on the fact that the consequences of behaviors have an influence on future behaviors.

The principles of establishing contingencies are really quite simple. Positive consequences of a behavior increase that behavior, whereas negative consequences decrease the behavior. For example, the Jones family had a household rule that prohibited smoking marijuana in the house. John, the patient, sometimes liked to smoke marijuana in his room, which his parents could easily smell. His parents decided to establish the contingency that John would lose ten dollars per week of spending money if he smoked in the house. If John smoked in the house more than once during the week, he would lose additional spending money. This contingency was helpful for addressing John's smoking in the house, but different strategies were necessary to reduce his marijuana use in other situations.

Using contingencies to alter substance abuse behavior is hard work and takes time, and this approach may not be feasible for some families. One common difficulty you might encounter is obtaining an accurate assessment of your relative's substance use behavior. If you can't measure this behavior, you won't know if you have changed it by providing consequences. Another problem some family members have is feeling bad when they have to deprive a patient of a particular privilege. Family members often feel sympathetic towards their relative's plight and are reluctant to contribute to making the patient's life any worse (such as by denying certain privileges), even if only temporarily. If you share this reluctance about providing negative consequences for substance use behavior, it may be helpful to remind yourself that reducing substance abuse is certainly in your relative's long-term best interest, and that he or she probably lacks the ability to stop the behavior on his or her own.

### Encouraging Participation in a Self-Help Group

A wide range of different self-help groups are available to persons with a substance abuse problem. Most of these groups are for anyone

## Steps in Establishing Contingencies for Patients

1. *Decide which behaviors you want to increase and which you want to decrease:*

- Work at increasing adaptive behaviors as well as decreasing maladaptive behaviors.

- Consider increasing behaviors that are alternatives to substance abuse.

- Identify one or two behaviors of each type to work on, but not more.

- Be as specific as possible.

2. *Decide how these behaviors will be measured, when, and by whom:*

- Look for objective measures of behavior (measures that more than one person can verify).

- Consider possible problems with measuring a behavior.

- Decide how often and at what times each behavior will be measured.

- Decide who will monitor and record the behaviors.

3. *Determine consequences for each behavior:*

- Identify positive consequences for behaviors that you want to increase.

- Choose positive consequences that are valued by your relative, you have control over, and which are readily available.

- Try to shape behaviors you want to increase by providing positive consequences for small steps in the right direction.

- Identify negative consequences for behaviors that you want to decrease.

- Choose negative consequences that involve the loss of something valued by your relative (such as a privilege), are under your control, and will not result in harm to your relative.

*continued on next page*

Figure 12.4

## Steps in Establishing Contingencies for Patients

4. *Draw up a specific plan to implement the program:*
   - Write down the plan, including:

     The definitions of the behaviors

     Who will measure the behaviors and when

     The specific consequences for each behavior
   - Who will provide the consequences and when.
   - Present the plan to your relative.
   - Decide on a time to meet again to follow up on the plan (not more than a week later).

5. *Follow up on the plan and modify it as necessary:*
   - Meet regularly to evaluate whether the plan is working as intended.
   - Check to see that consequences have been provided as planned.
   - Modify behaviors and consequences as necessary in order to promote more change.
   - If adaptive behaviors do not change, consider:

     Are the positive consequences really "positive" for the patient? If not, identify different positive consequences.

     Is too much behavioral change expected? If so, focus on a smaller increase in behavior and shape larger increases gradually over time.
   - If maladaptive behaviors do not change, consider:

     Are the negative consequences really "negative" for the patient? If not, identify other negative consequences.

     Is too much behavior change expected? If so, focus on a smaller decrease in behavior and gradually decrease the behavior more over time.

Figure 12.4

with such a problem, such as Alcoholics Anonymous (AA) or Rational Recovery, whereas others are for patients with a psychiatric disorder and substance abuse problems, "double trouble" groups. Many patients find participation in one of these groups provides them with much-needed support in combatting the urge to use drugs or alcohol. Encouraging your relative to try attending one of these groups may link him or her up with others who have overcome similar difficulties. You and other family members may find it helpful to attend self-help groups for relatives of persons with a substance use disorder, such as Al-Anon.

Self-help groups do not work for everyone. Obviously, to attend a self-help group your relative needs to have some awareness that his or her substance abuse is a problem. Even if your relative has this awareness, he or she may feel uncomfortable in the group setting. Patients often feel awkward at meetings in which most of the other participants do not have a psychiatric disorder (such as AA). Instead of feeling like they are members of a group of people with a common problem, they may feel isolated and different from the other participants. The personalities and dynamics of self-help groups for substance abuse problems vary from one group to the next, even within the same organization. If your relative is willing to consider a self-help group, it may be helpful to encourage him or her to shop around, attending several different groups to find one that is a particularly good match.

## Helping Your Relative Get Professional Treatment

We have emphasized the importance of long-term, comprehensive treatment for many patients who have substance use disorders. The need for long-term intervention is illustrated by the fact that many patients who participate in these programs show little change over the first one to two years, although significant improvement is usually evident after that. Do not blame yourself for not being able to solve your relative's problem on your own. Even though you can help your relative with his or her problem, the task of overcoming substance abuse is often too great to accomplish without professional help. If you succeed in engaging your relative in professional treatment for his or her substance abuse, you will have played a vital role in the recovery process.

# How Professionals Can Help

Mental health professionals provide a range of different services that can be useful in treating dual-diagnosis patients. We briefly describe these services below. Additional details about the nature of the treatments, their availability, and their appropriateness for your relative can be obtained by discussing it with professionals involved in your relative's treatment (case manager, social worker, psychiatrist), or by directly contacting service providers of substance abuse treatment for patients with a psychiatric disorder.

## Inpatient Treatment

When a patient has an extremely severe substance use disorder, especially if it is marked by physical dependence upon drugs or alcohol, inpatient treatment is sometimes used as a means of safely taking the person off the addictive substances ("detoxifying") and stabilizing his or her symptoms on medication. Inpatient treatment is usually quite brief. Most programs range from five days to one month in duration. The goals are limited to getting the alcohol and drugs out of the patient's system, temporarily breaking the substance abuse routine, and (hopefully) beginning the process of engaging the patient in longer term outpatient treatment.

## Outpatient Treatment

In the past, treatment of patients with a psychiatric disorder and a substance use disorder has been fragmented, with mental health services provided by some agencies and substance abuse services provided by others. Often the different agencies involved in providing treatment failed to communicate with each other, and sometimes they worked at odds with one another. This arrangement was particularly ill suited for patients with schizophrenia, who often failed to benefit from the traditional treatment approaches for substance use disorders. Fortunately, in recent years there has been a movement toward integrating mental health and substance abuse treatments for patients with serious psychiatric disorders. This means that the same professionals who provide treatment for your relative's schizophrenia may also be responsible for treating (or coordinating treatment of) his or her substance abuse disorder.

A variety of treatments may be available on an outpatient basis to address substance abuse problems in your relative. The specific programs will vary depending upon where you live. Treatment is often provided in the context of a day treatment program. Some day treatment programs are designed specifically to meet the needs of dual-diagnosis patients, while others are intended for the broader range of patients and contain special groups for patients with a substance abuse problem.

A number of different psychotherapeutic interventions appear to be helpful to patients with drug or alcohol problems. These interventions are usually provided on a group basis, although some individual sessions may also be conducted. *Persuasion groups* are designed to reach patients who are in denial about their substance abuse problem through involved discussions between group members and education about the effects of drugs and alcohol. *Stress management techniques* can provide patients with more adaptive strategies for handling their stress than resorting to drugs or alcohol. *Refusal skills training* uses social skills training techniques to bolster patients' ability to resist overtures from others to use substances. *Relapse prevention training* is a comprehensive cognitive-behavioral approach to addictive disorders centered around helping sober patients anticipate situations in which they are at high risk for drinking or drug use, as well as planning and practicing coping strategies to deal with those situations when they arise.

## Residential Treatment

For patients with a severe substance use disorder, residential treatment programs specifically designed for this population offer much promise. There are several unique advantages to these programs over other available treatments for dual-diagnosis patients. First, such programs provide a higher level of structure than can be achieved in ordinary outpatient settings. Many patients with schizophrenia who have severe problems with substance abuse require structured living settings in order to overcome their problems with addiction. Second, residential programs remove patients from their customary environments, thus decreasing or eliminating their exposure to many of the cues that trigger alcohol and drug use (such as friends, bars, parties). Third, the focus of residential programs—on helping patients manage urges to use substances and on developing alternative coping strategies, social skills, and a sense of personal self-control—provides a more intensive, integrated treatment than would otherwise be available. Fourth and last, residential programs provide a high level of monitoring of substance use behavior, which is helpful for patients who are prone to use drugs and alcohol at every available opportunity. Patients often need to live in a residential program for several years; however, preliminary research on these programs suggests that they can be quite beneficial.

## Assertive Community Treatment

The difficulties of engaging patients with schizophrenia and substance use disorders in treatment call for active interventions designed to meet patients' needs in the community. In contrast to traditional treatment approaches, Assertive Community Treatment (ACT) provides a range of critical services, including meeting with patients, family members, and other support persons in the community, and around-the-clock availability. One method of providing ACT in the community has been the establishment of *continuous treatment teams*, in which the responsibility for patients' treatment is shared by an interdisciplinary team of professionals. Another way of meeting the special needs of seriously impaired or dual-diagnosis patients is for an intensive case manager to be assigned. This person works closely with a small number of patients in the community.

Assertive community treatment is an approach to mental health service delivery that has evolved over the past two decades to overcome the limitations inherent in clinic-based treatment. The approach is not yet widely available, but increasing numbers of mental health centers have been adopting it, and it is likely to become more available in the future.

## Helping Yourself

Living with a relative who has schizophrenia and a substance use disorder can be strenuous and may create tension between family members. In your efforts to help your relative cope with this problem, it is important that you do not sacrifice your own and other family members' peace of mind. Ultimately, strong conflict and stressful family relationships will only increase your relative's symptoms, substance abuse, or both, making matters worse for everyone. It is vital that you attend to your own needs and those of family members other than your relative with schizophrenia.

In our experience, some patients with schizophrenia who have a serious substance use disorder cannot be effectively treated when living at home with family members, but can improve when they live in a more structured environment, such as a residential program or another type of structured living arrangement. It is very difficult for family members to closely monitor their relative's substance use behavior at home, and day-to-day activities tend to be less structured. If your relative lives at home and you have been unsuccessful in altering his or her dependence on drugs or alcohol, despite numerous attempts, we advise you to consider alternative living situations for your relative. You may feel as if you are "abandoning" your relative during this time of need, but you may actually be acting in his or her best interest. By not allowing your relative to continue to use drugs or alcohol in your home, you provide the most potent consequence of substance use available to you. Furthermore, you attend to the needs of all family members and recognize everyone's basic right to a quality life.

# 13

# Preventing and Responding to Crises

Sooner or later, if you have a family member with a serious illness, you will have to respond to a crisis, and this applies to both physical and mental disorders. Severe diabetes and asthma are examples of physical illnesses that can have a rocky course and can lead to frightening symptoms, midnight calls to physicians, visits to emergency rooms, and hospitalizations. Schizophrenia is a mental illness that can result in crisis situations affecting both patients and their relatives.

There are several characteristics of schizophrenia that can lead to crises:

- The symptoms of the illness fluctuate. Even when your relative is taking medication, he or she is vulnerable to relapse. This vulnerability is increased if medication is not taken.

- The nature of the symptoms themselves can contribute to crisis. For example, when patients have paranoid delusions they may react aggressively or violently to defend themselves.

- People with schizophrenia are prone to depression and suicidal thoughts and may try to hurt themselves.

The most severe kind of crises related to schizophrenia are those in which someone's safety is threatened. For example, violence, destructive behavior, suicide attempts, and threats of hurting oneself or others are all crisis situations that require immediate attention. Other situations also need attention, but allow you more time to respond, such as when your relative stops taking medication.

Dealing with any crisis takes a toll. Most family members have bad memories of their experiences dealing with crises, including spending hours in an emergency room, waiting for crisis teams or the police to respond to phone calls, attempting to reason with their relative when he or she is violent or suicidal, and negotiating the complicated involuntary commitment process. Family members often have especially strong memories of their worry and fear for their relative's welfare and of their feelings of helplessness.

You may have such nightmarish memories of trying to deal with a crisis that you don't even want to think about it, much less make plans for how to deal with it, should it happen again. Feeling this way is an understandable reaction. However, the expression "Those who forget the past are condemned to repeat it" applies here. You might prefer not to think about past crises, but reviewing these previous experiences and making plans for the future may be your best bet for preventing such crises from recurring.

Although this chapter focuses on crises, the entire book is intended to help you prevent them. By reading this book, learning as much as you can about the illness, and following the suggestions in other chapters, you are already taking important steps toward preventing crises. Managing the illness more effectively on a day-to-day basis, and noticing small changes or situations that need attention before they become problems, enables you to avoid crises. This chapter will help further prepare you by summarizing steps for preventing crises and providing guidelines for dealing with crises that do occur.

The major crises that are addressed in this chapter include violent or destructive behavior and suicidal thoughts or behavior. Procedures for involuntary commitment of psychiatric patients are also reviewed.

## Guidelines for Avoiding Crises

Strategies for averting crises related to schizophrenia can be grouped into three major categories: preventing relapses, creating a supportive environment, and directly addressing problems that arise from the illness. These areas have been addressed in detail in previous chapters and are briefly summarized here because of their relevance to preventing crises.

### Preventing Relapses

***Set firm expectations for taking medication.*** Research has shown that patients who do not take medication regularly are at higher risk for relapse. To encourage compliance, it helps for you to make sure that your relative understands the purpose of the medication and the side effects that might occur. It is also helpful to communicate with the doctor about how the medication is working and how side effects can be minimized (see Chapter 3).

*Respond quickly to early warning signs of relapse.* Make a list of early warning signs that are specific to your relative, and make a plan for what to do if they occur (see Chapter 4).

*Use community resources to get needed outpatient services.* Help your relative get the psychiatric and social services in the community that he or she needs and is eligible for. Such services can enable your relative to improve the quality of his or her life and ability to manage the illness. It is also helpful to have professionals involved in evaluating your relative on an ongoing basis (see Chapter 5).

## Creating a Supportive Environment

*Communicate clearly and reduce criticism.* Strive to create an atmosphere where people can talk freely to one another about their feelings. Avoid blame and excessive criticism. Keeping channels of communication open with your relative prevents unspoken resentments from developing and increases the chances that your relative will feel comfortable confiding in you when he or she does not feel well. In short, good communication can avert crises and relapses by maintaining a lower level of stress at home and by facilitating your ability to monitor your relative's symptoms (see Chapter 6).

*Use a problem-solving approach.* When you address problems directly and have a positive attitude about coming up with solutions, you can often prevent small problems from becoming crisis situations. Involve your relative and other family members whenever possible in coming up with a plan of action to solve problems as they arise (see Chapter 7).

*Prevent stress from building up.* Be alert to signs of stress and work to reduce the sources of the stress when possible. Develop coping techniques to reduce the impact of stress that cannot be avoided. This is important both for you and your relative (see Chapter 8).

*Establish household rules.* Patients with schizophrenia respond well to realistic, clear expectations. It is reassuring for them to know what is expected and how they can fulfill their responsibilities. Patients benefit from having a meaningful, but not too taxing, structure at home and in their other daily activities. Establishing household rules will result in a more peaceful family environment for everyone living at home (see Chapter 9).

## Addressing Problems Arising from Schizophrenia

*Help your relative cope with persistent symptoms.* Many patients with schizophrenia experience positive symptoms (such as hallucinations and delusions) and negative symptoms (such as apathy and blunted affect) between acute episodes. Helping your relative identify the symptoms that are most troublesome and develop strategies to cope more effectively will decrease the negative impact of these symptoms (see Chapter 10).

*Take action to reduce severe depression and anxiety in your relative.* Depression and anxiety are among the most common problems experienced by patients with schizophrenia and either one can be very debilitating. They can decrease motivation and hinder progress; they can also contribute to a higher risk of relapse or suicide. Helping your relative develop strategies to reduce these feelings may avert crises such as suicide attempts (see Chapter 11).

*Limit the use of alcohol and drugs.* Substance abuse is involved in many crises, among both psychiatric patients and nonpatients. Furthermore, drugs and alcohol act as biochemical stressors for persons with mental illness. Therefore, it is desirable to limit your relative's use of alcohol and drugs. For some patients, substance abuse is a chronic, difficult problem that can be overcome only with multifaceted, professional treatment (see Chapter 12).

*Evaluate current strategies.* These guidelines for preventing crises can require considerable time and energy to implement. However, in the long run you will reap the benefits of the time you invested in preventing crises. The Crisis Prevention Checklist is provided to help you evaluate the current status of these prevention strategies. Give yourself credit for what you are already doing, and note the areas of prevention that could be strengthened. Consult the corresponding chapters of this book to strengthen those areas in need.

## Suggestions for Dealing with Crises

Despite your best efforts, schizophrenia is an unpredictable illness, and you may not be able to prevent all crises. Therefore, in addition to working on prevention, we advise you to be prepared to respond to a crisis, should one occur. This is especially important if your relative has had a crisis in the past. For example, if your relative attempted suicide before, you could develop a plan for how to respond if he or she reported thoughts of suicide again.

The following guidelines will help you respond to most crises. We provide suggestions for dealing with specific crises later in this chapter.

*Use crisis services when necessary.* Make a list of phone numbers in advance. This list can include how to reach the treatment team, crisis hotline, suicide hotline, nearest emergency room, police, and any other services you think might be helpful in a crisis. Referring to a list is easier than trying to look up numbers in the phone book in the middle of an emergency.

## Crisis Prevention Checklist

*Instructions:* Check off those strategies you are currently using to prevent crises and those strategies that could be strengthened.

| Strategy | Using Effectively | Needs Work |
|---|---|---|
| 1. Set firm expectations about medication | _____ | _____ |
| 2. Respond quickly to early warning signs | _____ | _____ |
| 3. Use community resources | _____ | _____ |
| 4. Communicate clearly and reduce criticism | _____ | _____ |
| 5. Use a problem-solving approach | _____ | _____ |
| 6. Prevent stress from building up | _____ | _____ |
| 7. Establish household rules | _____ | _____ |
| 8. Use techniques for coping with persistent symptoms | _____ | _____ |
| 9. Reduce depression and anxiety | _____ | _____ |
| 10. Limit use of drugs and alcohol | _____ | _____ |

*Behave calmly.* Your primary task is to help your relative regain control. One of the best ways to do this is to show that you are in control of yourself. Speak slowly and clearly, and use a firm tone of voice. Keep communication brief. During a crisis, it is natural to feel anxious, frightened, or tense. Calmly stating that you are concerned about the situation is appropriate; panicking or acting hysterical can upset people even more. For example, shouting, hurrying around, or attempting to physically restrain your relative (unless there is no other recourse) can worsen the situation.

*Evaluate the urgency of the situation.* Many situations are upsetting, but do not constitute a crisis. For example, you may be disturbed if your relative refuses to bathe for a week, but this is not an emergency. Asking the following questions will help you determine if a situation is a crisis and requires immediate attention:

- Has anyone been hurt? Is your relative or someone else in danger of physical harm?

- Has property been damaged? Does it appear likely that it will be?

- Does the current behavior indicate that a serious relapse has occurred?

If the answer to any of these questions is "yes," the situation is a crisis and you need to take immediate action.

*Determine how much time you have to respond.* For example, if your relative reports hearing voices that tell him to hurt himself and he feels that he may do so, an immediate evaluation needs to be conducted either by his psychiatrist or at an emergency room. On the other hand, if your relative reports feeling irritable because of increased voices, it is probably sufficient to schedule an evaluation at the clinic the next day.

*Get help in handling the situation.* It is hard to stay calm and organized when you have the full responsibility for managing a crisis. When possible, enlist another family member, someone from the treatment team, or a neighbor or friend to help you deal with the situation. Working with another person to resolve a crisis will lighten your burden and may help you respond more effectively than if you had to work alone.

*Make a specific plan to manage the crisis.* Decide exactly what should be done about the crisis and determine the first step, second step, and so forth. Keep your plans simple and realistic. Determine what you need to carry out your plan: specific information, phone numbers, additional people. Take action as soon as possible in order to keep the situation from worsening. For example, if your relative began to have paranoid delusions that family members were trying to hurt him or her, your plan might include the following steps:

- Call the treatment team to let them know of the situation.

- Arrange an immediate evaluation at the clinic.

- Contact a relative or friend to drive you both to the clinic.

- Help your relative remain calm while waiting for the appointment by sitting with him or her and listening to favorite music.

*Keep safety in mind.* Although most people with schizophrenia are not aggressive or violent, there is an increased chance of such behavior during a crisis. Being aware of the importance of safety, therefore, can prevent someone from being hurt. For example, during a crisis it is best to avoid blocking your own or your relative's ways out of the room or other setting, in case your relative feels threatened. We discuss this issue in more detail later in this chapter.

## Learning from a Crisis

After a crisis has been resolved and it is still fresh in your mind, it may be useful to review what happened and to develop a plan for how a similar crisis could be prevented in the future. To review the crisis, arrange to meet individually with all the people who were involved in dealing with it, including relatives, friends, professionals, and (when possible) your ill relative. Alternatively, some people find it helpful to process the crisis in a group meeting, although this is not always practical. In either case, during your meetings try to take a positive, constructive approach and avoid blaming or finding fault. The Crisis Review Questionnaire can help you gather useful information. Note that it is not necessary to ask each question on the questionnaire; the questions are provided simply to aid your discussion. You may, however, wish to make a separate copy to use for each of the meetings.

After meeting with everyone involved you will be able to establish two plans. The first plan will address how you can *prevent* a similar crisis from occuring again. The second plan will involve how you can *respond* more effectively if a similar crisis happens again. The information you gather using the Crisis Review Quesionnaire can then be summarized on the Crisis Review Worksheet and used to develop action plans for preventing and responding to similar crises in the future. We urge you to take the opportunity now to consider your relative's most recent crisis, how to prevent another one, and how to cope more effectively should a similar crisis occur again. Even if it has been some time since your relative's last crisis, the information-gathering and planning process can still be performed, and may in the long run prove invaluable.

## Crisis Review Questionnaire

*Instructions:* Use these questions to guide your discussions with professionals, family members, your ill relative, and others to gain information about a past (or recent) crisis. You need not ask every person every question; they are intended simply as an aid.

*What was happening in the patient's life before the crisis occurred?*

- Was the patient under unusual stress? (See Chapter 8 for a reminder of what your relative experiences as stressful.)
- Has there been any changes in his or her routine?
- Had there been more arguments or other interpersonal conflicts?
- Was the patient taking medication as prescribed?
- Was he or she abusing drugs or alcohol?
- Was the patient more worried or anxious than usual?
- Had he or she shown signs of depression?
- Had the patient experienced a loss?

*What were the early signs that a crisis was building?*

- How did the patient's behavior change?
- Did his or her personal appearance change?
- What feelings did he or she express?
- Was there a change in the patient's relationships?
- Did the patient have difficulty with his or her thinking?
- Was there a disturbance in sleep or eating patterns?

*What was done to resolve the crisis?*

- What did each person involved do to try to improve the situation?
- What early interventions were tried?
- Did someone talk to the patient?
- Did someone talk to members of the treatment team?

- Did family members talk to each other?
- Who was called to intervene?
- How was safely assured?
- How did people stay calm?

*Which actions were effective in resolving the crisis?*

- What actions improved the situation?
- What actions made the situation worse?
- Were some interventions partly successful?

*What could have been done to better resolve the crisis?*

- Which actions should be used again?
- What should be done differently?
- What could have been done to resolve the crisis more rapidly or effectively?

*How might a similar crisis be prevented in the future?*

- How can you put into practice what you learned about the way this crisis developed?
- How could the crisis be stopped before it builds up?
- How can you put your ideas into a plan that can be followed?
- Who will be responsible for which parts of the plan?

*How might a similar crisis be resolved if it does occur?*

- How can you put into practice what you learned about how to respond better to a crisis like this?
- What could be done to intervene more quickly?
- How can your put your ideas into a plan that can be followed?
- Who will be responsible for the different tasks?

## Crisis Review Worksheet

*Instructions:* Use the information you have gathered from meeting with other people involved in your relative's most recent crisis (including your relative, if possible) to complete this worksheet. Enlist the aid of other family members, professionals, friends, and the patient (if appropriate) in planning for preventing and responding to future crisis.

Briefly describe the crisis.

What was happening in your relative's life before the crisis occured?

What were the early signs that a crisis was building?

What actions were taken to resolve the crisis? Place a star next to those actons that were effective.

What could have been done to improve how the crisis was resolved?

What is the plan of action for *preventing* a similar crisis in the future?
Steps in plan:

1.

2.

3.

4.

5.

What is the plan of action for *responding to* a similar crisis in the future?
Steps in plan:

1.

2.

3.

4.

5.

# Guidelines for Involuntary Commitment

Many family members have questions about how to get emergency psy-chiatric treatment in the middle of a crisis. If your relative presents a serious danger to others or to him- or herself during a crisis, he or she needs to be evaluated for admission to a psychiatric hospital. This can easily be arranged if you can convince your relative that an evaluation is in his or her best interest.

However, you may not be able to persuade your relative to go for a psychiatric evaluation, if for example, your relative has delusions that people are conspiring to harm him or her through hospitalization. If your relative will not agree to an evaluation, your next step is to seek an in-voluntary commitment. Each state has its own legal procedures for evalu-ating and hospitalizing psychiatric patients who present a danger to themselves or others but refuse voluntary treatment. Although the laws governing involuntary commitment in most states are similar, differences exist. We will use the laws of one state, Pennsylvania, to provide an ex-ample of the procedures for involuntary commitment.

In Pennsylvania, a concerned person, such as a family member or treatment provider, must file a petition for a warrant that requires the patient to submit to a psychiatric evaluation. These petitions are granted based on a combination of two factors which must have existed within the past 30 days: serious danger to the patient or to others and evidence of severe mental illness. The petitioner must have directly observed the patient behave in a way that presents an immediate threat of injury to the patient or others. The strongest evidence is an actual attempt to hurt oneself or another, for example, hitting someone, setting a fire, taking a medication overdose. Threats to hurt oneself or others that show serious intent can also be used as evidence, for example, locking oneself in the bathroom with a knife and threatening to slash one's wrists, having a weapon and threatening to kill someone.

To file a petition, the family member or professional must go to the nearest psychiatric emergency center, usually a community mental health center or a hospital emergency room. Once the petition is completed, the staff there contacts the Office of Mental Health for approval to obtain a warrant for involuntary psychiatric examination. If the petition is ap-proved, the police are then called, and they bring the patient to the near-est emergency facility.

If the examining psychiatrist determines that the patient meets the criteria for involuntary commitment to a hospital, the patient is commit-ted for treatment for a specified number of days at the nearest psychiatric hospital with an available bed. Within the specified period there will be a court hearing, in which the petitioner and the patient must appear be-fore a judge to determine if "probable cause" exists to hold the patient longer for treatment.

284 Coping with Schizophrenia

In some states, if the patient is unable to care for himself or herself and might die if left alone, he or she can be involuntarily hospitalized. For example, refusing to eat and drink for several days, walking outside in the snow barefoot, or going out in subzero temperatures without a coat present substantial dangers to the patient's health. In this circumstance, the patient is sometimes referred to as "gravely disabled" or "unable to care for himself or herself."

Commitment laws can be very complicated. One reason for this is that they must serve two purposes, which sometimes clash. First, they must provide a mechanism for protecting patients and others from harm that arises out of the psychiatric disorder. Second, the laws are designed to protect the rights of patients not to be hospitalized unnecessarily or for inappropriate reasons. Unfortunately, the laws sometimes seem to family members like cruel barriers to getting help for their ill relative. Consequently, it is best to become knowledgable about the specific laws and procedures for involuntary commitment in your state *before* a crisis arises. We recommend that you contact your treatment team, local psychiatric emergency room, or community mental health center to find out the necessary details. Then if a crisis occurs, you will be able to evaluate whether involuntary commitment is indicated, and you will know the necessary procedures for obtaining a commitment. The following are the general criteria for involuntary hospitalization in most states:

- The patient is dangerous to himself or herself.

- The patient is dangerous to other people.

- The patient is gravely disabled and unable to care for himself or herself.

It is preferable to go through the procedure of seeking an involuntary commitment before calling the police for transportation. However, if you are afraid that your relative or someone else is in imminent danger of being harmed, call the police immediately (usually 911). Safety is always of primary importance.

## Guidelines for Responding to Violent or Destructive Behavior

When a person with schizophrenia threatens others or acts in a violent manner, it may be that he or she is having a symptom relapse. For example, if a patient hears voices saying someone is trying to hurt him or her, the patient may strike out at that person in self-defense. Although only a small percentage of patients become violent, effective strategies are needed to minimize the risk these patients pose to others and themselves.

Research has shown that the patients who are most likely to become violent have been violent in the past. Other factors sometimes associated with violence in schizophrenia include difficulty controlling anger, high levels of tension, active hallucinations or delusions, and substance abuse. However, these factors are less important than a past history of violence.

## Responding to Violent Behavior

We provide here some suggestions that will help you respond effectively to threats of violence or violent behavior. These suggestions can be used in addition to the general guidelines described earlier for dealing with crises.

*Step 1: Evaluate the potential for actual violence.* If your relative threatens to hurt someone or break things, the best indication of whether he or she will act on these threats is past behavior. If your relative has been violent in the past few hours or days, threats of violence must be taken very seriously, because it is likely that he or she will be violent again. Similarly, if your relative has made threats in the past that were acted upon, there is a good chance he or she will act on the current threat. We emphasize, however, that even if your relative has never made threats in the past and does not have a history of violent behavior, it is best not to ignore threats of violence or destruction.

*Step 2: Take action to minimize the chance that someone will get hurt.* Try to avoid handling a situation in which there is a significant threat of violence by yourself. Don't be embarrassed to ask for help from professionals, other family members, or even the police. Also, don't be embarrassed to leave your house if you truly fear harm to yourself. Your safety and well-being are extremely important.

When dealing with a threatening relative, remember that people who make violent threats often feel threatened themselves. This can lead to violence when they feel cornered or under pressure to defend themselves. If you are in the same room, allow enough physical space so that your relative does not feel crowded, and avoid blocking his or her "escape route" from the room. Stand at least three feet away from your relative. Avoid approaching your relative suddenly, and carefully evaluate whether touching him or her might be perceived as threatening.

Speak in a firm but nonthreatening, nonchallenging manner. Acknowledge that your relative feels upset and try not to judge his or her feelings. Remember that even though your relative's perceptions may not be based in reality, to him or her the situation and dangers are very real. For example, you could say "I can understand that you're upset. I'd like to help you with this problem." People who feel angry and violent towards others are often confused and experience many different emotions. Do not attempt to interpret why your relative is upset; instead, focus on making the situation as safe as possible.

It may be necessary to remove any weapons or objects that could be used as weapons from your relative's access. Alert other people in the house to the situation. If they are not aware of what is happening, they may inadvertently provoke your relative. They may also be able to help you cope with the situation.

Remember, if at any time you believe that you are in imminent danger, leave the area as soon as possible. Try to avoid making sudden moves or being overly dramatic in your departure.

*Step 3: Rectify the immediate crisis.* Once safety issues have been assured, you can focus your attention on rectifying the situation. The usual first step is to contact your relative's treatment team to arrange for an immediate evaluation. If an evaluation cannot be arranged by the treatment team, your relative can be taken to the nearest emergency room. In some areas, local community mental health centers have emergency services to help families in crisis. If the patient refuses to be evaluated, you will need to seek an involuntary commitment.

*Step 4: Develop strategies to prevent violence from happening in the future.* After the immediate crisis is over, get together with family members (including the patient, when possible) to review what happened and to develop a plan for preventing a repetition of the situation. Use the Crisis Review Questionnaire and Worksheet to guide your discussion. In addition, it is important for your relative to acknowledge that someone was injured or could have been hurt or that property was damaged by his or her behavior. This can help your relative remember why a similar crisis needs to be prevented in the future. If your relative expresses concern over harm done and offers to pay any bills involved, it may help the other family members affected to feel less angry and more understanding toward the patient. After discussing the situation and completing the worksheet, you may be able to see what led up to the crisis and how such events could be prevented in the future.

In some cases, however, you may not be able to see a pattern that would have helped predict or prevent the crisis. Some violent episodes seem to come "out of the blue." When there is little or no predictability, or when a past episode contained a very high risk of actual harm (or someone was seriously hurt), we recommend that you seek alternative living arrangements for your relative. You can still maintain your relationship with your relative without exposing yourself to risk if he or she lives elsewhere, such as in a supervised residence in the community.

# Guidelines for Responding to Suicidal Thoughts or Attempts

It is very upsetting to family members when an ill relative has thoughts about hurting himself or herself or committing suicide. However, people with schizophrenia have a higher risk of having suicidal thoughts or trying to hurt themselves than people in the general population. As you may recall from Chapter 11, "Depression and Anxiety," about half of all patients with schizophrenia make a suicide attempt at some time during their life, and about one in every ten patients dies from suicide.

Although the risk of suicide attempts is significant, there are steps you can take to reduce the chances that your relative will hurt himself or herself. By becoming more aware of your relative's early warning signs, being willing to talk directly to him or her about suicidal thoughts, and taking action quickly when it is called for, you will be better prepared to deal with situations where suicidal thoughts or actions are involved.

The most important predictor of whether your relative will attempt suicide is a past history of attempts. The second most important indication is if he or she has had thoughts of suicide or seems preoccupied with death. Other patients who may be more vulnerable to suicide attempts include young men who have had frequent relapses and who are aware of the limitations imposed by their illness, patients with depression and strong feelings of hopelessness, and patients with a history of substance abuse.

## Common Myths About Suicide

Several common myths about suicide exist, which are important to dispel.

*Myth 1: Talking about suicide with your relative may give him or her the idea to try.* Talking about suicide does not cause patients to start thinking about it. Most patients who have been thinking about suicide experience some relief when asked about it. Patients who have not had such thoughts usually simply deny it. By asking questions about how your relative feels, you show that you are concerned about his or her welfare.

*Myth 2: People who talk about suicide don't act on it.* Threats of suicide should not be ignored. Most people who commit suicide have talked about it in advance. Even statements that are said jokingly, such as "I guess I'll just jump off a bridge," may indicate serious intent. Only by knowing your relative well and by asking questions will you be able to evaluate the seriousness of his or her talk.

*Myth 3: If someone really wants to commit suicide, no one can prevent it.* Most people who talk about suicide have mixed feelings about ending their life. Often, they want to live but find living very painful. Sometimes a patient's desire to end his or her life is a temporary urge that is difficult to resist; it may seem at the time like the only solution. Timely intervention can help the patient get past this urge and begin to address the most pressing problems in his or her life. Helping your relative address problems and painful feelings can relieve the pressure of the impulse to suicide.

## Suicide Prevention Guidelines

**Step 1: Be alert to warning signs of suicidal intent.** One important warning sign is symptoms of severe depression, including pervasive feelings of worthlessness, excessive guilt, and hopelessness about the future. Other signs include preoccupation with thoughts of death, the presence of voices telling the person to hurt himself or herself, and increased risky behavior, such as walking into traffic.

Pay close attention if your relative begins to talk about suicidal thoughts. Statements such as "I wish I were dead," "I would be better off dead," "I'm not afraid to die," and "I have nothing to live for," are reasons for concern. Your relative may also talk of a specific plan about how to hurt himself or herself or may refer to methods other people have used to commit suicide. This kind of talk can be a warning of serious suicidal intent.

Increases in symptoms, such as auditory hallucinations or delusions, often accompany suicidal thoughts in patients. Relapses that involve hearing extremely critical voices or voices that command the patient to hurt himself or herself are especially related to suicide attempts. If your relative experiences an increase in these types of symptoms, be alert to the risk of suicidal behavior.

**Step 2: Behave in a supportive manner.** If your relative is suicidal, it will probably help to express your concern and affection for him or her. Refusing to acknowledge your relative's suicidal thoughts, or trying to gloss over these feelings by saying things like "You don't really feel that way," only make matters worse. Speak calmly and try not to respond to your relative in a judgmental or harsh way. Talking with your relative keeps a vital channel of communication open, which may provide a ray of hope.

**Step 3: Evaluate the risk for self-harm.** Any threat of suicide should be taken seriously. It is impossible to predict perfectly when someone will follow through on a suicide threat. Evaluating suicidal intent is a complicated and difficult matter, and is usually best done by a professional. However, there are sometimes situations when the patient's treatment team cannot be reached immediately and family members need to evaluate whether there is an immediate danger of self-harm.

Unless your relative has already tried to harm himself or herself, you need to ask specific questions to evaluate the immediate danger. The following questions will elicit the kind of information necessary in evaluating your relative's potential for a suicide attempt:

- Have you been feeling sad or unhappy?

- Does it ever seem like things will never get better?

- Have you felt so badly that you thought about hurting yourself?

- Do you have any thoughts of ending your life?

- Have you had thoughts of how you might kill yourself?

- Have you made any plans to do so?

- What are your plans? When do you intend to do it?

- Is there anything that might hold you back, such as people you care about, religious beliefs, responsibilities to others, or something you wanted to live to do or see?

As you go down the list, the questions indicate progressively more danger of a suicide attempt. Thus, the danger is very high if the person feels hopeless about the future, has made a plan for carrying out his or her intentions, has already taken steps toward this plan, and feels that there is nothing to hold him or her back. If your relative expresses such conviction, he or she needs to be evaluated immediately by professionals, and steps must be taken to prevent him or her from carrying out the plan (see Step 4, below). Even when the danger is not immediate, the situation needs to be closely monitored and professional consultation sought. Do not try to handle the situation alone, as the circumstances can be very intense and demanding.

On rare occasions, people may develop a habit of threatening suicide when they do not sincerely feel that way. If your relative has a history of this behavior, talk it over with the treatment team and formulate a plan about how to deal with such threats. Bear in mind that no threat of suicide can be ignored.

*Step 4: Take steps to protect the person in the immediate situation.* Remove any potentially lethal instruments from the home (including guns, knives, sharp scissors, medicines, alcohol, and car keys), and do not leave your relative alone. Keep communication open. Your relative may experience some relief as a result of expressing his or her feelings, and family members can keep abreast of any changes in the seriousness of the threat. Although you need to give your relative space, stay within close enough proximity to keep a careful watch.

Talking with staff members at a suicide or crisis hotline can be helpful to both you and your relative. Keep the phone numbers of such hotlines, as well as other emergency numbers in a convenient spot.

*Step 5: Develop strategies to prevent suicide attempts in the future.* Completing the Crisis Review Worksheet will help you develop some prevention strategies and maintain good communication with your relative. If your relative can learn to describe his or her suicidal thoughts before making an attempt, you can intervene early enough before the urge becomes overwhelming. To encourage open communication, be receptive and listen to your relative when he or she expresses feelings, even if it is difficult to understand them.

Because many people who attempt suicide suffer from feelings of depression, it is also essential to monitor the symptoms of depression (see Chapter 11). Furthermore, being alert to life stressors, which can contribute to feelings of depression, may help you identify times when your relative is at greater risk for a suicide attempt.

# PART V

## Looking Ahead

# 14

# Improving Quality of Life

What *is* a quality life? "Quality of life" refers to the overall satisfaction or enjoyment of life that a person experiences. Surveys of psychiatric patients point to a number of different dimensions of living that together determine the quality of their lives: housing, rewarding social relationships (including both family and friends), work (or other purposeful activity), access to resources (such as health care and money), enjoyable leisure or recreational activities, and the absence of distress (such as depression or anxiety). Significant problems in any of these areas can interfere with your relative's ability to enjoy his or her life.

Although there is general agreement as to the areas that contribute to satisfaction with life, each patient is unique and has individual needs. It is your relative's own perceptions of enjoyment and quality of life that are most important, not any standards determined by society. For example, people in our society often assume that good "social adjustment" and a satisfactory "quality of life" require a person to work full-time and to live independently. However, your relative with schizophrenia may enjoy a better quality of life working only part-time and living at home or in a supervised residence. Recognizing the distinction (and often discrepancy) between what society deems desirable and what your relative wants is a key to helping him or her attain a satisfactory quality of life.

The lives of many patients with schizophrenia are difficult, and as a close family member you may be painfully aware of this. You may wonder whether the goal of helping your relative achieve a good quality of life is too lofty or "pie in the sky," when simply getting by is hard enough. These concerns are understandable. However, we believe there are good reasons to be optimistic that you can help your relative to *improve* the quality of his or her life. Rather than comparing your relative to other people, look at him or her as a unique individual and consider the small changes that might improve his or her enjoyment of life. We have been encouraged by our own experiences working with families and the reports of many family members that almost all patients are capable of experiencing a better quality of life.

## The Role of This Book

By reading this book and trying out some of the strategies we recommend, you have already begun to help your relative improve the quality of his or her life. The early chapters (Chapters 1 through 5) were devoted to providing you with critical information about schizophrenia, with the primary goals of helping you to monitor the course of your relative's disorder, to prevent or minimize relapses and rehospitalizations, and to gain access to available resources. Relapses of symptoms are often distressing for patients and result in temporary setbacks in achieving goals. Preventing or reducing the chances of a relapse will have positive effects on your relative's quality of life, by maintaining stability of his or her living arrangements and by avoiding the distress associated with a relapse.

The chapters focused on creating a supportive environment (Chapters 6 through 9) can help to improve the quality of family relationships and reduce the negative effects of stress on your relative. You and other family members may be the most important people in your relative's life. By strengthening your relationship through good communication, problem solving, and setting realistic expectations, you can help your relative to get more enjoyment out of life. Furthermore, stress reduction improves satisfaction with life by averting relapses and lowering distress.

Helping your relative cope with special problems and deal with crises can also directly affect the quality of his or her life. Most of the strategies we describe for managing symptoms are aimed at reducing distress either directly (anxiety or depression, Chapter 11) or indirectly (positive symptoms, Chapter 10). The methods described in Chapter 10 for coping with the common negative symptoms of apathy and anhedonia (lack of pleasure) are aimed at improving your relative's enjoyment of leisure-recreational activities. Likewise, preventing or responding effectively to crises has obvious benefits for your relative's overall experience of life.

In short, everything in this book is about improving the quality of your relative's life. However, there are three areas that, although they have been addressed at different points throughout the book, deserve additional consideration in this chapter: social relationships, work, and living arrangements. Therefore, this chapter focuses on how you can help your relative improve the quality of his or her life in these three areas.

# Social Relationships

We have previously discussed the basic ingredients of helping your relative improve his or her relationships with family members. However, many patients are also interested in making more friends, developing closer relationships outside the family, and having intimate relationships. If your relative has not expressed an interest in closer relationships with others, he or she may or may not be interested; the only way you can know is to ask. Some patients do *not* desire more intimate relationships, and find relationships in general to be stressful and burdensome. In our experience, however, most patients would like better relationships.

Some patients enjoy relationships with others, but on an infrequent, less intense basis. Avoid assuming that your relative would prefer to see others more often. Although seeing a friend once every two or three weeks might not be very satisfying to you, it may be sufficient to meet your relative's social needs. People's needs for interpersonal contact vary greatly, both among patients with schizophrenia and in the general population. Once again, the best way to understand your relative's needs is by talking about them with him or her.

If your relative is interested in having closer friends or more friends, some of the suggestions provided below may be helpful.

## *Attending to Personal Hygiene*

Some patients with schizophrenia have difficulty maintaining an adequate level of personal hygiene, such as bathing regularly, using deoderant, brushing teeth, shaving, and combing hair. Poor hygiene can be a major obstacle to establishing closer relationships. Thus, if this is a problem for your relative, working toward improving his or her hygiene may be an important first step to better relationships with others.

When broaching the topic of personal hygiene with your relative, it is best to avoid being judgmental or critical. Rather, express to your relative your understanding of how it can be difficult for him or her to perform particular self-care skills on a regular basis, being as specific as possible. Then, point out how attending to that specific skill can be important in improving relationships with others. Finally, offer to help your relative establish a plan to attend to that area of personal hygiene on a regular basis. For example:

| | |
|---|---|
| *Mother:* | Mike, I noticed that sometimes it seems to be a little hard for you to do some of your self-care skills, like brushing your teeth or taking a shower. |
| *Mike:* | Yeah. I sometimes forget. |
| *Mother:* | I can understand that it might be hard to remember to do some of those things. |

| *Mike:* | Sometimes I just don't want to do it. |
| *Mother:* | I can see how that might be tough. On the other hand, taking care of your hygiene can be important for making friends. |
| *Mike:* | I guess so. |
| *Mother:* | You've told me that you'd like to have closer friends. How about if I give you a hand in helping you improve some of these areas of personal hygiene? It might help you in making friends. |
| *Mike:* | OK, I'll give it a try. |

When you begin working with your relative on his or her personal hygiene, set attainable, realistic goals, and be willing to settle for a lower standard than you might for yourself. For example, showering two or three times per week might be a better goal for some patients than showering every day. Brushing teeth every morning is a good goal, not as ambitious as brushing twice daily, but better than not brushing at all. After making some progress toward these goals, you and your relative can meet to decide whether to modify the goal. Some guidelines for helping your relative improve his or her personal hygiene are provided in Figure 14.1.

---

### Guidelines for Helping Your Relative Improve Personal Hygiene

1. *Talk over why specific skill areas (such as showering, brushing teeth, use of deodorant) are important:*

- Explain why good personal hygiene can help your relative to make friends or get closer to people.

- Tactfully describe the effects of not attending to personal hygiene (for example, smelling bad because of not using deodorant).

- Point out any salient longer-term consequences of not attending to a particular area, such as the need for dental work if teeth are not brushed regularly.

2. *Agree on specific areas to work on:*

- Identify areas that are the biggest problem.

- Get your relative's feedback about the areas that you think are most important.

---

Figure 14.1

## Guidelines for Helping Your Relative Improve Personal Hygiene

3. *Set goals for each area of personal hygiene:*

- Aim for attainable goals; avoid being overly ambitious at first.
- Be specific in setting goals: How may times per day or week should a self-care skill be performed? If daily, approximately when? If weekly, on which days?

4. *Make a record sheet that your relative can use to record each day which skills he or she has performed:*

- The record sheet is both a reminder to do the skill and a measure of the success of the plan.
- Make the record sheet easy to use, with spaces to check off whether the skill was performed each day.
- Post the record sheet somewhere your relative will complete it regularly.

5. *Set up rewards for following through on the self-care plan (optional):*

- Talk about small, enjoyable rewards that can be provided each week (such as a special meal, going to the movies).
- Agree on exactly what self-care behaviors must be performed how often to qualify for the reward.
- Don't make the reward too difficult to achieve—program for success!

6. *Meet regularly to follow up on the plan:*

- Meet at least weekly at first.
- Praise your relative for any positive steps, no matter how small.
- Modify the plan as necessary, either to work toward larger goals or to set smaller goals.
- When setting new goals after success with a previous goal, take very small steps forward to avoid overwhelming your relative.
- Modify the rewards as necessary; make sure the reward is really desired by your relative.

Figure 14.1

## Social Activities

One way of helping your relative make friends is to encourage him or her to explore possible social activities. Some communities have special "clubhouses" or drop-in centers for psychiatric patients, in which the primary purpose is to provide a meeting place for people to socialize, with few or no other expectations. In many areas there are "consumer groups" of patients who meet regularly to socialize and provide support to one another. Day treatment programs also provide opportunities for socialization, but these opportunities are embedded within a more structured experience involving group meetings.

Your relative may also be interested in more social contacts with nonpatients. By exploring socially oriented activities in the community you may discover places for your relative to meet others, such as at lectures at libraries, talks and readings at bookstores, sing-alongs, coffee shops, or hobby clubs. An advantage to participating in some of these activities is that your relative can be around others without a strong expectation of engaging in a great deal of conversation. This allows your relative the flexibility of limiting involvement with others to the degree that he or she wants, while still meeting some of his or her needs for social contact.

## Social Skills

Social skills are the specific behaviors involved in interactions with others that enable people to be effective, to get their point across, and to meet their social needs. People with schizophrenia often have poor social skills, which interferes with their ability to make friends or deepen interpersonal relationships. For example, poor eye contact while speaking, lack of vocal inflection and facial expression, slowness when responding to others, and difficulty finding interesting conversational topics are common social skills problems for persons with schizophrenia.

Not everyone with schizophrenia has social skill deficits. In addition, not all patients with poor social skills are motivated to improve their skills for interacting. However, if your relative does lack certain social skills, and is motivated to have better relationships with others, helping him or her improve social skills may be beneficial.

### Considering Social Skills Training Programs

Over the past several decades, social skills training has become an increasingly popular method used by professionals to help psychiatric patients improve their personal interactions. Social skills training is a set of techniques that are "packaged" together to gradually teach specific skills to patients. These techniques include:

- Talking about the importance of a particular skill

- Demonstrating the skill to the patient in a role play (a simulated interaction)

- Engaging the patient in a role play to practice the skill

- Providing specific feedback about what the patient did well (positive feedback) and how he or she could do it better (corrective feedback)

- Engaging the patient in more role plays and providing more feedback

- Giving an assignment to use the skill somewhere else

- Following up to see how the skill worked and conducting additional training

Patients are taught either individually or in groups, with training taking place over several months, or even years.

Research on social skills training for patients with schizophrenia suggests that patients are capable of improving their social skills, and that changes in skills can result in better social functioning. Although skills training involves hard work on the part of patients, the positive nature of the practice and the feedback that is given often makes the learning an enjoyable experience.

If you and your relative agree that improving social skills is an important goal, you may find it useful to explore the availability of social skills training in your area. Many community mental health centers provide skills training programs that may meet your relative's needs. The specific programs available may differ from one center to another. One social skills training program for psychiatric patients that has become widely available in recent years is the Skills for Independent Living and Support (SILS) program, developed by Robert P. Liberman, M.D., and his colleagues at the University of California at Los Angeles.

The SILS program uses a highly standardized approach to improving patients' social skills in specific areas. Each social skill area is divided into a distinct module and training focuses on one module at a time. For example, modules have been developed or are being developed for skill areas such as medication management, conversational skills, friendship skills, symptom management, and recreation for leisure. Training in each module involves discussing the importance of specific skills, observing videotapes of people demonstrating the skill, practicing the skill in role plays, getting feedback, doing homework to practice the skill on one's own, and practicing problem solving to deal with obstacles to using the skill. Groups of three to eight patients meet two to four times per week, for about an hour each time. Between three and six months are usually required to complete each module. Encouraging your relative to improve his or her social skills by participating in a program such as this can help him or her develop more rewarding relationships with others.

### Implementing Your Own Social Skills Training

You may have difficulty locating social skills training programs in your area, or your relative may be reluctant to participate in those programs that are available locally. If your relative still wants to improve his or her social skills, and you are willing to help, you may be able to make some progress in this area. Improving skills takes time and patience; however, it is worth a try if other avenues are not available to you. We briefly provide below a ten-step method for helping your relative improve his or her social skills.

*Step 1: Discuss the long-term goal.* For your relative to be willing to work toward improving his or her social skills, it must be clear how these skills are related to long term goals that are valued by him or her.

For example, Eddie wanted to be able to make friends and he was also interested in having a girlfriend. However, he didn't have any friends and was quite shy around people.

*Step 2: Identify a short-term goal related to the long-term goal.* Long-term goals can be accomplished by attaining a series of shorter-term goals. By breaking down the goal into smaller, easier increments, gradual progress can be made. Identify the first, smallest step forward that your relative can make toward achieving the long-term goal. Identify a short-term goal that your relative is willing to work on.

Eddie talked with his parents about his long-term goal of making friends. In the discussion, it became apparent that one first step toward making friends was being able to start conversations with others. Eddie agreed that this was a good short-term goal to work on.

*Step 3: Assess your relative's skills for achieving the short-term goal.* Once you know what the short-term goal is, explore your relative's strengths and weaknesses in relation to that goal; talk with your relative about which situations are easier to handle and which are more difficult. Once you have identified situations where your relative has difficulty, you can set up some brief role plays to see how he or she handles these types of situations. In these role plays, you or another family member can play the other person and your relative can be himself or herself. Ask your relative to act as he or she ordinarily would in that situation. Praise your relative for any behaviors that were performed well in the role play.

Eddie indicated to his parents that he found it difficult to start conversations with almost anyone outside the family, including other patients at his day program. Eddie's parents set up a few role plays with him to see how he would try to start conversations with male or female patients. His parents praised him for his good posture in the role plays.

*Step 4: Select a specific behavior to work on.* Based on the role play, choose one or two behaviors to begin to work on helping your relative improve. Focus on behaviors that he or she is most likely to be successful in changing. Consider behaviors related to the style or manner in which your relative interacts (such as eye contact, tone and loudness of voice, facial expressions), as well as the content of what is said (such as its appropriateness and interest level). Don't work on more than one or two behaviors at once.

During Eddie's role plays, his parents observed that he tended to speak quietly and avoided looking at the other person. They described to him that this would be a good area to begin working on.

*Step 5: Demonstrate how to do the behavior.* Demonstrating the specific behavior for your relative makes it clear to him or her how to interact more effectively in the situation. People often find it easier to learn by observing others than by being told what to do. Before the demonstration, explain to your relative what you will be showing him or her in the role play. When the demonstration is over, ask your relative what he or she observed.

Eddie's parents talked with him about the importance of good eye contact and speaking up when starting conversations. Then his father demonstrated in a brief role play how to start a conversation, pretending his mother was another patient at the program. When the role play was over, they got Eddie's comments about what he observed.

*Step 6: Engage your relative in a role play to practice the skill.* Ask your relative to try using the skill in a brief role play, using the same situation you used to demonstrate the skill. Encourage him or her to pay particular attention to the behaviors that you previously focused on.

Eddie participated in a role play of starting a conversation with another patient at the program. His father pretended to be the other patient.

*Step 7: Provide positive feedback and suggestions for improvement.* Always provide positive feedback first about what your relative did well. Be specific and sincere. Praise his or her effort. Then identify one specific area that he or she could improve and suggest how to change this.

Eddie's parents praised him for choosing a good conversational topic in the role play (talking about a recent movie he had seen). They suggested he might be even more effective if he spoke more loudly next time.

*Step 8: Engage your relative in another role play of the same situation, and provide more feedback.* After one role play, try doing another, encouraging your relative to attend to your suggestion for how it could be done better. Then provide more positive feedback about what was done well. You can do additional role plays as before, or stop here and move onto the next step.

In the second role play, Eddie showed some improvement in the loudness of his voice, and he even did a third role play, in which he worked on improving his eye contact. Eddie's parents praised his work on these specific skills.

*Step 9: Plan an assignment for your relative to practice the skill on his or her own.* Select an actual situation your relative will encounter, and plan with him or her how to use the skill in that situation. Anticipate possible obstacles that might interfere with using the skill in that situation. Make the assignment as specific as possible.

Eddie and his parents agreed that starting one conversation each day at the day program with someone he knew would be a good first assignment, since he felt less anxious talking with acquaintances than with strangers.

*Step 10: Follow up on the assignment and decide what to do next.* Assignments to use the skill always need to be followed up on to see how they went. When problems are encountered, use troubleshooting or role plays to assess what went wrong, and provide feedback to bypass those problems or modify the assignment. If the assignment went well, consider whether to make it more difficult or to start working on the next skill related to the long term goal.

Eddie reported that trying to start conversations had gone allright. He felt a little nervous at first, but became more relaxed when the other person seemed interested. Eddie and his parents agreed that starting conversations with strangers would be a useful next assignment. When Eddie had become comfortable with this, he began to work on identifying more interesting topics for conversations, since he found that he ran out of things to say pretty quickly.

These steps provide just one way of helping your relative improve his or her social skills. The basic principles of practice, positive and specific feedback, and specific suggestions for improvement can be used in many different ways to improve skills and facilitate social interactions. The key to success is a willingness to work together on these skills. Further information on social skills training can be obtained by reading: *Social Skills Training for Psychiatric Patients,* by R. P. Liberman, W. T. DeRisi, and K. T. Mueser (Needham Heights, Mass.: Allyn and Bacon, 1989).

## Vocational Functioning

Most psychiatric patients, including those with schizophrenia, want to work. One of the most common frustrations of both patients and their family members is the difficulty in finding employment for persons with a mental illness. Many patients and family members assume that employment is out of the question if the patient has significant symptoms. You may find it surprising to learn that the severity of symptoms, or even a patient's specific psychiatric diagnosis, is not strongly related to his or her ability to work. Despite this fact, in most states the community mental health system is not geared toward helping patients find competitive employment (jobs on the open market); rather, the preponderance of services are geared toward day treatment programs, which may lead into jobs in programs tailored to patients, but often do not. Some of these "sheltered workshops" are intended to lead to competitive employment, and serve the purpose of gradually preparing patients to meet the demands of the competitive market. Others, however, are disappointing to patients because they resent working in an environment populated only by psychiatric patients, they prefer more stimulating tasks, or they feel the experience doesn't result in them getting "real jobs."

There are a number of reasons for helping your relative pursue employment if he or she is interested. As we have repeatedly stated, engagement in structured, meaningful activities such as work tends to decrease problematic positive and negative symptoms—in other words, work can be good therapy. Work also can improve self-esteem, especially paid work, because of the recognition that the person is contributing something valuable. Finally, another benefit of work is that it enables patients to have some contact with nonpatients, providing access to different role models and some degree of acceptance within the general population.

## Investigating Local Program Options

There is a range of options available to you in helping your relative obtain employment. At the most basic level, the first step to take is to explore employment-related programs or opportunities in your community for psychiatric patients. Most communities have an agency, such as the Office for Vocational Rehabilitation that assesses employment strengths and weaknesses and may provide training opportunities and job placement services for people with psychiatric and physical disabilities. The effectiveness of these agencies in locating and placing patients in jobs varies widely, with some agencies obtaining jobs for only a small fraction of those interested. Sometimes these agencies will provide funding for job training (such as classes in computer programming or typewriter repair), although you may need to be involved in finding which training programs are best suited to your relative. If you have not yet explored what your local vocational rehabilitation agency has to offer, it is worth doing so. If you have already tried and been dissatisfied, you have other options available as well.

One specific approach to psychosocial and vocational rehabilitation for psychiatric patients is the Fountain House model. This model got its start in New York City in the 1940s, and has been expanded to many other communities since that time. A unique aspect of the Fountain House model is that it is run entirely by patients with psychiatric illnesses, with minimal assistance from mental health professionals. Patients who join the "clubhouse" become "members," who can then take advantage of a wide variety of training and vocational opportunities available through the clubhouse. One of the primary expectations of members who join the clubhouse is that they will work to help run the house. Specific expectations are set for each patient in terms of the number of days he or she will attend the program and the activities the patient will engage in.

Clubhouses also establish liaisons with various businesses in the community, and are thus able to provide a range of different job experiences for members. Usually members begin by working at the clubhouse, and then progress to trying different jobs in the community, with the ongoing support of other members. This approach appears to be quite helpful for motivated patients. To find out whether a clubhouse based on the Fountain House model is located near you, contact the Fountain House Training and Education Center in New York City (see "Resources" appendix).

Many communities, especially in urban areas, have a wide range of different organizations designed to help unemployed people find jobs (charitable organizations, agencies funded by local governments). These organizations may not be geared toward psychiatric patients, but they may nevertheless be helpful. Some programs may even provide job coaches to ease patients into particular jobs. Exploring these options may provide useful job leads for your relative.

## Exploring Individual Alternatives

Some of the options discussed above may be productive, but it is also possible that they will not be sufficient to get your relative a job. At the present time, there are few programs designed to help psychiatric patients obtain employment that are also tailored to meeting the needs of individual people. One such program is the Individual Placement and Support (IPS) Program, developed by Robert E. Drake, M.D., Ph.D., and Deborah R. Becker, M.Ed. at Dartmouth Medical School. Although the IPS Program may not be available in your area, some of the basic principles and program philosophy may help you in assisting your relative to find employment.

In the IPS program, each patient is assigned a vocational specialist who helps him or her identify specific interests and vocational strengths, to explore (or create) employment opportunities, provide ongoing support and help when a job is obtained, and monitor progress toward vocational goals. The vocational specialist serves as a member of the patient's treatment team. More information about this program can be obtained by contacting the New Hampshire-Dartmouth Psychiatric Research Center, 105 Pleasant St., Concord, NH 03301.

If a service such as the IPS Program is not available in your area and your relative is interested in working, you can help him or her find employment if you are willing to invest the time and energy. Places to start include newspaper classified ads (under "Help Wanted") and bulletin boards. You can also ask your friends or relatives if they have any ideas or have heard about any jobs that might be appropriate for your relative. Sometimes parents of other psychiatric patients that you meet at self-help organizations such as the Alliance for the Mentally Ill can provide leads to jobs that are not suited to their relative but might be a good match for yours.

Nobody knows your relative better than you, which puts you in a unique position to help and support him or her in pursuing employment goals. To fulfill this important role, you will need to give yourself time to learn how to best work with and advocate for your relative, including both helping him or her locate possible job leads and maintaining contact with the treatment team to exchange pertinent information. Some patients are ready to enter competitive jobs immediately, although being able to gradually increase the amount of time spent on the job can be advantageous. Other patients may prefer to build up to competitive employment, developing their confidence by first working at a volunteer job. In searching for the best type of job, consider your relative's strengths, weaknesses, and interests. Above all, remember that the key to success is finding (or creating) a job that suits your relative's unique abilities and limitations, rather than trying to change your relative to fit the requirements of a particular job.

Tim, for example, had been attending a day treatment program for several years when his mother brought up the possibility of his working. Although Tim often heard auditory hallucinations and sometimes had trouble getting out of bed in the morning, he expressed some interest in a job. However, he was also concerned about meeting the demands of a job and about whether working would threaten his benefits. He and his mother discussed work and possible job interests on a number of occasions and he gradually warmed up to the idea. Tim preferred a job where he could work alone; he liked work that involved filing or cataloging and was especially interested in working at a library. He continued, however, to be concerned about meeting the demands of a competitive job. His mother suggested that a volunteer job might be suitable at first, for building up his confidence and getting him used to working a regular schedule.

Tim's mother explored possible volunteer jobs, and found a library that had positions available. Because Tim was very anxious at the prospect of the work, he and his mother paid a visit before he agreed to try working there. After obtaining the librarian's permission, Tim's mother took five books off the shelf and told Tim to reshelve the books. She told him she would meet him in the magazine section when he was done. He finished the job in about about ten minutes, and when he met his mother, he was excited that he had been able to do the task. His mother and the librarian confirmed that the books had been reshelved correctly. He practiced again, this time correctly shelving ten books, and they then met with the librarian to work out a schedule.

After working ten hours per week at the library for two months, Tim was interested in pursuing paid employment. The library where he had been working didn't have any paid positions, but they provided Tim and his mother with some leads for part-time jobs at other libraries and happily gave him a good recommendation. His mother found a library that was willing to pay Tim for 5 hours per week of book shelving, which he gradually increased over the next year to 10 and then 20 hours per week. Although Tim continued to be bothered by hearing voices, their intensity had decreased, and he reported feeling better about himself.

## Living Arrangements

Where your relative lives and his or her relationships with people in that setting can have an important bearing on his or her quality of life. For some patients, living with parents or siblings is best because of the social support they receive from relatives and their ability to fit in with the family routine, including following basic household rules. For others, living elsewhere is preferable because of tension between family members or the patient's need for greater structure. Ultimately, the best living arrangement is one that represents a balance between the needs of both your relative and other family members. Figure 14.2 contains a list of some factors indicating that your relative would be better off living somewhere other than your home.

The decision about when it is best for your relative to leave home and live elsewhere is not an easy one. Family members who decide to ask their relative to move out often feel guilty, thinking that they are "abandoning" their relative. However, if and when you contemplate this decision, you may find it helpful to think of your relative's moving to another living situation as a positive step toward greater independence, rather than as a setback. Furthermore, just because your relative doesn't live at home, doesn't mean that you can't continue to support him or her and maintain a good, close relationship. In fact, many relatives find that their relationship with the patient *improves* after their relative leaves home, because of the reduced tension felt by everyone.

When considering alternative living situations, the primary issues that need to be evaluated are your relative's need for structure and the cost of the housing. In our experience, most patients with schizophrenia require some supervision or assistance to meet their daily living needs, and benefit from a daily structure when they first move away from home. Therefore, most patients have difficulty moving directly into an independent, unsupervised apartment. Independent living is a viable goal for many patients, but it is usually best to pursue this goal gradually, by their living successfully in progressively less supervised residences. Different types of supervised living arrangements are described in Chapter 5, "Community Resources."

## Discussing "Moving Out" with Your Relative

Talking about moving out can be an emotional topic for you and your relative. If you decide to discuss this with your relative, advance preparation may allay some of your concerns and make it easier for your relative. The first and most fundamental issue you need to resolve before

---

### Indicators for the Patient Not to Live at Home

- The presence of a stressful or tense home environment
- Other family members (such as children) who are frightened of the patient
- Inability of the patient to follow basic household rules
- Persistent problems with setting limits or adhering to them
- Extremely disruptive behaviors at home, such as:

    Frequent angry outbursts

    Violent or threatening behavior

    Persistent problematic behaviors, such as waking family members up at night

    Grossly inappropriate behavior, such as walking around the house naked

    Severe substance abuse

- Consistent medication noncompliance
- Inability of family members to set realistic expectations for the patient
- Substantial conflict between other family members (such as issues between parents) regarding the patient
- Lack of meaningful structure for the patient

---

Figure 14.2

discussing alternative living arrangements with your relative is whether leaving is an open question or whether you have already decided that you want your relative to leave home. Knowing whether the question is still open has direct bearing on how you present the situation to your relative. If you have not decided whether you want your relative to leave, then the primary purpose of the discussion is to exchange views and find out whether your relative would like to move. On the other hand, if you have already made the decision that you want your relative to leave, it is best be clear about it at the beginning, to avoid misleading your relative.

If you live with other family members who share the role of caregiver with you, it can be helpful to come to an agreement about whether you want your relative to leave home before discussing the matter with him or her. By having settled disagreements between you, you will be able to support each other when presenting this issue to your relative. You will also be able to anticipate and plan for different possible responses your relative might give when asked to move out.

If you decide that you want your relative to move, you can present this to him or her in a family meeting. Arrange a time for this meeting when everyone is calm and a place that is free of distractions, such as TV or food. Present the decision to your relative in an honest, straightforward, unapologetic manner. Provide an explanation for your decision, but avoid justifying it. Also make it clear that your decision is not negotiable, while listening sympathetically to your relative's concerns and letting him or her know of your continued support.

Try to involve your relative as much as possible in planning the move to another living arrangement. Don't try to make all the necessary plans in a single meeting; give your relative some time to adjust to the idea of moving out. For example:

*Mother:*   John, your Dad and I have been doing a lot of talking recently, and we have come to the decision that it would be best for you to live somewhere else. Sometimes we feel quite a lot of tension around the home, and we both think that all of us would be better off if you had a different living situation.

*John:*   What? You're kicking me out of my home?

*Mother:*   We don't look at it that way. We still love you and want to support you, but we also feel that the time has come for you to move on. Moving away from home can be a positive step toward greater independence.

*John:*   But I don't want to go. This is my home and I like it here.

| | |
|---|---|
| *Father:* | I can understand your feelings. You've lived here your whole life and you feel comfortable here. However, your mother and I have decided we think that it is best now for you to live somewhere other than home. We think it is a step in the right direction. |
| *John:* | So now you're going to make me live in one of those group homes? |
| *Mother:* | We haven't decided what the best living arrangement for you is yet. We would like you to be involved in making some of these decisions. I understand that this is hard for you now, and we will need to talk more about this over the next few days and weeks. |
| *John:* | I don't like the whole idea. |
| *Father:* | I can see how this is upsetting to you, John. We wanted you to know that this is a decision your mother and I have made, but we also want you involved in it as much as possible. Why don't we stop here, and we can pick up talking about it a little later. OK? |
| *John:* | OK. |

In most cases, gentle persistence, presenting a unified front between involved caregivers, and trying to involve the patient are successful in making a smooth transition from living at home to living elsewhere. Sometimes, however, patients adamantly refuse to leave, and their lack of cooperation becomes a major obstacle. When this occurs, your choices naturally become more restricted.

One strategy used by many families is to initiate changes in the patient's living situation while he or she is temporarily in the hospital for treatment of a relapse. If your relative has recently been violent or has threatened violence, you may be able to petition to have him or her hospitalized. When the patient is in the hospital, you can inform the inpatient treatment team that the patient cannot return home after the hospitalization. The team then must assume responsibility for finding a suitable placement for your relative. If you take this route, you will need to be firm in presenting your position to the inpatient team (as well as to your relative), who may try to persuade you to allow him or her to return home. If your relative steadfastly refuses placements that the inpatient treatment team recommends, there is a small risk that he or she could be discharged with no living arrangement, although this is rare. More often, patients eventually see the light and agree to a placement.

If your relative refuses to leave home, but he or she cannot be hospitalized, there are even fewer recourses available to you. Legally, if you alone own your home, you can have him or her evicted. Most families do not see this as a viable option because of the level of confrontation involved. However, it may merit consideration in some very severe situations. If you are in this difficult predicament, it is essential that you work together with other family members toward evaluating strategies for encouraging your relative to leave. It may also be helpful to be in touch with your relative's treatment providers, who may be able to provide you with suggestions or support your decision during their interactions with your relative. Finally, the support and advice from other families who have been through the same experience is invaluable; help can be obtained through organizations such as local chapters of the Alliance for the Mentally Ill.

# 15

# The Importance of Siblings

When one family member has schizophrenia, it affects everyone. Each person is confronted with the effects of the symptoms of the illness, and each must make adjustments, depending on his or her relationship with the patient and role in the family. A great deal of attention has been devoted to understanding the effect of mental illness on the patient's parents. And indeed, parents are deeply affected by mental illness in an offspring, and many of the responsibilities of caring for a son or daughter with schizophrenia fall directly on them. Brothers and sisters of the patient, however, are also important, and experience their own unique difficulties due to the illness in the family. We believe that the feelings and responses of all family members need to be considered, and that addressing the special needs of siblings can strengthen their relationship with their ill relative.

This chapter contains information for both siblings and parents of persons with schizophrenia. The more everyone understands about each other's experience, the better for the whole family, including the patient. This chapter will describe feelings commonly experienced by siblings and the impact the illness has on their lives and on their relationships. We will also address some of the special concerns of siblings, including their worry about what level of involvement to have with their brother or sister. Finally, we provide some suggestions about what siblings can do to cope with having an ill relative and how parents can help their well children.

## The Experiences of Well Siblings

Just as no two parents experience the illness of schizophrenia in an offspring the same way, no two siblings have the exact same response when a brother or sister develops the illness. Much depends on the ages of the siblings when the illness developed, whether the ill sibling is older or younger, what kind of relationship they had prior to the illness, and whether the illness developed slowly or quickly. The following examples describe some of the different experiences siblings can have.

Alice was 10 when her brother Bill, age 16, started to develop symptoms of schizophrenia. Prior to his illness, Bill had always taken an active interest in Alice, and to her he was an idol, someone she really looked up to. He was a good student in high school and active in drama and music programs. Toward the end of his junior year, he began behaving in ways that seemed strange to Alice. He would come into her room in the middle of the night, complaining that other students in his class were against him and were spying on him in his bedroom. He started taking a different route to school each day to "keep those traitors off my trail." After three weeks of changing his route, he took a kitchen knife and barricaded himself in his room one morning, refusing to open the door, insisting "They're going to kill me." Alice's parents made her go to school anyway. When she came home, Bill was gone and she did not see him for a month. Alice's parents avoided her questions and did not allow her any visits or phone contact with Bill. Alice was very upset and confused. She did not find out until many years later that Bill's behavior was caused by a mental illness.

Dana, on the other hand, was four years older than his brother Mark. Dana was fond and protective of Mark, although he always seemed different than the other kids. He was especially shy and sometimes sounded peculiar when he talked. Everyone thought he would grow out of it. By high school he was keeping collections of objects that had special significance to him, including broken bottles, pieces of string, leaves, and bits of tin foil that he found on the street. His room became filled with these objects, scraps of food, and dirty laundry that he refused to put in the wash. Dana stopped bringing friends home because he was embarrassed by his brother's odd behavior. Mark's parents were very upset by his room and his poor personal hygiene. They had fierce arguments with him, which sometimes included Dana, who would defend his little brother. When Dana was in college, he received word that Mark had become increasingly seclusive and had refused to eat or drink for several days. His parents had to commit him involuntarily to the local psychiatric hospital. Mark was in and out of psychiatric facilities for the next 20 years.

Joanie was 11 years old and already had three brothers when her sister Kathy was born. She helped change Kathy's diapers and care for her as a baby, but never felt that they had much in common because of the big difference in their ages. There seemed to be nothing remarkable about Kathy until her first year of college, when she had trouble concentrating in class and studying. She began to develop ideas that she had a "past life" as a police officer, and was once arrested for trying to stop traffic in the middle of town. Joanie was married and had children by the time Kathy had her first psychotic episode at age 20. Her parents thought street drugs were to blame, and it was many years before anyone in the family knew Kathy's diagnosis of schizophrenia.

## Common Reactions of Siblings

Schizophrenia is a complex and confusing illness, both to family members and professionals. It is particularly worrisome to children and adolescents when someone they love develops symptoms that result in bizarre and sometimes frightening behavior. In addition, when a sibling becomes ill, the healthy sibling's feelings must be reconciled with usual feelings of affection and rivalry that occur in any family. The following examples describe feelings that siblings of patients with schizophrenia commonly report.

### Confusion and Frustration

Especially in the early stages of the illness, when the diagnosis has not been determined, it is very confusing for siblings to see their brother or sister do strange, unexplainable things. An example of baffling behavior is when an ill sibling is paranoid and accuses his sister of stealing and conspiring against him. It is also frustrating when the ill sibling does not respond to reason or behaves inappropriately in front of a sibling's friend. A very confusing situation occurs when the symptoms have been diagnosed as a mental illness and no one informs the well sibling. Being kept in the dark is a major source of distress for siblings, because they have no way of understanding their brother's or sister's behavior.

### Guilt

Healthy siblings often feel guilty that their lives are better than their ill sibling's. Although it is no one's fault that their relative became ill, well siblings are aware that it is not fair that the illness hits one person and not another. Healthy siblings can't help comparing their lives and prospects for the future with the patient's, and feeling guilty. "It shouldn't have been Bill," Alice complained, "He was so talented and I was just average."

### Fear and Anxiety

Well siblings often worry that whatever caused their brother's or sister's illness will cause them to become ill. If they have heard something about the genetic aspects of schizophrenia, they may be apprehensive, since they share the same parents. Even though the risk of developing schizophrenia is higher when someone in the immediate family has the illness, the chances are still against their developing the illness (see Chapter 1). Well siblings can talk to genetic counselors about concerns for themselves and for any children they may have. "It took a long time for me to relax and stop checking myself daily for symptoms," Dana said.

## Sadness

It makes siblings sad to see a brother or sister suffering. Especially if they have been close to their ill relative, they can empathize with how he or she is feeling. In many ways, well siblings grieve for the loss of the brother or sister they knew. For example, Alice missed the closeness she once had with her brother, and wished that she still had the kind of older brother she could turn to for advice and protection.

## Embarrassment

Sometimes persons with schizophrenia act in ways that can be embarrassing. Before his first hospitalization, Mark would frequently get into arguments with salesclerks and waiters when he was out with his family. As a teenager, Dana found it especially mortifying to have people's attention drawn to him. Even adults can be embarrassed when a brother or sister with schizophrenia behaves bizarrely. It can ease some of the intensity of the embarrassment to know that the behavior is prompted by the symptoms of a mental illness, that it is not the intention of the patient to embarrass someone. Although it is important for the ill sibling to get out of the house and be involved in activities, it may be helpful to plan outings so that the potential for embarrassing situations is minimized. For example, you might choose to go out to eat at an informal restaurant, where it is less likely that unusual behavior will stand out than in a more formal setting.

## Anger and Resentment

It is only natural to feel angry about having a brother or sister with schizophrenia. The illness disrupts the equilibrium of family life and requires enormous adjustments. Siblings may be aware that their ill brother or sister received the largest share of their parents' attention, and that no matter what they did, they couldn't get the same attention. Although nobody likes to feel resentful, it is an understandable emotion when faced with such disruption. Even though siblings may feel resentful about the effects of the illness, they can still care deeply for their brother or sister.

# Impact on Siblings

Because a family member's schizophrenia can affect so many aspects of family life, the illness is bound to have an impact on the development of well siblings. They seem to feel the strongest effects in the areas of relationships and level of involvement with their family.

## Relationship with Parents

As mentioned earlier, the well sibling may feel that parental energies center on the ill member of the family to the exclusion of himself or herself. Although intellectually they may understand that their ill sibling needs this attention, emotionally it may be difficult to accept. "I don't think my parents even knew I was on the honor roll my senior year," said one sibling, "because they were going through such a bad time with my sister." Well siblings who are used to their parents being capable of handling difficult situations are often jolted by seeing them upset by the ill sibling's behavior and uncertain about what to do. Seeing their parents suffer can also be anxiety provoking to the well sibling. "It was so scary watching Mom and Dad try to deal with Dean," said his sister. "Even though they worried about it all the time, no one seemed to know what to do."

## Relationship with the Ill Sibling

Depending on the age of the siblings and severity of the illness, schizophrenia can disrupt even a strong sibling relationship. "I thought I would always be able to turn to my older brother," said one young man, "but now he won't even talk to me because he thinks I'm poisoning his food." Even when the bond is not strong or when there is conflict between siblings, when one sibling develops schizophrenia it can alter the relationship. "I didn't have much in common with Rich before he got sick," said his sister, "but after it was impossible." In contrast to these experiences, some siblings actually may become closer after schizophrenia develops, because of the well sibling's strong empathy and willingness to help.

## Level of Involvement with the Whole Family

When a sibling becomes ill and the family dynamics change, reactions of the well sibling can range from withdrawal to overinvolvement. "I was a teenager when Marcia got sick," said her brother. "I felt so shaken up by her talking to voices and thinking the refrigerator was bugged that I ended up just staying away from the whole situation. I spent most of my time at friends' houses and hardly ever came home."

Adult siblings may likewise withdraw somewhat when a brother or sister becomes ill—calling and visiting less—out of confusion and distress, not out of a lack of concern.

However, sometimes healthy siblings find themselves overinvolved, acting less like a brother or a sister and more like a parent. They take on the role of protector, and may be the one who takes the patient to the emergency room and advocates for the best treatment possible. Well siblings may, in fact, focus so much on their brother or sister that they neglect their own interests and goals. "I never seemed to have time to find a boyfriend," said Elsa, "because I was so busy trying to keep Tom out of the hospital."

## Relationships with People Outside the Family

Relationships with people other than family members can be affected when a sibling develops schizophrenia. For example, well siblings may be afraid to bring a friend home because their ill brother or sister might behave inappropriately. "I was so embarrassed when Nick insisted on singing Frank Sinatra songs to my buddy that I always went to his house instead of mine after that," Carl said.

Some siblings find that they become more secretive with friends and acquaintances after their brother or sister falls ill. One healthy sibling reported, "I couldn't tell anyone what was happening at our house anymore or how I was feeling about it." Being cautious about disclosing your relative's schizophrenia is understandable, given the stigma of mental illness in our culture. Yet being excessively secretive can interfere with the ability to form close or intimate relationships, since no one can be confided in.

# Coping with Having an Ill Sibling

In spite of the many problems of having a brother or sister with schizophrenia, it is never too late to improve the situation. As a sibling, there are several strategies you can use that will help you cope more effectively.

## Educating Yourself about Schizophrenia

Learning more about schizophrenia will help you understand your ill brother or sister better. It is especially helpful to be familiar with the symptoms of the illness and how they affect behavior. Reading Chapters 1 and 2 of this book is a good start, because what you learn about symptoms may help explain some of the behavior you have seen in the past and help you to understand what your sibling has been going through. If you were not well informed about your sibling's problem in the past and felt "in the dark," you will benefit from learning as much as possible about schizophrenia. Publications are available in the library and through the National Alliance for the Mentally Ill (see Resources appendix).

To further your understanding, try discussing the illness directly with your parents and your ill sibling. When you show that you care and are interested in the answers, they will probably try to be open with you. You can find out a great deal about your sibling's history and about current symptoms by talking directly with him or her. If your sibling is reluctant to discuss such matters, respect his or her decision and consult your parents.

## Maintaining Some Form of Relationship

In spite of the changes your brother or sister has experienced since becoming ill, it is still possible for the two of you to have a relationship. This relationship may be different from the one you had before the illness; for example, you may not be able to spend as much time together or converse about the same subjects. But with effort you can form a new relationship that takes into consideration the limitations imposed by schizophrenia.

It is helpful to seek out aspects of your sibling's personality that you once enjoyed and are still present in some form. For example, many siblings can still enjoy each other's sense of humor, taste in music, or love of certain foods. "Before the illness, Jack and I used to talk about sports non-stop," said one brother, "and now we still enjoy watching a baseball game together on TV once in a while."

Avoid waiting until a crisis to become involved. If you only know your sibling in crisis, you will not get a sense of his or her strengths and capabilities.

## Determining Your Level of Involvement

Siblings differ in their degree of involvement with their ill brother or sister. A great deal depends on your relationship with your sibling and your other responsibilities. Some siblings are closely involved in day-to-day matters, and may even have their ill brother or sister live with them. Others feel comfortable keeping a greater distance, staying in touch by phone once a month and being supportive to the principal caregivers. "At first I thought there was nothing I could do," was one sibling's response, "but when I visited him in the hospital I could see that it did him good to just talk to me. So now, that's what I try to do—be available when he wants to talk about what's on his mind."

Another sibling chose a different level of involvement: "My brother lives with Mom and she does the lion's share of the work. But since neither of them drive, I give them rides to the grocery store and to appointments."

At a minimum, we recommend trying to remain informed about your ill sibling's status and treatment.

## Pursuing Your Own Interests

Avoid becoming so involved that you neglect pursuing your own interests and ambitions. It is important to balance your own needs with those of your ill relative. Everyone needs to determine his or her own level of involvement, but it is usually not beneficial to devote yourself solely to your sibling. "My sister was traveling everywhere, ending up in emergency rooms in every state," said Jane. "I used to take a train or fly to wherever she was and take her home. Now, instead, I spend time on the phone talking to the staff at the hospital, telling them which medication she is on, which medicines were tried in the past, how she might be convinced to be admitted, and so on. I think I'm still helping her, but now I have time for my own life, too."

## Seeking Support

Many siblings feel alone in having a mentally ill brother or sister. It can be helpful to find someone to talk to about your experiences, whether it is an understanding friend, a spouse, or a counselor. Many siblings benefit from being involved with support groups, such as the Sibling and Adult Children Network, a subgroup of the National Alliance for the Mentally Ill. This organization has branches in most states, and brings siblings together to talk about their experiences and to share strategies and information about resources. If you attend such a group, you are not required to speak. Some people prefer to listen, especially when they first attend. But whether they speak or listen, most siblings leave such meetings feeling relieved that they are not alone, that others share their experience, and that others care.

## Reminding Yourself of the Nature of the Illness

Sometimes siblings can lose touch with how much schizophrenia influences their relationship with their ill brother or sister. It helps to repeat the following reminders to yourself:

- Despite my relative's illness, he or she is still capable of having relationships and experiencing some enjoyment of life.

- Symptoms of the illness cause many of the upsetting behaviors of my brother or sister.

- My efforts to help my relative are important, no matter how big or how small.

- My relative may appreciate my involvement, even if it is difficult for him or her to show that appreciation.
- Underneath the illness, this is still my brother or sister.

# How Parents Can Help
# Their Healthy Children

Although healthy children themselves must decide how they will cope and what level of involvement they want with their ill brother or sister, there are many things that parents can do to help them in this process.

## Being Knowledgeable About Schizophrenia

Educating yourself about schizophrenia will, of course, help you cope better with your ill child. What you learn about such things as how to respond to symptoms will also help your well children, who often look to you as a model of how to behave. If you are well informed, your well children can also ask you questions about their siblings' illness, questions that may trouble them.

## Openly Discussing the Illness

Although all parents want to protect their children from upsetting information, most siblings report that they don't want to be kept in the dark. As one sibling said, "For years I knew something was wrong with Sam, but no one would tell me what it was." If you don't discuss it openly, your well children (even as adults) may imagine something worse than actually exists. "I was so surprised to hear that my kids thought Jeff was a dangerous criminal," said one parent, "They didn't realize that he had a mental illness."

Keep your well children informed about what's happening. If the patient is symptomatic, it is helpful to explain how the behavior is related to a specific symptom. They may also appreciate knowing about their sibling's treatment, including medication, counseling, and day programs. Well siblings feel less confused and more in control when they are told more of the facts.

## Maintaining a Balance

The needs of your ill relative are real and compelling. At times it is necessary to focus all your attention on averting a crisis or responding to a crisis caused by schizophrenia. However, it is important to balance the needs of your ill child with those of your well children. Try to make time to talk regularly with your well children, acknowledge their problems and achievements, and be available to support them in their efforts.

Sometimes it can be helpful to divide responsibilities with your spouse. For example, the mother might go to the well sibling's birthday dinner, while the father stays home with the ill sibling, who is too symptomatic to attend. Remember to avoid whenever possible one spouse being the one who always takes responsibility for the patient. This can cause undue stress on that spouse and does not allow him or her to experience some of the pleasures of being involved with the other children.

Sometimes friends or relatives can also help free up some time to spend with the healthier children. One parent said, "My sister has been invaluable—without her bringing over meals during the crises with Ethan, I never could have spent any time with Anna and Ben."

## Becoming Familiar with the Feelings of Your Healthy Children

Healthy children experience a range of emotions when a sibling has schizophrenia. These emotions will naturally include some negative ones, such as anger, fear, and resentment. Try to listen to your well children's feelings without being judgmental. These emotions are unavoidable, but if your well children are allowed to talk about their feelings, and see that you understand their position, they will be better able to cope. It may also be helpful to suggest professional counseling or a support group to your healthy children.

## Avoiding Pressure on Healthy Children

Some well siblings feel comfortable with their ill brother or sister, and want to be directly involved with helping care for him or her now and in the future. However, despite everyone's best efforts, others do not feel so comfortable with the patient and the illness and do not want to assume significant responsibility. Each person must determine on his or her own what is the right amount of contact and responsibility.

When people feel forced to be involved, they may comply at first, but feel resentment later. This resentment may be felt by the patient, which can be detrimental to his or her progress. As discussed elsewhere in this book, people with schizophrenia are very sensitive to feeling criticized or disliked; in fact, such feelings are experienced as stressful and may contribute to a relapse. Therefore, it is preferable not to force a healthy child into being involved when he or she does not really feel comfortable with it.

On the other hand, some siblings are more interested in being involved than you might think. "When Anna told me that she wanted Ethan to come to dinner at her house once a week, I was shocked," said her mother. Allowing your children to determine their own level of involvement will avoid the negative repercussions of trying to force a greater closeness or responsibility than they can handle.

## Special Concerns of Well Siblings

Surveys conducted with well siblings indicate they have two main questions on their minds: "What is the prognosis for my brother or sister?" and "What will be expected of me when my parents are no longer able to provide or supervise care for my ill sibling?" Although the answers to these questions are complicated, and depend a great deal on the individual circumstances involved, we will attempt to address these concerns here.

### Prognosis of the Ill Sibling

No one can predict exactly what will happen in the future. However, we do know that schizophrenia is a serious, long-term illness, with an episodic course. Some patients are less impaired, and may be able to live independently and hold a full-time job. Others are plagued by constant symptoms which interfere with their ability to work or take adequate care of themselves. Most patients are somewhere between these two extremes. Patients may also vary over time as to their abilities.

To understand a patient's prognosis, it is helpful to talk with his or her treatment team. Because of their knowledge of the patient and their extensive experience with others who have schizophrenia, they can discuss short-term and long-term goals for the patient. One sibling spoke to the psychiatrist of her brother and reported, "I didn't realize that Martin would be in the residential program for a long time. I thought it was just for a few weeks while he got back on his feet." It is helpful for well siblings to keep themselves informed of their relative's clinical status and treatment on an ongoing basis, so that they will have a perspective on his or her capabilities.

### Expectations of Well Siblings

As parents become less able to act as primary caregivers or supervisors of their ill child's care, the well siblings naturally wonder about the future. Many siblings are apprehensive about the amount of care and involvement that might be expected of them. "I never had much contact with Kathy because it was too upsetting for me," said her sister Joanie, "but I was petrified that when Mom died I would suddenly find out I had to take total responsibility." Obviously it is best if this scenario can be avoided and there are no such surprises for either the patient or the well sibling. It is best to make decisions about assuming responsibility after an open discussion of the situation that includes a review of the needs of the relative and considers all the options. This kind of discussion need not be postponed until the last minute, and it can involve as many family members as possible. It takes time to make this kind of significant decision.

It is crucial that well siblings make informed decisions about the level of responsibility they are willing to take. This depends on their relationship with the ill relative, their past involvement with him or her, their other responsibilities, their capabilities, and what they truly want to do. As mentioned earlier, pressure on a well sibling to be more involved than he or she wants can have negative consequences.

Siblings who decide that they do not want to assume responsibility for providing care for their ill relative may find other ways of being helpful. For instance, they can be active in discussions, helping to come up with possible solutions and offering to help the primary caregiver with specific tasks, such as taking their brother or sister shopping on a regular basis or being available during emergencies. For siblings who think that they want to be more involved in their brother or sister's long-term future, reading Chapter 16 will be helpful.

# 16

# Planning for
# Your Relative's Future

Planning for the future of a relative with schizophrenia is a natural extension of providing care and concern for that family member in the present. As parents who have been active caregivers become less able to care for their ill family member, it is necessary to think of the patient's future. Some family members sum it up as a simple question: "What will happen when we're gone?" Planning for the long-term care of a relative with serious mental illness can be a complex and emotional task, especially for aging parents and other relatives who have been the primary caregivers. It is difficult to know where to begin, who to consult, what areas to address, and how to legally safeguard your decisions.

You and other primary caregivers are rightfully concerned about the future of your ill relative. Whether you are providing daily assistance, lending an occasional hand, giving emotional support, or acting as an advocate for your relative, you may worry about how your relative will manage without you. You may want to do everything possible to assure that your ill relative will have a comfortable living situation, adequate funds, ongoing treatment for schizophrenia, and practical help if needed. Underlying those concerns may be your desire that your relative continue to have someone to care *about* him or her.

Some families address their concerns about the future directly by coming up with detailed plans for the ongoing care of their relative. Others find it difficult to talk openly about such matters. They tend to make assumptions about what other relatives will do to fill in the gaps, or they delay until the situation has become a crisis.

This chapter is designed to help you make choices, rather than leaving things to chance. We provide suggestions for assessing your relative's needs, establishing a dialogue with other family members, planning for the specific needs of your relative, and taking practical steps to make sure your decisions are carried out. The last section of the chapter concerns optimizing your ill relative's independence, so that he or she will be as prepared as possible for the future. Planning now can be a relief to both you and your relative, and can increase your ability to enjoy your time together.

## Assessing Your Relative's Needs

The first step in planning how your relative will be cared for in the future is to assess how his or her basic needs are being provided for now. Although this situation can change, the present and recent past are usually the best indicators of what will be needed in the future.

People with schizophrenia vary greatly when it comes to how independent they are and how much help they need. For example, Mike lives independently, manages his own money, does his own shopping and cooking, and occasionally turns to his family members for loans and social support. James lives with his parents, who do the cooking and laundry and provide his transportation. Jennifer lives in a community residence where the staff supervise her activities; she relies on her mother to bring extra money and cigarettes on a regular basis. When she gets upset or refuses to comply with the rules of the residence, staff members often call her mother to help reason with Jennifer.

The Independence Evaluation will help you assess your ill relative's current level of independent functioning. After you have completed this questionnaire, note the activities that require the most assistance. Are you providing that assistance? If you are, how would your ill relative continue to have his or her needs met if you were not providing that assistance? These are the kinds of questions to ask yourself as you prepare to plan for the future.

As a principal caregiver, it is helpful for you to consider what your ill relative will need most. Then, if other family members are available, we recommend you ask them to get together with you to help you discuss your relative's needs. Talking to your relative's treatment providers to get their ideas and advice can be helpful. It is preferable to delay making actual decisions until other family members (and concerned others) are consulted. If no other family members are available or willing to be involved, you will need to depend more on input from the treatment team.

## Involving Other Family Members in the Planning Process

Involving family members when making plans for the future of your ill relative can have several advantages. They may be able to provide new

## Independence Evaluation

*Instructions:* Rate how independently your relative performs each activity.

| Activity | Independently | With Prompting | With Help | Done by Someone Else |
|---|---|---|---|---|
| Managing money | ____ | ____ | ____ | ____ |
| Meal preparation | ____ | ____ | ____ | ____ |
| Shopping | ____ | ____ | ____ | ____ |
| Cleaning | ____ | ____ | ____ | ____ |
| Laundry | ____ | ____ | ____ | ____ |
| Taking medication | ____ | ____ | ____ | ____ |
| Making appointments | ____ | ____ | ____ | ____ |
| Keeping appointments | ____ | ____ | ____ | ____ |
| Transportation | ____ | ____ | ____ | ____ |
| Grooming and hygiene | ____ | ____ | ____ | ____ |

ideas or offer to help in ways that you cannot anticipate. Or they may have strong reservations about taking on responsibilities in the future. Meeting together to discuss the situation is the best way to understand each person's point of view and what he or she would like to contribute to the future care of your relative. An open discussion is the best way to come to decisions that will most benefit your relative.

When to involve your ill relative in the planning process depends on his or her ability to participate constructively. Patients who are very symptomatic or tend to become very anxious when talking about the future may benefit from being included only in the latter stages of planning. This does not mean that discussions should be kept a secret; however, your relative need not attend every meeting, especially in the early stages of planning. At the beginning it is helpful for family members to express their feelings openly, including some feelings that may be critical of the ill relative. After those feelings have been aired, however, the ill relative deserves a chance to express his or her opinions and preferences about the future. The fact that preferences and specific requests have been expressed does not, however, guarantee that the family can provide them. The planning process is similar to a negotiation, in that everyone's needs and abilities must be taken into consideration. For most families, compromises are necessary on everyone's part to come up with a workable plan.

Some parents hesitate to bring up the subject of what will happen when they're gone, feeling it is unlucky or pessimistic. Although bringing up the subject of planning for the future can initially cause some anxiety, the costs of not planning ahead are far greater. Without a clear plan, your ill relative could be left in an insecure, unstable situation, and your other relatives could be placed in a stressful, confusing position. Keeping family members involved and informed of the planning process will avoid the kind of surprises that can be so disruptive when caregivers are no longer available.

## Raising the Subject of Planning Ahead

Don't be surprised if you find that other family members have already been thinking about planning for the future. Even if they have not expressed their thoughts out loud, this subject is probably on their minds. Surveys have shown that most relatives are quite concerned about the future. For example, in a study of educational needs one of us (Kim Mueser) conducted, relatives and patients were asked to complete a questionnaire about topics in schizophrenia they wanted to learn more about. "What happens when parents are no longer available?" was among the top 5 topics (out of 45) most requested by both relatives and patients. Thus, raising this subject will probably not shock your relatives. Rather, it may be a relief to have it out in the open.

## *Initiating Family Meetings*

It is helpful to think through in advance how to approach family members about planning for the future. When raising this topic, be matter-of-fact and brief. Let your family members know your concerns and that you think it would be helpful to talk things over together. Suggest a day and time when as many people as possible can attend. Plan to keep the initial meetings relatively short, and expect that it will take several meetings over the course of weeks or even months before satisfactory plans can be worked out. For some families, group meetings are not practical. In such situations, you can talk with people individually and go through the same steps described below.

James was fortunate to have several family members who were interested in his well-being. When James's father turned 60, he decided that he needed to start planning for the future. Since James lived with his parents and they gave him extensive assistance, there were a number of issues to address. Although they planned to include James in the planning, his parents decided it was best to meet first with other family members and to ask James to join them at later meetings.

After evaluating James's independence using the Independence Evaluation, his father approached James's three siblings and his uncle in the following way: "Your mother and I would like to get together with you and the rest of the family to talk about James's future. It's been on our minds a lot, and maybe it's been on yours, too. We realize that it will take time to figure out what's best for James, so we think it's a good idea to get started thinking about things now. We'd like to get together Sunday after dinner, around seven o'clock, for about an hour. Can you come then? We'd appreciate it."

# Using Problem Solving Techniques to Plan for the Future

Planning for the future of your ill relative can be a complicated and emotional process, one that involves solving multiple problems and making decisions that affect people's lives. It can be helpful in such a process to use the suggestions provided in Chapter 7 to guide your planning efforts. The step-by-step method of solving problems described in that chapter has been found to be particularly useful to families who are trying to sort out complicated issues. You can use these steps in a group meeting or by yourself. To review, the steps are as follows:

1. Define the problem.

2. Generate options.

3. Evaluate each option.

4. Choose the best option.

5. Plan how to carry out the option.

6. Evaluate how the option is being carried out.

The following sections describe how to use the steps when planning for your relative's future.

## Defining Problems and Establishing a Common Goal

When your family first meets together, it is important to establish a common understanding of your relative's needs. Some family members may have limited contact with your relative and have little knowledge of his or her treatment, limitations, and strengths. Family members who have been more involved can help the others understand the situation better. In early meetings, avoid putting people on the spot, such as by asking them what they are going to do to help before they have had a chance to understand what they are getting into. If you request specific assistance prematurely, some family members may feel frightened of the responsibility and refuse. Alternatively, they may agree before they know if they can really follow through with the responsibility, and later back out. You may have to interrupt premature decision making, as James's father did, by saying, "Let's hold off on deciding who can do what until we know what exactly needs to be done."

Try to promote an atmosphere where family members feel free to ask questions, share information, and express their honest concerns. Open communication is crucial when dealing with the complicated issues of planning for the future. It is especially important for everyone to have an understanding of your relative's specific needs. For example, James's mother initially described him as "needing some help with cooking." When his sister Joan asked, "What exactly can he cook?" she found out that he could only fix cold cereal for himself for breakfast. Although everyone would have preferred that he be more independent in the kitchen, they needed to know the facts.

It is very helpful to think of planning for the patient's future as a family problem, something that all family members have an investment in seeing solved. This does not mean that all family members have the same capabilities or willingness to be closely involved with providing care, but it does imply that all family members would like to arrive at an adequate plan for their relative. When family members reflect on their mutual concern for their relative's welfare, they often see planning for the future as a common goal.

James's family discussed his needs at length, and began to think of the situation as "How can we help James to live a pleasant life in the future?" No single family member was pinpointed as being the answer to this problem. The family also made a list of the most important problems they needed to solve for James to be able to continue his present quality of life in the future. Their list included:

- A safe place to live

- A small amount of spending money in addition to his disability payment

- Help with meal preparation

- Help with laundry

- Transportation

- Someone to oversee his treatment and make sure he is getting what he needs

James's siblings and his uncle were surprised at how much assistance he needed for his daily living. No one felt capable of doing everything that James's parents had been doing.

Although it is important to know the overall extent of your relative's needs, you need not try to solve everything at once. Working on one or two problems at a time makes the overall task more manageable.

## Generating Options

After initial discussions focusing on understanding your relative's needs, it is time to start talking about possible options. Try to make early family discussions of options free and open, with as much brainstorming as possible, and avoiding evaluating the options or pressuring family members to assume certain roles. For example, James's brother Frank began the discussion of options by saying, "I think James should live with Joan, because she has the biggest house." Their father reminded him that they were just talking about options now, and "No one really knows what's best for James until we know what all the possibilities are."

Some families generate options for the "biggest" problem first (such as needing a safe place to live), whereas other families prefer to start with a problem that can be solved more quickly (such as needing someone to talk to). Still other families decide to group related problems together and generate options for the group (for example, meal preparation and laundry).

For many problems it will be necessary to investigate what the range of options are, such as community resources. For example, to decide what is the best living situation, it would be helpful to investigate the supervised community residences that might be available through the local Community Mental Health Center or private agencies. There are also boarding homes and group apartments that may be an option for your ill relative. The Community Mental Health Center could also be consulted to determine how your relative might receive transportation services. Many options for financial needs also require legal advice about such things as trusts and guardianships. (Financial issues are covered in a separate section of this chapter.) During the brainstorming session, family members need to suggest as many solutions as possible, even solutions they don't think they would use now. Having a variety of solutions in mind may be helpful in the future.

James's family decided to tackle first the problem of needing someone to monitor his treatment and see that he gets what he needs. They felt that deciding this question would have a bearing on many of the other problems they needed to solve. After consulting with James's therapist at the Community Mental Health Center about community resources, they generated the following options:

- His case manager could monitor treatment and whether he is receiving the appropriate benefits.

- James could be taught to monitor his own situation.

- The siblings could take turns monitoring him.

- His sister Joan could take primary responsibility for this task.

## Evaluating Options

Every option has its advantages and disadvantages. It can be complicated to evaluate options, so it is important to think as clearly as possible about how each option would affect the people involved. In some instances, it may be necessary to find out more about some options in order to evaluate them. For example, if you were interested in a supervised community residence, it would be important to know the admission criteria, the waiting period, and what the residence looks like.

It is also important to assess candidly the burden that certain options would place on individual family members. For example, James's sister Joan was very close to him and wanted to continue to be actively involved with him after their parents were no longer able. At the same time, she also had to consider her other responsibilities: 2-year-old twin sons and a 6-year-old daughter with asthma. Thus, when it came to evaluating the option of her acting as an overseer, being able to help her brother was a strong advantage, whereas adding an additional responsibility to her life was a disadvantage. In this case, Joan felt that the additional responsibility would be manageable.

## Choosing the Best Option

There is no one right solution to any of the problems involved in planning for the future. The best you can do is to choose an option that has a good chance of meeting the needs of your ill relative and has the smallest chance of being a burden to another relative. In general, the solutions that seem to work best are those that attempt to balance the needs of everyone involved. One way to accomplish this balance is to consider distributing responsibilities between relatives and outside services. If this option is selected, it will be important to consider who will assume the responsibility of overseeing your relative's overall care.

This stage of the planning process is a good time to make sure your relative is included. After all, his or her future is at stake. If your relative has not been involved in previous meetings, you can update him or her on the options being considered and the advantages and disadvantages that have been raised so far. Ask if there is anything your relative would like to add and solicit his or her opinions and preferences. It may be necessary to keep the meetings short to optimize your relative's ability to concentrate and to minimize his or her anxiety.

James agreed with the problems as listed. As the family discussed the particular problem of his needing someone to monitor his treatment and living situation, he added a disadvantage to the idea of his relatives' taking turns. He said that he would be confused if too many people were involved and that he preferred to have just one person. No one felt comfortable leaving everything to the case manager. Since Joan expressed a willingness to take on the role of monitoring James's treatment and living situation, the family, including James, agreed upon that as the best option.

## Planning How to Carry Out Options

Once a decision has been made, it is important to make a plan to accomplish it. Some parts of the plan can be implemented immediately, whereas others take more time. For example, in James's situation, for Joan to oversee his treatment, she needed to get to know his treatment providers and the details of his treatment. She also needed to know more about how he spent his days and what he would need to maintain his quality of life. Contacting the treatment team did not take long, but getting to know the details of his treatment, and getting to know James better, took more time.

Some decisions require very intensive planning, especially such tasks as changing your relative's living situation, working out the financial terms of a will, and improving his or her independence. In such instances, it is helpful for family members to divide responsibility for completing various tasks. It is also important to set a realistic timeframe for each task that is planned, and to schedule a follow-up meeting to determine whether the steps are being accomplished. Family members need to support each other as they work on the steps necessary to following through on plans.

## *Evaluating How the Solution Is Being Carried Out*

When planning for the future, it is critical that your plans are followed through on and that they are accomplishing what you hoped. For example, if you decide to establish a trust fund for your relative, the lawyer needs to be contacted and the papers must be drawn up. If this task is delayed, the financial security you planned for your relative may not exist at the critical time. Similarly, in James's situation, if his sister Joan did not develop a relationship with his treatment team, the smooth transition that his family envisioned would not come about, which could also negatively affect other plans. James's family set a date for a follow-up meeting in one month.

Another consideration when planning for the future is that of periodically reevaluating whether the plans are still relevant: Does your relative have the same needs, and are the same resources available? We suggest that you reevaluate plans for your relative at least every year. For example, in James's situation, it would be necessary to modify the plans if his sister returned to full-time employment and had less time to devote to him.

# Special Issues to Consider When Planning for the Future

Although many of the problems encountered in planning for the future can be solved by following the steps described above, some topics require special information and preparation. Such topics include estate planning and consideration of organizations designed specifically to provide "lifetime assistance" to mentally ill persons.

## *Estate Planning*

When planning for your relative's financial security, it is important to keep in mind that he or she may be receiving benefits that are based on financial need, such as Supplemental Security Income (SSI), and public assistance, or welfare (see Chapter 5). If someone receiving such benefits has an inheritance that is not legally safeguarded, federal or state officials can claim that the person is no longer eligible for financial assistance. Furthermore, SSI and public assistance are tied to health care benefits, such as medicaid, which help pay for inpatient and outpatient medical and mental health expenses. Even if your relative no longer needs to rely on financial benefits, he or she will almost invariably continue to need health care benefits.

If you wish to leave money or property to your relative after you die and still maintain his or her eligibility for benefits, we recommend that you consult a lawyer who is knowledgeable about wills and trust funds for the mentally ill. In addition to safeguarding your relative's eligibility for government benefit programs, such a lawyer can help protect your relative's inheritance itself from government agencies and from your relative's own inability to manage funds. The lawyer can also help you understand state and federal laws as they relate to your individual situation. The Alliance for the Mentally Ill in your area may have a list of lawyers with the expertise you need. Some lawyers may even have a reduced rate if you have limited financial resources.

Although each family's situation is different and each state has specific laws, it may be helpful to review here some of the estate planning options that can be used by families who have a mentally ill relative.

### Full Inheritance

*Full inheritance* means that you leave funds and assets directly to your relative. This option is rarely chosen by families because it jeopardizes the patient's receipt of government benefits. One must also exercise extreme caution in using this option because the person receiving such an inheritance would be put under the stress of managing assets and investments. Given that the course of schizophrenia can be variable over time, even if your relative is functioning independently now, a recurrence of symptoms could alter his or her judgment and ability to handle finances.

### Disinheritance

*Disinheritance* means that you do not leave anything directly to your ill family member. You can, for example, disinherit your ill relative and leave your assets to another relative with the understanding that he or she will care for the patient. If the obligations of your healthy relative are informal, this option will not jeopardize your relative's eligibility for government programs. For some families this works very well, especially if there is a relative who has an ongoing and close relationship with your family member. However, many families hesitate to use this option because disinheritance can be perceived by your relative as a sign of lack of affection. Also, the assets left to the well relative are vulnerable to his or her judgment and creditors. For example, if the well relative divorces, the inheritance may become a part of the couple's assets, subject to distribution. Finally, if you disinherit your relative, another relative is not legally obligated to care for him or her.

### Supplemental Needs Trust

Many families choose to place their assets in a trust fund for their relative. This can be in the form of an *inter vivos trust* (during lifetime) or *testamentary trust* (in a will). A *supplemental needs trust* can appoint a trustee to distribute the funds on behalf of your relative, and can stipulate that the funds are meant to pay for *supplemental needs,* that is, costs not paid for by governmental programs, such as medicaid or SSI. Such a trust can stipulate that income or principal cannot be used for food, clothing, or shelter. If properly drafted, such a trust would mean that neither the income nor the principal would be considered an available resource by government agencies determining eligibility for their programs.

### Trustees

The *trustee* is the individual or financial institution who distributes assets based on the specific provisions of the trust. It is extremely important to choose as trustee a person or institution whose judgment you trust and who will have your relative's best interests at heart. It is also important to spell out your wishes as specifically as possible when drafting a trust, so that the trustee can carry them out. For example, decide if you want the funds of the trusts used for recreation, special services, trips, musical equipment, classes, and so on. Keep in mind that the trustee will not have authority over your ill relative, only over the funds.

## Organizations That Provide "Lifetime Assistance" to the Mentally Ill

In recent years, several organizations have been founded to provide services for people with serious mental illness whose parents or relatives are either deceased or no longer able to care for them. These organizations usually have staff members who monitor the needs of the mentally ill person, obtain financial and health care benefits, attempt to preserve or improve the quality of their clients' lives, and respond to crises. The staff generally develop individual care plans and schedule regular appointments to meet with their clients to evaluate their needs. Naturally, these organizations charge fees to provide their extensive services.

One example of such an organization is the Planned Lifetime Assistance Network (PLAN). Like other similar organizations, it requires a membership fee and a gift in trust (part of an inheritance given to the organization). The PLAN organization exists in many different states. To locate PLAN in your area, or another nonprofit organization that assists family members in planning for the future of an ill relative, contact your local Alliance for the Mentally Ill chapter. The National Alliance for the Mentally Ill has established a Guardian and Trusts Network, which has information about organizations that provide long-term care as well as information about estate planning in general. The network can be reached at 2101 Wilson Boulevard, Suite 302, Arlington, VA 22201; 703-524-7600.

Because lifetime care organizations are a relatively recent innovation, they need to be evaluated very carefully. Basic questions to ask include the following:

- How long has the organization been in existence?
- How many clients have you provided services to?
- How is your money invested?
- How financially secure is your organization?
- May I talk to someone who has used your services?
- What exactly is provided in return for the fees you require?

For some families, lifetime care organizations may be a very good solution to planning for the future; for others they may not be suitable.

## Optimizing Your Ill Relative's Independence

In planning for the future, family members frequently find themselves wishing that there were more options for their relative. Many times the options are limited by how much the family member can do for him or herself. For example, in James's situation, he was not able to take care of his own meals, laundry or transportation. If he had more skills, he might be able to live alone or in a shared apartment arrangement.

Many times family members underestimate what their relative can do, or they find it simpler to do things for him or her. In the short run, it may feel good to provide a service your relative needs. However, in the long run, you may not really be doing him or her a favor. If your relative relies on you too much, he or she will not be prepared for the future, when you will no longer be able to do these tasks.

In contrast, taking steps to increase your relative's independence may be one of the best ways you can help. Even small improvements in independence can lead to a better quality of life. The following are suggestions for improving your relative's independence.

*Choose a specific area to work on.* Assess carefully the areas where your relative needs the most help. Reviewing the Independence Evaluation can be a good start to identifying specific areas to focus on. Concentrate on improving your relative's skills in one area at a time. It is usually best to start with an area where it is likely that improvement can be made more readily. For example, James is able to serve himself a cold breakfast, but cannot do any food preparation beyond that. His family might start by helping him to expand what he can prepare in the kitchen.

*Set a series of modest, attainable goals.* It is unrealistic to expect dramatic improvement in a short time. Instead, start small and build your relative's confidence and willingness to keep trying. For example, James's mother began by praising how well he prepared his breakfast and asking him to help her fix sandwiches for lunch. He was surprised to be asked, but was willing to go along with the idea. The first day, she explained where the supplies for ham sandwiches were kept (in the refrigerator and the pantry) and asked him to lay out the supplies on the counter. She thanked him for his help and proceeded to make the ham sandwiches.

The next day she asked him to lay out the supplies and to take out the appropriate number of slices of bread. Two days later, she demonstrated the steps of putting on the ham and mustard. Each time he accomplished a step, she thanked him and told him specifically what he had done well. If he missed a step, she let him know specifically what the step should have been. Within a few weeks, James was able to make sandwiches for himself and his parents.

James's mother slowly added to his repertoire in the kitchen: making salads, boiling spaghetti, cooking eggs. She only taught how to prepare a new dish when James showed confidence in the previous one. She did not expect that he would become adept at complicated dishes, but she did want him to be able to "survive" in the kitchen.

Her next goal was to help him do his own laundry, starting with gauging how much laundry could fit in a single load.

**Expect that the process will not be smooth.** When someone is accustomed to having another person do certain tasks, he or she may resist change. It is helpful to reassure your ill relative of your affection and that asking him or her to do more is a sign that you care about his or her independence. Let your relative know that you appreciate his or her efforts, and praise even small steps toward greater independence.

**Initiate difficult transitions as soon as possible.** Some plans for the future involve making major changes, such as moving to a new living situation. It is usually best if you are available to assist your relative in making such a transition. This can involve making a change before it is absolutely necessary, but is usually a gentler process for your relative. For example, James had lived at home his entire life. If he and his family agreed that the best option for his future was for him to move to a supervised apartment, it would be best to begin the process while he was still living with his parents. He could look at apartments while he was still living at home, and could perhaps begin to live in an apartment while he could visit his parents on weekends. This kind of gradual transition is usually easier for people with schizophrenia, although some people are unable to follow through on changes until they have no other choice. Your relative will benefit, however, from whatever support you can provide while he or she is moving toward greater independence.

# Resources

## Agencies and Organizations

### Self-Help and Advocacy Organizations

**Compeer**, 259 Monroe Avenue, Suite B-1, Rochester, NY 14607; 716-546-8280. This organization helps psychiatric patients develop friendships through volunteers.

**Fountain House**, 425 West 47th Street, New York, NY 10036; 212-582-0340. This organization is run by consumers (persons with psychiatric difficulties) to enable them to gain vocational experiences. Interested persons can call to find the "clubhouse" closest to where they live.

**Friends and Advocates of the Mentally Ill (FAMI)**, 381 Park Avenue South, Suite 620, New York, NY 10016; 212-684-3264.

**The Judge David L. Bazelon Center for Mental Health Law**, 1101 15th Street NW, Suite 1212, Washington, DC 20005; 202-467-5730. This advocacy organization aids families and patients regarding legal issues and mental illness.

**National Alliance for Mental Patients**, P.O. Box 618, Sioux Falls, SD 57101.

**National Alliance for the Mentally Ill (NAMI)**, 2101 Wilson Blvd., Suite 302, Arlington, VA 22201. NAMI is the largest advocacy and self-help organization in the United States for relatives of persons with a psychiatric disorder. It also publishes a monthly newspaper, *The Advocate*. Local affiliates can be identified by looking up Alliance for the Mentally Ill (AMI) in the telephone directory or by calling the NAMI help line at 800-950-6264.

**National Mental Health Association**, 1021 Prince Street, Alexandria, VA 22314; 703-684-7722.

**National Mental Health Consumers Self-Help Clearinghouse,** 311 South Juniper Street, Suite 1000, Philadelphia, PA 19107; 800-553-4539.

**National Sibling Network,** P.O. Box 300040, Minneapolis, MN 55403; 612-872-1565. This is a self-help organization for persons with a mentally ill sibling which also publishes a quarterly newsletter, *The Sibling Bond.*

**Schizophrenics Anonymous Mental Health Association,** 15920 West Twelve Mile, Southfield, MI 48076; 313-557-6777.

**Training and Education Center (TEC) Network,** at the Mental Health Association of Southeastern Pennsylvania, 311 South Juniper Street, Suite 902, Philadelphia, PA 19107; 215-735-2465.

## Professional Organizations

**American Association for Partial Hospitalization,** 901 North Washington, #600, Alexandria, VA 22314; 703-836-2274.

**American Psychiatric Association,** 1400 K Street NW, Washington, DC 20002; 202-336-5500.

**American Psychological Association,** 750 First Street NW, Washington, DC 20002; 202-336-5500.

**International Association of Psychosocial Rehabilitation Services,** 10025 Governor Warfield Parkway, Suite 301, Columbia, MD 21044.

**Mental Health Policy Resource Center,** 1730 Rhode Island Avenue NW, #308, Washington, DC 20036; 202-775-8826.

**Mental Illness Foundation,** 420 Lexington Avenue, Suite 2104, New York, NY 10170; 212-682-4699.

**National Association of Social Workers,** 750 First Street NE, Washington, DC 20002; 202-408-8600.

**National Association of State Mental Health Program Directors,** 66 Canal Center Plaza, Suite 302, Alexandria, VA 22314; 703-739-9333.

**National Council of Community Mental Health Centers,** 12300 Twinbrook Parkway, Suite 320, Rockville, MD 20852; 301-984-6200.

**National Rehabilitation Association,** 1910 Association Drive, #205, Reston, VA 22091; 703-715-9090.

## Federal Agencies and Programs

**Center for Mental Health Services,** Office of Consumer, Family, and Public Information; 301-443-0747 (public information and answers to questions).

**Equal Employment Opportunity,** Americans with Disabilities Act, Equal Employment Opportunity Commission, 1801 L Street NW, Washington, DC 20507; 800-669-3362.

**Fair Housing,** Department of Housing and Urban Development (HUD), Office of Fair Housing and Equal Opportunity; 202-708-4252.

**Medicaid,** Health Care Financing Administration, Medical Information; 410-966-5659.

**Medicare,** Health Care Financing Administration, Medical Bureau Public Affairs Office; 202-690-6113.

**SSI and SSDI,** Social Security Administration, Public Information; 800-772-1213.

**State Vocational Rehabilitation,** U.S. Department of Education, Rehabilitation Services Administration; 202-205-8303.

**Substance Abuse and Mental Health Services Administration (SAMSA);** 301-443-4513 (public information and answers to questions).

# Further Reading

## Books for Families About Schizophrenia

These books provide more information about the nature of schizophrenia, written at a level accessible to nonprofessionals.

*Coping with Schizophrenia: A Survival Manual for Parents, Relatives, and Friends,* by M. Wasow. Palo Alto, Calif.: Science and Behavior Books, 1982.

*The Family Face of Schizophrenia,* by P. Backlar. New York: Tarcher/Putnam, 1994.

*Living with Schizophrenia: A Question and Answer Guide for Patients and Their Families,* by A. P. Hyde. Chicago: Contemporary Books, 1985.

*Schizophrenia Genesis: The Origins of Madness,* by I. I. Gottesman. New York: W. H. Freeman, 1991.

*Schizophrenia: Straight Talk for Families and Friends,* by M. Walsh. New York: Morrow, 1985.

*Surviving Schizophrenia: A Family Manual* (revised edition), by E. F. Torrey. New York: Harper & Row, 1988.

*Understanding Schizophrenia,* by R. S. E. Keefe and P. D. Harvey. New York: Free Press, 1994.

## Books for Families About Mental Illness

*The Broken Brain: The Biological Revolution in Psychiatry,* by N. C. Andreasen. New York: Harper & Row, 1984.

*The Caring Family: Living with the Chronic Mental Patient,* by K. F. Bernheim, R. R. J. Beale, and C. T. Beale. New York: Random House, 1982.

*Families in Pain,* by P. Vine. New York: Pantheon, 1982.

*A Family Affair: Helping Families Cope with Mental Illness,* by the Committee on Psychiatry and the Community, Group for the Advancement of Psychiatry. New York: Brunner/Mazel Publishers, 1986.

*Hidden Victims: An Eight-Stage Healing Process for Families and Friends of the Mentally Ill,* by J. T. Johnson. New York: Doubleday, 1988.

*Mental Illness: A Homecare Guide,* by A. H. Esser and S. D. Lacey. New York: John Wiley and Sons, 1989.

*My Parent's Keeper: Adult Children of the Emotionally Disturbed,* by E. M. Brown. Oakland, Calif.: New Harbinger Publications, 1989.

*Out of Our Minds: How to Cope with the Everyday Problems of the Mentally Ill—A Guide for Patients and Their Families,* by S. Garson. Buffalo, N.Y.: Prometheus Books, 1986.

*Surviving Mental Illness: Stress, Coping, and Adaptation,* by A. B. Hatfield and H. P. Lefley. New York: Guilford Press, 1993.

*When Someone You Love Has a Mental Illness,* by R. Wollis. New York: Putnam, 1992.

## First Person Accounts by Relatives of Their Experience

These books describe what it is like to live with a close family member who has schizophrenia. The primary focus is on the *relative's* experience, rather than the patient's experience with the illness.

*Breaking Points,* by J. Hinckley and J. Hinckley with E. Sherrill. Grand Rapids: Chosen Books, 1985.

*Families Helping Families: Living with Schizophrenia,* by N. Dearth, B. J. Labenski, M. E. Mott, and L. M. Pellegrini. New York: Norton, 1986.

*The Four of Us,* by E. Swados. New York: Farrar, Straus, and Girou, 1991. (A first-person account of the impact of schizophrenia on the family, told from each person's perspective.)

*My Sister's Keeper,* by M. Moorman. New York: Norton, 1992. (A first-person account of a woman learning how to cope with her sister's schizophrenia.)

*Schizophrenia: The Experiences of Patients and Families,* reprint from *Schizophrenia Bulletin.* Rockville, Md.: National Institute of Mental Health, 1987.

*Tell Me I'm Here: One Family's Experience of Schizophrenia,* by A. Deveson. New York: Penguin, 1991.

## The Experience of Schizophrenia

These books focus on helping the reader understand what the experience of schizophrenia is like from the perspective of the patient.

*Autobiography of a Schizophrenic Girl,* by M. Sechehaye. New York: New
    American Library, 1970.

*The Inner World of Mental Illness,* by B. Kaplan. New York: Harper & Row,
    1964.

*Is There No Place on Earth for Me?* by S. Sheehan. New York: Vintage, 1982.

*Operators and Things: The Inner Life of the Schizophrenic,* by B. O'Brien. Cam-
    bridge, Mass.: Arlington Books, 1958.

*Schizophrenia: The Experiences of Patients and Families,* reprint from *Schizo-
    phrenia Bulletin.* Rockville, Md.: National Institute of Mental Health,
    1987.

*The Voices of Robbie Wilde,* by E. Kytle. Washington, D.C.: Seven Locks
    Press, 1987.

## Research on Schizophrenia

These books and journals contain information about recent advances
in research on schizophrenia. The readings are intended primarily for professionals, but family members who are especially interested in current
research may find them helpful.

*A Clinical Guide for the Treatment of Schizophrenia,* A.S. Bellack, editor. New
    York: Plenum Press, 1989.

*Handbook of Schizophrenia,* volumes I–IV, A.H. Nasrallah, general editor.
    Amsterdam: Elsevier Press, 1988–1992.

*Innovations and Research*—published quarterly by the National Alliance for
    the Mentally Ill and the Center for Psychiatric Rehabilitation, Sar-
    gent College of Allied Health Professions, Boston University (730
    Commonwealth Avenue, Boston, MA 02115; 617-353-3549).

*Innovations in the Psychological Management of Schizophrenia: Assessment,
    Treatment and Services,* M. Birchwood and N. Tarrier, editors. Chi-
    chester, England: John Wiley and Sons, 1992.

*Psychosocial Rehabilitation Journal*—published quarterly by the Interna-
    tional Association of Psychosocial Rehabilitation Services and the
    Department of Rehabilitation Counseling, Sargent College of Allied
    Health Professions, Boston University (730 Commonwealth Avenue,
    Boston, MA 02115; 617-353-3549).

*Schizophrenia,* S.R. Hirsch and D. Weinberger, editors. Oxford: Blackwell
    Scientific Publications, in press.

*Schizophrenia: A Practical Overview,* D. Kavanagh, editor. London: Chap-
    man and Hall, 1992.

*Schizophrenia Bulletin*—published quarterly by the National Institute of
    Mental Health. This journal contains mostly invited articles by ex-
    perts on selected topics and brief first-person accounts by patients

and their relatives. Covers are composed of artwork by persons with the illness. For subscription information contact Superintendent of Documents, U.S. Government Printing Offices, Washington, D.C. 20402.

*Schizophrenia Research*—published bimonthly by Elsevier Press.

# Chapter References

## Chapter 1

Andreasen, N. C. 1984. *The broken brain: The biological revolution in psychiatry.* New York: Harper and Row.

Angermeyer, M. C., and L. Kuhn. 1988. Gender differences in age at onset of schizophrenia: An overview. *European Archives of Psychiatry and Neurological Sciences* 237:351–364.

Asarnow, J.R., and M. J. Goldstein. 1986. Schizophrenia during adolescence and early adulthood: A developmental perspective on risk research. *Clinical Psychology Review* 6:211–235.

Bateson G., D. D. Jackson, J. Haley, and J. Weakland. 1956. Toward a theory of schizophrenia. *Behavioral Science* 1:251–264.

Beckmann, H., and E. Franzek. 1992. Deficit of birthrates in winter and spring months in distinct subgroups of mainly genetically determined schizophrenia. *Psychopathology* 25:57–64.

Bleuler, E. [1911] 1950. *Dementia praecox or the group of schizophrenias,* translated by J. Zinkin. New York: International Universities Press.

Braff, D. L., R. Heaton, J. Kuck, M. Cullum, J. Moranville, I. Grant, and S. Zisook. 1991. The generalized pattern of neuropsychological deficits in outpatients with chronic schizophrenia with heterogeneous Wisconsin Card Sorting Test results. *Archives of General Psychiatry* 48:891–898.

Carpenter, W. T., R. W. Buchanan, B. Kirkpatrick, C. Tamminga, and F. Wood. 1993. Strong inference, theory testing, and the neuroanatomy of schizophrenia. *Archives of General Psychiatry* 50:825–831.

Ciompi, L. 1980. Aging and schizophrenic psychosis. *Acta Psychiatrica Scandinavica* 71:93–105.

Ciompi, L. 1980. The natural history of schizophrenia in the long term. *British Journal of Psychiatry* 136:413–420.

Ciompi, L. 1987. Toward a coherent multidimensional understanding and therapy of schizophrenia: Converging new concepts. In *Psychosocial treatment of schizophrenia: Multidimensional concepts, psychological, family, and self–help perspectives,* edited by J. S. Strauss, W. Boker, and H. D. Brenner. Toronto: Hans Huber Publishers.

Cornblatt, B.A., and J. G. Keilp. 1994. Impaired attention, genetics, and the pathophysiology of schizophrenia. *Schizophrenia Bulletin* 20:31–46.

Davis, K. L., R. S. Kahn, G. Ko, and M. Davidson. 1991. Dopamine in schizophrenia: A review and reconceptualization. *American Journal of Psychiatry* 148:1474–1486.

Dworkin, R. H., B. A. Cornblatt, R. Friedmann, L. M. Kaplansky, J. A. Lewis, A. Rinaldi, C. Shilliday, and L. Erlenmeyer-Kimling. 1993. Childhood precursors of affective vs. social deficits in adolescents at risk for schizophrenia. *Schizophrenia Bulletin* 19:563–577.

Frith, C. D. 1992. *The cognitive neuropsychology of schizophrenia.* Hove, England: Lawrence Erlbaum Associates.

Goldman, H. H., A. A. Gattozzi, and C. A. Taube. 1981. Defining and counting the chronically ill. *Hospital and Community Psychiatry* 32:21–27.

Goldstein, J. M. 1988. Gender differences in the course of schizophrenia. *American Journal of Psychiatry* 145:684–689.

Gottesman, I. I. 1991. *Schizophrenia genesis: The origins of madness.* New York: W. H. Freeman.

Harding, C. M., G. W. Brooks, T. Ashikaga, J. S. Strauss, and A. Breier. 1987. The Vermont longitudinal study of persons with severe mental illness: I. Methodology, study sample, and overall status 32 years later. *American Journal of Psychiatry* 144:718–726.

Harding, C. M., G. W. Brooks, T. Ashikaga, J. S. Strauss, and A. Breier. 1987. The Vermont longitudinal study of persons with severe mental illness: II. Long-term outcome of subjects who retrospectively met DSM-III criteria for schizophrenia. *American Journal of Psychiatry* 144:727–735.

Hatfield, A. B., and H. P. Lefley, eds. 1987. *Families of the mentally ill: Coping and adaptation.* New York: Guilford Press.

Hatfield, A. B., and H. P. Lefley, eds. 1993. *Surviving mental illness: Stress, coping, and adaptation.* New York: Guilford Press.

Holzman, P. S., and S. Matthysse. 1990. The genetics of schizophrenia: A review. *Psychological Science* 1:279–286.

Kaplan, B. 1964. *The inner world of mental illness.* New York: Harper and Row.

Kendler, K. S., and S. R. Diehl. 1993. The genetics of schizophrenia. *Schizophrenia Bulletin* 19:261–285.

Kendler, K. S., M. T. Tsuang, and P. Hays. 1987. Age at onset in schizophrenia: A familial perspective. *Archives of General Psychiatry* 44:881–890.

Kirch, D. G. 1993. Infection and autoimmunity as etiologic factors in schizophrenia: A review and reappraisal. *Schizophrenia Bulletin* 19:355–370.

Klassen, D., and W. A. O'Conor. 1988. Predicting violence in schizophrenic and non–schizophrenic patients: A prospective study. *Journal of Community Psychology* 16:217–227.

Kraepelin, E. [1919] 1971. *Dementia praecox and paraphrenia,* translated by R. M. Barclay. New York: Robert E. Krieger Publishing.

Lefley, H. P., and D. L. Johnson, eds. 1990. *Families as allies in treatment of the mentally ill: New directions for mental health professionals.* Washington D.C.: American Psychiatric Press.

Liberman, R. P., and K. T. Mueser. 1989. Schizophrenia: Psychosocial treatment. In *Comprehensive textbook of psychiatry V,* edited by H. I. Kaplan and B. J. Sadock. Baltimore: Williams and Wilkins.

Lindqvist, P., and P. Allebeck. 1990. Schizophrenia and crime: A longitudinal follow-up of 644 schizophrenics in Stockholm. *British Journal of Psychiatry* 157:345–350.

McNeil, T. F. 1987. Perinatal influences in the development of schizophrenia. In *Biological perspectives of schizophrenia,* edited by H. Helmchen and F. A. Henn. New York: John Wiley and Sons.

Mueser, K. T., A. S. Bellack, J. H. Wade, S. L. Sayers, and C. K. Rosenthal. 1992. An assessment of the educational needs of chronic psychiatric patients and their relatives. *British Journal of Psychiatry* 160:674–680.

Murray, R. M., and S. W. Lewis. 1987. Is schizophrenia a neurodevelopmental disorder? *British Medical Journal* 295:681–682.

Nasrallah, H. A. 1990. Brain structure and functions in schizophrenia: Evidence for fetal neurodevelopmental impairment. *Current Opinion in Psychiatry* 3:74–78.

Neale, J. M., and T. F. Oltmans. 1980. *Schizophrenia*. New York: John Wiley and Sons.

Nuechterlein, K. H. 1986. Childhood precursors of adult schizophrenia. *Journal of Child Psychology and Psychiatry* 27:133–144.

Nuechterlein, K. H., and M. E. Dawson. 1984. A heuristic vulnerability/stress model of schizophrenic episodes. *Schizophrenia Bulletin* 10:300–312.

Nuechterlein, K. H., and M. E. Dawson, M. Gitlin, J. Ventura, M. J. Goldstein, K. S. Snyder, C. M. Yee, and J. Mintz. 1992. Developmental processes in schizophrenic disorders: Longitudinal studies of vulnerability and stress. *Schizophrenia Bulletin* 18:387–425.

Robins, L. N., and D. A. Regier, eds. 1991. *Psychiatric disorders in America*. New York: Free Press.

Robins, L. N., and M. Rutter, eds. 1990. *Straight and devious pathways from childhood to adulthood*. New York: Cambridge University Press.

Rodrigo, G., M. Lusiardo, G. Briggs, and A. Ulmer. 1991. Differences between schizophrenics born in winter and summer. *Acta Psychiatrica Scandinavica* 84:320–322.

Sacchetti, E., A. Calzeroni, A. Vita, A. Terzi, F. Pollastro, and C. L. Cazzullo. 1992. The brain damage hypothesis of the seasonality of births in schizophrenia and major affective disorders: Evidence from computerised tomography. *British Journal of Psychiatry* 160:390–397.

Sechehaye, M. 1970. *Autobiography of a schizophrenic girl*. New York: New American Library.

Sheehan, S. 1982. *Is there no place on earth for me?* New York: Vintage Books.

Sharfstein, S. S. 1984. Sociopolitical issues affecting patients with chronic schizophrenia. In *Schizophrenia: Treatment, management, and rehabilitation*, edited by A. S. Bellack. Orlando: Grune and Stratton.

Susser, E., and S. Lin. 1992. Schizophrenia after prenatal exposure to the Dutch Hunger Winter of 1944–1945. *Archives of General Psychiatry* 49:983–988.

Talbott, J. A. 1984. The chronic mental patient: A national perspective. In *The chronically mentally ill: Research and services*, edited by M. Mirabi. New York: SP Medical and Scientific Books.

Terkelsen, K. G. 1983. Schizophrenia and the family: II. Adverse effects of family therapy. *Family Process* 22:191–200.

Torrey, E. F., A. E. Bowler, R. Rawlings, and A. Terrazas. 1993. Seasonality of schizophrenia and stillbirths. *Schizophrenia Bulletin* 19:557–562.

Volavka, J., and M. Krakowski. 1989. Schizophrenia and violence. *Psychological Medicine* 19:559–562.

Walker, E., G. Downey, and A. Caspi. 1991. Twin studies of psychopathology: Why do the concordance rates vary? *Schizophrenia Research* 5:211–221.

Walker, E., and R. J. Lewine. 1990. Prediction of adult–onset schizophrenia from childhood home movies of the patients. *American Journal of Psychiatry* 147:1052–1056.

Watt, D. C., K. Katz, and M. Shepherd. 1983. The natural history of schizophrenia: A 5-year prospective follow-up of a representative sample of schizophrenics by means of a standardized clinical and social assessment. *Psychological Medicine* 13:663–670.

Weinberger, D. R. 1987. Implications of normal brain development for the pathogenesis of schizophrenia. *Archives of General Psychiatry* 44:660–669.

Wyatt, R. J., R. C. Alexander, M. F. Egan, and D. G. Kirch. 1988. Schizophrenia, just the facts. What do we know, how well do we know it? *Schizophrenia Research* 1:3–18.

Zigler, E., and M. Glick. 1986. *A developmental approach to adult psychopathology.* New York: John Wiley and Sons.

Zubin, J., and B. Spring. 1977. Vulnerability: A new view of schizophrenia. *Journal of Abnormal Psychology* 86:103–126.

## Chapter 2

Alpert, M. 1985. The signs and symptoms of schizophrenia. *Comprehensive Psychiatry* 26:103–112.

American Psychiatric Association. 1994. *The Diagnostic and Statistical Manual for Psychiatric Disorders IV.* Washington D.C.: American Psychiatric Press.

Anderson, C. M., D. J. Reiss, and G. E. Hogarty. 1986. *Schizophrenia and the family.* New York: Guilford Press.

Andreasen, N. C., and W. T. Carpenter Jr. 1993. Diagnosis and classification of schizophrenia. *Schizophrenia Bulletin* 19:199–214.

Andreasen, N. C., and M. Flaum. 1991. Schizophrenia: The characteristic symptoms. *Schizophrenia Bulletin* 17:27–49.

Andreasen, N. C., M. Flaum, and S. Arndt. 1992. The Comprehensive Assessment of Symptoms and History (CASH). *Archives of General Psychiatry* 49:615–623.

Chapman, J. 1966. The early symptoms of schizophrenia. *British Journal of Psychiatry* 112:225–251.

Cloninger, C. R., R. L. Martin, S. B. Guze, and P. J. Clayton. 1985. Diagnosis and prognosis in schizophrenia. *Archives of General Psychiatry* 42:12–25.

Goodwin, F. K., and K. R. Jamison. 1990. *Manic-depressive illness.* New York: Oxford University Press.

Grossman, L.S., M. Harrow, J. F. Goldberg, and C. G. Fichtner. 1991. Outcome of schizoaffective disorder at two long-term follow–ups: Comparisons with outcome of schizophrenia and affective disorders. *American Journal of Psychiatry* 148:1359–1365.

Keith, S. M., and S. M. Matthews. 1991. The diagnosis of schizophrenia: A review of onset and duration issues. *Schizophrenia Bulletin* 17:51–67.

Maj, M., F. Starace, and R. Pirozzi. 1991. A family study of DSM-III-R schizoaffective disorder, depressive type, compared with schizophrenia and psychotic and nonpsychotic major depression. *American Journal of Psychiatry* 148:612–616.

Maneros, A., and M. T. Tsuang, eds. 1986. *Schizoaffective psychosis.* Berlin: Springer-Verlag.

Matarazzo, J. D. 1983. The reliability of psychiatric and psychological diagnosis. *Clinical Psychology Review* 3:103–145.

McGhie, A., and J. Chapman. 1961. Disorders of attention and perception in early schizophrenia. *British Journal of Medical Psychology* 34:103–116.

Mellor, C. S. 1970. First rank symptoms of schizophrenia: I. The frequency in schizophrenics on admission to hospital. II. Differences between individual first rank symptoms. *British Journal of Psychiatry* 117:15–23.

Mueser, K. T., A. S. Bellack, and E. U. Brady. 1990. Hallucinations in schizophrenia. *Acta Psychiatrica Scandinavica* 82:26–29.

Rice, J. P., and A. A. Todorov. 1994. Stability of diagnosis: Application to phenotype definition. *Schizophrenia Bulletin* 20:185–190.

Spitzer, R. L., J. B. W. Williams, M. Gibbon, and M. B. First. 1992. The Structured Clinical Interview for DSM-III-R (SCID): I. History, rationale, and description. *Archives of General Psychiatry* 49:624–629.

Williams, J. B. W., M. Gibbon, M. B. First, R. L. Spitzer, M. Davies, J. Borus, M. J. Howes, J. Kane, H.G. Pope Jr., B. Rounsaville, and H. Wittchen. 1992. The Structured Clinical Interview for DSM-III-R (SCID): II. Multisite test–retest reliability. *Archives of General Psychiatry* 49:630–636.

## Chapter 3

Blackwell, B. 1976. Treatment adherence. *British Journal of Psychiatry* 129:513–531.

*British Journal of Psychiatry.* 1992. Clozapine—the atypical antipsychotic. *British Journal of Psychiatry* 160, supplement 17 (entire issue).

Christison, G. W., D. G. Kirch, and R. J. Wyatt. 1991. When symptoms persist: Choosing among alternative somatic treatments for schizophrenia. *Schizophrenia Bulletin* 17:217–245.

Corrigan, P. W., R. P. Liberman, and J. D. Engle. 1990. From noncompliance to collaboration in the treatment of schizophrenia. *Hospital and Community Psychiatry* 41:1203–1211.

Davis, J. M. 1974. Dose equivalence of the antipsychotic drugs. *Journal of Psychiatric Research* 11:65–69.

Davis, J. M. 1975. Overview: Maintenance therapy in psychiatry: I. Schizophrenia. *American Journal of Psychiatry* 132:1237–1245.

Deniker, P. 1983. Discovery of the clinical uses of neuroleptics. In *Discoveries in pharmacology*, vol. 1, *Psycho and neuropharmacology*, edited by M. J. Parnham and J. Bruinvels. New York: Elsevier Science Publishers.

Enns, M. W., and J. P. Reiss. 1992. Electroconvulsive therapy. *Canadian Journal of Psychiatry* 37:671–678.

Gratz, S. S., and G.M. Simpson. 1992. Psychopharmacology. In *Research in psychiatry: Issues, strategies, and methods*, edited by L. K. G. Hsu and M. Hersen. New York: Plenum Press.

Hoyberg, O. J., C. Fensbo, J. Remvis, O. Lingjaerderde, M. Sloth–Nielsen, and I. Salvesen. 1993. Risperidone versus perphenazine in the treatment of chronic schizophrenic patients with acute exacerbations. *Acta Psychiatrica Scandinavica* 88:395–402.

Jeste, D. V., and M. P. Caligiuri. 1993. Tardive dyskinesia. *Schizophrenia Bulletin* 19:303–315.

Judd, L. L., and M. Rapaport. 1994. Risperidone: A new antipsychotic medication for the treatment of schizophrenia. *Innovations and Research* 3:1–7.

Kahn, R. S., M. Davidson, L. Siever, S. Gabriel, S. Apter, and K. L. Davis. 1993. Serotonin function and treatment response to clozapine in schizophrenic patients. *American Journal of Psychiatry* 150:1337–1342.

Kane, J. M. 1985. Compliance issues in outpatient treatment. *Journal of Clinical Psychopharmacology* 5:22–27.

Kane, J. M. 1993. Depot neuroleptic therapy. *Today's Therapeutic Trends* 11:93–102.

Kane, J., G. Honigfeld, J. Singer, and H. Meltzer. 1988. Clozapine for the treatment–resistant schizophrenic. *Archives of General Psychiatry* 45:789–796.

348    Coping with Schizophrenia

Kane, J. M., and J. A. Lieberman, eds. 1992. *Adverse effects of psychotropic drugs*. New York: Guilford Press.

Kane, J. M., and S. R. Marder. 1993. Psychopharmacologic treatment of schizophrenia. *Schizophrenia Bulletin* 19:287–302.

Kane, J. M., M. Woerner, J. A. Lieberman, P. Weinhold, W. Florio, M. Rubinstein, J. Rotrosen, J. Kurucz, S. Mukherjee, K. Bergmann, and N. R. Schooler. 1985. The prevalence of tardive dyskinesia. *Psychopharmacology Bulletin* 21:136–139.

Levenson, D. F. 1991. Pharmacologic treatment of schizophrenia. *Clinical Therapeutics* 13:326–352.

Long, J. W. 1993. *The essential guide to prescription drugs 1993*. New York: HarperPerennial.

Marder, S. R. 1992. Pharmacological treatment of schizophrenia. In *Schizophrenia: An overview and practical handbook*, edited by D. Kavanagh. London: Chapman and Hall.

Meltzer, H. Y., ed. 1987. *Psychopharmacology: The third generation of progress*. New York: Raven.

Meltzer, H. Y. 1992. Treatment of the neuroleptic–nonresponsive schizophrenic patient. *Schizophrenia Bulletin* 18:515–542.

Meltzer, H. Y., S. Burnett, B. Bastani, and L. F. Ramirez. 1990. Effects of six months of clozapine treatment on the quality of life of chronic schizophrenia patients. *Hospital and Community Psychiatry* 41:892–897.

Moller, H. J. 1993. Neuroleptic treatment of negative symptoms in schizophrenic patients: Efficacy problems and methodological difficulties. *European Neuropsychopharmacology* 3:1–11.

Plasky, P. 1991. Antidepressant usage in schizophrenia. *Schizophrenia Bulletin* 17:649–657.

Schooler, N. R. 1991. Maintenance medication for schizophrenia. *Schizophrenia Bulletin* 17:311–324.

Simhandl, C., and K. Meszaros. 1992. The use of carbamazepine in the treatment of schizophrenic and schizoaffective psychosis: A review. *Journal of Psychiatry and Neuroscience* 17:1–14.

Siris, S. G., D. P. van Kammen, and J. P. Docherty. 1978. Use of antidepressant drugs in schizophrenia. *Archives of General Psychiatry* 35:1368–1377.

Small, J. G. 1985. Efficacy of electroconvulsive therapy in schizophrenia, mania, and other disorders: I. Schizophrenia. *Convulsive Therapy* 1:263–270.

Strauss, M. E., K. S. Reynolds, G. Jayaram, and L. E. Tune. 1990. Effects of anticholinergic medication on memory in schizophrenia. *Schizophrenia Research* 3:127–129.

Wolkowitz, O. M., and D. Pickar. 1991. Benzodiazepines in the treatment of schizophrenia: A review and reappraisal. *American Journal of Psychiatry* 148:14–26.

## Chapter 4

Docherty, J. P., D. P. van Kammen, S. G. Siris, and S. R. Marder. 1978. Stages of onset of schizophrenic psychosis. *American Journal of Psychiatry* 135:420–426.

Freedman, B., and L. J. Chapman. 1973. Early subjective experience in schizophrenic episodes. *Journal of Abnormal Psychology* 82:45–54.

Green, M. F., K. H. Nuechterlein, J. Ventura, and J. Mintz. 1990. The temporal relationship between depressive and psychotic symptoms in recent-onset schizophrenia. *American Journal of Psychiatry* 147:179–182.

Heinrichs, D. W., B. P. Cohen, and W. T. Carpenter Jr. 1985. Early insight and the management of schizophrenic decompensation. *Journal of Nervous and Mental Disease* 173:133–138.

Herz, M. I., and C. Melville. 1980. Relapse in schizophrenia. *American Journal of Psychiatry* 137:801–805.

Hirsch, S. R., and A. G. Jolley. 1989. The Dysphoric Syndrome in schizophrenia and its implications for relapse. *British Journal of Psychiatry* 155:46–50.

MacMillan, F., M. Birchwood, and J. Smith. 1992. Predicting and controlling relapse in schizophrenia: Early warning signs monitoring. In *Schizophrenia: An overview and practical handbook*, edited by D. Kavanagh. London: Chapman and Hall.

Malla, A. K., and R. M. G. Norman. 1994. Prodromal symptoms in schizophrenia. *British Journal of Psychiatry* 164:487–493.

Stein, W. 1967. The sense of becoming psychotic. *British Journal of Psychiatry* 30:262–275.

Subotnik, K. L., and K. H. Nuechterlein. 1988. Prodromal signs and symptoms of schizophrenic relapse. *Journal of Abnormal Psychology* 97:405–412.

Ventura, J., K. H. Nuechterlein, D. Lukoff, and J. P. Hardesty. 1989. A prospective study of stressful life events and schizophrenic relapse. *Journal of Abnormal Psychology* 98:407–411.

## Chapter 5

Bellack, A. S., and K. T. Mueser, 1993. Psychosocial treatment for schizophrenia. *Schizophrenia Bulletin* 19:317–336.

Bellack A. S, S. M. Turner, M. Hersen, and R. F. Luber. 1984. An examination of the efficacy of social skills training for chronic schizophrenic patients. *Hospital and Community Psychiatry* 35:1023–1028.

Dietzen, L. L., and G. R. Bond. 1993. Relationship between case manager contact and outcome for frequently hospitalized psychiatric clients. *Hospital and Community Psychiatry* 44:839–843.

Eckman, T. A., W. C. Wirshing, S. R. Marder, R. P. Liberman, K. Johnston-Cronk, K. Zimmermann, and J. Mintz. 1992. Technique for training schizophrenic patients in illness self-management: A controlled trial. *American Journal of Psychiatry* 149:1549–1555.

Falloon, I. R. H., J. L. Boyd, C. W. McGill, M. Williamson, J. Razani, H. B. Moss, A. M. Gilderman, and G. M. Simpson. 1985. Family management in the prevention of morbidity of schizophrenia: Clinical outcome of a two year longitudinal study. *Archives of General Psychiatry* 42:887–896.

Hogarty G. E., C. M. Anderson, D. J. Reiss , S. J. Kornblith, D. P. Greenwald, C. D. Javna, and M. J. Madonia. 1986. Family psychoeducation, social skills training, and maintenance chemotherapy in the aftercare treatment of schizophrenia: I. One-year effects of a controlled study on relapse and expressed emotion. *Archives of General Psychiatry* 43:633–642.

Hogarty G. E., C. M. Anderson, D. J. Reiss, S. J. Kornblith, D. P. Greenwald, R. F. Ulrich, and M. Carter. 1991. Family psychoeducation, social skills training, and maintenance chemotherapy in the aftercare treatment of schizophrenia: II. Two-year effects of a controlled study on relapse and adjustment. *Archives of General Psychiatry* 48:340–347.

Kanter, J. 1989. Clinical case management: Definition, principles, components. *Hospital and Community Psychiatry* 40:361–368.

Leff, J., L. Kuipers, R. Berkowitz, and D. Sturgeon. 1985. A control trial of social intervention in the family of schizophrenic patients: Two-year follow-up. *British Journal of Psychiatry* 146:594–600.

Liberman, R. P., K. T. Mueser, and C. J. Wallace. 1986. Social skills training for schizophrenics at risk for relapse. *American Journal of Psychiatry* 143:523–526.

Linn, M. W., E. M. Caffey, J. Klett, G. E. Hogarty, and R. Lamb. 1979. Day treatment and psychotropic drugs in the aftercare of schizophrenic patients. *Archives of General Psychiatry* 36:1055–1066.

Marder S. R., W. C. Wirshing, T. Eckman, R. P. Liberman, T. Van Putten, K. Johnston-Cronk, M. Lebell, and J. McKenzie. 1993. Psychosocial and pharmacological strategies for maintenance therapy: Effects on two-year out-come. *Schizophrenia Research* 9:260.

May, P. R. A. 1968. *Treatment of schizophrenia: A comparative study of five treatment methods.* New York: Science House.

McFarlane, W. R. 1990. Multiple family groups and the treatment of schizophrenia. In *Handbook of Schizophrenia,* vol. 4, *Psychosocial Treatment of Schizophrenia,* edited by M. I. Herz, S. J. Keith, and J. P. Docherty. Amsterdam: Elsevier Science Publishers.

McFarlane, W. R., E. Dunne, E. Lukens, M. Newmark, J. McLaughlin-Toran, S. Deakins, and B. Horen. 1993. From research to clinical practice: Dissemination of New York State's Family Psychoeducation Project. *Hospital and Community Psychiatry* 44:265–270.

Mueser, K. T., and H. Berenbaum. 1990. Psychodynamic treatment of schizophrenia: Is there a future? *Psychological Medicine* 20:253–262.

Mueser, K. T., and S. M. Glynn. 1993. Efficacy of psychotherapy for schizophrenia. In *Handbook Of Effective Psychotherapy,* edited by T. R. Giles. New York: Plenum Press.

Parker, S., and J. K. Groll III. 1990. Partial hospitalization: An update. *American Journal of Psychiatry* 147:156–160.

Randolph, E. T., S. Eth, S. Glynn, G. B. Paz, G. B. Leong, A. L. Shaner, A. Strachan, W. Van Vort, J. Escobar, and R. P. Liberman. 1994. Behavioral family management in schizophrenia: Outcome from a clinic-based intervention. *British Journal of Psychiatry* 164:501–506.

Solomon, P. 1992. The efficacy of case management services for severely mentally disabled clients. *Community Mental Health Journal* 28:163–180.

Stein, L. I., and M. A. Test, eds. 1985. *The training in community living model: A decade of experience,* no. 26 of *New Directions for Mental Health Services.* San Francisco: Jossey-Bass.

Tarrier N., C. Barrowclough, C. Vaughn, J. Bamrah, K. Porceddu, S. Watts, and H. Freeman. 1989. Community management of schizophrenia: A two-year follow-up of a behavioral intervention with families. *British Journal of Psychiatry* 154:625–628.

## Chapter 6

Corrigan, P. W., and M. F. Green. 1993. Schizophrenic patients' sensitivity to social cues: The role of abstraction. *American Journal of Psychiatry* 150:589–594.

Cramer, P., J. Bowen, and M. O'Neill. 1992. Schizophrenics and social judgement: Why do schizophrenics get it wrong? *British Journal of Psychiatry* 160:481–487.

Falloon, I. R. H., M. Laporta, G. Fadden, and V. Graham-Hole. 1993. *Managing stress in families.* London: Routledge.

Gottman, J., C. Notarius, J. Gonso, and H. Markman. 1976. *A couples guide to communication.* Champaign, Ill.: Research Press.

McKay, M., M. Davis, and P. Fanning. 1983. *Messages: The communication skills book.* Oakland, Calif: New Harbinger Publications.

Mueser, K. T., and S. M. Glynn. In press. *Behavioral family therapy for psychiatric disorders.* Needham Heights, Mass.: Allyn and Bacon.

## Chapter 7

Bellack, A. S., R. L. Morrison, and K. T. Mueser. 1989. Social problem solving in schizophrenia. *Schizophrenia Bulletin* 15:101–116.

Bellack, A. S., M. Sayers, K. T. Mueser, and M. Bennett. 1994. Evaluation of social problem solving in schizophrenia. *Journal of Abnormal Psychology* 103:371–378.

D'zurilla, T. J. 1986. *Problem–solving therapy: A social competence approach to clinical intervention.* New York: Springer.

D'zurilla, T. J., and M. R. Goldfried. 1971. Problem solving and behavior modification. *Journal of Abnormal Psychology* 78:107–126.

Donahoe, C. P., M. J. Carter, W. D. Bloem, G. L. Hirsch, N. Laasi, and C. J. Wallace. 1990. Assessment of interpersonal problem-solving skills. *Psychiatry* 53:329–339.

Falloon, I. R. H., J. L. Boyd, and C. W. McGill. 1984. *Family care of schizophrenia.* New York: Guilford Press.

Falloon, I., K. Mueser, S. Gingerich, S. Rappaport, C. McGill, and V. Hole. 1988. *Behavioural family therapy: A workbook.* Buckingham, England: Buckingham Mental Health Services.

Isen, A. M., K. A. Daubman, and G. P. Nowicki. 1987. Positive affect facilitates creative problem solving. *Journal of Personality and Social Psychology* 52:1122–1131.

Mueser, K. T., and S. M. Glynn. In press. *Behavioral family therapy for psychiatric disorders.* Needham Heights, Mass.: Allyn and Bacon.

Nezu, A. M., C. M. Nezu, and M. G. Perri. 1989. *Problem-solving therapy for depression: Theory, research, and clinical guidelines.* New York: John Wiley and Sons.

Scott, G. G. 1990. *Resolving conflict with others and within yourself.* Oakland, Calif.: New Harbinger Publications.

## Chapter 8

Charlesworth, E. A., and R. G. Nathan. 1984. *Stress management: A comprehensive guide to wellness.* New York: Ballantine.

Girdano, D., and G. Everly. 1979. *Controlling stress and tension.* Englewood Cliffs, N.J.: Prentice Hall.

Matheny, K. B., and R. J. Riordan. 1992. *Stress and strategies for lifestyle management.* Atlanta: Georgia State University Press.

Steinberg, H. R., and J. Durell. 1968. A stressful social situation as a precipitant of schizophrenic symptoms: An epidemiological study. *British Journal of Psychiatry* 114:1097–1105.

Woolfolk, R. L., and P. M. Lehrer, eds. 1984. *Principles and practice of stress management.* New York: Guilford Press.

## Chapter 9

Esser, A. H., and S. D. Lacey. 1989. *Mental illness: A homecare guide.* New York: John Wiley and Sons.

Mueser, K. T., and S. Gingerich. 1991. *Educational family therapy for schizophrenia.* Philadelphia: Mueser and Gingerich.

Woolis, R. 1992. *When someone you love has a mental illness.* New York: Putnam.

## Chapter 10

Andreasen, N. 1982. Negative symptoms in schizophrenia. *Archives of General Psychiatry* 39:784–788.

352    Coping with Schizophrenia

Andreasen, N. C., M. Flaum, V. W. Swayze, G. Tyrrell, and S. Arndt. 1990. Positive and negative symptoms in schizophrenia. *Archives of General Psychiatry* 47:615–621.

Bentall, R. P., P. J. Higson, and C. F. Lowe. 1987. Teaching self-instructions to chronic schizophrenic patients: Efficacy and generalization. *Behavioural Psychotherapy* 15:58–76.

Berenbaum, H., R. Snowhite, and T. F. Oltmans. 1987. Anhedonia and emotional responses to affect evoking stimuli. *Psychological Medicine* 17:677–684.

Booker, W., H. D. Brenner, G. Gerstner, F. Keller, J. Muller, and L. Spichtig. 1984. Self-healing strategies among schizophrenics: Attempts at compensation for basic disorders. *Acta Psychiatrica Scandinavica* 69:373–378.

Breier. A., and J. S. Strauss. 1983. Self–control in psychotic disorders. *Archives of General Psychiatry* 40:1141–1145.

Carpenter, W. T., D. W. Heinrichs, and A. M. I. Wagman. 1988. Deficit and nondeficit forms of schizophrenia: The concept. *American Journal of Psychiatry* 145:578–583.

Carr V. 1988. Patients' techniques for coping with schizophrenia: An exploratory study. *British Journal of Medical Psychology* 61:339–352.

Falloon, I. R. H., and R. E. Talbot. 1981. Persistent auditory hallucinations: Coping mechanisms and implications for management. *Psychological Medicine* 11:329–339.

Greden, J. F., and R. Tandon, eds. 1991. *Negative schizophrenic symptoms: pathophysiology and clinical implications.* Washington D.C.: American Psychiatric Press.

Green, M. F., and M. Kinsbourne. 1990. Subvocal activity and auditory hallucinations: Clues for behavior treatment? *Schizophrenia Bulletin* 16:617–625.

Heilbrun, A. B., R. Diller, R. Fleming, and L. Slade. 1986. Strategies of disattention and auditory hallucinations in schizophrenics. *Journal of Nervous and Mental Disease* 174:265–273.

Huber, G., and G. Gross. 1989. The concept of basic symptoms in schizophrenic and schizoaffective psychosis. *Recenti Progressi in Medicina* 80:646–652.

Liddle, P. F., and T. R. E. Barnes. 1988. The subjective experience of deficits in schizophrenia. *Comprehensive Psychiatry* 29:157–164.

Matousek, N., J. Edwards, H. J. Jackson, R. P. Rudd, and N. E. McMurray. 1992. Social skills training and negative symptoms. *Behavior Modification* 16:39–63.

Mueser, K. T., M. S. Douglas, A. S. Bellack, and R. L. Morrison. 1991. Assessment of enduring deficit and negative symptom subtypes in schizophrenia. *Schizophrenia Bulletin* 17:565–582.

Shepherd, G. 1988. Practical aspects of the management of negative symptoms. *International Journal of Mental Health* 16:75–97.

Silverstein M. L., and M. Harrow. 1978. First rank symptoms in the post acute schizophrenic: A follow-up study. *American Journal of Psychiatry* 135:1481–1486.

Takai, A., M. Uematsu, H. Kaiya, M. Inoue, and H. Ueki. 1990. Coping styles to basic disorders among schizophrenics. *Acta Psychiatrica Scandinavica* 82:289–294.

Tarrier, N. 1992. Management and modification of residual positive psychotic symptoms. In *Innovations in the psychological management of schizophrenia,* edited by M. Birchwood and N. Tarrier. England: John Wiley and Sons.

Tarrier, N., R. Beckett, S. Harwood, A. Baker, L. Yusupoff, and I. Ugarteburu. 1993. A trial of two cognitive-behavioural methods of treating drug–resistant residual psychotic symptoms in schizophrenic patients: I. Outcome. *British Journal of Psychiatry* 162:524–532.

Tarrier N., L. Sharpe, R. Beckett, S. Harwood, A. Baker, and L. Yusupoff. 1993. A trial of two cognitive behavioral methods of treating drug–resistant residual psychotic symptoms in schizophrenic patients: II. Treatment-specific changes in coping and problem-solving skills. *Social Psychiatry and Psychiatric Epidemiology* 28:5–10.

## Chapter 11

Argyle, N. 1990. Panic attacks in chronic schizophrenia. *British Journal of Psychiatry* 157:430–433.

Barlow, D. H. 1988. *Anxiety and its disorders: The nature and treatment of anxiety and panic*. New York: Guilford Press.

Becker, R. E. 1988. Depression in schizophrenia. *Hospital and Community Psychiatry* 39:1269–1275.

Birchwood, M., R. Mason, F. MacMillan, and J. Healy. 1993. Depression, demoralization and control over psychotic illness: A comparison of depressed and non-depressed patients with a chronic psychosis. *Psychological Medicine* 23:387–395.

Burns, D. 1980. *Feeling good: The new mood therapy*. New York: William Morrow.

Burns, D. 1989. *The feeling good handbook*. New York: William Morrow.

Drake, R. E., C. Gates, A. Whitaker, and P. G. Cotton. 1985. Suicide among schizophrenics: A review. *Comprehensive Psychiatry* 26:90–100.

Elk, R., B. J. Dickman, and A. F. Teggin. 1986. Depression in schizophrenia: A study of prevalence and treatment. *British Journal of Psychiatry* 149:228–229.

Ellis, A., and Harper, R. A. 1975. *A new guide to rational living*. Hollywood, Calif.: Wilshire Book Company.

Heinssen, R. K., Jr., and C. R. Glass. 1990. Social skills, social anxiety, and cognitive factors in schizophrenia. In *Handbook of social and evaluation anxiety*, edited by H. Leitenberg. New York: Plenum Press.

Lewinsohn, P. M., R. F. Munoz, M. A. Youngren, and A. M. Zeiss. 1992. *Control your depression*, rev. ed. New York: Simon and Schuster.

Miller, F., J. Dworkin, M. Ward, and D. Barone. 1990. A preliminary study of unresolved grief in families of seriously mentally ill patients. *Hospital and Community Psychiatry* 41:1321–1325.

Penn, D., D. A. Hope, W. D. Spaulding, and J. Kucera. 1994. Social anxiety in schizophrenia. *Schizophrenia Research* 11:277–284.

Papolos, D., and J. Papolos. 1992. *Overcoming depression*, rev. ed.. New York: HarperCollins Publishers.

Roy, A., ed. 1986. *Suicide*. Baltimore: Williams and Wilkins.

Williams, R., and J. T. Darby, eds. 1989. *Depression in schizophrenia*. New York: Plenum Press.

## Chapter 12

Carey, K. B. 1989. Treatment of the mentally ill chemical abuser: Description of the Hutchings day treatment program. *Psychiatric Quarterly* 60:303–316.

Dixon, L., G. Haas, P. J. Weiden, J. Sweeney, and A. J. Francis. 1991. Drug abuse in schizophrenic patients: Clinical correlates and reasons for use. *American Journal of Psychiatry* 148:224–230.

Drake, R. E., S. J. Bartels, G. B. Teague, D. L. Noordsy, and R. E. Clark. 1993. Treatment of substance abuse in severely mentally ill patients. *Journal of Nervous and Mental Disease* 181:606–611.

Drake, R. E., F. C. Osher, D. Noordsy, S. C. Hurlbut, G. B. Teague, and M. S. Beudette. 1990. Diagnosis of alcohol use disorders in schizophrenia. *Schizophrenia Bulletin* 16:57–67.

Drake, R. E., F. C. Osher, and M. A. Wallach. 1989. Alcohol use and abuse in schizophrenia: A prospective community study. *Journal of Nervous and Mental Disease* 177:408–414.

Drake, R. E., and M. A. Wallach. 1993. Moderate drinking among people with severe mental illness. *Hospital and Community Psychiatry* 44:780–782.

Evans, K., and J. M. Sullivan. 1990. *Dual diagnosis: Counseling the mentally ill substance abuser.* New York: Guilford Press.

Lindqvist, P., and P. Allebeck. 1990. Schizophrenia and assaultive behaviour: the role of alcohol and drug abuse. *Acta Psychiatrica Scandinavica* 82:191–195.

Linszen, D. H., P. M. Dingemans, and M. E. Lenior. 1994. Cannabis abuse and the course of recent-onset schizophrenic disorders. *Archives of General Psychiatry* 51:273–279.

Minkoff, K., and R. E. Drake, eds. 1991. *Dual diagnosis of major mental illness and substance disorder,* no. 50 of *New Directions for Mental Health Services.* San Francisco: Jossey–Bass.

Mueser, K. T., A. S. Bellack, and J. J. Blanchard. 1992. Co-morbidity of schizophrenia and substance abuse: Implications for treatment. *Journal of Consulting and Clinical Psychology* 60:845–856.

Mueser, K. T., P. R. Yarnold, and A. S. Bellack. 1992. Diagnostic and demographic correlates of substance abuse in schizophrenia and major affective disorder. *Acta Psychiatrica Scandinavica* 85:48–55.

Mueser, K. T., P. R. Yarnold, D. F. Levinson, H. Singh, A. S. Bellack, K. Kee, R. L. Morrison, and K. G. Yadalam. 1990. Prevalence of substance abuse in schizophrenia: Demographic and clinical correlates. *Schizophrenia Bulletin* 16:31–56.

Noordsy, D. L., R. E. Drake, G. B. Teague, F. C. Osher, S. C. Hurlbut, M. S. Beaudette, and T. S. Paskus. 1991. Subjective experiences related to alcohol use among schizophrenics. *Journal of Nervous and Mental Disease* 179:410–414.

Regier, D. A., M. E. Farmer, D. S. Rae, B. Z. Locke, S. J. Keith, L. L. Judd, and F. K. Goodwin. 1990. Comorbidity of mental disorders with alcohol and other drug abuse: Results from the Epidemiologic Catchment Area (ECA) study. *Journal of the American Medical Association (JAMA)* 264:2511–2518.

Test, M. A., L. S. Wallisch, D. J. Allness, and K. Ripp. 1989. Substance use in young adults with schizophrenic disorders. *Schizophrenia Bulletin* 15:465–476.

## Chapter 13

Aguilera, D. C. 1990. *Crisis intervention: Theory and methodology,* 6th ed. St. Louis: The C. V. Mosby Company.

Barrowclough, C., and N. Tarrier. 1990. *Families of schizophrenic patients: Cognitive behavioural intervention.* London: Chapman and Hall.

Hatfield, A. 1990. *Family education in mental illness.* New York: Guilford Press.

Hatfield, A. 1992. *Coping with aggressive behavior.* Arlington, Va.: National Alliance for the Mentally Ill.

Roberts, A. R., ed. 1990. *Crisis intervention handbook: Assessment, treatment and research.* Belmont, Calif.: Wadsworth Publishing.

Straznickas, K. A., D. E. McNiel, and R. L. Binde. 1993. Violence toward family caregivers by mentally ill relatives. *Hospital and Community Psychiatry* 44:385–387.

Wyatt, R. J. 1994. *Practical psychiatric practice: Forms and protocols for clinical use.* Washington D.C.: American Psychiatric Press.

## Chapter 14

Becker, D. R., and R. E. Drake. 1993. *A working life: The individual placement and support (IPS) Program.* Concord, N.H.: New Hampshire-Dartmouth Psychiatric Research Center.

Becker, D. R., and R. E. Drake. 1994. Individual placement and support: A community mental health center approach to vocational rehabilitation. *Community Mental Health Journal* 30:193–206.

Black, B. J., ed. 1986. *Work as therapy and rehabilitation for the mentally ill.* New York: Altro Health and Rehabilitation Services.

Bond, G. R. 1992. Vocational rehabilitation. In *Handbook of psychiatric rehabilitation,* edited by R. P. Liberman. New York: Macmillan.

Ciardiello, J. A., and M. D. Bell, eds. 1988. *Vocational rehabilitation of persons with prolonged psychiatric disorders.* Baltimore: Johns Hopkins University Press.

Farkas, M. D., and W. A. Anthony, eds. 1989. *Psychiatric rehabilitation programs.* Baltimore: Johns Hopkins University Press.

Levitt, A. J., T. P. Hogan, and C. M. Bucosky. 1990. Quality of life in chronically mentally ill patients in day treatment. *Psychological Medicine* 20:703–710.

Liberman, R.P., ed. 1992. *Handbook of psychiatric rehabilitation.* New York: MacMillan.

Liberman, R. P., W. R. DeRisi, and K. T. Mueser. 1989. *Social skills training for psychiatric patients.* Needham Heights, Mass.: Allyn and Bacon.

Mueser, K. T., A. S. Bellack, M. S. Douglas, and J. H. Wade. 1991. Prediction of social skill acquisition in schizophrenic and major affective disorder patients from memory and symptomatology. *Psychiatry Research* 37:281–296.

Wallace, C. J., R. P. Liberman, S. J. MacKain, G. Blackwell, and T. A. Eckman. 1992. Effectiveness and replicability of modules for teaching social and instrumental skills to the severely mentally ill. *American Journal of Psychiatry* 149:654–658.

## Chapter 15

Gerace, L. M., D. Camilleri, and L. Ayres. 1993. Sibling perspectives on schizophrenia and the family. *Schizophrenia Bulletin* 19:637–647.

Horwitz, A. V., R. C. Tessler, G. A. Fisher, and G. M. Gamache. 1992. The role of adult siblings in providing social support to the severely mentally ill. *Journal of Marriage and Family* 54:233–241.

Landeen, J., C. Whelton, S. Dermer, J. Cardamone, H. Munroe-Blum, and J. Thorton. 1992. Needs of well siblings of persons with schizophrenia. *Hospital and Community Psychiatry* 43:266–269.

Moorman, M. 1992. *My sister's keeper.* New York: Norton.

Swados, E. 1991. *The four of us.* New York: Farrar, Straus, and Giroux.

Vine, P. 1982. *Families in pain.* New York: Pantheon.

## Chapter 16

Russell, L. M., A. E. Grant, and S. M. Joseph. 1993. *Planning for the future: Providing a meaningful life for a child with a disability.* Evanston, Ill.: American Publishing.

Silver, D. 1992. *A parent's guide to wills and trusts.* Los Angeles: Adams Hall.

Turnbull, J. R., A. P. Turnbull, G. L. Bronicki, J. A. Summers, C. Roeder–Gorden. 1992. *Disability and the family: A guide to decisions for adulthood.* Baltimore: Paul H. Brooks.

# Other New Harbinger Self-Help Titles

*When Anger Hurts Your Kids*, $12.95
*The Addiction Workbook*, $17.95
*The Mother's Survival Guide to Recover*, $12.95
*The Chronic Pain Control Workbook, Second Edition*, $17.95
*Fibromyalgia & Chronic Myofacial Pain Sybndrome*, $19.95
*Diagnosis and Treatment of Sociopaths*, $44.95
*Flying Without Fear*, $12.95
*Kid Cooperation: How to Stop Yelling, Nagging & Pleading and Get Kids to Cooperate*, $12.95
*The Stop Smoking Workbook: Your Guide to Healthy Quitting*, $17.95
*Conquering Carpal Tunnel Syndrome and Other Repetitive Strain Injuries*, $17.95
*The Tao of Conversation*, $12.95
*Wellness at Work: Building Resilience for Job Stress*, $17.95
*What Your Doctor Can't Tell You About Cosmetic Surgery*, $13.95
*An End of Panic: Breakthrough Techniques for Overcoming Panic Disorder*, $17.95
*On the Clients Path: A Manual for the Practice of Solution-Focused Therapy*, $39.95
*Living Without Procrastination: How to Stop Postponing Your Life*, $12.95
*Goodbye Mother, Hello Woman: Reweaving the Daughter Mother Relationship*, $14.95
*Letting Go of Anger: The 10 Most Common Anger Styles and What to Do About Them*, $12.95
*Messages: The Communication Skills Workbook, Second Edition*, $13.95
*Coping With Chronic Fatigue Syndrome: Nine Things You Can Do*, $12.95
*The Anxiety & Phobia Workbook, Second Edition*, $17.95
*Thueson's Guide to Over-The Counter Drugs*, $13.95
*Natural Women's Health: A Guide to Healthy Living for Women of Any Age*, $13.95
*I'd Rather Be Married: Finding Your Future Spouse*, $13.95
*The Relaxation & Stress Reduction Workbook, Fourth Edition*, $17.95
*Living Without Depression & Manic Depression: A Workbook for Maintaining Mood Stability*, $17.95
*Belonging: A Guide to Overcoming Loneliness*, $13.95
*Coping With Schizophrenia: A Guide For Families*, $13.95
*Visualization for Change, Second Edition*, $13.95
*Postpartum Survival Guide*, $13.95
*Angry All The Time: An Emergency Guide to Anger Control*, $12.95
*Couple Skills: Making Your Relationship Work*, $13.95
*Handbook of Clinical Psychopharmacology for Therapists*, $39.95
*The Warrior's Journey Home: Healing Men, Healing the Planet*, $13.95
*Weight Loss Through Persistence*, $13.95
*Post-Traumatic Stress Disorder: A Complete Treatment Guide*, $39.95
*Stepfamily Realities: How to Overcome Difficulties and Have a Happy Family*, $13.95
*Leaving the Fold: A Guide for Former Fundamentalists and Others Leaving Their Religion*, $13.95
*Father-Son Healing: An Adult Son's Guide*, $12.95
*The Chemotherapy Survival Guide*, $11.95
*Your Family/Your Self: How to Analyze Your Family System*, $12.95
*Being a Man: A Guide to the New Masculinity*, $12.95
*The Deadly Diet, Second Edition: Recovering from Anorexia & Bulimia*, $13.95
*Last Touch: Preparing for a Parent's Death*, $11.95
*Consuming Passions: Help for Compulsive Shoppers*, $11.95
*Self-Esteem, Second Edition*, $13.95
*I Can't Get Over It, A Handbook for Trauma Survivors*, $13.95
*Concerned Intervention, When Your Loved One Won't Quit Alcohol or Drugs*, $12.95
*Dying of Embarrassment: Help for Social Anxiety and Social Phobia*, $12.95
*The Depression Workbook: Living With Depression and Manic Depression*, $17.95
*The Marriage Bed: Renewing Love, Friendship, Trust, and Romance*, $11.95
*Focal Group Psychotherapy: For Mental Health Professionals*, $44.95
*Hot Water Therapy: Save Your Back, Neck & Shoulders in 10 Minutes a Day* $11.95
*Prisoners of Belief: Exposing & Changing Beliefs that Control Your Life*, $12.95
*Be Sick Well: A Healthy Approach to Chronic Illness*, $11.95
*Men & Grief: A Guide for Men Surviving the Death of a Loved One.*, $13.95
*When the Bough Breaks: A Helping Guide for Parents of Sexually Abused Childern*, $11.95
*Love Addiction: A Guide to Emotional Independence*, $12.95
*When Once Is Not Enough: Help for Obsessive Compulsives*, $13.95
*The New Three Minute Meditator*, $12.95
*Getting to Sleep*, $12.95
*Beyond Grief: A Guide for Recovering from the Death of a Loved One*, $13.95
*Leader's Guide to the Relaxation & Stress Reduction Workbook, Fourth Edition*, $19.95
*The Divorce Book*, $13.95
*Hypnosis for Change: A Manual of Proven Techniques, 2nd Edition*, $13.95
*When Anger Hurts*, $13.95
*Free of the Shadows: Recovering from Sexual Violence*, $12.95
*Lifetime Weight Control*, $11.95
*Love and Renewal: A Couple's Guide to Commitment*, $13.95

Call **toll free, 1-800-748-6273**, to order. Have your Visa or Mastercard number ready. Or send a check for the titles you want to New Harbinger Publications, Inc., 5674 Shattuck Ave., Oakland, CA 94609. Include $3.80 for the first book and 75¢ for each additional book, to cover shipping and handling. (California residents please include appropriate sales tax.) Allow four to six weeks for delivery.

*Prices subject to change without notice.*